WILLMINGTON'S NOTES ON THE
NEW TESTAMENT: GOSPELS

"In the beginning was the Word, and the Word was with God, and the Word was God." ~ John 1:1

LIBERTY HOME BIBLE INSTITUTE
ACCELERATED LEARNING PROGRAM

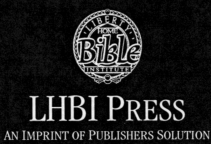

LHBI PRESS
AN IMPRINT OF PUBLISHERS SOLUTION

ISBN: 978-1-937925-03-1

LHBI PRESS

AN IMPRINT OF PUBLISHERS SOLUTION
www.PublishersSolution.com

14805 Forest Rd., Suite 205
Forest, VA 24551
www.LHBIonline.com/press

Cover & Interior Design by the Publishers Solution Design Team

TELL ME THE STORY OF JESUS

FANNY J. CROSBY, 1920-1915

JOHN R. SWENEY, 1837-1899

1. Tell me the sto-ry of Je-sus; Write on my heart ev-ery word.
2. Fast-ing a-lone in the des-ert, Tell of the days that are past,
3. Tell of the cross where they nailed Him, With-ing in an-guish and pain;
Refrain: Tell me the sto-ry of Je-sus; Write on my heart ev-ery word.

Tell me the sto-ry most pre-cious, Sweet-est that ev-er was heard.
How for our sins He was tempt-ed, Yet was tri-um-phant at last.
Tell of the grave where they laid Him. Tell how He liv-eth a-gain.
Tell me the sto-ry most pre-cious, Sweet-est that ev-er was heard.

Tell how the an-gels in cho-rus Sang as they wel-comed His birth:
Tell of the years of His la-bor; Tell of the sor-row He bore.
Love in that sto-ry so ten-der, Clear-er than ev-er I see.

"Glo-ry to God in the high-est! Peace and good tid-ings to earth."
He was de-spised and af-flict-ed, Home-less, re-ject-ed and poor.
Stay, let me weep while you whis-per, Love paid the ran-som for me.

THE WONDERS OF THE WONDROUS ONE

The Old Testament opens with man made in the likeness of God. The New Testament opens with God made in the likeness of man.

In the Old Testament the sovereign Creator created his creatures. In the New Testament the sinful creatures crucified their sovereign Creator.

These statements, in essence, summarize the person and work of Jesus Christ, who is both the Lamb of God and the Lion of Judah.

It has been estimated that some 40 billion individuals have lived upon this earth since Adam. What a contrast can be seen in this vast multitude of humanity. It includes black men, white men, brown men, and yellow men. These men have explored and settled in every corner of this earth. They speak dozens of languages, practice multitudes of religions, and have formulated numerous cultures.

But every single human being in this 40 billion number shares one vital thing in common. His purpose of life down here and his eternal destiny afterwards depend completely upon his personal relationship with the subject of this study—the Lord Jesus Christ. It is therefore absolutely impossible to overemphasize the importance of his life. The key question of the universe continues to be, "What think ye of Christ?" (Mt. 22:42).

Jesus said, "Search the scriptures; for in them ye think ye have eternal life: and they are they which testify of me" (Jn. 5:39). Note the following:

❋ To the artist he is the one altogether lovely	(Song. 5:16)
❋ To the architect he is the chief Cornerstone	(1 Pet. 2:6)
❋ To the astronomer he is the Sun of righteousness	(Mal. 4:2)
❋ To the baker he is the Bread of Life	(Jn. 6:35)
❋ To the banker he is the hidden treasure	(Mt. 13:44)
❋ To the builder he is the sure foundation	(Isa. 28:16)
❋ To the carpenter he is the door	(Jn. 10:7)
❋ To the doctor he is the Great Physician	(Jer. 8:22)
❋ To the educator he is the new and living way	(Heb. 10:20)
❋ To the farmer he is the sower and the Lord of the harvest	(Lk.10:2)

THE SCRIPTURES AND THE SAVIOR

* Both are the Word of God: The Scriptures are the written Word..........................(Exod. 31:18) and the Savior is the Living Word...(Jn. 1:14)
* Both are eternal...(1 Pet. 1:23; Heb. 13:8)
* Both came from heaven...(Psa. 119:89; Jn. 3:13)
* Both came to bless a lost world...(Lk.11:28; Acts 3:26)
* Both partook of the human and the divine.......................................(2 Pet. 1:20-21; 1 Tim. 3:16)
* Both enjoyed angelic support.....................................(Acts 7:53; Gal. 3:19; Mt. 4:11; Lk.22:43)
* Both are faultless..(Prov. 30:5; 1 Jn. 3:5)
* Both are sources of life..(Heb 4:12; Jn. 14:6)
* Both are sources of light..(Psa. 119:130; Jn. 1:4, 9)
* Both are absolute truth...(Jn. 17:17; Jn. 14:6)
* Both provide food for the soul...(Dt. 8:3; Jn. 6.35)
* Both provide cleansing...(Jn. 15:3; 1 Jn. 1:9)
* Both produce fruit..(Mt. 13:23; Jn. 15:5)
* Both give peace..(Psa. 119:165; Jn. 14:27)
* Both are like a sword...(Eph. 6:17; Rev. 19:15)
* Both are called wonderful...(Psa. 119:18; Isa. 9:6)
* Both are called the power of God...(Rom. 1:1.6; 1 Cor. 1:2.4)
* Both successfully complete their assignments............................(Isa. 55:10-11; Jn. 17:4; 19:30)
* Both produce fruit..(Mt. 13:23; Jn. 15:5)
* Both give peace..(Psa. 119:165; Jn. 14:27)
* Both are like a sword...(Eph. 6:17; Rev. 19:150)
* Both are called wonderful...(Psa. 119:18; Isa. 9:6)
* Both are called the power of God...(Rom. 1:16; 1 Cor. 1:24)
* Both successfully complete their assignments............................(Isa. 55:10-11; Jn. 17:4; 19:30)
* Both must be received for salvation...(Jn. 8:31-32; Jn. 1:12)
* Both have been attacked by sinners...(Jer. 36:27-28; Jn. 10:31)
* Both have been rejected by sinners...(Mk. 7:9; Isa. 53:3)
* Both will eventually judge all sinners...(Rom. 2:12; 3:19; Jn. 5:22)

INTRODUCTION

The most concise and practical "user-friendly" fact-filled volume overviewing the earthly life of Jesus ever published.

Especially prepared for Christian leaders and lay people alike, providing literally hundreds of relevant and ready-to-use fingertip facts in tracing the steps of our Savior.

LIBERTY HOME BIBLE INSTITUTE: *Accelerated Learning Program*

CONTENTS

One: ANALYTICAL

Twelve Key Periods And Events In The Earthly Life Of Jesus:

Two: TOPICAL

A Brief Consideration Of The Following Topics:

Three: CHRONOLOGICAL

Four: BIOGRAPHICAL

Five: VISUAL

Six: GEOGRAPHICAL

Seven: POLITICAL & THEOLOGICAL

Eight: NUMERICAL

Nine: PERSONAL

An Alliterated Outline Overview Of Each Of The Four Gospels:

One: ANALYTICAL

Special studies examining twelve key time periods and events in the earthly life of Jesus:

- ➢ His Genealogies

- ➢ His Birth

- ➢ His Early Years in Nazareth

- ➢ His Baptism

- ➢ His Temptation

- ➢ His Soul Winning Activities

- ➢ His Preaching Activities

- ➢ His Promise to Build the Church

- ➢ His Transfiguration

- ➢ His Final Week

- ➢ His Crucifixion

- ➢ His Resurrection Appearances And Ascension

THE GENEALOGIES OF JESUS

MATTHEW'S GENEALOGY

Mt. 1:1-17

- Matthew begins with Abraham and goes forward in time to Joseph
    1. He gives the royal line of Joseph.
    2. He traces this line through Solomon, David's first son.
    3. His list includes forty-one names, four of which are women.

- This genealogy is remarkable for several reasons:
    1. It contains the names of four women–Oriental and Mid-eastern genealogies rarely do this.
    2. All four women had questionable backgrounds.
        a. Tamar was an ex-harlot (Mt. 1:3; Gen. 38:13-30).
        b. Rahab was an ex-harlot (Mt. 1:5; Josh. 2:1).
        c. Ruth was a former pagan (Mt. 1:5; Ruth 1:4).
        d. Bath-Sheba was a former adulteress (Mt. 1:6; 2 Sam. 11:1-5).

- But through the manifold and marvelous grace of God, the first of these women (Tamar) became the distantly removed grandmother of King David; the second (Rahab) became his great-great-grandmother; the third (Ruth) was his great-grandmother; and the fourth (Bath-Sheba) became his beloved wife and mother of Solomon. (See Ruth 4:18-22.).

- Matthew opens and closes his genealogical account with three names.

    "The book of the generation of Jesus Christ, the son of David, the son of Abraham...So all the generations from Abraham to David are fourteen generations; and from David until the carrying away into Babylon are fourteen generations; and from the carrying away into Babylon unto Christ are fourteen generations." (Mt. 1:1, 17)

- It can be seen that his genealogy records 41 generations consisting of three groups of 14 each:
    1. From Abraham to David
    2. From David to the Babylonian Captivity
    3. From the Babylonian Captivity to Christ

- To make these three groups of 14 each, Matthew omitted three generations, those of Ahaziah, Joash, and Amaziah. Chronologically they should appear between the two names, "Jehoram begat Uzziah" in Mt. 1:8. There were probably several reasons why Matthew used this approach:
    1. As a memory device
    2. The number 14 is twice seven, the number of perfection.
    3. The name David, Israel's greatest king, has a numerical value in the Hebrew language which totals 14

LUKE'S GENEALOGY

Lk. 3:23-38

- Luke begins with Joseph and goes back to Adam.
    1. He gives the racial line of Mary.
    2. He traces this line through Nathan, David's second son.
    3. His list includes seventy-four names.

- Joseph's father is said by Matthew to be Jacob (Mt. 1:16), while Luke says he was Heli's son (Lk. 3:23). The ancient world often referred to their sons-in-law as their own sons. Thus it is possible that Heli was actually the father of Mary and the father-in-law of Joseph.

- Satan was keenly aware of the fact that the line leading to Christ would go through David's seed. He thus apparently attempted to break a link in the royal chain. With the advent of King Jeconiah (the 19th "link" from David), it appeared that the devil had succeeded, for God pronounced the following curse upon this wicked young ruler: *"Thus saith the LORD, Write ye this man childless, a man that shall not prosper in his days: for no man of his seed shall prosper, sitting upon the throne of David, and ruling any more in Judah." (Jer. 22:30).*

- This declaration did not mean he would have no children, for in 1 Chron. 3:17-18, some are named. (See also Mt. 1:12.) What it did mean is that by divine judgment this king would be considered childless as far as the throne of Judah was concerned. Whatever it meant, it seemed the royal line of David and Solomon had ground to a stop with Jeconiah (also called Coniah and Jehoiachin in the Old Testament) (See Jer. 22:24; 2 Kings 24:8.) But what a rude shock when the devil learned that God was not limited to one line. David had another son named Nathan, and it was through this line that Mary, the mother of Jesus, came.

THE BIRTH OF JESUS

THE INCARNATION OF JESUS

I. PART ONE: Events Preceding His Birth

A. The Three Announcements
1. To Zacharias, About the Birth of John the Baptist

"There was in the days of Herod, the king of Judaea, a certain priest named Zacharias, of the course of Abia: and his wife was of the daughters of Aaron, and her name was Elisabeth. And they were both righteous before God, walking in all the commandments and ordinances of the Lord blameless. And they had no child, because that Elisabeth was barren, and they both were now well stricken in years. And it came to pass, that while he executed the priest's office before God in the order of his course, According to the custom of the priest's office, his lot was to burn incense when he went into the temple of the Lord. And the whole multitude of the people were praying without at the time of incense. And there appeared unto him an angel of the Lord standing on the right side of the altar of incense. And when Zacharias saw him, he was troubled, and fear fell upon him. But the angel said unto him, Fear not, Zacharias: for thy prayer is heard; and thy wife Elisabeth shall bear thee a son, and thou shalt call his name John. And thou shalt have joy and gladness; and many shall rejoice at his birth. For he shall be great in the sight of the Lord, and shall drink neither wine nor strong drink; and he shall be filled with the Holy Ghost, even from his mother's womb. And many of the children of Israel shall he turn to the Lord their God. And he shall go before him in the spirit and power of Elias, to turn the hearts of the fathers to the children, and the disobedient to the wisdom of the just; to make ready a people prepared for the Lord. And Zacharias said unto the angel, Whereby shall I know this? for I am an old man, and my wife well stricken in years. And the angel answering said unto him, I am Gabriel, that stand in the presence of God; and am sent to speak unto thee, and to shew thee these glad tidings. And, behold, thou shalt be dumb, and not able to speak, until the day that these things shall be performed, because thou believest not my words, which shall be fulfilled in their season. And the people waited for Zacharias, and marvelled that he tarried so long in the temple. And when he came out, he could not speak unto them: and they perceived that he had seen a vision in the temple: for he beckoned unto them, and remained speechless. And it came to pass, that, as soon as the days of his ministration were accomplished, he departed to his own house. And after those days his wife Elisabeth conceived, and hid herself five months, saying, Thus hath the Lord dealt with me in the days wherein he looked on me, to take away my reproach among men." (Lk. 1:5-25)

■ This old couple doubtless had many things going for them:
1. Both had experienced the new birth.
2. Both were walking in the will of God.
3. Each was apparently enjoying good health.

■ We are informed in Luke 1:5 that Zacharias was from the course (or division) of Abijah. Because the priests became so numerous, and they could not all officiate at the altar, David divided them into twenty-four courses or classes. This act is described in 1 Chron. 24, which mentions the curse of Abia (Abijah in Hebrew) as the eighth one. Josephus says that in his day there were about 20,000 priests. The Talmud says there were even more.

At Passover, Pentecost, and the Feast of Tabernacles, all of the priests served, but the rest of the year was divided up among the courses. Since there were so many in each course (an average of nearly 850, if Josephus' figure is accurate), the various duties were assigned by the casting of lots.

■ The archangel Gabriel appeared to Zacharias the priest as he burned incense at the golden altar in the Jerusalem temple (see Ex. 30:7; 2 Chron. 29:11). This is the first spoken message from heaven in more than 400 years. The last person before Zacharias to receive a message given by angels was named Zechariah (see Zech. 1-6).

■ The name Gabriel means "God's hero," or "mighty man of God." He is one of the two most powerful and important good angels in the entire Bible. The other is Michael (Dan. 10:13, 21; Jude 9; Rev. 12:7). Both probably hold the title of archangel. How thrilling to realize that even in the birth announcement of Christ's forerunner, God chose the very best.

■ This is the eighth of nine biblical births in which God himself intervened. They are:
   1. The birth of Isaac to Abraham and Sarah (Gen. 21:1)
   2. The birth of Jacob and Esau to Isaac and Rebekah (Gen. 25:21)
   3. The birth of Reuben to Jacob and Leah (Gen. 29:31)
   4. The birth of Issachar to Jacob and Leah (Gen. 30:17-18)
   5. The birth of Joseph to Jacob and Rachel (Gen. 30:22-24)
   6. The birth of Samuel to Elkanah and Hannah (1 Sam. 1:19)
   7. The birth of Samson to Manoah and his wife (Judg. 13:1-2)
   8. The birth of John to Zacharias and Elisabeth (Lk. 1:57)
   9. The birth of Jesus to Mary (Lk. 2:7)

■ The child was to be called John, which means *the grace of Jehovah.* The name Zacharias means "God remembers," and the name Elisabeth means "his oath." Thus, at the birth of John the Baptist, God was remembering his covenant of grace made in Psa. 89:34-37 concerning David's seed, Jesus, to which John would serve as a forerunner. Note:

   "My covenant will I not break, nor alter the thing that is gone out of my lips. Once have I sworn by my holiness that I will not lie unto David. His seed shall endure for ever, and his throne as the sun before me. It shall be established for ever as the moon, and as a faithful witness in heaven" (Psa. 89:34-37). "And he [John] shall go before him [Jesus] in the spirit and power of Elijah ... to make ready a people for the Lord." (Lk. 1:17)

■ John was to function as a Nazarite (Lk. 1:15). There is a difference between a Nazarite and a Nazarene:
   1. A Nazarite had to do with vocation. This is to say that the Nazarite took upon him a threefold vow (Num. 6:2-6).
      a. He would abstain from wine.
      b. He would not have his hair cut.
      c. He would not come in contact with a dead body.

2. A Nazarene had to do with location. This is to say that if one lived in the city of Nazareth, he was known as a Nazarene. Thus, while John was a Nazarite, Jesus became a Nazarene (Mt. 2:23). In fact, our Lord did not observe any of the three Nazarite vows.

    a. He did partake of the fruit of the vine. He both created it (Jn. 2:1-10) and served it (Mt. 26:26-29).

    b. He did cut his hair. Jesus was often looked upon as a Jewish rabbi, and it is known that they did cut their hair (Jn. 3:2).

    c. He did come in contact with dead bodies. In fact, our Lord broke up every funeral he ever attended by raising the corpse (Lk. 7:14; 8:54; Jn. 11:43).

■ John would be filled with the Holy Spirit from his mother's womb. This is said also about two other men:

    1. Jeremiah (Jer. 1:5)

    2. Paul (Gal. 1:15)

■ He would turn many Israelites to the Lord. This he did at the Lord's first coming, as Elijah will someday do at Christ's second coming (Mal. 4:5-6).

■ As both he and his wife were advanced in years, Zacharias had some difficulty believing all this as once did Abraham and Sarah (see Gen. 17:17; 18:12). The old priest is rebuked for this unbelief and would not be able to speak until the child was born (Lk. 1:20).

■ The waiting crowd soon realized that something very strange had happened to Zacharias and that he could not pronounce the expected blessing upon them. No doubt many in that waiting crowd were there to help Zacharias celebrate a very special event, the burning of incense upon the golden altar. A priest could do this only once in his entire life. Others in the multitude were expecting to hear him pronounce the great Levitical blessing. In Num. 6:22-27 we read:

"And the LORD spake unto Moses, saying, Speak unto Aaron and unto his sons, saying, On this wise ye shall bless the children of Israel, saying unto them, The LORD bless thee, and keep thee: The LORD make his face shine upon thee, and be gracious unto thee: The LORD lift up his countenance upon thee, and give thee peace. And they shall put my name upon the children of Israel, and I will bless them."

■ But on that day there was no celebration or benediction. Something far more exciting and eternal was about to happen. Zacharias returned home and soon his old and barren wife conceived a child.

---

2. To Mary, About the Birth of Jesus the Messiah

"And in the sixth month the angel Gabriel was sent from God unto a city of Galilee, named Nazareth, To a virgin espoused to a man whose name was Joseph, of the house of David; and the virgin's name was Mary. And the angel came in unto her, and said, Hail, thou that art highly favoured, the Lord is with thee: blessed art thou among women. And when she saw him, she was troubled at his saying, and cast in her mind what manner of salutation this should be. And the angel said unto her, Fear not, Mary: for thou hast found favour with God. And, behold, thou shalt conceive in thy womb, and bring forth a son, and shalt call his name JESUS. He shall be great, and shall be called the Son of the Highest: and the Lord God shall give unto him the throne of his father David: And he shall reign over the house of Jacob for ever; and of his kingdom there shall be no end.

Then said Mary unto the angel, How shall this be, seeing I know not a man? And the angel answered and said unto her, The Holy Ghost shall come upon thee, and the power of the Highest shall overshadow thee: therefore also that holy thing which shall be born of thee shall be called the Son of God. And, behold, thy cousin Elisabeth, she hath also conceived a son in her old age: and this is the sixth month with her, who was called barren. For with God nothing shall be impossible. And Mary said, Behold the handmaid of the Lord; be it unto me according to thy word. And the angel departed from her." (Lk. 1:26-38)

■ The angel did not say Mary was to be blessed above women, but among women. Note also that Luke tells us the first recorded person to call Jesus Savior was Mary. *"And Mary said, My soul doth magnify the Lord, And my spirit hath rejoiced in God my Saviour" (Lk. 1:46-47).* Mary needed salvation, as did all others (see Rom. 3:23).

■ At this point, two questions can be raised regarding Luke 1:34-35:

1. What was the real mystery involved in the incarnation and where did it take place? The supernatural element in the incarnation was not the birth of Christ, but rather his conception. He was born as all humans are born. It is vital to make this distinction, for he was not only as completely God as though he had never been man; he was also as completely man as though he had never been God. Thus, the actual miracle occurred not at Bethlehem, but in Nazareth.

2. Why did the angel Gabriel rebuke Zacharias for his question and not rebuke Mary for her question?
   Zacharias: *"Whereby shall I know this? For I am an old man, and my wife well stricken in years." (Lk. 1:18)*
   Mary: *"How shall this be, seeing I know not a man?" (Lk. 1:34)*

3. **Answer**: Zacharias had for many years been praying for a son (Lk. 1:13), but when the announcement came, he doubted God's power to do this. When something wonderful happens sometimes the most surprised individual on earth is that very Christian who has been fervently praying for it to happen. However, there is no reason to believe that Mary had been praying to become the mother of Jesus.

   Another classic example is found in the book of Acts. Peter was in prison awaiting execution, and when the Jerusalem believers heard of it, "prayer was made without ceasing of the church unto God for him" (Acts 12:5). At God's command an angel staged a spectacular jailbreak. Upon being set free, Peter hurried to the prayer meeting to announce the good news. Note the amusing account: *"And when he had considered the thing, he came to the house of Mary the mother of John, whose surname was Mark; where many were gathered together praying. And as Peter knocked at the door of the gate, a damsel came to hearken, named Rhoda. And when she knew Peter's voice, she opened not the gate for gladness, but ran in, and told how Peter stood before the gate. And they said unto her, Thou art mad. But she constantly affirmed that it was even so. Then said they, It is his angel. But Peter continued knocking: and when they had opened the door, and saw him, they were astonished" (Acts 12:12-16).* Peter had a harder time getting into that prayer meeting than he had had getting out of prison.

■ Gabriel's response to Mary's question is thrilling indeed: *"For with God nothing shall be impossible." (Lk. 1:37)*

■ Some twenty centuries previous to this, another woman had heard similar words: *"Is any thing too hard for the LORD? At the time appointed I will return unto thee, according to the time of life, and Sarah shall have a son." (Gen. 18:14)*

  3. To Joseph, About the Purity of Mary

"Now the birth of Jesus Christ was on this wise: When as his mother Mary was espoused to Joseph, before they came together, she was found with child of the Holy Ghost. Then Joseph her husband, being a just man, and not willing to make her a publick example, was minded to put her away privily. But while he thought on these things, behold, the angel of the LORD appeared unto him in a dream, saying, Joseph, thou son of David, fear not to take unto thee Mary thy wife: for that which is conceived in her is of the Holy Ghost. And she shall bring forth a son, and thou shalt call his name JESUS: for he shall save his people from their sins. Now all this was done, that it might be fulfilled which was spoken of the Lord by the prophet, saying, Behold, a virgin shall be with child, and shall bring forth a son, and they shall call his name Emmanuel, which being interpreted is, God with us. Then Joseph being raised from sleep did as the angel of the Lord had bidden him, and took unto him his wife: And knew her not till she had brought forth her firstborn son: and he called his name JESUS." (Mt. 1:18-25)

■ Note especially several key phrases in this passage:
1. *"Thou shalt call his name JESUS"* (1:21a). This name, meaning "Jehovah is salvation" is found over 800 times in the New Testament which both opens and closes its pages with it! *"The book of the generation of Jesus Christ, the son of David, the son of Abraham"* (Mt. 1:1). *"The grace of our Lord Jesus Christ be with you all. Amen"* (Rev. 22:21).
2. *"He shall save his people from their sins"* (1:21b). Thus, Jesus would come to rescue us NOT from our errors, or our shortcomings, but from our SINS!
3. *"Spoken... through the prophet"* (1:22).

■ This prophecy was of course a fulfillment of Isaiah 7:14 (see Mt. 1:23). Some have questioned (unsuccessfully) the Hebrew word Almah in Isa. 7:14, saying it does not always mean virgin. However, there is absolutely no doubt whatsoever about the Greek word for virgin, which is parthenos and always, without exception, refers to a young girl totally devoid of sexual experience.

■ Joseph arranged to make Mary his full, legal wife. Joseph must be considered by all standards of measurement a truly just man, with the spiritual maturity of a David, Moses, or Paul. In fact, the New Testament Joseph may be favorably compared to the Old Testament Joseph. Both had fathers named Jacob. Both had amazing maturity. Both received visions from God. Both were in Egypt. One was a type of Christ; the other was his legal guardian. In fact, had it not been for Judah's sin, Joseph would have been ruling from Jerusalem as the rightful king when Christ was born. It was he and not Herod who had the proper credentials to sit upon the throne of Israel.

B. The Three Songs of Praise
   1. The Praise of Elisabeth to God

"And Mary arose in those days, and went into the hill country with haste, into a city of Juda; And entered into the house of Zacharias, and saluted Elisabeth. And it came to pass, that, when Elisabeth heard the salutation of Mary, the babe leaped in her womb; and Elisabeth was filled with the Holy Ghost: And she spake out with a loud voice, and said, Blessed art thou among women, and blessed is the fruit of thy womb. And whence is this to me, that the mother of my Lord should come to me? For, lo, as soon as the voice of thy salutation sounded in mine ears, the babe leaped in my womb for joy. And blessed is she that believed: for there shall be a performance of those things which were told her from the Lord." (Lk. 1:39-45)

■ Never in the history of childbirth did two expectant mothers have more to talk about than these two women.

   1. Here was Elisabeth, well past the childbearing years, but anticipating a baby.

   2. Here was Mary, a young virgin, but now with child. This was the case because *"with God nothing shall be impossible" (Lk. 1:37).*

   It should be noted that Elisabeth's unborn child is referred to twice as *"the babe" (Lk. 1:41, 44),* indicating Scripture's position on abortion. From the beginning, John was not looked upon as a developing mass of human tissue or a fetus, but as "the babe."

■ But what about a therapeutic abortion? Consider the following: A therapeutic abortion occurs when a pregnant woman is persuaded (often by her doctor) that her unborn child presents an emotional or mental threat to her general well-being. Therefore, the most practical and painless solution (for the mother at least) is simply to kill the offending baby. There are two wellknown instances in history in which this attitude toward unborn human life could certainly have been applied.

   The first case involved that of an older woman, the wife of a respected religious leader, living in a large southern city. Present-day advice to her would have been: "Do you really feel it wise to complete this birth? Consider your age. The psychological strain upon you will be much greater than it would be on a younger woman. Then too, as an older parent, don't you think you'll have real problems adjusting to this infant? I mean, it might even affect your relationship with your husband. No, all things considered, it would be far better to terminate the potential problem right now."

   The second case had to do with a teenage girl, engaged to a struggling young tradesman, living in a small northern town. Here there could be no doubt. A quick abortion would immediately solve the embarrassment and downright hostility which would certainly develop if the unborn baby was not destroyed.

   Two simple and clear-cut cases for therapeutic abortion. Not quite. Could even the most calloused present-day abortion mill operator stomach the thought of Elisabeth (the older woman) and Mary (the teenager) with trembling hands and hearts awaiting the sharp instrument of some ancient abortionist?

---

2. The Praise of Mary to God

   "And Mary said, My soul doth magnify the Lord, And my spirit hath rejoiced in God my Saviour. For he hath regarded the low estate of his handmaiden: for, behold, from henceforth all generations shall call me blessed. For he that is mighty hath done to me great things; and holy is his name. And his mercy is on them that fear him from generation to generation. He hath shewed strength with his arm; he hath scattered the proud in the imagination of their hearts. He hath put down the mighty from their seats, and exalted them of low degree. He hath filled the hungry with good things; and the rich he hath sent empty away." (Lk. 1:46-53)

■ In these verses Mary quotes from at least fifteen Old Testament sources and worships God for displaying His manifold characteristics! She refers to:

   1. His grace (Lk. 1:46-48)

   2. His power (Lk.1:51)

   3. His mercy (Lk.1:50)

   4. His holiness (Lk.1:49)

5. His goodness (Lk.1:53)

6. His faithfulness (Lk.1:54-56)

---

3. The Praise of Zacharias to God

"And his father Zacharias was filled with the Holy Ghost, and prophesied, saying, Blessed be the Lord God of Israel; for he hath visited and redeemed his people, And hath raised up an horn of salvation for us in the house of his servant David; As he spake by the mouth of his holy prophets, which have been since the world began: That we should be saved from our enemies, and from the hand of all that hate us; To perform the mercy promised to our fathers, and to remember his holy covenant; The oath which he sware to our father Abraham, That he would grant unto us, that we being delivered out of the hand of our enemies might serve him without fear, In holiness and righteousness before him, all the days of our life. And thou, child, shalt be called the prophet of the Highest: for thou shalt go before the face of the Lord to prepare his ways; To give knowledge of salvation unto his people by the remission of their sins, Through the tender mercy of our God; whereby the dayspring from on high hath visited us, To give light to them that sit in darkness and in the shadow of death, to guide our feet into the way of peace." (Lk. 1:67-79)

■ In this marvelous passage the old priest thanks God for keeping his promise regarding the fulfilling of two all-important Old Testament covenants, the Abrahamic Covenant (verse 73) and the Davidic Covenant (verse 69).

1. The Abrahamic Covenant had to do with seed and soil. God promised Abraham he would father a great nation (seed) and be given a special land (soil). (See Gen. 12-15.)

2. The Davidic Covenant had to do with a Sovereign God. God promised David that a male descendant from his line (Christ) would someday rule over that seed upon that soil (see 2 Sam. 7). *"He shall be great, and shall be called the Son of the Highest: and the Lord God shall give unto him the throne of his father David: And he shall reign over the house of Jacob for ever; and of his kingdom there shall be no end"* (Lk. 1:32-33).

■ Zacharias predicted that his son would be called "the prophet of the Highest," as contrasted to Gabriel, who referred to Jesus as "the Son of the Highest!"

II. PART TWO: Events Accompanying and Following His Birth

A. From Nazareth to Bethlehem

"And it came to pass in those days, that there went out a decree from Caesar Augustus that all the world should be taxed. (And this taxing was first made when Cyrenius was governor of Syria.) And all went to be taxed, every one into his own city. And Joseph also went up from Galilee, out of the city of Nazareth, into Judaea, unto the city of David, which is called Bethlehem; (because he was of the house and lineage of David:) To be taxed with Mary his espoused wife, being great with child." (Lk. 2:1-5)

■ Joseph and Mary were brought to Bethlehem because of an enrollment decree which commanded each Hebrew citizen to be counted from that town where he or she was born. Note: This is the third all-important trip made to Bethlehem. Ruth and Naomi made the first journey (see Ruth 1:22). Samuel the prophet made the second (see 1 Sam. 16).

■ Had it not been for the first trip, Ruth would not have met Boaz, both who would later become the great-grandparents of King David (Ruth 4:21-22).

■ Were it not for the second trip, David would not have been anointed as King by Samuel!

■ This is the only occasion in the scripture where Bethlehem is called the city of David. In all other instances Jerusalem is that city.

B. At Bethlehem

"And so it was, that, while they were there, the days were accomplished that she should be delivered. And she brought forth her firstborn son, and wrapped him in swaddling clothes, and laid him in a manger; because there was no room for them in the inn. And there were in the same country shepherds abiding in the field, keeping watch over their flock by night. And, lo, the angel of the Lord came upon them, and the glory of the Lord shone round about them: and they were sore afraid. And the angel said unto them, Fear not: for, behold, I bring you good tidings of great joy, which shall be to all people. For unto you is born this day in the city of David a Saviour, which is Christ the Lord. And this shall be a sign unto you; Ye shall find the babe wrapped in swaddling clothes, lying in a manger. And suddenly there was with the angel a multitude of the heavenly host praising God, and saying, Glory to God in the highest, and on earth peace, good will toward men. And it came to pass, as the angels were gone away from them into heaven, the shepherds said one to another, Let us now go even unto Bethlehem, and see this thing which is come to pass, which the Lord hath made known unto us. And they came with haste, and found Mary, and Joseph, and the babe lying in a manger. And when they had seen it, they made known abroad the saying which was told them concerning this child. And all they that heard it wondered at those things which were told them by the shepherds. But Mary kept all these things, and pondered them in her heart And the shepherds returned, glorifying and praising God for all the things that they had heard and seen, as it was told unto them. And when eight days were accomplished for the circumcising of the child, his name was called JESUS, which was so named of the angel before he was conceived in the womb. (Lk. 2:6-21)

■ Some have considered the words of Lk. 2:7 as describing the fifth greatest day in human history! If this be the case, then:

   1. The fourth greatest day would occur some 34 years later on a hill outside the city of Jerusalem–

      "And when they were come to the place, which is called Calvary, there they crucified him, and the malefactors, one on the right hand, and the other on the left." (Lk. 23:33)

   2. The third greatest day happened on a Sunday morning beside an empty tomb as announced by an angel–

      "And the angel answered and said unto the women, Fear not ye: for I know that ye seek Jesus, which was crucified. He is not here: for he is risen, as he said. Come, see the place where the Lord lay." (Mt. 28:5-6)

   3. The second greatest day transpired nearly six weeks later on Mt. Olivet immediately following Jesus' parting words to His apostles:

      "But ye shall receive power, after that the Holy Ghost is come upon you: and ye shall be witnesses unto me both in Jerusalem, and in all Judaea, and in Samaria, and unto the uttermost part of the earth. And when

---

he had spoken these things, while they beheld, he was taken up; and a cloud received him out of their sight."
(Acts 1:8-9)

4. The greatest day however is yet to occur. John the apostle describes it by the following thrilling words:

"Therefore are they before the throne of God, and serve him day and night in his temple: and he that sitteth on the throne shall dwell among them." (Rev. 7:15)

■ One may favorably contrast Lk. 2:7 with Dan. 2:11. In this Old Testament passage King Nebuchadnezzar had just ordered the death of his wise men because of their inability to relate a dream he had just experienced. These astrologers thereupon protested, exclaiming: *"And it is a rare thing that the king requireth, and there is no other that can shew it before the king, except the gods, whose dwelling is not with flesh."* But at the advent of the fifth greatest day in history all this would change.

■ In Jn. 1:14 we read that the Word was made flesh. One of the most glorious truths of the incarnation was its eternality. This simply means that the results of this day will last forever. He still has and always will have a body of flesh and bone (see Lk. 24:39).

■ In the 1960s an American astronaut wrote a book entitled Moon Walk. In it he related how he had left a pleasant, familiar, and safe place called earth and had landed on an alien, dangerous, and unfamiliar planet known as the moon. When rightly understood, Lk. 2:7 is the divine account of Earth Walk, for it begins the story of how God's Son left the beauty and safety of heaven to dwell upon an alien and sin-cursed planet, the wicked world of mankind.

■ To rephrase the familiar nursery rhyme:

Mary had a little Lamb, His life was pure as snow.
And everywhere the Father led, the Lamb was sure to go.
He followed Him to Calvary, one dark and dreadful day,
And there the Lamb that Mary had washed all my sins away.

■ Note just how the angels announced the birth of Jesus to the shepherds: *"For unto you is born this day in the city of David a Saviour, which is Christ the Lord." (Lk. 2:11)*

An unknown author has written:

If our greatest need had been information
God would have sent us an educator.
If our greatest need had been technology
God would have sent us a scientist.
If our greatest need had been money
God would have sent us an economist.
If our greatest need had been pleasure
God would have sent us an entertainer.
But, alas, our greatest need was forgiveness and redemption
So ... God sent us a Savior.

- Observe how the shepherds came, and how they left.
  1. They *"came with haste" (Lk. 2:16)*.
  2. They left and *"made known abroad....concerning this child" (Lk. 2:17)*.

- At this point, let us stop and consider several questions that may be raised concerning those events leading up to the birth of the Savior.
  1. Why did Joseph and Mary wait so long before coming to Bethlehem? We know that both believed the angel's message about the Babe in Mary's womb, and they doubtless were well aware of the prophecy in Micah 5:2 which stated that Christ was to be born in Bethlehem.

     Why did they wait until the last moment to come? In fact, one is somewhat led to believe that had it not been for the decree of Caesar Augustus they might not have come at all. Answer: No satisfactory answer has been found by this author. It is best to conclude that Joseph (man of God that he was) had good reasons for acting in the manner that he did. The reader may desire to explore this further.
  2. Why didn't Mary and Joseph stay with their relatives in Bethlehem? The inns of those days were rather notorious, and Joseph must have been desperate to subject his pregnant wife to the sin and noise of such a place. But, of course, they were denied even this. Answer: It would have been too difficult to explain (or to expect them to understand) the nature of the virgin birth. Every gossip in town doubtless knew by this time that Joseph and Mary had been married only six months, and there she was, expecting a baby at any moment. Was the father Joseph? Did the child belong to some stranger? Thus, to spare his beloved wife all this, Joseph did not call upon their relatives.
  3. Why was Jesus born in a place which apparently housed animals? Answer: Because lambs are usually born in barns. This was God's Lamb.
  4. Why did the angels appear to the shepherds first? Answer: What other earthly group than shepherds would better understand what God had just accomplished? These were men who raised lambs and later sold them for sacrificial purposes in the temple (see John 1:29; 10:11).

     Note: They would eventually understand that in the past the sheep had died for the shepherd, but soon the Shepherd planned to die for the sheep (see John 10:11).
  5. Why did God use the angels in the first place? Answer:
     a. He Because angels are interested in the things of salvation (see 1 Pet. 1:12; Exod. 25:20; Dan. 12:5-6; Lk. 15:10; Eph. 3:10).
     b. Because they were present at the creation of this world and shouted for joy (Job 38:7). It is only logical, therefore, that God would allow them to be on hand at the presentation of the Savior of this world.

- Finally, Luke records Mary's reaction to all this:

  "But Mary kept all these things, and pondered them in her heart" (Lk. 2:19).

  It can be rightly said Mary probably had more to ponder than any other person in human history! Consider:
  1. As she first held the tiny infant in her arms, Mary may have pondered:

     "This is incredible! My little babe, not yet five minutes old, is already infinitely older than His mother and as old as His Father!"
  2. As he received the milk from her breast, perhaps she pondered.

     "Miracles of miracles! I'm actually feeding the Bread of Life who once fed my ancestors with bread from heaven during their 40 years trek in the wilderness!"

3. As she washed his soiled diapers, she might have marveled:

"Who would believe it? I'm performing this thankless task for that One who once created the earth, the sun, moon, and stars!"

C. In Jerusalem

"And when the days of her purification according to the law of Moses were accomplished, they brought him to Jerusalem, to present him to the Lord; (As it is written in the law of the LORD, Every male that openeth the womb shall be called holy to the Lord;) And to offer a sacrifice according to that which is said in the law of the Lord, A pair of turtledoves, or two young pigeons. And, behold, there was a man in Jerusalem, whose name was Simeon; and the same man was just and devout, waiting for the consolation of Israel: and the Holy Ghost was upon him. And it was revealed unto him by the Holy Ghost, that he should not see death, before he had seen the Lord's Christ. And he came by the Spirit into the temple: and when the parents brought in the child Jesus, to do for him after the custom of the law, Then took he him up in his arms, and blessed God, and said," (Lk. 2:22-28).

■ Jesus was brought to the temple to be dedicated to the Lord.
1. He was at least forty days old at this time, for Mary would have been considered ceremonially impure until forty days had elapsed following childbirth (see Lev. 12:2-4; Exod. 13:2)
2. Two offerings were to be brought (Lev. 12:6).
   a. A yearling lamb as a burnt offering
   b. A young pigeon or turtledove as a sin offering
3. However, if the family was poor, God would accept two birds (Lev. 12:8). Joseph and Mary offered these birds in place of the lamb.

■ Simeon describes Mary's small son in seven-fold fashion. He was and would become:
1. The Lord's Christ (2:25)
2. God's salvation (2:30)
3. The light of the Gentiles (2:32a)
4. The consolation of Israel (2:25)
5. The glory of Israel (2:32b)
6. The judge of the lost (2:34a)
7. The joy of the saved (2:34b)

■ Note Simeon's prophecy in 2:35:

Some thirty-four years later, Mary would stand at the foot of a hideous Roman cross outside the city of Jerusalem, watching her firstborn Son die in agony. Surely at that awful moment the full significance of Simeon's strange words would fall with crushing weight upon her soul.

D. Back in Bethlehem

"Now when Jesus was born in Bethlehem of Judaea in the days of Herod the king, behold, there came wise men from the east to Jerusalem, Saying, Where is he that is born King of the Jews? for we have seen his star in the east, and are come to worship him. When Herod the king had heard these things, he was troubled, and all Jerusalem with him. And when he had gathered all the chief priests and scribes of the people together, he demanded of them where Christ should be born. And they said unto him, In Bethlehem of Judaea: for thus it is written by the prophet, And thou Bethlehem, in the land of Juda, art not the least among the princes of Juda: for out of thee shall come a Governor, that shall rule my people Israel. Then Herod, when he had privily called the wise men, enquired of them diligently what time the star appeared. And he sent them to Bethlehem, and said, Go and search diligently for the young child; and when ye have found him, bring me word again, that I may come and worship him also. When they had heard the king, they departed; and, lo, the star, which they saw in the east, went before them, till it came and stood over where the young child was. When they saw the star, they rejoiced with exceeding great joy. And when they were come into the house, they saw the young child with Mary his mother, and fell down, and worshipped him: and when they had opened their treasures, they presented unto him gifts; gold, and frankincense and myrrh. And being warned of God in a dream that they should not return to Herod, they departed into their own country another way." (Mt. 2:1-12)

■ Here is a concise two-fold summary of Herod the Great, second son of Antipater, and a descendant of Esau.

1. Herod the brutal—He became King of the Jews through the favor of the Romans. Able and courageous, but jealous and cruel, he became half-insane toward the close of his life and tried to murder everybody who seemed to threaten his throne. He killed his wife Marianne and three of his sons. He killed his son Antipater just five days before his own death. He commanded a large group of the nobles among the Jews to be assembled and killed at his death in order that there should be a sufficient amount of mourning.

2. Herod the builder—Josephus, the Jewish historian, writes:

"To conciliate the Jews, who had been alienated by his cruelties, he with much address proposed to reconstruct their ancient temple which Solomon had originally built, though it has been shrewdly suspected that he entertained the sinister motive to possess himself of the public genealogies collected there, especially those relating to the priestly families, unto whom they were of paramount importance and interest. It is said that he thereby hoped to destroy the genealogy of the expected Messiah, lest He should come and usurp His kingdom. However, that may be, he endeavored to make the Jewish nation understand that he was doing them a great kindness without cost to them, and he promised that he would not attempt to build them a new temple, but merely restore to its ancient magnificence the one originally built by David's son. For the restoration made by Zerubbabel upon the return of Israel from the captivity of Babylon seems to have fallen short in architectural measurement, in height some sixty cubits, and the whole was becoming marked with decay. To this end Herod took down the old temple to its very foundations, and engaged one thousand wagons to draw stones and ten thousand skilled workmen to teach the priests the art of stonecutting and carpentering."

The temple proper which he erected was one hundred cubits in length and twenty cubits in height. It was constructed of white stone, each one being twenty-five cubits long and eight in height. Surmounting this structure was a great white dome adorned with a pinnacle of gold, suggestive of a mountain of snow as seen from afar.

The Jewish tradition holds that the temple itself was built by the priests in one year and six months, when they celebrated its completion with Jewish feasts and sacrifices; but that the cloisters and outer enclosures were eight years in building. However that may be, additions were made continuously from year to year, so that though Herod began the rebuilding in 20 B.C., as a whole it was literally true that the temple was built in forty and six years, when the Jews so asserted to Jesus (Jn. 2:20).

But the end was not yet, for the work was really continued until A.D. 64, just six years before the final destruction of the temple (Ant. XV. Ch. 11).

■ A brief overview of the wise men's visit might consist of eight questions and answers:

1. Who were these wise men? It is thought that they were perhaps a group of religious astronomers living in the Mesopotamian area.

2. How did they associate the star with Christ? There are several possibilities. In the fourteenth century, B.C., a prophet from their area named Balaam had spoken of this star (see Num. 24:17). They also had the writings of Daniel, who had been prime minister of both Babylon and Persia some six centuries before Christ. Daniel, of course, wrote much about the second coming.

3. Why did they come? These men were doubtless acquainted with the various religions of the East and knew the emptiness of them all. It would seem that they followed this star to find peace and purpose for their lives.

4. When did they arrive in Bethlehem? It was perhaps not until some two years after the angels announced his birth to the shepherds. He is referred to as "the young child" (Mt. 2:9, 11, 13-14), and is not a tiny babe at this time. When Herod later attempted to destroy this unknown Babe, he had all children in the Bethlehem area two years and under slain (Mt. 2:16).

5. How many wise men came? There is no evidence that there were three. On the contrary, the group may have numbered from two to several hundred or more. Tradition, however, claims that there were but three and that their names were Caspar, Melchior, and Balthazar.

6. Why did the star, after leading the wise men to Jerusalem, apparently disappear for a brief time and then reappear, taking them directly to Bethlehem? It may be that God intended this visit for the sake of the Jewish leaders. However, they had degenerated to such a level that they were unwilling to travel down the road a few miles from Jerusalem to Bethlehem to see if their Messiah had really come. But here was a group of sincere Gentiles who had traveled across a hostile and extended desert to find him.

7. Was the star a regular one? The astronomer Kepler said there was a conjunction of the planets Jupiter and Saturn about this time in history. However, by no stretch of the imagination could a planet or star located thousands of millions of miles from earth function in the precise way this star did as recorded by Matthew: *"The star. .. came and stood over where the young child was"* (Mt. 2:9). It is not at all unreasonable, however, to suggest that the star was actually a New Testament appearance of that Old Testament Shekinah Glory cloud that led Israel across the desert.

8. What gifts did they offer him?
   a. They gave him gold, which spoke of his deity.
   b. They gave him frankincense, which spoke of his humanity.
   c. They gave him myrrh, which spoke of his future sufferings. Reg Grant writes:

"During her life, Mary would see Jesus receive the gift of myrrh on five occasions; twice from Gentiles and three times from Jews."

(1) On the first occasion, the Magi brought myrrh from the east in honor of Jesus as King of kings (Mt. 2:11). This event anticipated the worship Christ will receive from the Gentile nations in the future kingdom.

(2) The second occasion found Jesus in the home of Simon the Pharisee receiving myrrh from the loving hand of a contrite woman who approached Jesus as her great High Priest, the One who could forgive her many sins (Lk. 7:36-50).

(3) The third offering of myrrh came from the devout Mary of Bethany as she anointed Christ for his burial prior to his death. This showed that she understood the sacrificial nature of his ministry in a way that even his closest disciples had failed to grasp.

(4) Just before the crucifixion, the Roman soldiers offered Christ a fourth 'gift' of myrrh mixed with wine—a kind of narcotic to dull the pain—but he refused it.

(5) The fifth and final offering came from the hand of Nicodemus when he provided a mixture of myrrh and aloes for anointing Christ's body following his crucifixion. (Jn. 19:39) (*Kindred Spirit*, Winter 1988, pp. 13-14.)

E. From Bethlehem to Egypt

"And when they were departed, behold, the angel of the Lord appeareth to Joseph in a dream, saying, Arise, and take the young child and his mother, and flee into Egypt, and be thou there until I bring thee word: for Herod will seek the young child to destroy him. When he arose, he took the young child and his mother by night, and departed into Egypt: And was there until the death of Herod: that it might be fulfilled which was spoken of the Lord by the prophet, saying, Out of Egypt have I called my son. Then Herod, when he saw that he was mocked of the wise men, was exceeding wroth, and sent forth, and slew all the children that were in Bethlehem, and in all the coasts thereof, from two years old and under, according to the time which he had diligently enquired of the wise men. Then was fulfilled that which was spoken by Jeremy the prophet, saying, In Rama was there a voice heard, lamentation, and weeping, and great mourning, Rachel weeping for her children, and would not be comforted, because they are not." (Mt. 2:13-18)

■ A divine irony is seen here. In the Old Testament God led his chosen people out of Egypt to escape Satan's wrath, but in the New Testament he leads his beloved Son into Egypt to escape this same wrath.

F. From Egypt to Nazareth

"But when Herod was dead, behold, an angel of the Lord appeareth in a dream to Joseph in Egypt, Saying, Arise, and take the young child and his mother, and go into the land of Israel: for they are dead which sought the young child's life. And he arose, and took the young child and his mother, and came into the land of Israel. But when he heard that Archelaus did reign in Judaea in the room of his father Herod, he

was afraid to go thither: notwithstanding, being warned of God in a dream, he turned aside into the parts of Galilee: And he came and dwelt in a city called Nazareth: that it might be fulfilled which was spoken by the prophets, He shall be called a Nazarene." (Mt. 2:19-23)

■ This passage records the final of three dreams given by God to Joseph in relation to the incarnation of Jesus (see Mt. 1:20; 2:13, 20).

■ It also marks the only occasion where Jesus is personally referred to as a Nazarene (Mt. 2:23). In a later passage His followers are described as belonging to "the sect of the Nazarenes" (Acts 24:5).

THE EARLY YEARS OF JESUS IN NAZARETH

THE SILENT YEARS OF JESUS IN NAZARETH

I. From Age Two to Twelve

"And when they had performed all things according to the law of the Lord, they returned into Galilee, to their own city Nazareth. And the child grew, and waxed strong in spirit, filled with wisdom: and the grace of God was upon him ... And he went down with them, and came to Nazareth, and was subject unto them: but his mother kept all these sayings in her heart. And Jesus increased in wisdom and stature, and in favour with God and man." (Lk. 2:39-40, 51-52)

■ How did Jesus develop as a human being?

While most liberal theologians tend to deny the deity of Jesus, evangelicals often downplay his humanity. As has been often observed, while upon this planet, our Lord was as much God had he never been man, but also as much man had he never been God. The second part of this statement is vital in rightly understanding his earthly ministry, lest we think of him in terms of gliding about down here with angelic movements, always looking upwards at the golden halo which surrounded his head. All this of course is pious nonsense, as demonstrated by the two key words "grew" and "increased," as found in Luke 2. How, then, did Jesus develop as a human being?

1. He increased in wisdom (mental maturity). Nowhere are we told he possessed total knowledge, allowing him to instantly understand all things as a baby. In fact, to the contrary, most conservative theologians believe that while he indeed retained his divine attributes, such as his omniscience, he did not, however, use them, but depended completely upon the Holy Spirit (see Phil. 2:5-8; Lk. 4:18; Jn. 3:34.)

    Thus, later in his ministry Jesus employed the Scriptures in a very effective way indeed in dealing with both his friends (Lk. 24:25-27) and his foes (Mt. 4:1-11; 22:29), but only because he had faithfully studied the Hebrew Bible as a lad.

2. He increased in stature (physical maturity). There is positive evidence in the Gospel accounts that our Lord was a strong and powerfully built man. An indication of this can be seen by his ability to intimidate on two separate occasions the greedy money changers in the temple (see Jn. 2:13-16; Mt. 21:12-13).

    We are told that Joseph was a carpenter (Mt. 13:55), and it is not unreasonable to conclude that Jesus also learned this trade as a boy. However, in New Testament times a carpenter probably worked more with stone than wood, due to the abundance of the first. Our Lord thus had the opportunity to build strong muscles by diligently moving and molding those stones.

3. He increased in favor with God (spiritual maturity). Even though he was the unique Son of God and had, before Bethlehem, enjoyed unparalleled fellowship with his Father (Jn. 17:5), he nevertheless cultivated his quiet time with God during long hours of prayer upon the hills surrounding Nazareth. The time involved was

probably early morning, as suggested by his adult prayer habit: *"And in the morning, rising up a great while being day, he went out, and departed into a solitary place, and there prayed." (Mk. 1:35)*

Not only was he faithful in prayer but also in attending his Father's house to hear the Word of God expounded. *"And he came to Nazareth, where he had been brought up: and, as his custom was, he went into the synagogue on the sabbath day, and stood up for to read." (Lk. 4:16)*

4. He increased in favor with man (social maturity). Although he was sinless, Jesus apparently did not display his righteousness in a way that turned people off. To the contrary, he seemed to be well received among the citizens of Nazareth. It is true that his younger half brothers would later turn against him (Jn. 7:5). However, for the most part he was viewed in a positive light. This characteristic was carried over into his public ministry. We are told *"the common people heard him gladly" (Mk. 12:37)*. Crowds flocked to hear him (Lk. 8:19; 19:3). Parents brought their children to him (Mk. 10:13). Both the sick (Mt. 9:18) and needy sinners sought him out (Lk. 19:1-4).

What is the primary lesson from all the above? Simply this: While on earth, as a human being, Jesus Christ carefully and consistently developed his mental, physical, spiritual, and social features in such a way as to bring the greatest possible amount of glory to his Father and the greatest possible good to his fellow man. As redeemed human beings, God desires for us to do the exact same thing.

■ Did he go to school? Some would say no, based on these verses in John's gospel: *"Now about the midst of the feast Jesus went up into the temple, and taught. And the Jews marvelled, saying, How knoweth this man letters, having never learned? Jesus answered them, and said, My doctrine is not mine, but his that sent me." (Jn. 7:14-16)*

However, the phrase "having never learned" may have referred to the learning offered in a rabbinical school. In other words, the Jewish leaders were amazed that Christ could speak with such spiritual knowledge and authority, since he had never been enrolled in their religious schools.

Jesus as a boy had doubtless learned Hebrew, Aramaic, and Greek. He later would read from a Hebrew scroll in Nazareth (Lk. 4), teach the multitudes in Aramaic, and converse with Pilate in Greek. He may have read the Testaments of the Twelve Patriarchs, which was a noncanonical account relating the testimony of Jacob's twelve sons. He surely also would have been familiar with well-known Jewish books on the sacred Law and writings.

■ Do we know anything concerning his early years? In reality we possess no hard facts whatsoever about Jesus from age two to age twelve.

II. At Age Twelve

"Now his parents went to Jerusalem every year at the feast of the passover. And when he was twelve years old, they went up to Jerusalem after the custom of the feast And when they had fulfilled the days, as they returned, the child Jesus tarried behind in Jerusalem; and Joseph and his mother knew not of it. But they, supposing him to have been in the company, went a day's journey; and they sought him among their kinsfolk and acquaintance. And when they found him not, they turned back again to Jerusalem, seeking him. And it came to pass, that after three days they found him in the temple, sitting in the midst of the doctors, both hearing them, and asking them questions. And all that heard him were astonished at his understanding and answers. And when they saw him, they were amazed: and his mother said unto him, Son, why hast thou thus

dealt with us? behold, thy father and I have sought thee sorrowing. And he said unto them, How is it that ye sought me? wist ye not that I must be about my Father's business? And they understood not the saying which he spake unto them." (Lk. 2:41-50)

■ This is but the first of many incidents in which people were astonished at the words and wisdom of Christ. This is recorded:

1. Following his Sermon on the Mount (Mt. 7:28)
2. At the end of his lecture in Nazareth (Mt. 13:54)
3. During his debate with the Pharisees in Jerusalem (Mt. 22:33)

■ Note also that Jesus spoke his first recorded words: *"I must be about my Father's business."* Compare these with the words he spoke en route from heaven's glory to Bethlehem's manger. *"Wherefore when he cometh into the world, he saith, Sacrifice and offering thou wouldest not, but a body hast thou prepared me ... Then said I, Lo, I come (in the volume of the book it is written of me,) to do thy will, O God." (Heb. 10:5, 7)*

■ Our Lord thus began His ministry by referring to the Father. Some twenty years later He would complete it in similar fashion, as seen through His first and last utterance on the cross:

"Then said Jesus, Father, forgive them; for they know not what they do. And they parted his raiment, and cast lots." (Lk. 23:34)

"And when Jesus had cried with a loud voice, he said, Father, into thy hands I commend my spirit: and having said thus, he gave up the ghost." (Lk. 23:46)

III. From Age Twelve to Thirty

"And Jesus himself began to be about thirty years of age, being (as was supposed) the son of Joseph, which was the son of Heli." (Lk. 3:23)

"And it came to pass, that when Jesus had finished these parables, he departed thence. And when he was come into his own country, he taught them in their synagogue, insomuch that they were astonished, and said, Whence hath this man this wisdom, and these mighty works? Is not this the carpenter's son? is not his mother called Mary? and his brethren, James, and Joses, and Simon, and Judas? And his sisters, are they not all with us? Whence then hath this man all these things?" (Mt. 13:53-56)

■ Here it can be readily seen that with the exception of His birth, worship by the shepherd and wise men, and temple visit at twelve, we know almost nothing regarding the first thirty years of our Lord's earthly walk.

■ In fact, of the 89 chapters in the four gospel accounts, only four are given over in describing the first thirty years of His life!

The Baptism of Jesus

"Then cometh Jesus from Galilee to Jordan unto John, to be baptized of him. But John forbad him, saying, I have need to be baptized of thee, and comest thou to me? And Jesus answering said unto him, Suffer it to be so now: for thus it becometh us to fulfil all righteousness. Then he suffered him. And Jesus, when he was baptized, went up straightway out of the water: and, lo, the heavens were opened unto him, and he saw the Spirit of God descending like a dove, and lighting upon him: And lo a voice from heaven, saying, This is my beloved Son, in whom I am well pleased." (Mt. 3:13-17)

I. The Three Persons Involved

■ This is the clearest illustration of the doctrine of the Trinity in the entire Bible:

1. The Father speaks from heaven.
2. The Son stands in the water.
3. The Holy Spirit descends.

■ This marks the first of three occasions on which the Father orally expressed his approval of the Son.

1. Here at the baptism
2. On the Mount of Transfiguration (Mt. 17:5)
3. In Jerusalem (Jn. 12:28)

■ This first approval is especially significant because of when it occurred. At this time our Lord had yet to perform one miracle or preach one sermon. Yet his life had already won the favor of the Father. We are prone to reverse this, assuming God awaits spectacular works before he can officially approve us. But to the contrary, divine sanction rests upon present day attitudes and not upon future achievements. In fact, the first is the root from which the second becomes the fruit.

An example of this principle can be seen in the life of Timothy, whom Paul praised in the most glowing manner: *"I hope in the Lord Jesus to send Timothy to you soon, that I also may be cheered when I received news about you. I have no one else like him, who takes a genuine interest in your welfare. For everyone looks out for his own interests, not those of Jesus Christ. But you know that Timothy has proved himself, because as a son with his father he has served with me in the work of the gospel." (Phil. 2:19-22, NW)*

This, then, described the fruit of Timothy's ministry. But what of the root? The apostle speaks of this during his final epistle: *"But continue thou in the things which thou hast learned and hast been assured of, knowing of whom thou hast learned them; And that from a child thou hast known the holy scriptures, which are able to make thee wise unto salvation through faith which is in Christ Jesus." (2 Tim. 3:14-15)*

- Apparently the divine approval from heaven was given to reassure BOTH John and Jesus as seen by the three gospel accounts. Thus:
  1. Matthew records the Father as saying, "This is my beloved Son." (Mt. 3:17)
  2. Mark and Luke record the Father as saying, "You are my beloved son." (Mk. 1:11; Lk. 3:21)
  3. Finally, the event gives us the first reference to Jesus' prayer life: *"Now when all the people were baptized, it came to pass, that Jesus also being baptized, and praying, the heaven was opened." (Lk. 3:21)*

II. The Five Reasons Involved

- Why was Christ baptized? Here it may be stated that his baptism totally refutes that false doctrine of baptismal regeneration, that is, the claim that one must be baptized to be saved. The Savior of all people did not need to be saved himself. But why, then, was he baptized?
  1. He was baptized in order to identify with the message of John the Baptist. Actually, there were two aspects to John's message:
     a. *"God's kingdom is at hand! The Messiah is here!"*
     b. *"Repent therefore of your sin and be baptized to demonstrate this repentance."* Thus Christ was baptized to identify with the first part of John's message, while the converts fulfilled the second aspect.
  2. He was baptized so that John would know that Jesus was the true Messiah. *"And I knew him not: but he that sent me to baptize with water, the same said unto me, Upon whom thou shalt see the Spirit descending, and remaining on him, the same is he which baptizeth with the Holy Ghost." (Jn. 1:33)*
  3. He was baptized to signal the beginning of his work as the Messiah. This was similar to the Old Testament minister who began his ministry at age thirty after a special ordination service.
  4. He was baptized to identify himself with the office of the prophet, priest, and king. In the Old Testament, all three were anointed in connection with their office. In Lev. 8 is described the threefold anointing of a priest. He was first washed with water, then anointed with oil, then finally with blood. Christ submitted to the first two of these (water baptism and the oil of the Spirit), but not to the third.
  5. He was baptized to show that he had the total approval and support of both other members of the Trinity, the Father and Holy Spirit.

III. The Six Examples Involved

- This is the first of various baptisms mentioned in the Gospel accounts. The word baptism means *"to identify with."*
  1. The baptism of John the Baptist—This was national baptism (see Mk. 1:4)
  2. The baptism of Jesus
     a. With water by John (Mt. 3:15)
     b. With the Holy Spirit by the Father (Mt. 3:16)
  3. The baptism of sin upon Christ at Calvary (Lk. 12:50; Mt. 20:22)
  4. The baptism of the Holy Spirit upon believers at Pentecost (Mt. 3:11b)
  5. The baptism of God's wrath upon sinners during the tribulation (Mt. 3:11b; 3:12; 13:30)
  6. The baptism of believers (Mt. 28:19)

THE TEMPTATION OF JESUS

"Then was Jesus led up of the spirit into the wilderness to be tempted of the devil. And when he had fasted forty days and forty nights, he was afterward an hungered And when the tempter came to him, he said, If thou be the Son of God, command that these stones be made bread. But he answered and said, It is written, Man shall not live by bread alone, but by every word that proceedeth out of the mouth of God. Then the devil taketh him up into the holy city, and setteth him on a pinnacle of the temple, And saith unto him, If thou be the Son of God, cast thyself down: for it is written, He shall give his angels charge concerning thee: and in their hands they shall bear thee up, lest at any time thou dash thy foot against a stone. Jesus said unto him, It is written again, Thou shalt not tempt the Lord thy God. Again, the devil taketh him up into an exceeding high mountain, and sheweth him all the kingdoms of the world, and the glory of them; And saith unto him, All these things will I give thee, if thou wilt fall down and worship me. Then saith Jesus unto him, Get thee hence, Satan: for it is written, Thou shalt worship the Lord thy God, and him only shalt thou serve. Then the devil leaveth him, and, behold, angels came and ministered unto him." (Mt. 4:1-11)

I. Temptation and the Son of God

■ In what ways can the temptations experienced by the first Adam and the second Adam be compared and contrasted?

1. The comparison—In his first epistle, John separated all temptations into three general categories or groups (1 John 2:16). These are: the lust of the flesh, the lust of the eyes, and the pride of life.
   a. The first Adam was tempted in each area (Gen. 3:6).
      (1) *"The tree was good for food"* (the lust of the flesh).
      (2) *"It was pleasant to the eyes"* (the lust of the eyes).
      (3) *"A tree desired to make one wise"* (the pride of Iife).
   b. The second Adam was tempted in each area.
      (1) *"Command that these stones be made bread"* (the lust of the flesh).
      (2) *"The devil...showeth him all the kingdoms of the world and the glory of them"* (the lust of the eyes).
      (3) *"Cast thyself down: for.. he shall give his angels charge concerning thee"* (the pride of life).

2. The contrast
   a. The first Adam was tempted in a beautiful garden, while the second Adam met Satan in a desolate wilderness.
   b. The first Adam experienced total failure, while the second Adam was completely victorious.

■ Did Satan know whom he was tempting? He did indeed. The account in Mt. 4:3 and 4:6 is in the indicative mode in the Greek and should be rendered, *"Since you are the Son of God."*

■ What benefits did Satan offer him?

1. First temptation: To fill his stomach (and thus depend upon his own resources).

2. Second temptation: To jump off the temple (and thus force the hand of the Father).

3. Third temptation: To grasp the kingdoms of this world (and thus refuse Calvary).

■ What trick did Satan use during the second temptation? He attempted to confuse Christ by quoting Scripture out of context (compare Mt. 4:6 with Psa. 91:11-12). In essence, he did the same thing in dealing with the first Adam (Gen. 3:1).

■ Why are Jesus' temptations associated with a period of forty days? This number is often one of tempting or testing as found in the Bible. Examples would be:

1. Moses (Ex. 24:18; 34:28)

2. Israel (Deut. 8:2-3)

3. Elijah (1 Kings 19:8)

4. Goliath (1 Sam. 17:16)

■ Did Satan really have the right to offer Christ *"all the kingdoms of the world and the glory of them"* (Mt. 4:8)?

1. In a shallow and temporary sense, yes (see John 14:30; Eph. 2:2; 6:12; 1 John 5:19; Rev. 13:7).

2. In the deepest and most eternal sense, no. *"Yet have I set my king upon my holy hill of Zion. I will declare the decree: the LORD hath said unto me, Thou art my Son; this day have I begotten thee. Ask of me, and I shall give thee the heathen for thine inheritance, and the uttermost parts of the earth for thy possession. Thou shalt break them with a rod of iron; thou shalt dash them in pieces like a potters vessel"* (Psa. 2:6-9). *"And the seventh angel sounded; and there were great voices in heaven, saying, The kingdoms of this world are become the kingdoms of our Lord, and of his Christ; and he shall reign for ever and ever."* (Rev. 11:15)

■ How did Christ answer Satan? By the Word of God.

1. First temptation: *"It is written, man shall not live by bread alone, but by every word that proceedeth out of the mouth of God."* (Compare Mt. 4:4 with Deut. 8:3.)

2. Second temptation: *"It is written again, Thou shalt not tempt the Lord thy God."* (Compare Mt. 4:7 with Deut. 6:16.)

This temptation was probably an attempt for him to prematurely (and wrongly) fulfill Malachi 3:1: *"Behold, I will send my messenger, and he shall prepare the way before me: and the LORD, whom ye seek, shall suddenly come to his temple, even the messenger of the covenant, whom ye delight in: behold, he shall come, saith the LORD of hosts."*

Satan's supreme object in the temptation ordeal was to cause Christ to act by himself, independent of the Father. Just what does it mean to tempt God? Israel is said to have tempted God on ten specific occasions en route to the promised land (see Num. 14:11, 22; Heb. 3:9). It means simply to presume upon the goodness of God. It refers to using this goodness in a selfish way. It means to force God's hand on something. Had Christ actually jumped from this temple pinnacle, God would have been forced to step in and save Christ from smashing his physical body on the ground below.

3. Third temptation: *"Get thee hence, Satan: for it is written, thou shalt worship the Lord thy God, and him only shalt thou serve."* (Compare Mt. 4:10 with Deut. 6:13. See also James 4:7.)

■ Is this the only time Satan tempted Christ? No. In Lk.4:13 we are told: *"And when the devil had ended all the temptation, he departed from him for a season."* Note especially the last three words. Satan tempted Christ all through his ministry. At least three specific instances come to mind here in which, at a later date, Satan continued his tempting work against Christ.

1. As expressed by the 5,000 men Christ fed— *"When Jesus therefore perceived that they would come and take him by force, to make him a king, he departed again into a mountain himself alone" (Jn. 6:15).* "Bypass the cross and grab the crown!"

2. As expressed by Simon Peter— *"from that time forth began Jesus to shew unto his disciples, how that he must go unto Jerusalem, and suffer many things of the elders and chief priests and scribes, and be killed, and be raised again the third day. Then Peter took him, and began to rebuke him, saying, Be it far from thee, Lord.-this shall not be unto thee. But he turned, and said unto Peter, Get thee behind me, Satan: thou art an offence unto me: for thou savourest not the things that be of God, but those that be of men" (Mt. 16:21-23).* "Don't even talk about the Cross!"

3. As expressed by the mob at Calvary— *"And they that passed by reviled him, wagging their heads, And saying, Thou that destroyest the temple, and buildest it in three days, save thyself. If thou be the Son of God, come down from the cross" (Mt. 27:39-40).* "Come down from the cross!"

■ What happened after the wilderness temptation? *"Then the devil leaveth him, and, behold, angels came and ministered unto him." (Mt. 4:11)* Heaven's angels played an important part in the earthly ministry of Christ.

1. They announced his birth (Lk. 1-2; Mt. 1).
2. They later ministered to him in Gethsemane (Lk. 22:43).
3. They announced his resurrection (Mt. 28:6).

■ Could Christ have sinned during the temptation experience? He could not; God cannot sin. The Bible declares:

1. He knew no sin (2 Cor. 5:21).
2. He did no sin (1 Pet. 2:22; Heb. 4:15).
3. He had no sin (1 John 3:5; John 14:30). (See also Heb. 7:26.)

■ What then was the purpose for the temptation? The purpose was not to see if he would, but to prove that he could not sin. During the settling of the West a railroad company faced a problem. A bridge spanning a deep chasm gained the reputation of being unsafe. Careful examination by railroad officials showed this to be totally unfounded, but the rumor persisted. Finally, a train was formed made up of only heavy locomotives. For an entire day as hundreds watched, this train crossed and recrossed the bridge. Why was this done? Did the railroad engineers arrange the experiment to see if the bridge would hold, or did they do it to prove it would hold? The obvious answer here may be applied to the purpose of Christ's temptations. The purpose was to provide the believer with an experienced high priest (see Heb. 4:15; 2:18).

II. Temptation and the Saint of God

■ Were both God and Satan involved in the temptation of Christ? Is this the case also, when we are tempted? The answer to both questions is yes. The reason for this is seen in the twofold meaning of the word temptation.

1. First meaning—To test in a good sense with the goal of confirming one in matters of righteousness
   a. As experienced by Jesus— *"Then was Jesus led up of the spirit into the wilderness to be tempted of the devil" (Mt. 4:1). "For we have not an high priest which cannot be touched with the feeling of our infirmities; but was in all points tempted like as we are, yet without sin." (Heb. 4:15)*
   b. As experienced by believers— *"And it came to pass after these things, that God did tempt Abraham, and said unto him, Abraham: and he said, Behold, here I am." (Gen. 22:1)*

2. Second meaning—
   a. As experienced by Jesus--Satan made a desperate attempt to entice Jesus into evil.
   b. As experienced by believers— *"And Satan stood up against Israel, and provoked David to number Israel" (1 Chron. 21:1). "Let no man say when he is tempted, I am tempted of God., for God cannot be tempted with evil, neither tempteth he any man: But every man is tempted, when he is drawn away of his own lust, and enticed." (James 1:13-14)*

■ In light of this, is it ever (or always) a sin for the believer to be tempted? It all depends upon just who has led us into the temptation itself!

1. If our guide has been the Holy Spirit (as was the case here in Matthew 4), then it can be said that not only is temptation not a sin, it is actually both an honor and an opportunity.
   a. It is an honor because it demonstrated that God can trust us. He knows just how much we can withstand (Ps. 103:13-14), and will not allow the temptation to go beyond that limit (1 Cor. 10:13). This is why both James and Peter could describe temptation in such a positive light. *"My brethren, count it all joy when ye fall into divers temptations. Blessed is the man that endureth temptations for when he is tried, he shall receive the crown of life, which the Lord hath promised to them that love him." (James 1:2, 12) "Wherein ye greatly rejoice, though now for a season, if need be, ye are in heaviness through manifold temptations: That the trial of your faith, being much more precious than of gold that perisheth, though it be tried with fire, might be found unto praise and honour and glory at the appearing of Jesus Christ." (1 Pet. 1:6-7)*
   b. It is an opportunity because we can use it to grow spiritually and to strengthen our faith. Paul writes of this: *"And lest I should be exalted above measure through the abundance of the revelations, there, was given to me a thorn in the flesh, the messenger of Satan to buffet me, lest I should be exalted above measure. For this thing I besought the Lord thrice, that it might depart from me. And he said unto me, My grace is sufficient for thee: for my strength is made perfect in weakness. Most gladly therefore will I rather glory in my infirmities, that the power of Christ may rest upon me. Therefore I take pleasure in infirmities, in reproaches, in necessities, in persecutions, in distresses for Christ's sake: for when I am weak, then am I strong." (2 Cor. 12:7-10)*

2. If, however, our guide has been the old nature (as is often the case with us), then the temptation will prove harmful and even disastrous. James had this kind of guide in mind when he warned: *"Let no man say when he is tempted, I am tempted of God., for God cannot be tempted with evil, neither tempteth he any man: But every man is tempted, when he is drawn away of his own lust, and enticed. Then when lust hath conceived, it bringeth forth sin: and sin, when it is finished, bringeth forth death." (James 1:13-15)*

   James was saying that we should not "tempt" temptation. Note the admonition of Solomon: "Can a man take fire in his bosom, and his clothes not be burned? Can one go upon hot coals, and his feet not be burned? So he that goeth in to his neighbour's wife; whosoever toucheth her shall not be innocent." (Prov. 6:27-29)

It has been correctly observed that while a believer may find it impossible to control himself under certain circumstances, he or she can always control the circumstances themselves. An airline captain who had flown gigantic Boeing 747 passenger jetliners for years was once asked to define what constituted a great pilot. He replied: "A great pilot is an expert flier who never allows his plane to encounter those flying conditions which would require all of his greatness and expertise."

THE SOUL WINNING ACTIVITIES OF JESUS

I. The Personal Encounters of Jesus

A. Jesus and His First Apostles
  1. Andrew and Peter

> *"Again the next day after John stood, and two of his disciples; And looking upon Jesus as he walked, he saith, Behold the Lamb of God. And the two disciples heard him speak, and they followed Jesus Then Jesus turned, and saw them following, and saith unto them, What seek ye?, They said unto him, Rabbi, (which is to say, being interpreted, Master,) where dwellest thou? He saith unto them, Come and see. They came and saw where he dwelt, and abode with him that day for it was about the tenth hour One of the two which heard John speak, and followed him, was Andrew, Simon Peters brother. He first findeth his own brother Simon, and saith unto him, We have found the Messias, which is, being interpreted, the Christ And he brought him to Jesus And when Jesus beheld him, he said, Thou art Simon the son of Jona: thou shalt be called Cephas, which is by interpretation, A stone." (Jn. 1:35-42)*

■ Andrew called Jesus "Messias" [Messiah] (Jn. 1:41). This title is found only three other times in the entire Bible:
  1. As used (twice) by the angel Gabriel (Dan. 9:25-26)
  2. As used by the Samaritan woman (Jn. 4:25)

■ Jesus calls Peter "Cephas," which is translated, "a stone." God's purpose is to change people's names (and character). (See Rev. 3:12.)
  1. He changed Abram to Abraham (Gen. 17:5).
  2. He changed Sarai to Sarah (Gen. 17:15).
  3. He changed Jacob to Israel (Gen. 32:28).
  4. He changed Saul to Paul (Acts 13:9).
       Note, however, that Peter at this point was anything but a rock. He was, in fact, in a practical sense, *"tossed to and fro, and carried about with every wind of doctrine"* (Eph. 4:14). Actually, Jesus' description of Peter here can be compared to the one he once gave the timid Gideon in the Old Testament, referring to him as *"thou mighty man of valour"* (Judg. 6:12). But for Peter, all this would change after Pentecost.

■ Without realizing it, Andrew answered Job's perplexing question:
  1. Job: *"Oh that I knew where I might find him!"* (23:3).
  2. Andrew (to Peter): *"We have found the Messias, which is, being interpreted, the Christ"* (Jn. 1:41).

  2. Philip and Nathanael

"The day following Jesus would go forth into Galilee, and findeth Phillip, and saith unto him, Follow me. Now Philip was of Bethsaida, the city of Andrew and Peter. Phillip findeth Nathanael, and saith unto him, We have found him, of whom Moses in the law, and the prophets, did write, Jesus of Nazareth, the son of Joseph. And Nathanael said unto him, Can there any good thing come out of Nazareth? Philip saith unto him, Come and see. Jesus saw Nathanael coming to him, and saith of him, Behold an Israelite indeed, in whom is no guile! Nathanael saith unto him, Whence knowest thou me? Jesus answered and said unto him, Before that Phillip called thee, when thou wast under the fig tree, I saw thee. Nathanael answered and saith unto him, Rabbi, thou art the Son of God; thou art the King of Israel. Jesus answered and said unto him, Because I said unto thee, I saw thee under the fig tree, believest thou? thou shalt see greater things than these. And he saith unto him, Verily, verily, I say unto you, Hereafter ye shall see heaven open, and the angels of God ascending and descending upon the Son of man." (Jn. 1:43-51)

■ We note that Philip, a new convert, did not have a full understanding of the virgin birth, but he was still an effective witness. (He refers to Jesus as *"the son of Joseph."*) Nathanael was bothered by Philip's "Jesus of Nazareth" title. He doubtless realized that the Messiah would be born in Bethlehem. In addition, he probably had a low view of Galileans. Nazareth was the town which housed the Roman garrison for the northern regions of Galilee. In light of this, most Jews would have little to do with that city. In fact, those who lived there were looked down upon as compromisers. Thus, to call one a "Nazarene" was to use a term of utter contempt.

■ Philip wisely refused to argue, but invited him to "come and see." His approach was the one suggested in the Psalms: *"O taste and see that the Lord is good: blessed is the man that trusteth in him."(Psa. 34:8)*

■ Nathanael was amazed that Jesus knew he had been sitting under a fig tree when Philip talked to him. The Savior always dealt with people on their own level.

   1. He dealt with Nathanael under a fig tree (Jn. 1:48).

   2. He dealt with Zacchaeus up a sycamore tree (Lk. 19:4-5).

   3. He dealt with a dying thief on a cruel tree (Lk. 23:39-43).

■ Nathanael was promised he would someday see heaven open and the angels ascending and descending upon Christ. This happened at the ascension (see Acts 1:9-11).

■ Although Nathanael addressed him as the Son of God and King of Israel (1:49), our Lord referred to himself as the Son of man (1:51). This was by far his favorite title for himself. He used it more times than any other name. Nathanael and Philip are the first to hear it.

■ Note: It is thrilling to observe that our Lord's first recorded prediction was not concerning his suffering, death, or even resurrection, but the promise that he would someday ascend. As Isaiah once declared of God: *"Remember the former things of old: for I am God, and there is none else; I am God, and there is none like me, Declaring the end from the beginning, and from ancient times the things that are not yet done, saying, My counsel shall stand, and I will do all my pleasure." (46:9-10)*

B. Jesus and Nicodemus

"There was a man of the Pharisees, named Nicodemus, a ruler of the Jews: The same came to Jesus by night, and said unto him, Rabbi, we know that thou art a teacher come from God: for no man can do these miracles that thou doest, except God be with him. Jesus answered and said unto him, Verily, verily, I say unto thee, Except a man be born again, he cannot see the kingdom of God. Nicodemus saith unto him, How can a man be born when he is old? can he enter the second time into his mothers womb, and be born? Jesus answered, Verily, verily, I say unto thee, Except a man be born of water and of the Spirit, he cannot enter into the kingdom of God. That which is born of the flesh is flesh; and that which is born of the Spirit is spirit. Marvel not that I said unto thee, Ye must be born again. The wind bloweth where it listeth, and thou hearest the sound thereof, but canst not tell whence it cometh, and whither it goeth: so is every one that is born of the Spirit. Nicodemus answered and said unto him, How can these things be? Jesus answered and said unto him, Art thou a master of Israel, and knowest not these things? Verily, verily, I say unto thee, We speak that we do know, and testify that we have seen; and ye receive not our witness. If I have told you earthly things, and ye believe not, how shall ye believe, if I tell you of heavenly things? And no man hath ascended up to heaven, but he that came down from heaven, even the Son of man which is in heaven. And as Moses lifted up the serpent in the wilderness, even so must the Son of man be lifted up: That whosoever believeth in him should not perish, but have eternal fife. For God so loved the world, that he gave his only begotten Son, that whosoever believeth in him should not perish, but have everlasting life." (Jn. 3:1-16)

◼ Note the character of this man:

1. He was a Jewish religious leader (Jn. 3:1).
2. He was a member of the Pharisees (Jn. 3:1).
3. He was a well-known teacher (Jn. 3:10).
4. He was, however, lost!

◼ Why did he come by night? We do not know, and it is unfair to brand him a coward. Perhaps the heavy schedules of both men required this.

◼ What did Nicodemus know about Jesus? He knew he was from God because of his supernatural miracles. (Compare Jn. 3:2 with 20:30-31.)

◼ Nicodemus was told he had to be born again. This is the first of but three occasions on which the term "born again" is found in the Word of God (see Jn. 3:3, 7; 1 Pet. 1:23). However, John often uses the phrase "born of God" (see Jn. 1:31; 1 Jn. 3:9; 4:7; 5:18).

◼ What did Jesus mean by his expression, *"Except a man be born of water and of the Spirit, he cannot enter into the Kingdom of God" (Jn. 3:5)*? Here five main views have been offered:

1. He was referring to baptismal regeneration. This, of course, is totally refuted by other biblical passages (see Eph. 2:8-9; 1 Cor. 1:17; Rom. 5:1).
2. He was referring to that watery sac, the placenta, which accompanies physical birth. Thus he contrasted physical birth with spiritual birth.
3. He was saying that the one requirement to live on this earth is to have had a physical birthday; and likewise, the one requirement to someday live in heaven is to have a spiritual birthday. Those who hold this view point to 3:6 where they feel Jesus clarifies his position.

4. He was referring to John's baptism of repentance in the Jordan, which baptism the Pharisees had rejected. (Compare Lk. 3:3 with 7:30.)

5. He was referring to the Word of God (the water) and the Spirit of God (Spirit), without which no man can ever be saved (see Jn. 16:8-11; Rom. 11:6-15). Advocates of this position point out that water in the Bible is often the recognized symbol for the Word of God (see Psa. 119:9; Jn. 4:14; Eph. 5:25-26; Titus 3:5).

■ Although this man was both a ruler and a religious leader, he needed the new birth. Note Jesus' question in 3:10, *"Art thou a master of Israel, and knoweth not these things?"* In the Greek the definite article is used, meaning, *"Are you the teacher in Israel?"* Nicodemus may have been the most famous teacher of his day.

■ In John 3:12, Jesus connects earthly things with heavenly things, indicating that a right view of the second is based squarely on a right view of the first. This only serves to emphasize the supreme importance of accepting at face value the historical words of Moses concerning creation (Gen. 1-2), as one would do with Christ's words concerning redemption.

■ Jesus illustrated his visitor's need by referring to Moses and the brazen serpent. (Compare John 3:14 with Num. 21:9.) On this occasion in the Old Testament account, God had sent poisonous serpents to punish rebellious Israel. The people repented and a cure was provided. A serpent of brass was placed atop a wooden pole where all could view it. Anyone bitten needed only to look upon the brass serpent to be healed.

To paraphrase, here is what Jesus told Nicodemus: "Nicodemus, like those Old Testament Israelites, you have been bitten by a serpent--the serpent of sin. It is an incurable and fatal bite. But soon God is going to erect a crosslike pole just outside Jerusalem. And on that cross he will place a Savior."

■ It may be said that one cannot fully grasp the most famous verse in the Bible, John 3:16, unless he has some understanding of its background, which is found in John 3:14. *"And as Moses lifted up the serpent in the wilderness, even so must the Son of man be lifted up."*

■ Did Nicodemus accept Jesus as Savior? Two later events strongly testify that he did indeed!

1. He defends Jesus before the Pharisees

"Nicodemus saith unto them, (he that came to Jesus by night, being one of them,) Doth our law judge any man, before it hear him, and know what he doeth? They answered and said unto him, Art thou also of Galilee? Search, and look: for out of Galilee ariseth no prophet." (Jn. 7:50-52)

2. He helps in preparing the body of Jesus for burial

"And there came also Nicodemus, which at the first came to Jesus by night, and brought a mixture of myrrh and aloes, about an hundred pound weight. Then took they the body of Jesus, and wound it in linen clothes with the spices, as the manner of the Jews is to bury. Now in the place where he was crucified there was a garden; and in the garden a new sepulchre, wherein was never man yet laid. There laid they Jesus therefore because of the Jews' preparation day; for the sepulchre was nigh at hand." (Jn. 19:39-42)

■ If Jesus quoted the words in John 3:16, then Nicodemus had the supreme honor of being the very first person to hear both the most important and greatest verse in all the Bible!

1. It is the most important verse, because it contains the gospel in a nutshell.

2. It is the greatest verse, because it contains nine of the most profound truths ever recorded:

"For God!" —The greatest Person

"So loved the world" —The greatest truth

"That he gave" —The greatest act

"His only begotten Son" —The greatest gift

"That whosoever" —The greatest number

"Believeth in him" —The greatest invitation

"Should not perish" —The greatest promise

"But have" —The greatest certainty

"Everlasting life" —The greatest destiny

■ The following features may be observed in summarizing Jesus' dealings with Nicodemus:

1. He was accessible. We are told (3:2) that Nicodemus came *"by night."* All too often a busy and successful Christian leader is anything but accessible to those who may desperately need godly counsel.

2. He was single-minded. The only issue Jesus wanted to discuss was the born again experience. He refused to be side-tracked by the opening flattery of Nicodemus. Note the first statement from each man:

   Nicodemus: *"Rabbi, we know that thou art a teacher come from God; for no man can do these miracles that thou doest, except God be with him"* (Jn. 3:2). **Jesus**: *"Verily, verily, I say unto thee, Except a man be born again, he cannot see the kingdom of God"* (John 3:3).

3. He was clear and concise. Realizing Nicodemus's confusion, Jesus related three helpful illustrations to explain the new birth.

   a. A physical illustration— *"Jesus answered, Verily, verily, I say unto thee, Except a man be born of water and of the Spirit, he cannot enter into the kingdom of God. That which is born of the flesh is flesh; and that which is born of the Spirit is spirit"* (Jn. 3:5-6).

   b. A natural illustration— *"The wind bloweth where it listeth, and thou hearest the sound thereof but canst not tell whence it cometh, and whither it goeth: so is every one that is born of the Spirit"* (Jn. 3:8).

   c. A scriptural illustration— *"And as Moses lifted up the serpent in the wilderness, even so must the Son of man be lifted up"* (Jn. 3:14).

4. He was well-informed. He knew the background of Nicodemus. *"Jesus answered and said unto him, Art thou a master of Israel, and knowest not these things?"* (Jn. 3:10)

5. He was impartial. Even though Nicodemus was no doubt well-known and successful in the political, financial, and religious world, our Lord dealt with him for what he was, a poor lost sinner.

C. Jesus and the Samaritan Woman

"When therefore the LORD knew how the Pharisees had heard that Jesus made and baptized more disciples than John, (Though Jesus himself baptized not, but his disciples,) He left Judaea, and departed again into Galilee. And he must needs go through Samaria. Then cometh he to a city of Samaria, which is called Sychar, near to the parcel of ground that Jacob gave to his son Joseph. Now Jacob's well was there. Jesus therefore, being wearied with his journey, sat thus on the well. and it was about the sixth hour. There cometh a woman of Samaria to draw water: Jesus saith unto her, Give me to drink. (For his disciples were gone away unto the city to buy meat.) Then saith the woman of Samaria unto him, How is it that thou,

being a Jew, askest drink of me, which am a woman of Samaria? for the Jews have no dealings with the Samaritans Jesus answered and said unto her, If thou knewest the gift of God, and who it is that saith to thee, Give me to drink; thou wouldest have asked of him, and he would have given thee living water The woman saith unto him, Sir, thou hast nothing to draw with, and the well is deep: from whence then halt thou that flying water? Art thou greater than our father Jacob, which gave us the well, and drank thereof himself, and his children, and his cattle? Jesus answered and said unto her, Whosoever drinketh of this water shall thirst again: But whosoever drinketh of the water that I shall give him shall never thirst; but the water that I shall give him shall be in him a well of water springing up into everlasting life. The woman saith unto him, Sir, give me this water, that I thirst not, neither come hither to draw Jesus saith unto her, Go, call thy husband, and come hither. The woman answered and said, I have no husband. Jesus said unto her, Thou hast well said, I have no husband: For thou hast had five husbands; and he whom thou now hast is not thy husband- in that saidst thou truly. The woman saith unto him, Sir, I perceive that thou art a prophet Our fathers worshipped in this mountain; and ye say, that in Jerusalem is the place where men ought to worship. Jesus saith unto her, Woman, believe me, the hour cometh, when ye shall neither in this mountain, nor yet at Jerusalem, worship the Father. Ye worship ye know not what: we know what we worship: for salvation is of the Jews But the hour cometh, and now is, when the true worshippers shall worship the Father in spirit and in truth: for the Father seeketh such to worship him. God is a Spirit and they that worship him must worship him in spirit and in truth. The woman saith unto him, I know that Messias cometh, which is called Christ: when he is come, he will tell us all things. Jesus saith unto her, I that speak unto thee am he. And upon this came his disciples, and marvelled that he talked with the woman: yet no man said, What seekest thou? or, Why talkest thou with her? The woman then left her waterpot, and went her way into the city, and saith to the men, Come, see a man, which told me all things that ever I did: is not this the Christ? Then they went out of the city, and came unto him. In the mean while his disciples prayed him, saying, Master, eat. But he said unto them, I have meat to eat that ye know not of Therefore said the disciples one to another, Hath any man brought him ought to eat? Jesus saith unto them, My meat is to do the will of him that sent me, and to finish his work. Say not ye, There are yet four months, and then cometh harvest? behold, I say unto you, Lift up your eyes, and look on the fields; for they are white already to harvest. And he that reapeth receiveth wages, and gathereth fruit unto life eternal: that both he that soweth and he that reapeth may rejoice together. And herein is that saying true, One soweth, and another reapeth. I sent you to reap that whereon ye bestowed no labour: other men laboured, and ye are entered into their labours. And many of the Samaritans of that city believed on him for the saying of the woman, which testified, He told me all that ever I did. So when the Samaritans were come unto him, they besought him that he would tarry with them: and he abode there two days And many more believed because of his own word; And said unto the woman, Now we believe, not because of thy saying: for we have heard him ourselves, and know that this is indeed the Christ, the Saviour of the world." (Jn. 4:1-42)

■ After realizing that the Pharisees were pitting him against John in a baptismal contest, Jesus quickly left the Judean area. Our Lord did not come to compete with John, but rather to be crucified for him, along with all other sinners.

■ Note the phrase, *"He must needs go through Samaria."* H. A. Ironsides observed: "An orthodox Jew would cross the Jordan near Jericho and make his way up through Perea, and then cross back near the Sea of Galilee in the north. But the Lord Jesus Christ did not take that route. A stern legalist would not go through Samaria; but the

Lord Jesus Christ took that direct road because of the very fact that He was anxious to meet these poor Samaritan sinners that He might reveal the truth to them. 'He must needs go through Samaria.' Long before the creation of the world it had been settled in the counsels of eternity that he was to meet a poor, sinful, Samaritan woman that day. He could not forego that appointment." (*Gospel of John*, John Loizeaux Brothers, N.Y., 1954, p. 138.)

■ Our Lord's perfect humanity is clearly revealed through the following word in 4:6— "*Jesus, therefore, being wearied with his journey...*"

   He would later again experience this utter exhaustion in a boat during a storm (Mk. 4:35-38). In addition, Jesus knew extreme hunger (Mt. 4:2), and thirst (Jn. 19:38). Jesus was thus as much God had He been not man, but also as much man had He not been God.

■ During His conversation with the Samaritan woman, Jesus contrasted two things:
   1. Living water with liquid water (4:13-14).
   2. Real worship with ritual worship (4:20-24).

■ The woman spoke of a mountain in 4:20 -- The mountain referred to here was Mount Gerizim, especially sacred to the Samaritans.
   1. Abraham and Jacob had built altars in that general vicinity (Gen. 12:7; 33:20).
   2. The people of Israel had been blessed from this mountain (Deut. 11:29; 27:12).
   3. The Samaritans had built a temple on Mount Gerizim around 400 B.C., which had later been destroyed by the Jews.

■ Jesus reveals an incredible fact about the Father at this time:

   "*But the hour cometh, and now is, when the true worshippers shall worship the Father in spirit and in truth: for the Father seeketh such to worship him.*" (Jn. 4:23)

   The implications here are staggering indeed! We are told that the omnipresent, omnipotent, omniscient, eternal, sovereign and holy creation actually desires indeed, seeks the worship of His finite and sinful creatures!

■ It was at this time that Christ made the first recorded announcement that he indeed was the anticipated Messiah. This revelation was given to an immoral woman (Jn. 4:26). Later, the Savior would make the first resurrection appearance in his new body before another woman, who had been possessed of devils — Mary Magdalene (Jn. 20:11-18).

■ Note the progressive revelation regarding the identity of Jesus as given by the Holy Spirit to this woman:
   1. "*How is it that thou, being a Jew...?*" (4:9)
   2. "*Art thou greater than our father Jacob...?*" (4:12)
   3. "*I perceive that thou are a prophet.*" (4:19)
   4. "*Is this not the Christ?*" (4:29)

■ The Samaritan woman will thus become one of the two greatest soul winners in the entire gospel account and both were former pagan Gentiles! Compare her tremendous testimony in Jn. 4:28-30, 39, with that of a former demon possessed man from Gadara (Mk. 5:18-20).

- The title given to Jesus by the Samaritan man, *"Savior of the world" (4:42)* is found only here and in 1 John 4:14— *"And we have seen and do testify that the Father sent the Son to be the Saviour of the world."*

- This passage contains one of the greatest examples for soul winners in the entire Bible. Note a few of its practical points:

    1. Jesus refused to argue with the woman.

    2. He avoided getting entangled by various theological concepts.

    3. He never browbeat her, even though she was a great sinner.

    4. He repeatedly spoke of the living water, which was the real (and only) issue.

    5. He concluded by pointing her to himself (4:26).

    6. The Christian has only to lift up his eyes to see the bountiful harvest of lost souls all around him.

    7. Christians sometimes sow seed that will be reaped by others, but they often reap seed planted by another. God alone gives the increase (see 1 Cor. 3:5-9).

D. Jesus and the Woman Taken In Adultery

"Jesus went unto the mount of Olives. And early in the morning he came again into the temple, and all the people came unto him; and he sat down, and taught them. And the scribes and Pharisees brought unto him a woman taken in adultery; and when they had set her in the midst, They say unto him, Master, this woman was taken in adultery, in the very Acts Now Moses in the law commanded us, that such should be stoned: but what sayest thou? This they said, tempting him, that they might have to accuse him. But Jesus stooped down, and with his finger wrote on the ground, as though he heard them not. So when they continued asking him, he lilted up himself, and said unto them, He that is without sin among you, let him first cast a stone at her. And again he stooped down, and wrote on the ground. And they which heard it, being convicted by their own conscience, went out one by one, beginning at the eldest, even unto the last: and Jesus was left alone, and the woman standing in the midst. When Jesus had lifted up himself, and saw none but the woman, he said unto her, Woman, where are those thine accusers? hath no man condemned thee? She said, No man, Lord. And Jesus said unto her, Neither do I condemn thee: go, and sin no more." (Jn. 8:1-11)

- The wicked Jewish leaders altered the Law somewhat as seen by their statement in verse 5.

    1. The manner of execution was not prescribed unless the woman was a betrothed virgin (Deut. 22:23-24).

    2. The Law also required both parties to be killed (Lev. 20:10; Deut. 22:22).

- There is only one Old Testament instance in which this law was carried out (see Num. 25:7-8).

- This account is the only one in the gospel record where Jesus is described as writing something.

- What did he write? It has been suggested that he may have written down the names of those Pharisees standing there who had secretly committed adultery. Consider Paul's words at a later date: *"Behold, thou art called a Jew, and restest in the law, and makest thy boast of God... thou that sayest a man should not commit adultery, dost thou commit adultery? thou that abhorrest idols, dost thou commit sacrilege?" (Rom. 2:17, 22)*

■ The reason of course why Jesus did not write or author a book while here on earth was that, in the ultimate sense He was a book! John begins his gospel account by referring to this: *"In the beginning was the Word, and the Word was with God, and the Word was God." (Jn. 1:1)*

The Greek term Logos (here translated word) denotes a thought, a concept, an expression. In other words the very life of Jesus served to reveal both God's thoughts and work!

■ In essence it can be seen that Jesus dealt with this poor sinful woman in three-fold fashion:

1. He was accessible— *"And early in the morning he came again into the temple, and all the people came unto him; and he sat down, and taught them" (Jn. 8:2)*. Note: In John 3, Nicodemus met Christ late at night. Here the woman taken in adultery would meet him *"early in the morning."*

2. He did not condemn her, nor did he permit the self-righteous Pharisees to condemn her. Our Lord did not come to damn sinners, but rather to deliver them. *"A bruised reed shall he not break, and smoking flax shall he not quench, till he send forth judgment unto victory." (Mt. 12:20)*

3. He both forgave and instructed her. *"Neither do I condemn thee: go, and sin no more." (Jn. 8:11)*

E. Jesus and A Rich Young Ruler

■ Here we will allow both Matthew and Mark to record this meeting:

"And, behold, one came and said unto him, Good Master, what good thing shall I do, that I may have eternal life? And he said unto him, Why callest thou me good? there is none good but one, that is, God, but if thou wilt enter into life, keep the commandments. He saith unto him, Which? Jesus said, Thou shalt do no murder, Thou shalt not commit adultery, Thou shalt not steal, Thou shalt not bear false witness, Honour thy father and thy mother: and, Thou shalt love thy neighbour as thyself. The young man saith unto him, All these things have I kept from my youth up. what lack I yet? Jesus said unto him, If thou wilt be perfect, go and sell that thou hast, and give to the poor, and thou shalt have treasure in heaven: and come and follow me. But when the young man heard that saying, he went away sorrowful: for he had great possessions. Then said Jesus unto his disciples, Verily I say unto you, That a rich man shall hardly enter into the kingdom of heaven. And again I say unto you, it is easier for a camel to go through the eye of a needle, than for a rich man to enter into the kingdom of God. When his disciples heard it, they were exceedingly amazed, saying, Who then can be saved? But Jesus beheld them, and said unto them, With men this is impossible, but with God all things are possible." (Mt. 19:16-26)

"And when he was gone forth into the way, there came one running, and kneeled to him, and asked him, Good Master, what shall I do that I may inherit eternal life? And Jesus said unto him, Why callest thou me good? there is none good but one, that is, God Thou knowest the commandments, Do not commit adultery, Do not kill, Do not steal, Do not bear false witness, Defraud not, Honour thy father and mother. And he answered and said unto him, Master, all these have I observed from my youth. Then Jesus beholding him loved him, and said unto him, One thing thou lackest: go thy way, sell whatsoever thou hast, and give to the poor, and thou shalt have treasure in heaven: and come, take up the cross, and follow me. And he was sad at that saying, and went away grieved: for he had great possessions." (Mk. 10:17-22)

■ The rich young ruler was confused in regards to four things. Jesus corrects all four errors.

■ First confusion and correction—

1. The confusion: concerning the deity of Christ— *"There came one running, and kneeled to him, and asked him, Good Master…" (Mk. 10:17)*

2. The correction— *"And Jesus said unto him, Why callest thou me good? there is none good but one, that is, God." (Mk. 10:18)*

   The rabbis had no room whatsoever in their theology for the idea that the promised Old Testament Messiah would actually be God himself. Thus, Jesus may have been saying, *"In light of the fact that God alone is good, are you still willing to call me good Master?"*

■ Second confusion and correction—

1. The confusion: concerning the vanity of works— *"What good thing shall I do, that I might have eternal life?" (Mt. 19:16)*

2. The correction— *"If thou wilt enter into life, keep the commandments." (Mt. 19:17)*
   (Note: Christ then lists five of the Ten Commandments.)

   a. Honor thy father and mother (fifth)

   b. Thou shalt do no murder (sixth)

   c. Thou shalt not commit adultery (seventh)

   d. Thou shalt not steal (eighth)

   e. Thou shalt not bear false witness (ninth)

      He does not, however, list the first commandment (Thou shalt have no other gods before me), nor the tenth (Thou shalt not covet), the very two already broken by the rich young ruler. Apparently Christ wanted him to come to this conclusion himself.

■ Third confusion and correction—

1. The confusion: concerning the depravity of man— *"The young man lath unto him, All these things have I kept from my youth up: what lack I yet" (Mt. 19:20)*? Had he really done this?

   A case could be made concerning the possibility of observing the first nine commandments, but only in an outward and external manner. However, no human could ever even remotely keep the Tenth Commandment, which is an inward law, dealing with the heart— *"Thou shalt not covet" (Exod. 20:17)*.

2. The correction— *"Jesus said unto him, If thou wilt be perfect, go and sell that thou hast, and give to the poor, and thou shalt have treasure in heaven: and come and follow me." (Mt. 19:21)*

■ Fourth confusion and correction—

1. The confusion: concerning the captivity of riches— *"But when the young man heard that saying, he went away sorrowful: for he had great possessions" (Mt. 19:22)*.

   A rabbi once visited a miserly old man who was known far and wide for his greed. Pointing out the window, the rabbi asked him what he saw. "Well," he said, "I see children playing and adults walking." The rabbi then placed a mirror in front of the old man. "Now," he asked, "what do you see?" "Oh," replied the man, "I see myself!" In a quiet tone, the rabbi observed: "I have just shown you two pieces of glass. Concerning the first, you saw people, but concerning the second, you saw only yourself. The reason you could not see human beings through the second was because it has been coated with a thin layer of silver."

2. The correction—*"Then said Jesus unto his disciples, Verily I say unto you, That a rich man shall hardly enter into the kingdom of heaven, And again I say unto you, It is easier for a camel to go through the eye of a needle, than for a rich man to enter into the kingdom of God. When his disciples heard it, they were exceedingly amazed, saying, Who then can be saved? But Jesus beheld them, and said unto them, With men this is impossible; but with God all things are possible." (Mt. 19:23-26)*

■ In conclusion, five facts may be seen in regards to the rich young ruler:

1. He asked the right question — "How can I receive eternal life?"

2. He asked in the right way — He ran and knelt.

3. He asked the right person — He addressed his concerns to Jesus.

4. He asked at the right time — This may have been his first and only encounter with Jesus.

5. He however, tragically, responded in the wrong way.

F. Jesus and Zacchaeus

■ As seen from the perspective of the publican:

1. Zacchaeus the sinner— *"And Jesus entered and passed through Jericho. And, behold, there was a man named Zacchaeus, which was the chief among the publicans, and he was rich." (Lk. 19:1-2)*

2. Zacchaeus the seeker—This man wanted to meet Jesus but had a problem.
   a. The source of his problem— *"And he sought to see Jesus who he was; and could not for the press, because he was little of stature." (Lk. 19:3)*
   b. The solution to his problem— *"And he ran before, and climbed up into a sycamore tree to see him: for he was to pass that way." (Lk. 19:4)*

3. Zacchaeus the saved
   a. The request of the Savior— *"And when Jesus came to the place, he looked up, and saw him, and said unto him, Zacchaeus, make haste, and come down; for to day I must abide at thy house." (Lk. 19:5)*
   b. The response of the publican— *"And he made haste, and came down, and received him joyfully." (Lk. 19:6)*
   c. The reaction of the crowd— *"And when they saw it, they all murmured, saying, That he was gone to be guest with a man that is a sinner." (Lk. 19:7)*

4. Zacchaeus the Spirit-controlled
   a. As witnessed by his own testimony— *"And Zacchaeus stood, and said unto the Lord; Behold, Lord, the half of my goods I give to the poor; and If I have taken any thing from any man by false accusation, I restore him fourfold." (Lk. 19:8)*
   b. As witnessed by Jesus' testimony— *"And Jesus said unto him, This day is salvation come to this house, forsomuch as he also is a son of Abraham. For the Son of man is come to seek and to save that which was lost." (Lk. 19:9-10)*

■ As seen from the perspective of the Savior:

1. Jesus saw Zacchaeus. *"And when Jesus came to the place, he looked up, and saw him" (Lk. 19:5a).*

2. Jesus knew Zacchaeus. *"And said unto him, Zacchaeus" (Lk. 19:5b).*

3. Jesus loved Zacchaeus. *"Make haste, and comedown; for today I must abide at thy house"* (Lk. 19:5c).

4. Jesus saved Zacchaeus. *"And he made haste, and came down, and received him joyfully. And Jesus said unto him, This day is salvation come to this house, forsomuch as he also is a son of Abraham"* (Lk. 19:6, 9).

THE PREACHING ACTIVITIES OF JESUS

THE PREACHING ACTIVITIES OF JESUS AND HIS DISCIPLES

On five specific occasions Jesus went out on an extended preaching mission. On two specific occasions he sent his disciples out on an extended preaching mission.

■ The preaching tours of Jesus:

1. First tour — *"And Jesus returned in the power of the Spirit into Galilee: and there went out a fame of him through all the region round about. And he taught in their synagogues, being glorified of all." (Lk. 4:14-15)*

   a. This tour took place shortly after his temptation in the wilderness (Lk. 4:1-13).

   b. All his preaching missions apparently were centered in the Galilean area and not in Judea and Jerusalem. The reason for this seemed to be the intense hostility he experienced whenever he was in Jerusalem (see Jn. 10:31; 11:8).

2. Second tour — *"And Jesus went about all Galilee, teaching in their synagogues, and preaching the gospel of the kingdom, and healing all manner of sickness and all manner of disease among the people. And his fame went throughout all Syria: and they brought unto him all sick people that were taken with divers diseases and torments, and those which were possessed with devils, and those which were lunatick, and those that had the palsy; and he healed them. And there followed him great multitudes of people from Galilee, and from Decapolis, and from Jerusalem, and from Judaea, and from beyond Jordan." (Mt. 4:23-25)* This was undoubtedly his most successful crusade, with people flocking to hear him from Galilee, Judea, Syria, and the surrounding country.

3. Third tour — *"And Jesus went about all the cities and villages, teaching in their synagogues, and preaching the gospel of the kingdom, and healing every sickness and every disease among the people." (Mt. 9:35)*

   a. Here we are told the motivation prompting all his tours. *"But when he saw the multitudes, he was moved with compassion on them, because they fainted, and were scattered abroad, as sheep having no shepherd." (Mt. 9:36)*

   b. This tour also has a command attached to it. *"Then saith he unto his disciples, The harvest truly is plenteous, but the labourers are few; Pray ye therefore the Lord of the harvest, that he will send forth labourers into his harvest." (Mt. 9:37-38)*

4. Fourth tour — *"And it came to pass, when Jesus had made an end of commanding his twelve disciples, he departed thence to teach and to preach in their cities" (Mt. 11:1)*

   a. Just prior to this tour our Lord had sent out his twelve disciples (Mt. 10)

   b. During this tour he is visited by two messengers sent by the imprisoned John the Baptist (Mt. 11:2).

5. Fifth tour — *"And it came to pass afterward, that he went throughout every city and village, preaching and shewing the glad tidings of the kingdom of God: and the twelve were with him, And certain women, which*

had been healed of evil spirits and infirmities, Mary called Magdalene, out of whom went seven devils, And Joanna the wife of Chuza Herod's steward, and Susanna, and many others, which ministered unto him of their substance." (Lk. 8:1-3)

These women, converted during his final preaching crusade would later render fruitful service to their Savior.

    a. They were present at the crucifixion (Mt. 27:56; Mk. 15:40-41; Lk. 23:49, 55)

    b. They were present at the resurrection (Lk. 24:1-11)

    c. Mary Magdalene was the first human being to see the risen Christ (Jn. 20:11-18)

■ The preaching tours of Jesus' disciples—As has been previously noted, Jesus sent a group of his disciples out on two occasions. These events are described in Matthew 10 and in Luke 10. The following offers both a contrast and comparison between these two groups:

1. The group in Matthew 10

    a. The number involved was 12 (Mt. 10:1)

    b. All 12 are named (Mt. 10:2-4)

    c. They were to preach a specific message. *"And as ye go, preach, saying, The kingdom of heaven is at hand." (Mt. 10:7)*

    d. They were given power to *"heal the sick, cleanse the lepers, raise the dead, and to cast out devils"* (Mt. 10:8).

    e. They were to preach only to Jews. *"These twelve Jesus sent forth, and commanded them, saying, Go not into the way of the Gentiles, and into any city of the Samaritans enter ye not: But go rather to the lost sheep of the house of Israel." (Mt. 10:5-6)*

    f. They were to travel lightly. *"Provide neither gold, nor silver, nor brass in your purses, Nor scrip for your journey, neither two coats, neither shoes, nor yet staves: for the workman is worthy of his meat." (Mt. 10:9-10)*

    g. They were to expect persecution. *"Behold, I send you forth as sheep in the midst of wolves: be ye therefore wise as serpents, and harmless as doves. But beware of men: for they will deliver you up to the councils, and they will scourge you in their synagogues; And ye shall be brought before governors and kings for my sake, for a testimony against them and the Gentiles"* (Mt. 10:16-18)

    h. They were promised the anointing of the Holy Spirit. *"But when they deliver you up, take no thought how or what ye shall speak: for it shall be given you in that same hour what ye shall speak. For it is not ye that speak, but the Spirit of your Father which speaketh in you." (Mt. 10:19-20)*

    i. The results of their preaching trip are not recorded.

2. The group in Luke 10

    a. The number involved was 70 (Lk. 10:1).

    b. None of the 70 are named.

    c. They were to preach a specific message. *"Say unto them, The kingdom of God is come nigh unto you." (Lk. 10:9)*

    d. They were given power to heal the sick and to cast out demons (Lk. 10:9, 17).

    e. They were not restricted to preach only to the Jews. *"After these things the LORD appointed other seventy also, and sent them two and two before his face into every city and place, whither he himself would come." (Lk. 10:1)*

f. They were to travel lightly (Lk. 10:4).

g. They were to expect persecution. *"Go your ways: behold, I send you forth as lambs among wolves"* *(Lk. 10:3).*

h. They were promised the anointing of the Father (implied in Lk. 10:21).

i. The results of their preaching trip are recorded. *"And the seventy returned again with joy, saying, Lord, even the devils are subject unto us through thy name. And he said unto them, I beheld Satan as lightning fall from heaven. Behold, I give unto you power to tread on serpents and scorpions, and over all the power of the enemy: and nothing shall by any means hurt you. Notwithstanding in this rejoice not, that the spirits are subject unto you; but rather rejoice, because your names are written in heaven."* (Lk. 10:17-20)

THE PROMISE OF JESUS TO BUILD THE CHURCH

JESUS' PROMISE TO BUILD HIS CHURCH

I. The Probing By Jesus

> *"When Jesus came into the coasts of Caesarea Philippi, he asked his disciples, saying, Whom do men say that I the Son of man am? And they said, Some say that thou art John the Baptist: some, Elias; and others, Jeremias, or one of the prophets. He saith unto them, But whom say ye that I am?" (Mt. 16:13-15)*

■ How are we to account for the various rumors concerning Jesus' identity? Some, influenced by Herod Antipas, confused Jesus with John the Baptist, whom they felt had been raised from the dead (Mt. 14:2). Others identified Jesus with the prophet Elijah, whose coming had been predicted by Malachi (4:5-6). The apocryphal book 2 Esdras predicted the return of Isaiah and Jeremiah (2:18). It was commonly believed among the Jews that at the Messiah's coming the prophets would rise again. "The nearer still the 'kingdom of heaven' came, by so much the more did they dream of the resurrection of the prophets."

■ Note the phrase, *"But whom say ye?"* Jesus both was, and is now, far more interested in what his people think about him than what the world might say about him.

II. The Person of Jesus

> *"And Simon Peter answered and said, Thou art the Christ, the Son of the living God. And Jesus answered and said unto him, Blessed art thou, Simon Barjona: for flesh and blood hath not revealed it unto thee, but my Father which is in heaven." (Mt. 16:16-17)*

■ Luke provides for us the reason for this timely revelation, namely, the request of Christ to his Father. *"And it came to pass, as he was alone praying, his disciples were with him: and he asked them, saying, Whom say the people that I am?" (Lk. 9:18)*

III. The Promise of Jesus

> *"And I say also unto thee, That thou art Peter, and upon this rock I will build my church; and the gates of hell shall not prevail against it. And I will give unto thee the keys of the kingdom of heaven: and whatsoever thou shalt bind on earth shall be bound in heaven: and whatsoever thou shalt loose on earth shall be loosed in heaven." (Mt. 16:18-19)*

■ Was Jesus building his church upon Peter and planning to make him its first Pope? It may be clearly stated that he was not, for the following reasons:

1. Christ later gave the same responsibilities to the other apostles which he here gives to Peter. (Compare Mt. 16:19 with Jn. 20:22-23.)

2. The New Testament clearly presents Christ and Christ only as the foundation of his Church (see Acts 4:11-12; 1 Cor. 3:11; 1 Pet. 2:4-8).

3. The New Testament clearly presents Christ and Christ only as the Head of his Church (see Eph. 1:20-23; 5:23; Col. 1:18; 2:18-19).

4. In the Greek language, there is a play upon words in this verse. Jesus said, *"Thou art Peter* [petros, a little stone,] *and upon this rock* [petra, massive cliff or rock] *I will build my church."*

5. Peter's testimony denies it (see 1 Pet. 5:1-4).

6. James and not Peter later officiated at the Jerusalem church (see Acts 15:13, 19).

■ What then, was Christ doing? The answer is given in Ephesians. *"Now therefore ye are no more strangers and foreigners, but fellow citizens with the saints, and of the household of God; And are built upon the foundation of the apostles and prophets, Jesus Christ himself being the chief corner stone; In whom all the building fitly framed together groweth unto an holy temple in the Lord: In whom ye also are builded together for an habitation of God through the Spirit."* (Eph. 2:19-22)

■ What did he mean by *"the gates of hell shall not prevail against it"*? J. Vernon McGee wrote: "The gates of hell refer to the 'gates of death'." The word used here is the hades and sheol of the Old Testament, which refers to the unseen world and means death. The gates of death shall not prevail against Christ's church (Matthew, Vol. II, p. 23). This glorious event is called the rapture (see 1 Thes. 4:13-18; 1 Cor. 15:51-57).

■ What were the *"keys of the kingdom of heaven"* that Jesus gave Peter? A key, of course, unlocks doors and makes available something which was previously closed. Jesus here predicts that Peter would be given the privilege of opening the door of salvation to various peoples. This he later did.

1. He opened the door of Christian opportunity to Israel at Pentecost (Acts 2:38-42)

2. He did the same thing for the Samaritans (Acts 8:14-17)

3. He performed this ministry to the Gentiles at Cornelius' house at Caesarea (Acts 10)

■ What did Christ mean by the binding and loosing of Matthew 16:19? This authority was given to all the apostles as well as to other believers (see Mt. 18:18; Jn. 20:22-23). W. A. Criswell writes: "In Greek the future perfect tense is used to express the double notion of an action terminated in the past but whose effects are still existing in the present. 'Having been bound and still bound,' and 'having been loosed and still loosed.' The meaning is: if the disciples act in their proper capacity as stewards, they will be acting in accordance with the principles and elective purposes ordained beforehand in heaven." (Expository Notes on Matthew, p. 101)

In other words, all the actions of the Spirit-filled believer, whether positive or negative in nature, will carry with them the awesome authority of heaven itself.

IV. The Prohibition By Jesus

"Then charged he his disciples that they should tell no man that he was Jesus the Christ," (Mt. 16:20)

V. The Passion of Jesus

"From that time forth began Jesus to shew unto his disciples, how that he must go unto Jerusalem, and suffer many things of the elders and chief priests and scribes, and be killed, and be raised again the third day." (Mt. 16:21)

■ This shocking and sobering truth would be hammered home repeatedly by the Savior. Examples: *"And while they abode in Galilee, Jesus said unto them, The Son of man shall be betrayed into the hands of men: And they shall kill him, and the third day he shall be raised again. And they were exceeding sorry"* (Mt. 17:22-23). *"Behold, we go up to Jerusalem; and the Son of man shall be betrayed unto the chief priests and unto the scribes, and they shall condemn him to death, And shall deliver him to the Gentiles to mock, and to scourge, and to crucify him: and the third day he shall rise again." (Mt. 20:18-19)*

VI. The Plot Against Jesus

"Then Peter took him, and began to rebuke him, saying, Be it far from thee, Lord: this shall not be unto thee. But he turned, and said unto Peter, Get thee behind me, Satan: thou art an offence unto me: for thou savourest not the things that be of God, but those that be of men." (Mt. 16:22-23)

■ Here Satan employs a familiar tactic, using a secondary source through which to spew forth his poison. The first successful attempt occurred in the Garden of Eden. *"Now the serpent was more subtil than any beast of the field which the LORD God had made. And he said unto the woman, Yea, hath God said, Ye shall not eat of every tree of the garden?" (Gen. 3:1)*

THE TRANSFIGURATION OF JESUS

I. The Prophecy Involved

"Verily I say unto you, There be some standing here, which shall not taste of death, till they see the Son of man coming in his kingdom." (Mt. 16:28)

II. The Place Involved

"a high mountain" *(Mt. 17:1)* This was probably Mt. Hermon.

III. The Purpose Involved

"He ... went up ... to pray" (Lk. 9:28)

IV. The Personalities Involved

■ There were seven:
1. Peter, James, and John
2. The Savior
3. The Father
4. Moses and Elijah

V. The Particulars Involved

"And was transfigured before them: and his face did shine as the sun, and his raiment was white as the light. And, behold, there appeared unto them Moses and Elias talking with him. Then answered Peter, and said unto Jesus, Lord, it is good for us to be here: if thou wilt, let us make here three tabernacles; one for thee, and one for Moses, and one for Elias. While he yet spake, behold, a bight cloud overshadowed them and behold a voice out of the cloud, which said, This is my beloved Son, in whom I am well pleased; hear ye him. And when the disciples heard it, they fell on their face, and were sore afraid. And Jesus came and touched them, and said, Arise, and be not afraid. And when they had lifted up their eyes, they saw no man, save Jesus only." (Mt. 17:2-8)

■ The Scriptures suggest that this may have been a night scene, for the three disciples had just awakened from a deep sleep (see Lk. 9:32).

■ Note that the, light was from within, and not from some giant cosmic spotlight suddenly focusing down upon Jesus. His countenance was affected first, then his garments. This was the same glory that shone in both the Old Testament tabernacle (Exod. 40) and the temple (1 Kings 8). It would later be withdrawn because of Israel's sin in the days of Ezekiel (Ezek. 10-11). Later it was revealed to the shepherds (Lk. 2:9), to the disciples (Acts 1:9), to Stephen (Acts 7:55), to Saul (Acts 9:3), and to John the apostle (Rev. 1:16). Finally, at Christ's second coming this glory will be revealed to the whole world. "And then shall appear the sign of the Son of man in heaven: and then shall all the tribes of the earth mourn, and they shall see the Son of man coming in the clouds of heaven with power and great glory." (Mt. 24:30)

Christ's eternal glory was not surrendered at the time of the incarnation, but rather was covered and contained by his fleshly body. The body of Christ was to the disciples what the veil of the tabernacle was to Old Testament Israel.

1. Both "veils" housed and protected the glory of God from within.

2. Both "veils" were broken at Calvary. *"And he took bread, and gave thanks, and brake it, and gave unto them, saying, This is my body which is given for you: this do in remembrance of me" (Lk. 22:19). "And, behold, the veil of the temple was rent in twain from the top to the bottom; and the earth did quake, and the rocks rent" (Mt. 27:51).* Satan tried, unsuccessfully, to imitate this inward splendor of Christ (2 Cor. 11:14).

■ The word "transfigured" is metamorphoo in the Greek language. We get our word "metamorphosis" from it. It brings to mind a caterpillar in the cocoon coming forth as a butterfly. The transfiguration of Christ does not set forth his deity, but rather his humanity. Transformation is the goal of humanity. We shall experience this at the rapture. Adam and Eve may well have been clothed by a light of innocence proceeding from within. But all this was lost through sin.

■ Note the previous description of Jesus as offered by John the Apostle:

"And the Word was made flesh, and dwelt among us, (and we beheld his glory, the glory as of the only begotten of the Father,) full of grace and truth" (Jn. 1:14).

A case could be made here that, in all the universe, the strongest object ever created by God was the earthly body of Jesus! Ponder this amazing thought: for 34 years this vessel of clay actually contained and confined the resplendent glory of Almighty God Himself, only allowing for one brief moment a tiny ray to escape, which temporarily blinded Peter, James, and John!

■ Why the appearance of both Moses and Elijah?

1. Because of what they represented—The main reason for the writing of the Old Testament was to prepare us for Christ. Jesus himself testified of this:—*"Search the scriptures ... they... testify of me" (Jn. 5:39). "And beginning at Moses and all the prophets, he expounded unto them in all the scriptures, the things concerning himself " (Lk. 24:27).* While he was on earth, Jesus had a very simple way of summarizing the entire Old Testament: *"Think not that I am come to destroy the law, or the prophets, I am not come to destroy, but to fulfil" (Mt. 5:17).* Why then the appearance of these two men?
   a. Moses was there because he represented the Law.
   b. Elijah was there because he represented the prophets.

2. Because of who they represented—Why were Moses and Elijah, of all Old Testament people, present on this occasion? Perhaps these two men and the disciples suggest all the categories of people who will be in Jesus' coming kingdom. The disciples represent individuals who will be present in physical bodies. Moses represents saved individuals who have died or will die. Elijah represents saved individuals who will not experience death, but will be caught up to heaven alive (1 Thes. 4:17). These three groups will be present when Christ institutes his kingdom on earth. Furthermore, the Lord will be in his glory as he was at the transfiguration, and the kingdom will take place on earth, as this event obviously did. The disciples were thus enjoying a foretaste of the promised kingdom of the Lord (Mt. 16:28). (*The Bible Knowledge Commentary*, Victor Books, Wheaton, Ill., 1983, p. 59)

3. Because of their future ministry during the great tribulation—Many believe that Moses and Elijah will be the two witnesses referred to in Rev. 11:3-12 (see also Mal. 4:4-5). If this is true, the transfiguration event would thus serve as a "trial run." In fact, Jesus had suggested this very thing on the way down from the mountain. *"And Jesus answered and said unto them, Elias truly shall first come, and restore all things" (Mt. 17:11).*

■ If the two witnesses in Rev. 11 are indeed Moses and Elijah, then consider:

1. During the transfiguration they speak of Christ's death in the city of Jerusalem. *"Who appeared in glory, and spake of his decease which he should accomplish at Jerusalem." (Lk. 9:31)*

2. During the tribulation they themselves will die in the city of Jerusalem. *"And when they shall have finished their testimony, the beast that ascended out of the bottomless pit shall make war against them, and shall overcome them, and kill them. And their dead bodies shall lie in the street of the great city, which spiritually is called Sodom and Egypt, where also our Lord was crucified." (Rev. 11:7-8)*

■ Both Moses and Elijah had previously experienced a special revelation from God (see Exod. 33:17-23 and 1 Kings 19:9-13), and at the same place (Mount Sinai/Horeb). The transfiguration answered Moses' twofold request:

1. To see the glory of God (Exod. 33:18)

2. To enter the promised land (Deut. 3:23-25)

■ Peter here thoughtlessly suggests the building of three booths. It may be that at this time the Feast of Tabernacles (booths) was being celebrated in Jerusalem. This was to be a type of the coming Millennium as well as a reminder of Israel's redemption from Egypt (see Lev. 23:34-44). But before this (the Millennium) could happen, another feast would take place—the Passover (see Lev. 23:4-8 and Mt. 26-27). *"For even Christ, our passover, is sacrificed for us" (1 Cor. 5:7).*

■ Peter would never forget this great event. He later wrote about it (see 2 Pet. 1:16-18).

■ Jesus spoke to Moses and Elijah concerning his "decease" (Lk. 9:31). The word here is actually "exodus," and is used by Peter at a later date in describing his approaching death (see 2 Pet. 1:13-14).

■ Mark concluded the transfiguration event with the following words: *"And as they came down from the mountain, he charged them that they should tell no man what things they had seen, till the Son of man were risen from the dead. And they kept that saying with themselves, questioning one with another what the rising from the dead should mean." (Mk. 9:9-10).* The Jews were familiar with the doctrine of the resurrection (see Job 19:25-26; Isa. 25:8; 26:19; Hosea 13:14), but the resurrection of the Son of man astonished them, for their theology had no place for a suffering and dying Messiah. This is seen especially in John 12:32-39.

THE FINAL WEEK OF JESUS

THE FINAL EIGHT DAYS OF JESUS' MINISTRY

INTRODUCTION: There are a total of 89 chapters in the four Gospel accounts of Matthew, Mark, Luke, and John. Of these, only four record the first 30 years of Jesus' earthly life (Mt. 1, 2; Lk. 1, 2). However, of the remaining 85, no less than 24 describe the final eight days of His life (Mt. 21-27; Mk. 11-15; Lk. 20-23; Jn. 12-19). In other words, as measured by the scriptural space given it, the last week or so of our Lord's ministry was some eight times more important than the first 30 years. These eight "dreadful days of divine destiny" began with a conspiracy by sinners. They would end with a crucifixion for sinners. This all important time span will be overviewed in a two-fold manner.

    I. A Basic Outline Summary of Each Day

    II. An Extended Analytical Summary of Each Day

In both accounts we will use the Roman system of reckoning time as employed by the Apostle John (see Jn. 19:14) which begins at both midnight and noon. This, of course, is our system today. Matthew, Mark, and Luke, however, use the Hebrew system which begins the new day at 6:00 P.M. (sunset).

I. A Basic Outline Summary of Each Day

A. Saturday

■ His anointing by Mary in Bethany

B. Sunday

■ The triumphal entry

C. Monday

■ The cursing of the fig tree
■ The second temple cleansing
■ The request by some Greeks to see Jesus

D. Tuesday

- The confrontation with the Pharisees
- The condemnation of the Pharisees
- Jesus commends a poor widow
- Jesus weeps over Jerusalem
- Jesus delivers the Mt. Olivet Discourse

E. Wednesday

- The final predictions by Jesus
- The final plots against Jesus

F. Thursday

- Events in the Upper Room

G. Friday

- Jesus delivers His Vine and Branch Discourse
- He prays His Great High Priestly Prayer
- His prayers in Gethsemane
- His unfair trials
    1. Before Annas
    2. Before Caiaphas
    3. Before the entire Sanhedrin
    4. Before Pilate (first time)
    5. Before Herod Antipas
    6. Before Pilate (second time)
    7. Before the Roman soldiers
- The denial by Peter
- The death of Judas
- The crucifixion of Jesus
- The burial of Jesus

H. Saturday

- The sealing of the tomb

II. An Extended Analytical Summary of Each Day

A. Saturday

■ His anointing by Mary in Bethany

"Then Jesus six days before the passover came to Bethany, where Lazarus was, which had been dead, whom he raised from the dead. There they made him a supper; and Martha served: but Lazarus was one of them that sat at the table with him. Then took Mary a pound of ointment of spikenard, very costly, and anointed the feet of Jesus, and wiped his feet with her hair: and the house was filled with the odour of the ointment. Then saith one of his disciples, Judas Iscariot, Simon's son, which should betray him, Why was not this ointment sold for three hundred pence, and given to the poor? This he said, not that he cared for the poor; but because he was a thief, and had the bag, and bare what was put therein. Then said Jesus, Let her alone: against the day of my burying hath she kept this. For the poor always ye have with you; but me ye have not always ... Verily I say unto you, Wheresoever this gospel shall be preached throughout the whole world, this also that she hath done shall be spoken of for a memorial of her." (Jn. 12:1-8; Mk. 14:9)

1. This was the only anointing His body would receive. In spite of the many times Christ had warned of His suffering and death (see Mt. 16:21; 20:18-19), apparently the only person to take him seriously was Mary (see also Jn. 10:11, 17-18).
2. The 300 pence (denarii) was roughly a year's wages. In present-day finances this would have represented some 20 to 25 thousand dollars. There is a possibility that Mary inherited this, or that it represented her life's savings.
3. Even prior to his betrayal of Jesus we are told the following facts regarding Judas Iscariot:
   a. He belonged to Satan from the very beginning (Jn. 6:70)
   b. He was a shameless hypocrite
   c. He was a thief

B. Sunday

■ The triumphal entry

"And when they drew nigh unto Jerusalem, and were come to Bethphage, unto the mount of Olives, then sent Jesus two disciples, Saying unto them, Go into the village over against you, and straightway ye shall find an ass tied, and a colt with her: loose them, and bring them unto me. And if any man say ought unto you, ye shall say, The Lord hath need of them; and straightway he will send them. All this was done, that it might be fulfilled which was spoken by the prophet, saying, Tell ye the daughter of Sion, Behold, thy King cometh unto thee, meek, and sitting upon an ass, and a colt the foal of an ass. And the disciples went, and did as Jesus commanded them, And brought the ass, and the colt, and put on them their clothes, and they set him thereon. And a very great multitude spread their garments in the way; others cut down branches from the trees, and strawed them in the way. And the multitudes that went before, and that followed, cried, saying, Hosanna to the son of David: Blessed is he that cometh in the name of the Lord; Hosanna in the highest. And when he was come into Jerusalem, all the city was moved, saying, Who is this? And the multitude said, This is Jesus the prophet of Nazareth of Galilee." (Mt. 21:1-11)

1. This marks the only "ticker tape parade" our Lord would receive during His earthly ministry, and it was, to say the least, short-lived. The disciples were no doubt excited over all this attention, but Jesus was not, for He knew what the future held, realizing the Jewish cries of celebration would soon turn into those of condemnation. Note the contrast:

   a. The cries on Palm Sunday— *"Blessed is the King that cometh in the name of the Lord" (Lk. 19:38). "Blessed is the King of Israel" (Jn. 12:13).*

   b. The cries on Good Friday— *"When Pilate therefore heard that saying, he brought Jesus forth, and sat down in the judgment seat in a place that is called the Pavement, but in the Hebrew, Gabbatha. And it was the preparation of the passover, and about the sixth hour: and he saith unto the Jews, Behold your King! But they cried out, Away with him, away with him, crucify him. Pilate saith unto them, Shall I crucify your King? The chief priests answered, We have no king but Caesar." (Jn. 19:13-15)*

   "And when they had platted a crown of thorns, they put it upon his head, and a reed in his right hand: and they bowed the knee before him, and mocked him, saying, Hail, King of the Jews!" (Mt. 27:29)

2. On this occasion Jesus chose to enter Jerusalem on the foal of an ass. He did this for two reasons:

   a. To fulfill prophecy— *"All this was done, that it might be fulfilled which was spoken by the prophet, saying, Tell ye the daughter of Sion, Behold, thy King cometh unto thee, meek, and sitting upon an ass, and a colt the foal of an ass" (Mt. 21:4-5)*. This act of Christ was thus a direct fulfillment of the Old Testament prophecy written by Zechariah: *"Rejoice greatly, O daughter of Zion; shout, O daughter of Jerusalem: behold, thy King cometh unto thee: he is just, and having salvation; lowly, and riding upon an ass, and upon a colt the foal of an ass." (Zech. 9:9)*

   b. To demonstrate the value of little things—Jesus often used the insignificant things to accomplish His divine will.

      (1) Here he used a small animal.

      (2) He had once used a little boy's lunch (Jn. 6:9-11), some empty pots (Jn. 2:6-9), and some clay (Jn. 9:6-7). With these he provided food for the multitudes, wine for a wedding, and healing for the sightless. Paul later expounds upon this: *"But God hath chosen the foolish things of the world to confound the wise; and God hath chosen the weak things of the world to confound the things which are mighty; And base things of the world, and things which are despised, hath God chosen, yea, and things which are not, to bring to nought things that are: That no flesh should glory in his presence." (1 Cor. 1:27-29)*

3. Note the word hosanna as used by the crowd (Mt. 21:9). This word is only found five times in the Bible and all but one occur during the triumphal entry event.

   W. E. Vine comments: "Hosanna in the Hebrew means, 'save, we pray.' The word seems to have become an utterance of praise rather than of prayer, though originally, probably a cry for help. The people's cry at the Lord's triumphal entry into Jerusalem (Mt. 21:9, 15; Mk. 11:9-10; Jn. 12:13) was taken from Ps. 118, which was recited at the Feast of Tabernacles in the great Halle Psalms 113-118 in responses with the priest, accompanied by the waving of palms and willow branches. The last day of the feast was called 'the great Hosanna, and the boughs called hosannas'." (*Vine's Expository Dictionary of New Testament Words*, p. 564).

■ The cursing of the fig tree for a detailed account of this event, see the section overviewing the 35 miracles of Jesus.

■ The second temple cleansing

"And they come to Jerusalem: and Jesus went into the temple, and began to cast out them that sold and bought in the temple, and overthrew the tables of the moneychangers, and the seats of them that sold doves; And would not suffer that any man should carry any vessel through the temple. And he taught, saying unto them, Is it not written, My house shall be called of all nations the house of prayer? but ye have made it a den of thieves. And the scribes and chief priests heard it, and sought how they might destroy him: for they feared him, because all the people was astonished at his doctrine." (Mk. 11:15-18)

As observed, this marks the final of two temple cleansings. These two may be favorably compared.

1. Both occurred at Passover time. The first introduced Jesus' public ministry, while the second concluded it.
2. His death and resurrection is predicted on both occasions.
    a. First occasion— *"Then answered the Jews and said unto him, What sign shewest thou unto us, seeing that thou doest these things? Jesus answered and said unto them, Destroy this temple, and in three days I will raise it up. Then said the Jews, Forty and six years was this temple in building, and wilt thou rear it up in three days? But he spake of the temple of his body." (Jn. 2:18-21)*
    b. Second occasion— *"Verily, verily, I say unto you, Except a corn of wheat fall into the ground and die, it abideth alone: but if it die, it bringeth forth much fruit... Now is my soul troubled; and what shall I say? Father, save me from this hour: but for this cause came I unto this hour. And I, if I be lifted up from the earth, will draw all men unto me. This he said, signifying what death he should die." (Jn. 12:24, 27, 32-33)*
3. His glory was revealed just prior to the first cleansing. "This beginning of miracles did Jesus in Cana of Galilee, and manifested forth his glory; and his disciples believed on him." (Jn. 2:11)
4. His glory was revealed just after the second cleansing. *"Father, glorify thy name. Then came there a voice from heaven, saying, I have both glorified it, and will glorify it again." (Jn. 12:28)*
5. The Father is associated with both events.
    a. First cleansing— *"And said unto them that sold doves, Take these things hence; make not my Father's house an house of merchandise. And his disciples remembered that it was written, The zeal of thine house hath eaten me up." (Jn. 2:16-17)*
    b. Second cleansing— *"And Jesus went into the temple of God, and cast out all them that sold and bought in the temple, and overthrew the tables of the moneychangers, and the seats of them that sold doves, And said unto them, It is written, My house shall be called the house of prayer; but ye have made it a den of thieves." (Mt. 21:12-13)*
6. Several factors no doubt invoked His wrath against the money changers on each occasion:
    a. They were selling cattle, sheep, and doves in the court of the Gentiles, the only place where non-Jews could come and pray.
    b. They may have been selling blemished animals.
    c. They could have been overcharging.
    d. They were obviously filled with greed.

7. John Grassmick observes: "When Jesus arrived in Jerusalem, he went into the temple area, the large outer court of the Gentiles surrounding the inner sacred courts of the temple itself. No Gentile was allowed beyond this outer court. In it the high priest Caiaphas had authorized a market (probably a recent economic innovation) for the sale of ritually pure items necessary for temple sacrifice: wine, oil, salt, approved sacrificial animals and birds.

8. Observe Jesus' words concerning His Father's house. *"And he taught, saying unto them, Is it not written, My house shall be called of all nations the house of prayer? but ye have made it a den of thieves." (Mk. 11:17)*

    Here Jesus quotes from Jeremiah's sermon delivered some six centuries earlier in the same temple area, condemning Israel for the same thing. *"Is this house, which is called by my name, become a den of robbers in your eyes? Behold, even I have seen it, saith the LORD." (Jer. 7:11)* Our Lord also refers to a prophecy of Isaiah concerning Gentile people and the temple during the Millennium. *"Even them will I bring to my holy mountain, and make them joyful in my house of prayer: their burnt offerings and their sacrifices shall be accepted upon mine altar; for mine house shall be called an house of prayer for all people." (Isa. 56:7)*

■ The request by some Greeks to see Jesus

"And there were certain Greeks among them that came up to worship at the feast: The same came therefore to Philip, which was of Bethsaida of Galilee, and desired him, saying, Sir, we would see Jesus. Philip cometh and telleth Andrew: and again Andrew and Philip tell Jesus. And Jesus answered them, saying, The hour is come, that the Son of man should be glorified. Verily, verily, I say unto you, Except a corn of wheat fall into the ground and die, it abideth alone: but if it die, it bringeth forth much fruit. He that loveth his life shall lose it; and he that hateth his life in this world shall keep it unto life eternal. If any man serve me, let him follow me; and where I am, there shall also my servant be: if any man serve me, him will my Father honour. Now is my soul troubled; and what shall I say? Father, save me from this hour: but for this cause came I unto this hour. Father, glorify thy name. Then came there a voice from heaven, saying, I have both glorified it, and will glorify it again. The people therefore, that stood by, and heard it, said that it thundered: others said, An angel spake to him. Jesus answered and said, This voice came not because of me, but for your sakes. Now is the judgment of this world: now shall the prince of this world be cast out. And I, if I be lifted up from the earth, will draw all men unto me." (Jn. 12:20-32)

1. Note two phrases at this point, one referred to here and the second in (Jn. 20):
   a. *"Sir, we would see Jesus" (Jn. 12:21).*
   b. *"Then were the disciples glad, when they saw the Lord" (Jn. 20:20).*
2. The wise pastor or Sunday School teacher will seek to make the first statement a reality in their presentation of God's Word, thus assuring that all those who hear them will experience the second statement!
3. It is interesting to observe the Greeks wanted Philip to show them the Son, and that, he, Philip, would later ask Jesus to show him the Father (Jn. 14:8). Jesus' response would indicate Philip still had much to learn about the Son of God! *"Jesus saith unto him, Have I been so long time with you, and yet hast thou not known me, Philip? he that hath seen me hath seen the Father; and how sayest thou then, Shew us the Father? Believest thou not that I am in the Father, and the Father in me? the words that I speak unto you I speak not of myself: but the Father that dwelleth in me, he doeth the works." (Jn. 14:9-10)*

■ Jesus' statement, *"The hour is come, that the Son of man should be glorified" (12:23)* is revealing indeed, especially the words *"hour"* and *"glorified."* Both terms refer directly to His death. Note:

1. Regarding the word *"hour"* —
   a. *"Jesus saith unto her, Woman, what have I to do with thee? mine hour is not yet come." (Jn. 2:4)*
   b. *"Then they sought to take him: but no man laid hands on him, because his hour was not yet come." (Jn. 7:30)*
   c. *"These words spake Jesus in the treasury, as he taught in the temple: and no man laid hands on him; for his hour was not yet come." (Jn. 8:20)*
   d. *"Now before the feast of the passover, when Jesus knew that his hour was come that he should depart out of this world unto the Father, having loved his own which were in the world, he loved them unto the end." (Jn. 13:1)*
   e. *"Then cometh he to his disciples, and saith unto them, Sleep on now, and take your rest: behold, the hour is at hand, and the Son of man is betrayed into the hands of sinners." (Mt. 26:45)*
   f. *"And he went forward a little, and fell on the ground, and prayed that, if it were possible, the hour might pass from him." (Mk. 14:35)*

2. Regarding the word *"glorified"* —
   a. *"(But this spake he of the Spirit, which they that believe on him should receive: for the Holy Ghost was not yet given; because that Jesus was not yet glorified.)" (Jn. 7:39)*
   b. *"These things understood not his disciples at the first: but when Jesus was glorified, then remembered they that these things were written of him, and that they had done these things unto him." (Jn. 12:16)*
   c. *"Jesus answered, He it is, to whom I shall give a sop, when I have dipped it. And when he had dipped the sop, he gave it to Judas Iscariot, the son of Simon. And after the sop Satan entered into him. Then said Jesus unto him, That thou doest, do quickly... He then having received the sop went immediately out: and it was night. Therefore, when he was gone out, Jesus said, Now is the Son of man glorified, and God is glorified in him." (Jn. 13:26-27, 30-31)*
   d. *"The God of Abraham, and of Isaac, and of Jacob, the God of our fathers, hath glorified his Son Jesus; whom ye delivered up, and denied him in the presence of Pilate, when he was determined to let him go." (Acts 3:13)*

D. Tuesday

■ Jesus' Confrontations with the Pharisees. All throughout His ministry, Jesus had tangled with the Pharisees who had constantly attempted to either accuse or ensnare Him.

1. Prior Confrontations—They said:
   a. He violated the Sabbath

   "Therefore said some of the Pharisees, This man is not of God, because he keepeth not the Sabbath day. Others said, How can a man that is a sinner do such miracles? And there was a division among them." (Jn. 9:16)
   b. He had transgressed the traditions of the Father (Mk. 7:5-9, 13)
   c. He did not insist upon His disciples observing the many feasts (Mk. 2:18-20)
   d. He ate and associated with sinners (Mk. 2:15-17)
   e. He was a blasphemer
      (1) Because He claimed to forgive sin (Mt. 9:1-3)
      (2) Because He claimed to be God (Jn. 10:31-33)
   f. He was actually energized by Satan himself (Mt. 12:22, 24)

---

2. Passion Tuesday Confrontations
   a. Concerning the source of His authority

   "And they come again to Jerusalem: and as he was walking in the temple, there come to him the chief priests, and the scribes, and the elders, And say unto him, By what authority doest thou these things? and who gave thee this authority to do these things? And Jesus answered and said unto them, I will also ask of you one question, and answer me, and I will tell you by what authority I do these things. The baptism of John, was it from heaven, or of men? answer me. And they reasoned with themselves, saying, If we shall say, From heaven; he will say, Why then did ye not believe him? But if we shall say, Of men; they feared the people: for all men counted John, that he was a prophet indeed. And they answered and said unto Jesus, We cannot tell. And Jesus answering saith unto them, Neither do I tell you by what authority I do these things." (Mk. 11:27-33)

   b. Concerning paying tribute to Caesar

   "And they asked him, saying, Master, we know that thou sayest and teachest rightly, neither acceptest thou the person of any, but teachest the way of God truly: Is it lawful for us to give tribute unto Caesar, or no? But he perceived their craftiness, and said unto them, Why tempt ye me? Shew me a penny. Whose image and superscription hath it? They answered and said, Caesar's. And he said unto them, Render therefore unto Caesar the things which be Caesar's, and unto God the things which be God's. And they could not take hold of his words before the people: and they marvelled at his answer, and held their peace." (Lk. 20:21-26)

   c. Concerning the resurrection

   "The same day came to him the Sadducees, which say that there is no resurrection, and asked him, Saying, Master, Moses said, If a man die, having no children, his brother shall marry his wife, and raise up seed unto his brother. Now there were with us seven brethren: and the first, when he had married a wife, deceased, and, having no issue, left his wife unto his brother: Likewise the second also, and the third, unto the seventh. And last of all the woman died also. Therefore in the resurrection whose wife shall she be of the seven? for they all had her. Jesus answered and said unto them, Ye do err, not knowing the scriptures, nor the power of God. For in the resurrection they neither marry, nor are given in marriage, but are as the angels of God in heaven. But as touching the resurrection of the dead, have ye not read that which was spoken unto you by God, saying, I am the God of Abraham, and the God of Isaac, and the God of Jacob? God is not the God of the dead, but of the living. And when the multitude heard this, they were astonished at his doctrine." (Mt. 22:23-33)

   This ignorance of God's Word had always been Israel's problem. The Old Testament prophets often testified of this: *"The ox knoweth his owner, and the ass his master's crib: but Israel doth not know, my people doth not consider." (Isa. 1:3)* *"My people are destroyed for lack of knowledge: because thou hast rejected knowledge, I will also reject thee, that thou shalt be no priest to me: seeing thou hast forgotten the law of thy God, I will also forget thy children"* (Hos. 4:6). *"Behold, the days come, saith the Lord GOD, that I will send a famine in the land, not a famine of bread, nor a thirst for water, but of hearing the words of the LORD: And they shall wander from sea to sea, and from the north even to the east, they shall run to and fro to seek the word of the LORD, and shall not find it." (Amos 8:11-12)*

   d. Concerning the greatest commandment

   "And one of the scribes came, and having heard them reasoning together, and perceiving that he had answered them well, asked him, Which is the first commandment of all? And Jesus answered him, The

first of all the commandments is, Hear, O Israel; The Lord our God is one Lord: And thou shalt love the Lord thy God with all thy heart, and with all thy soul, and with all thy mind, and with all thy strength: this is the first commandment. And the second is like, namely this, Thou shalt love thy neighbour as thyself. There is none other commandment greater than these. And the scribe said unto him, Well, Master, thou hast said the truth: for there is one God; and there is none other but he: And to love him with all the heart, and with all the understanding, and with all the soul, and with all the strength, and to love his neighbour as himself, is more than all whole burnt offerings and sacrifices. And when Jesus saw that he answered discreetly, he said unto him, Thou art not far from the kingdom of God. And no man after that durst ask him any question" (Mk. 12:28-34)

The *"Hear, O Israel"* phrase (12:29) is known as the "shema," named after the first word of Deuteronomy 6:4 in Hebrew which means "hear." The Shema became the Jewish confession of faith, which was recited by pious Jews every morning and evening. To this day it begins every synagogue service.

As Jesus stated, the Ten Commandments are aptly summarized by these two statements:

(1) The first statement is vertical in nature, and covers commands 1-4 (Exod. 20:3-11).

(2) The second statement is horizontal in nature, and covers commands 5-10 (Exod. 20:12-17).

e. Concerning the deity of the Messiah

"While the Pharisees were gathered together, Jesus asked them, Saying, What think ye of Christ? whose son is he? They say unto him, The son of David. He saith unto them, How then doth David in spirit call him Lord, saying, The LORD said unto my Lord, Sit thou on my right hand, till I make thin enemies thy footstool? if David then call him Lord, how is he his son? And no man was able to answer him a word, neither durst any man from that day forth ask him any more questions. " (Mt. 22:41-46)

■ Jesus' condemnation of the Pharisees

1. Their words and their works were totally unrelated— *"Then spake Jesus to the multitude, and to his disciples, Saying The scribes and the Pharisees sit in Moses' seat: All therefore whatsoever they bid you observe, that observe and do; but do not ye after their works: for they say, and do not."* (Mt. 23:1-3)

2. They placed grievous weights of their own vain traditions upon the shoulders of men (23:4).

3. They dressed and performed only for the praise of men.

   a. Wearing fancy prayer boxes (23:5)

   b. Displaying lavish garments (23:5)

   c. Occupying prominent places at feasts and in synagogues (23:6)

   d. Demanding to be addressed by their full titles (23:7)

4. They not only refused to enter into the kingdom of heaven, but stood in the doorway to prevent others from entering (23:13).

5. They cheated poor widows out of their homes (23:14).

6. They repeated long and insincere prayers (23:14).

7. They made converts and taught them their evil ways— *"Woe unto you, scribes and Pharisees, hypocrites! for ye compass sea and land to make one proselyte, and when he is made, ye make him twofold more the child of hell than yourselves."* (Mt. 23:15)

8. They uttered their oaths of promise with forked tongues (23:16-22).

9. They had, in their legalistic bondage, perverted the very Law of Moses.

a. In their tithing—*"Woe unto you, scribes and Pharisees, hypocrites! for ye pay tithe of mint and anise and cummin, and have omitted the weightier matters of the law, judgment, mercy, and faith: these ought ye to have done, and not to leave the other undone. Ye blind guides, which strain at a gnat, and swallow a camel." (Mt. 23:23-24)*

In their deceitful tithing practices, they had actually done violence to their own parents. Mark records Jesus' word on this: *"For Moses said, Honour thy father and thy mother; and, Whoso curseth father or mother, let him die the death: But ye say, If a man shall say to his father or mother, it is Corban, that is to say, a gift, by whatsoever thou mightest be profited by me; he shall be free." (Mk. 7:10-11)*

Thus, by this despicable method, the wicked Jewish leaders were deliberately violating the Fifth Commandment. Centuries before, Isaiah had written concerning this sad and sordid thing: *"Wherefore the Lord said, Forasmuch as this people draw near me with their mouth, and with their lips do honour me, but have removed their heart far from me, and their fear toward me is taught by the precept of men" (Isa. 29:13).*

Note the phrase, "swallow a camel." The strict Pharisee would carefully strain his drinking water through a cloth to make sure he did not unknowingly swallow a gnat, the smallest of unclean creatures. But, in a figurative sense, by his double standard of life, he would knowingly swallow a camel, one of the largest of unclean creatures.

b. In their ritual washings—*"Woe unto you, scribes and Pharisees, hypocrites! for ye make clean the outside of the cup and of the platter, but within they are full of extortion and excess. Thou blind Pharisee, cleanse first that which is within the cup and platter, that the outside of them may be clean also" (Mt. 23:25-26).*

10. They had polished exteriors, but polluted interiors (23:27-28)—*"Woe unto you, scribes and Pharisees, hypocrites! for ye are like unto whited sepulchres, which indeed appear beautiful outward, but are within full of dead men's bones, and of all uncleanness." (Mt. 23:27)*

11. They revered the memories of their murderous fathers (23:29-32).

12. They were, in fact, descendants from a race of religious snakes (23:33)

13. They would later kill God's prophets—*"Wherefore, behold, I send unto you prophets, and wise men, and scribes: and some of them ye shall kill and crucify; and some of them shall ye scourge in your synagogues, and persecute them from city to city." (Mt. 23:34)*

14. They had already killed God's prophets—*"That upon you may come all the righteous blood shed upon the earth, from the blood of righteous Abel unto the blood of Zacharias son of Barachias, whom ye slew between the temple and the altar. " (Mt. 23:35)*

Here Jesus summarized the past cruel action of the unsaved Jewish leaders by referring to the first and last Old Testament martyrs. The killing of Abel is recorded in Genesis 4:8, in Scripture's first book; and the killing of Zechariah in 2 Chronicles 24:20-22, the final book of the Hebrew Bible.

■ Jesus commends a poor widow

"And he looked up, and saw the rich men casting their gifts into the treasury. And he saw also a certain poor widow casting in thither two mites. And he said, Of a truth I say unto you, that this poor widow hath cast in more than they all: For all these have of their abundance cast in unto the offerings of God: but she of her penury hath cast in all the living that she had." (Lk. 21:1-4)

Her sacrificial gift here was in stark contrast to the hypocritical giving of many rich people. Our Lord warned of this during His Sermon on the Mount.

"Take heed that ye do not your alms before men, to be seen of them: otherwise ye have no reward of your Father which is in heaven. Therefore when thou doest thine alms, do not sound a trumpet before thee, as the hypocrites do in the synagogues and in the streets, that they may have glory of men. Verily I say unto you, They have their reward. But when thou doest alms, let not thy left hand know what thy right hand doeth: That thine alms may be in secret: and thy Father which seeth in secret himself shall reward thee openly." (Mt. 6:1-4)

■ Jesus weeps over the City of Jerusalem

1. First occasion

"And when he was come near, he beheld the city, and wept over it, Saying, If thou hadst known, even thou, at least in this thy day, the things which belong unto thy peace! but now they are hid from thine eyes. For the days shall come upon thee, that thine enemies shall cast a trench about thee, and compass thee round, and keep thee in on every side, And shall lay thee even with the ground, and thy children within thee, and they shall not leave in thee one stone upon another; because thou knewest not the time of thy visitation." (Lk. 19:41-44)

The famous Bible student, Sir Robert Anderson, has attached great meaning to the three words, "this thy day." According to the prophecy in Dan. 9:24-27 (often called the 70-week prophecy) God told Daniel he would deal with Israel for yet another 70 "weeks," which is usually interpreted as 490 years. The prophecy continued that after 69 of these "weeks," or 483 years, the Messiah would be "cut off" (rejected and crucified.) The prophecy was to start on March 14, 445 B.C. Mr. Anderson suggests that if one begins counting forward from that day, he discovers that the 483 years (173,880 days) runs out on April 6, A.D. 32. It was on this exact day that Jesus rode into Jerusalem on the foal of an ass and, although welcomed by the masses, was officially rejected by Israel's leaders. According to Sir Robert, all this was in mind when our Lord uttered the words of this statement.

2. Second occasion

"O Jerusalem, Jerusalem, thou that killest the prophets, and stonest them which are sent unto thee, how often would I have gathered thy children together, even as a hen gathereth her chickens under her wings, and ye would not! Behold, your house is left unto you desolate. For I say unto you, Ye shall not see me henceforth, till ye shall say, Blessed is he that cometh in the name of the Lord." (Mt. 23:37-39)

Note especially Jesus' reference to *"your house"* (the temple) here as contrasted to the *"my house"* statements of John 2:16 and Matthew 21:13. At this point Israel is set aside for the duration of the Church age (see Mt. 21:33-46). Jesus' statement in 23:39 will someday be gloriously fulfilled. *"Blessed be he that cometh in the name of the Lord: we have blessed you out of the house of the Lord." (Psa. 118:26)*

■ Jesus delivers the Mt. Olivet Discourse

Note: for an expanded overview of this discourse, see the section entitled, "The Sermons of Jesus."

E. Wednesday

■ Jesus is secretly betrayed by Judas

"Then entered Satan into Judas surnamed Iscariot, being of the number of the twelve. And he went his way, and communed with the chief priests and captains, how he might betray him unto them." (Lk. 22:3-4)

This is the first of two recorded occasions when Satan himself entered into Judas (see also Jn. 13:27). This can be said about no other person in the Bible.

"And said unto them, What will ye give me, and I will deliver him unto you? And they covenanted with him for thirty pieces of silver. And from that time he sought opportunity to betray him." (Mt. 26:15-16)

Note: For an expanded overview of this betrayal, see the chart section under Wednesday.

F. Thursday

■ Jesus prepares for the Upper Room events

"And he sent Peter and John, saying, Go and prepare us the passover, that we may eat. And they said unto him, Where wilt thou that we prepare? And he said unto them, Behold, when ye are entered into the city, there shall a man meet you, bearing a pitcher of water; follow him into the house where he entereth in. And ye shall say unto the goodman of the house, The Master saith unto thee, Where is the guestchamber, where I shall eat the passover with my disciples? And he shall shew you a large upper room furnished: there make ready. And they went, and found as he had said unto them: and they made ready the passover." (Lk. 22:8-13)

1. The purpose behind this somewhat strange instruction of Jesus was probably to keep the actual location of the final Passover from Judas as long as possible. Our Lord was, of course, aware of the wicked plot against him.

2. This is the first reference to the Upper Room, a place that would become very important in the life of the early church.

    a. Jesus instituted the Lord's Supper in this room (Lk. 22:14-15).

    b. He later appeared here to ten of his apostles on the first Easter Sunday night (Jn. 20:19).

    c. He showed his nail-pierced hands to Thomas a week later (Jn. 20:24-26).

    d. The apostles gathered for both a prayer meeting and a business meeting in this room (Acts 1:12-26).

    e. The Holy Spirit came upon them here (Acts 2:1).

■ Jesus presides over the Upper Room events

1. He partakes of the Passover.

    "Now before the feast of the passover, when Jesus knew that his hour was come that he should depart out of this world unto the Father, having loved his own which were in the world, he loved them unto the end. And supper being ended, the devil having now put into the heart of Judas Iscariot, Simon's son, to betray him." (Jn. 13:1-2)

    This involved roasting the lamb, setting out the unleavened bread and wine, and preparing bitter herbs along with a sauce made of dried fruit moistened with vinegar and wine and combined with spices.

2. He washes their feet

    "Jesus knowing that the Father had given all things into his hands, and that he was come from God, and went to God; He riseth from supper, and laid aside his garments; and took a towel, and girded himself. After that he poureth water into a bason, and began to wash the disciples' feet, and to wipe them with the towel wherewith he was girded. Then cometh he to Simon Peter: and Peter saith unto him, Lord, dost thou wash my feet? Jesus answered and said unto him, What I do thou knowest not now; but thou shalt know hereafter. Peter saith unto him, Thou shalt never wash my feet. Jesus answered him, If I wash thee not, thou hast no part with me. Simon Peter saith unto him, Lord, not my feet only, but also my hands and my head. Jesus saith to him, He that is washed needeth not save to wash his feet, but is clean every whit: and ye are clean, but not all. For he knew who should betray him; therefore said he, Ye are not all clean." (Jn. 13:3-11)

3. He speaks to them regarding servanthood (Jn. 13:12-19)

4. He announces His impending betrayal

"When Jesus had thus said, he was troubled in spirit, and testified, and said, Verily, verily, I say unto you, that one of you shall betray me." (Jn. 13:21)

5. His disciples are dumb struck

"And they were exceeding sorrowful, and began every one of them to say unto him, Lord, is it I?" (Mt. 26:22)

"Now there was leaning on Jesus' bosom one of his disciples, whom Jesus loved. Simon Peter therefore beckoned to him, that he should ask who it should be of whom he spake. He then lying on Jesus' breast saith unto him, Lord, who is it?" (Jn. 13:23-25)

To their credit, they did not say, "Lord, is it such and such?" or "Lord, I'm sure I know who it is."

"Then Judas, which betrayed him, answered and said, Master, is it I? He said unto him, Thou hast said." (Mt. 26:25)

Here Judas called Jesus "Rabbi" (Master), and not "Lord," as did the other apostles in the Upper Room.

6. Jesus hints in regards to the traitor's identification

"Jesus answered, He it is, to whom I shall give a sop, when I have dipped it. And when he had dipped the sop, he gave it to Judas Iscariot, the son of Simon. And after the sop Satan entered into him. Then said Jesus unto him, That thou doest, do quickly. Now no man at the table knew for what intent he spake this unto him. For some of them thought, because Judas had the bag, that Jesus had said unto him, Buy those things that we have need of against the feast; or, that he should give something to the poor. He then having received the sop went immediately out: and it was night." (Jn. 13:26-30)

Apparently Judas had played his deceitful role so well that the eleven still did not realize he was the traitor, in spite of Christ's obvious statement.

7. He predicts His disciples would soon all forsake Him (Mt. 26:31).

8. He promises to meet them in Galilee following His resurrection (Mt. 26:32).

9. He predicts Peter's denials

"Peter answered and said unto him, Though all men shall be offended because of thee, yet will I never be offended. Jesus said unto him, Verily I say unto thee, That this night, before the cock crow, thou shalt deny me thrice. Peter said unto him, Though I should die with thee, yet will I not deny thee. Likewise also said all the disciples. Then cometh Jesus with them unto a place called Gethsemane, and saith unto the disciples, Sit ye here, while I go and pray yonder." (Mt. 26:33-36)

"And the Lord said, Simon, Simon, behold, Satan hath desired to have you, that he may sift you as wheat: But I have prayed for thee, that thy faith fail not: and when thou art converted, strengthen thy brethren." (Lk. 22:31-32)

The devil once requested permission from God to test and torment another choice servant of God, Job (see Job 1-2). Here Satan apparently asked for the same power over Simon Peter. The apostle may have had this very event in mind when he wrote concerning the devil and the believer in one of his epistles (see 1 Pet. 5:7-11). At any rate, it should be a great comfort for all believers to know that the resurrected Savior is, even today, at this very moment, praying for them in glory (see Rom. 8:34; 1 John 2:1; Heb. 7:25; 9:24).

10. He institutes the Lord's Supper from the remains of the Passover meal.

"And as they were eating, Jesus took bread, and blessed it, and brake it, and gave it to the disciples, and said, Take, eat; this is my body. And he took the cup, and gave thanks, and gave it to them, saying, Drink ye all of it; For this is my blood of the new testament, which is shed for many for the remission of sins. But

I say unto you, I will not drink henceforth of this fruit of the vine, until that day when I drink it new with you in my Father's kingdom." (Mt. 26:26-29)

11. He speaks to them regarding discipleship, heaven, His relationship with the Father, and the coming ministry of the Holy Spirit (Jn. 13:31-14:31).

12. He concludes the meeting with a song and they depart for the Mt. of Olives. *"And when they had sung an hymn, they went out into the mount of Olives." (Mt. 26:30)*

Six Psalms are called the "Hallel" Psalms. These are: 113, 114, 115, 116, 117, and 118. All of these were to be sung on the eve of the Passover. This is what Jesus and the disciples sang. Note some of the verses in these Psalms: *"The sorrows of death compassed me, and the pains of hell gat hold upon me: I found trouble and sorrow" (116:3). "I will take the cup of salvation, and call upon the name of the Lord" (116:13). "The stone which the builders refused is become the head stone of the corner. This is the Lord's doing; it is marvelous in our eyes. This is the day which the Lord hath made; we will rejoice and be glad in it" (118:22-24). "Blessed is he that cometh in the name of the Lord..." (118:26).*

G. Friday

■ Jesus lectures His disciples on fruit bearing en route to the Mt. of Olives

"I am the true vine, and my Father is the husbandman. Every branch in me that beareth not fruit he taketh away: and every branch that beareth fruit, he purgeth it, that it may bring forth more fruit. Now ye are clean through the word which I have spoken unto you. Abide in me, and I in you. As the branch cannot bear fruit of itself, except it abide in the vine; no more can ye, except ye abide in me. I am the vine, ye are the branches: He that abideth in me, and I in him, the same bringeth forth much fruit: for without me ye can do nothing." (Jn. 15:1-5)

Note: For a detailed overview of John 15 and 16, see the section under Jesus' sermons.

■ Jesus prays His Great High Priestly Prayer

Question: Where in the New Testament is the Lord's Prayer recorded, and what does it say?

Answer: Many Christians would mistakenly turn to Matt. 6 and begin reading those familiar words: "Our Father which art in heaven, Hallowed be thy name" (Mt. 6:9). However, this is not the Lord's Prayer, but rather the Disciple's Prayer. In reality, the Lord's Prayer is found here in John 17. In this prayer, our great High Priest prays for Himself, for His apostles, and for His Church.

During His prayer, Jesus refers to God as "Father" on six occasions (17:1, 5, 11, 21, 24, and 25). This awesome title is extremely rare in the Old Testament. Our Lord is the first to use it in the New Testament. In fact, He employs two titles found only in this prayer. They are:

(1) Holy Father (17:11)

(2) Righteous Father (17:25)

1. Jesus prays for Himself

"These words spake Jesus, and lifted up his eyes to heaven, and said, Father, the hour is come; glorify thy Son, that thy Son also may glorify thee: As thou hast given him power over all flesh, that he should give eternal life to as many as thou hast given him. And this is life eternal, that they might know thee the only true God, and Jesus Christ, whom thou hast sent. I have glorified thee on the earth: I have finished the work which

thou gavest me to do. And now, O Father, glorify thou me with thine own self with the glory which I had with thee before the world was." (Jn. 17:1-5)

a. The request of Jesus here to receive glory is absolute proof of his deity, when compared with Isaiah's statement: *"I am the Lord: that is my name: and my glory will I not give to another, neither my praise to graven images" (Isa. 42:8).* Did the Father hear and answer this request? Note Jesus' previous testimony along this line: *"Then they took away the stone from the place where the dead was laid. And Jesus lifted up his eyes, and said, Father, I thank thee that thou hast heard me. And I knew that thou hearest me always: but because of the people which stand by I said it, that they may believe that thou hast sent me." (Jn. 11:41-42)*

b. Our Lord here tells the Father He had finished the divine assignment given Him (17:4). This marks the third of four occasions where Jesus had or would speak of this. Note:

"Then they went out of the city, and came unto him." (Jn. 4:30)

"But I have greater witness than that of John: for the works which the Father hath given me to finish, the same works that I do, bear witness of me, that the Father hath sent me." (Jn. 5:36)

"When Jesus therefore had received the vinegar, he said, It is finished: and he bowed his head, and gave up the ghost." (Jn. 19:30)

2. Jesus prays for His disciples

Our Lord prayed (and prays) constantly for His own.

a. He prayed before He chose them. *"And it came to pass in those days, that he went out into a mountain to pray, and continued all night in prayer to God. And when it was day, he called unto him his disciples: and of them he chose twelve, whom also he named apostles." (Lk. 6:12-13)*

b. He prayed for them during His ministry. *"And when he had sent the multitudes away, he went up into a mountain apart to pray: and when the evening was come, he was there alone. And in the fourth watch of the night Jesus went unto them, walking on the sea." (Mt. 14:23, 25)*

c. He prayed for them at the end of His ministry (Jn. 17:9).

d. He now prays for them (and all believers) in heaven. *"Who is he that condemneth? It is Christ that died, yea rather, that is risen again, who is even at the right hand of God, who also maketh intercession for us" (Rom. 8:34). "Wherefore he is able also to save them to the uttermost that come unto God by him, seeing he ever liveth to make intercession for them." (Heb. 7:25)*

"I have manifested thy name unto the men which thou gavest me out of the world: thine they were, and thou gavest them me; and they have kept thy word. Now they have known that all things whatsoever thou hast given me are of thee. For I have given unto them the words which thou gavest me; and they have received them, and have known surely that I came out from thee, and they have believed that thou didst send me. I pray for them: I pray not for the world, but for them which thou hast given me; for they are thine. And all mine are thine, and thine are mine; and I am glorified in them. And now I am no more in the world, but these are in the world, and I come to thee. Holy Father, keep through thine own name those whom thou hast given me, that they may be one, as we are. While I was with them in the world, I kept them in thy name: those that thou gavest me I have kept, and none of them is lost, but the son of perdition; that the scripture might be fulfilled. And now come I to thee; and these things I speak in the world, that they might have my joy fulfilled in themselves. I have given them thy word; and the world hath hated them, because they are not of the world, even as I am not of the world. I pray not that thou shouldest take them out of the world, but that thou shouldest keep them from the evil. They are not of the world, even as I am not of the world. Sanctify them through thy truth: thy word is truth. As thou hast sent

me into the world, even so have I also sent them into the world. And for their sakes I sanctify myself, that they also might be sanctified through the truth." (Jn. 17:6-19)

3. Jesus prays for all believers who would ever live

"Neither pray I for these alone, but for them also which shall believe on me through their word; That they all may be one; as thou, Father, art in me, and I in thee, that they also may be one in us: that the world may believe that thou hast sent me. And the glory which thou gavest me I have given them; that they may be one, even as we are one: I in them, and thou in me, that they may be made perfect in one; and that the world may know that thou hast sent me, and hast loved them, as thou hast loved me. Father, I will that they also, whom thou hast given me, be with me where I am; that they may behold my glory, which thou hast given me: for thou lovedst me before the foundation of the world. O righteous Father, the world hath not known thee: but I have known thee, and these have known that thou hast sent me. And I have declared unto them thy name, and will declare it: that the love wherewith thou hast loved me may be in them, and I in them." (Jn. 17:20-26)

He thus asked the Father:

a. That the Church might be spiritually united (17:21-22)

b. That the Church might be spiritually mature (17:23)

c. That the Church might behold His glory (17:24)

■ Jesus' ordeal in Gethsemane

Here is how Matthew, Mark, and Luke describe this terrible ordeal:

"And they came to a place which was named Gethsemane: and he saith to his disciples, Sit ye here, while I shall pray. And he taketh with him Peter and James and John, and began to be sore amazed, and to be very heavy; And saith unto them, My soul is exceeding sorrowful unto death: tarry ye here, and watch. And he went forward a little, and fell on the ground, and prayed that, if it were possible, the hour might pass from him. And he said, Abba, Father, all things are possible unto thee; take away this cup from me: nevertheless not what I will, but what thou wilt" (Mk. 14:32-36). "And there appeared an angel unto him from heaven, strengthening him. And being in an agony he prayed more earnestly: and his sweat was as it were great drops of blood falling down to the ground." (Lk. 22:43-44)

"And he cometh unto the disciples, and findeth them asleep, and saith unto Peter, What, could ye not watch with me one hour? Watch and pray, that ye enter not into temptation: the spirit indeed is willing, but the flesh is weak. He went away again the second time, and prayed, saying, O my Father, if this cup may not pass away from me, except I drink it, thy will be done. And he came and found them asleep again: for their eyes were heavy. And he left them, and went away again, and prayed the third time, saying the same words. Then cometh he to his disciples, and saith unto them, Sleep on now, and take your rest: behold, the hour is at hand, and the Son of man is betrayed into the hands of sinners. Rise, let us be going: behold, he is at hand that doth betray me." (Mt. 26:40-46)

1. This marks the second of two severe periods of mental strain, suffering, and satanic stress in the life of Jesus.

a. The first occurred in the wilderness of Judea (Mt. 4:1).

b. The second now occurs in the Garden of Gethsemane.

2. The book of Hebrews summarizes both periods.

a. The wilderness of Judea— *"For we have not an high priest which cannot be touched with the feeling of our infirmities; but was in all points tempted like as we are, yet without sin." (Heb. 4:15)*

b. The Garden of Gethsemane—*"Who in the days of his flesh, when he had offered up prayers and supplications with strong crying and tears unto him that was able to save him from death, and was heard in that he feared." (Heb. 5:7)*

3. A number of striking similarities can be seen at this point in the lives of David and Jesus.

   a. Both crossed the brook Kedron in the hour of personal crisis (2 Sam. 15:23; Jn. 18:1).

   b. Both would leave the city of Jerusalem rejected by its citizens (2 Sam. 15:13; Jn. 1:11).

   c. Both would be betrayed by a close friend (2 Sam. 15:31; Mt. 26:14-16).

   d. Both of their traitors would later hang themselves (2 Sam. 17:23; Mt. 27:3-5).

   e. Both would weep over all of this (2 Sam. 15:23, 30; Lk. 19:41).

   f. Both would climb the Mount of Olives and pray (2 Sam. 15:30-32; Mt. 26:30; Jn. 17:1-26).

   g. Both would condemn the use of a sword by a follower to defend them (2 Sam. 16:9-12; Mt. 26:51-53; Jn. 18:10-11).

   h. Both would forgive their tormentors (2 Sam. 16:5-13; 19:18-23; Lk. 23:34).

   i. Both would be victorious over their enemies (2 Sam. 18:6-8; Rev. 19:11-21).

   j. Both would return in triumph to Jerusalem (2 Sam. 19:8-9, 15, 25; Rev. 21:1-4).

4. Many artists and songwriters have depicted this prayer for us, and their descriptions usually show a hushed and tranquil scene, with the light from heaven falling upon a kneeling Savior, his hands clasped devoutly in front, his eyes cast heavenward, and his lips moving faintly as he prays his "cup of suffering" prayer. All is silent, subdued, and serene. But this is not the biblical account at all. The careful student can almost hear the shrieks of demons and the crackling flames which filled the gentle Garden of Gethsemane that awful night. Notice our Lord's own description of his feelings during that hour. He says he was:

   a. "Sore amazed"—that is, he was suddenly struck with surprised terror (Mk. 14:33).

   b. "Very heavy"—that is, he experienced the totally unfamiliar, which bore down upon his soul and filled it with uncertainty and acute distress (suggested exegesis here by the late Kenneth S. Wuest, a Greek professor at Moody Bible Institute).

   c. *"Exceeding sorrowful unto death"*—that is, he was so completely surrounded and encircled by grief that it threatened his very life. From all this it becomes evident that the devil made an all-out effort to murder the Savior in the garden in order to prevent his blood being shed a few hours later on the cross. Our Lord realized this and responded accordingly, as we are told in Heb. 5:7: *"Who in the days of his flesh, when he had offered up prayers and supplications with strong crying and tears unto him that was able to save him from death, and was heard in that he feared."*

5. The Father heard his cry for aid and sent angels to strengthen him (See Lk. 22:43).

   We are told that he wrestled his way through three prayer sessions in the garden, and he referred to the "cup" during each prayer. What was this cup his soul so dreaded to drink from? Some say it was the cup of human suffering, but our Lord was no stranger to suffering and pain, for he had known these things throughout his ministry. Others claim it was the cup of physical death that our Lord abhorred here. But again, it must be realized that he was the Prince of Life, and therefore, death would hold no terror for him.

   What then was the nature of this cursed cup? We are not left groping in the dark here, for the Scriptures plainly inform us that the Gethsemane cup was filled with the sins of all humanity. Our Lord looked deeply into the cesspool of human sin that dark night and groaned as he smelled its foul odor and viewed the rising poisonous fumes. Was there no other way to redeem humanity than by drinking this corrupt cup? There was no other way. In a few short hours he would drain that container of its last bitter drop of human depravity. Heb. 2:9: *"But we see Jesus, who was made a little lower than the angels for the suffering of death, crowned with glory and honour; that he by the grace of God should taste death for every man."* (See also Isa. 53; Rom. 4:25; 1 Pet. 2:24; 3:18; 2 Cor. 5:21.)

6. The double title, "Abba, Father," used by Christ here occurs only two other times in the Bible. Abba was the common way young Jewish children addressed their fathers. It conveyed a sense of intimacy and familiarity. Because of the marvelous work of redemption our blessed Lord would accomplish on the cross, the most humble believer could actually refer to the infinite, omnipresent, omniscient, omnipotent, and eternal Creator of the universe as...'Abba, Father'." The last stanza of Charles Wesley's great hymn, "Arise My Soul, Arise," summarizes this beautiful theological truth: 'To God, I'm reconciled./ His pardoning voice I hear;/He owns me for his child—/ I can no longer fear;/ with confidence I now draw nigh, and 'Father, Abba, Father' cry!"

7. These are the three "Not my will, but thy will be done" prayers that Jesus would offer up in Gethsemane (see Mt. 26:39, 42, 44). Contrast this submissive will of Christ to that selfcentered will of Lucifer. *"How art thou fallen from heaven, O Lucifer, son of the morning! how art thou cut down to the ground, which didst weaken the nations! For thou hast said in thine heart, I will ascend into heaven, I will exalt my throne above the stars of God: I will sit also upon the mount of the congregation, in the sides of the north: I will ascend above the heights of the clouds; I will be like the most High"* (Isa. 14:12-14). Consider the awesome significance of those four words, *"Thy will be done."*

    a. If a repentant sinner says them to God, they result in heaven.

    b. If God says them to an unrepentant sinner, they result in hell.

■ Jesus' arrest in Gethsemane

1. Judas betrays Jesus with a kiss

    "And while he yet spake, lo, Judas, one of the twelve, came, and with him a great multitude with swords and staves, from the chief priests and elders of the people. Now he that betrayed him gave them a sign, saying, Whomsoever I shall kiss, that same is he: hold him fast. And forthwith he came to Jesus, and said, Hail, master; and kissed him." (Mt. 26:47-49)

    "But Jesus said unto him, Judas, betrayest thou the Son of man with a kiss?" (Lk. 22:48)

    This is the final of three biblical kisses of deceit.

    a. Jacob kissed Isaac (Gen. 27:26-27).

    b. Joab kissed Amasa (2 Sam. 20:9).

    c. Judas kissed Jesus.

2. Jesus restores a severed ear

    "Jesus therefore, knowing all things that should come upon him, went forth, and said unto them, Whom seek ye? They answered him, Jesus of Nazareth. Jesus saith unto them, I am he. And Judas also, which betrayed him, stood with them. As soon then as he had said unto them, I am he, they went backward, and fell to the ground. Then asked he them again, Whom seek ye? And they said, Jesus of Nazareth. Jesus answered, I have told you that I am he: if therefore ye seek me, let these go their way: That the saying might be fulfilled, which he spake, Of them which thou gavest me have I lost none. Then Simon Peter having a sword drew it, and smote the high priest's servant, and cut off his right ear. The servant's name was Malchus." (Jn. 18:4-10)

    "And Jesus answered and said, Suffer ye thus far. And he touched his ear, and healed him." (Lk. 22:51)

3. Jesus rebukes Peter

"Then said Jesus unto him, Put up again thy sword into his place: for all they that take the sword shall perish with the sword. Thinkest thou that I cannot now pray to my Father, and he shall presently give me more than twelve legions of angels? But how then shall the scriptures be fulfilled, that thus it must be? In that same hour said Jesus to the multitudes, Are ye come out as against a thief with swords and staves for to take me? I sat daily with you teaching in the temple, and ye laid no hold on me." (Mt. 26:52-55)

4. Jesus is arrested

"Then the band and the captain and officers of the Jews took Jesus, and bound him." (Jn. 18:12)

5. Jesus is forsaken by all

"And they all forsook him, and fled. And there followed him a certain young man, having a linen cloth cast about his naked body; and the young men laid hold on him: And he left the linen cloth, and fled from them naked." (Mk. 14:50-52)

Some Bible students believe that this young man was John Mark, who accompanied Paul during his first missionary journey and later wrote the Gospel of Mark.

■ Jesus suffers His first unfair trial (before Annas, the ex-High Priest)

"And led him away to Annas first; for he was father in law to Caiaphas, which was the high priest that same year. Now Caiaphas was he, which gave counsel to the Jews, that it was expedient that one man should die for the people... The high priest then asked Jesus of his disciples, and of his doctrine. Jesus answered him, I spake openly to the world; I ever taught in the synagogue, and in the temple, whither the Jews always resort; and in secret have I said nothing. Why askest thou me? ask them which heard me, what I have said unto them: behold, they know what I said. And when he had thus spoken, one of the officers which stood by struck Jesus with the palm of his hand, saying, Answerest thou the high priest so? Jesus answered him, If I have spoken evil, bear witness of the evil: but if well, why smitest thou me?" (Jn. 18:13-14, 19-23) Here we are told Jesus was struck in the face. This was just the beginning of the terrible ordeals suffered during His trials. He would thus be:

1. Misquoted (Mt. 26:60-61)
2. Spit upon (Mt. 26:67; 27:30)
3. Struck with fists (Mt. 26:67; 27:30)
4. Repeatedly slapped (Mt. 26:67)
5. Ridiculed (Mt. 26:68; Lk. 23:11)
6. Blindfolded (Mk. 14:65)
7. Falsely accused (Lk. 23:2, 10)
8. Insulted (Lk. 22:65)
9. Stripped of His clothes (Mt. 27:28)
10. Flogged (Mk. 15:13)

■ Jesus suffers His second unfair trial (before Caiaphas, the current High Priest)

"And they that had laid hold on Jesus led him away to Caiaphas the high priest, where the scribes and the elders were assembled. But Peter followed him afar off unto the high priest's palace, and went in, and sat with the servants, to see the end. Now the chief priests, and elders, and all the council, sought false witness against Jesus, to put him to death; But found none: yea, though many false witnesses came, yet found they

none. At the last came two false witnesses, And said, This fellow said, I am able to destroy the temple of God, and to build it in three days. And the high priest arose, and said unto him, Answerest thou nothing? what is it which these witness against thee? But Jesus held his peace, And the high priest answered and said unto him, I adjure thee by the living God, that thou tell us whether thou be the Christ, the Son of God. Jesus saith unto him, Thou hast said: nevertheless I say unto you, Hereafter shall ye see the Son of man sitting on the right hand of power, and coming in the clouds of heaven. Then the high priest rent his clothes, saying, He hath spoken blasphemy; what further need have we of witnesses? behold, now ye have heard his blasphemy. What think ye? They answered and said, He is guilty of death. Then did they spit in his face, and buffeted him; and others smote him with the palms of their hands." (Mt. 26:57-67)

1. Jesus both warned his foes and promised his friends that he would come again. Compare this passage with John 14:1-3.

2. We are told here that Caiaphas tore his clothes.

    The high priest was forbidden to do this under the Mosaic Law. *"And he that is the high priest among his brethren, upon whose head the anointing oil was poured, and that is consecrated to put on the garments, shall not uncover his head, nor rend his clothes." (Lev. 21:10)*

3. This shameful session ends by the Jewish leaders spitting upon Jesus.

    To spit in one's face was considered by the Jews to be an act of total repudiation and gross personal insult.

    a. A person was considered disgraced for seven days after having his face spit upon (Num. 12:14).

    b. Job's enemies showed their utter contempt for the suffering patriarch by spitting in his face (Job 30:10).

    c. The Savior himself had predicted all this through the prophet Isaiah some seven centuries before it actually happened. *"I gave my back to the smiters, and my cheeks to them that plucked off the hair: I hid not my face from shame and spitting" (Isa. 50:6).*

4. After being blindfolded, they demanded that he tell them who struck him. This reflected a traditional test of Messianic status based on a rabbinic interpretation of Isa. 11:2-4. According to this view the true Messiah could know who was hitting him even though blindfolded.

■ Simon Peter denies Jesus at this time. (Mt. 26:58, 69-75; Mk. 14:54, 66-72; Lk. 22:54b-62; Jn. 18:15-18, 25-27)

    Note: An exact chronological arrangement of these denials is impossible. In fact, it has even been suggested that Peter denied his Lord not three times on one occasion, but six times on two occasions, and that Christ predicted both events.

1. The first warning

    a. Place: The Upper Room

    b. Prophecy: That Peter would deny Christ three times before the cock crowed at all (see Jn. 13:38; Lk. 22:34).

2. The second warning

    a. Place: On the way to Gethsemane

    b. Prophecy: That Peter would deny Christ three times before the cock crowed twice (see Mk. 14:30).

■ Whatever the chronology, note the characters, the charges, the concealment, and the contrition in this sordid account.

1. The characters

    a. Peter and John

        John went inside— *"And Simon Peter followed Jesus, and so did another disciple: that disciple was known unto the high priest, and went in with Jesus into the palace of the high priest." (Jn. 18:15)*

Peter waited outside— *"But Peter stood at the door without. Then went out that other disciple, which was known unto the high priest, and spake unto her that kept the door, and brought in Peter." (Jn. 18:16)*

    b. Several servant maids

    c. Some officers

    d. A kinsman of Malchus

2. The charges

    a. *"Then saith the damsel that kept the door unto Peter, Art not thou also one of this man's disciples?" (Jn. 18:17)*

    b. *"And thou also wast with Jesus of Nazareth." (Mk. 14:67b)*

    c. *"Thou art one of them: for thou art a Galilean, and thy speech agreeth thereto." (Mk. 14:70b)*

    d. *"One of the servants of the high priest, being his kinsman whose ear Peter cut off, saith, Did not I see thee in the garden with him?" (Jn. 18:26)*

3. The concealment

    a. *"I know not, neither understand I what thou sayest." (Mk. 14:68)*

    b. *"Woman, I know him not." (Lk. 22:57)*

    c. *"Man, I know not what thou sayest." (Lk. 22:60)*

    d. *"But he began to curse and to swear, saying, I know not this man of whom ye speak." (Mk. 14:71)*

4. The contrite

    a. The lie of Peter—"And Peter said, Man, I know not what thou sayest. And immediately, while he yet spake, the cock crew." (Lk. 22:60)

    b. The look of Jesus— *"And the Lord turned, and looked upon Peter. And Peter remembered the word of the Lord, how he had said unto him, Before the cock crow, thou shalt deny me thrice. And Peter went out, and wept bitterly." (Lk. 22:61-62)*

5. The conclusion

    The Shakespearean character Juliet once said, "What's in a name?" Here we could rephrase it to read, "What's in a look?" The Lord turned and looked upon Peter. Apparently he had also heard the awful cursing and denials. Peter was stricken in his thoughts and went out, weeping bitterly. It is not our sin that causes us to weep. It is rather seeing the Savior that we have sinned against that causes our tears.

    Note the phrase, *"Peter... wept bitterly."* It is indeed a fact--you can't judge a book by its cover. Imagine yourself in the vicinity of the Garden of Gethsemane on a warm April night some two thousand years ago. As you watch, a man walks up to Jesus and begins kissing him. You would probably conclude, "How this man must love the Master!" Shortly after this you would be shocked to hear another man bitterly cursing Christ. Your conclusions about this would be, "How this man must hate the Master!" But both times you would be wrong. Judas, the man who kissed Christ, really hated him, and Peter, the one who cursed him, really loved him.

◼ Jesus suffers His third unfair trial (before the assembled Sanhedrin)

    "And as soon as it was day, the elders of the people and the chief priests and the scribes came together, and led him into their council, saying, Art thou the Christ? tell us. And he said unto them, If I tell you, ye will not believe: And if I also ask you, ye will not answer me, nor let me go. Hereafter shall the Son of man sit on the right hand of the power of God. Then said they all, Art thou then the Son of God? And he said unto them, Ye say that I am. And they said, What need we any further witness? for we ourselves have heard of his own mouth." (Lk. 22:66-71)

"When the morning was come, all the chief priests and elders of the people took counsel against Jesus to put him to death." (Mt. 27:1)

■ Judas Iscariot hangs himself at this time

"Then Judas, which had betrayed him, when he saw that he was condemned, repented himself, and brought again the thirty pieces of silver to the chief priests and elders, Saying, I have sinned in that I have betrayed the innocent blood. And they said, What is that to us? See thou to that. And he cast down the pieces of silver in the temple, and departed, and went and hanged himself. And the chief priests took the silver pieces, and said, It is not lawful for to put them into the treasury, because it is the price of blood. And they took counsel, and bought with them the potter's field, to bury strangers in. Wherefore that field was called, The field of blood, unto this day. Then was fulfilled that which was spoken by Jeremy the prophet, saying, And they took the thirty pieces of silver, the price of him that was valued, whom they of the children of Israel did value; And gave them for the potter's field, as the Lord appointed me." (Mt. 27:3-10)

Question: How are we to understand Judas' repentance in this passage? In essence, the word itself has a two-fold meaning:

1. To turn from something or someone
2. To turn to something or someone

Both meanings are seen in the following verses:

"Unto you first God, having raised up his Son Jesus, sent him to bless you, in turning away every one of you from his iniquities... Testifying both to the Jews, and also to the Greeks, repentance toward God, and faith toward our Lord Jesus Christ... For they themselves shew of us what manner of entering in we had unto you, and how ye turned to God from idols to serve the living and true God." (Acts 3:26; 20:21; 1 Thess. 1:9)

With this in mind it is apparent by his subsequent suicide that Judas' repentance involved only the first but none of the second. The same would be said about Esau:

"For ye know how that afterward, when he would have inherited the blessing, he was rejected: for he found no place of repentance, though he sought it carefully with tears." (Heb. 12:17)

In fact it can be concluded both Esau and Judas experienced some kind of remorse, but no real repentance whatsoever!

■ Jesus suffers His fourth unfair trial (before Pilate for the first time)
(See Mt. 27:2, 11-14; Mk. 15:1b-5; Lk. 23:1-5; Jn. 18:28-38.)

1. Round One: Pilate and the Jews

"Then led they Jesus from Caiaphas unto the hall of judgment: and it was early; and they themselves went not into the judgment hall, lest they should be defiled; but that they might eat the passover. Pilate then went out unto them, and said, What accusation bring ye against this man? They answered and said unto him, If he were not a malefactor, we would not have delivered him up unto thee. Then said Pilate unto them, Take ye him, and judge him according to your law. The Jews therefore said unto him, It is not lawful for us to put any man to death: That the saying of Jesus might be fulfilled, which he spake, signifying what death he should die." (Jn. 18:28-32)

The passage here in 18:28 records what is probably the most blatant example of raw hypocrisy in the entire Bible! The Pharisees, now involved in an all-out effort to murder their own Messiah, take great care lest they defile themselves by entering a Gentile room which might have contained leaven! These Jewish leaders had previously illustrated this twisted standard of morality:

"For the Son of man is Lord even of the Sabbath day. And when he was departed thence, he went into their synagogue: And, behold, there was a man which had his hand withered. And they asked him, saying, Is it lawful to heal on the Sabbath days? that they might accuse him. And he said unto them, What man shall there be among you, that shall have one sheep, and if it fall into a pit on the Sabbath day, will he not lay hold on it, and lift it out? How much then is a man better than a sheep? Wherefore it is lawful to do well on the Sabbath days. Then saith he to the man, Stretch forth thine hand. And he stretched it forth; and it was restored whole, like as the other." (Mt. 12:8-13)

2. Round Two: Pilate and the Savior

"Then Pilate entered into the judgment hall again, and called Jesus, and said unto him, Art thou the King of the Jews? Jesus answered him, Sayest thou this thing of thyself, or did others tell it thee of me? Pilate answered, Am I a Jew? Thine own nation and the chief priests have delivered thee unto me: what hast thou done? Jesus answered, My kingdom is not of this world: if my kingdom were of this world, then would my servants fight, that I should not be delivered to the Jews: but now is my kingdom not from hence. Pilate therefore said unto him, Art thou a king then? Jesus answered, Thou sayest that I am a king. To this end was I born, and for this cause came I into the world, that I should bear witness unto the truth. Every one that is of the truth heareth my voice. Pilate saith unto him, What is truth? And when he had said this, he went out again unto the Jews, and saith unto them, I find in him no fault at all." (Jn. 18:33-38)

Note Pilate's question to Jesus, "What is truth?"

This is undoubtedly the second most important and profound question in all the Bible—indeed, in all of history.

a. The first was asked by a frightened Philippian jailor, *"Sirs, what must I do to be saved?"* (Acts 16:30)

b. The second was asked by a frustrated Roman governor: *"What is truth?"* The tragedy here is that while the jailor awaited his answer and was saved (Acts 16:31), the governor impatiently walked out and was lost.

■ Jesus suffers His fifth unfair trial (before Herod Antipas)

"And they were the more fierce, saying, He stirreth up the people, teaching throughout all Jewry, beginning from Galilee to this place. When Pilate heard of Galilee, he asked whether the man were a Galilaean. And as soon as he knew that he belonged unto Herod's jurisdiction, he sent him to Herod, who himself also was at Jerusalem at that time. And when Herod saw Jesus, he was exceeding glad: for he was desirous to see him of a long season, because he had heard many things of him; and he hoped to have seen some miracle done by him. Then he questioned with him in many words; but he answered him nothing. And the chief priests and scribes stood and vehemently accused him. And Herod with his men of war set him at nought, and mocked him, and arrayed him in a gorgeous robe, and sent him again to Pilate. And the same day Pilate and Herod were made friends together: for before they were at enmity between themselves." (Lk. 23:5-12)

There is a tragic truth to be seen here in that the person and work of Jesus Christ serves to reconcile enemies through two totally different methods:

1. Unifying them in their love for Him

"That in the dispensation of the fulness of times he might gather together in one all things in Christ, both which are in heaven, and which are on earth; even in him." (Eph. 1:10)

2. Unifying them in their hatred for Him

"The kings of the earth stood up, and the rulers were gathered together against the Lord, and against his Christ. For of a truth against thy holy child Jesus, whom thou hast anointed, both Herod, and Pontius Pilate, with the Gentiles, and the people of Israel, were gathered together." (Acts 4:26-27)

■ Jesus suffers His sixth unfair trial (before Pilate for the final time)

(See Mt. 27:15-26; Mk. 15:6-15; Lk. 23:13-25; Jn. 18:39-19:1, 4-16a.) It is very difficult to place all those events transpiring during the sixth trial in exact proper order. The following is a suggested chronological outline.

1. Pilate and the Jewish leaders (First encounter)

"And Pilate, when he had called together the chief priests and the rulers and the people, Said unto them, Ye have brought this man unto me, as one that perverteth the people: and, behold, I, having examined him before you, have found no fault in this man touching those things whereof ye accuse him: No, nor yet Herod: for I sent you to him; and, lo, nothing worthy of death is done unto him. I will therefore chastise him, and release him. (For of necessity he must release one unto them at the feast.) And they cried out all at once, saying, Away with this man, and release unto us Barabbas: (Who for a certain sedition made in the city, and for murder, was cast into prison). Pilate therefore, willing to release Jesus, spake again to them. But they cried, saying, Crucify him, crucify him ... And Pilate gave sentence that it should be as they required." (Lk. 23:13-21, 24)

2. Pilate and his wife

There are two significant occasions in the scriptures when a non-Jewish wife offered counsel to her husband.

a. Some bad advice which was tragically heeded —

"Haman said moreover, Yea, Esther the queen did let no man come in with the king unto the banquet that she had prepared but myself; and to morrow am I invited unto her also with the king. Yet all this availeth me nothing, so long as I see Mordecai the Jew sitting at the king's gate. Then said Zeresh his wife and all his friends unto him, Let a gallows be made of fifty cubits high, and to morrow speak thou unto the king that Mordecai may be hanged thereon: then go thou in merrily with the king unto the banquet. And the thing pleased Haman; and he caused the gallows to be made." (Esther 5:12-14)

b. Some good advice which was tragically not heeded —

"When he was set down on the judgment seat, his wife sent unto him, saying, Have thou nothing to do with that just man: for I have suffered many things this day in a dream because of him." (Mt. 27:19)

3. Pilate and Jesus (First encounter)

"Then Pilate therefore took Jesus, and scourged him." (Jn. 19:1)

This was obviously done in an attempt to appease and satisfy the demands of the blood thirsty leaders in hopes it would allow Jesus to be released.

4. Pilate and the Jewish leaders (Second encounter)

"Pilate therefore went forth again, and saith unto them, Behold, I bring him forth to you, that ye may know that I find no fault in him. Then came Jesus forth, wearing the crown of thorns, and the purple robe. And Pilate saith unto them, Behold the man! When the chief priests therefore and officers saw him, they cried out, saying, Crucify him, crucify him. Pilate saith unto them, Take ye him, and crucify him: for I find no fault in him. The Jews answered him, We have a law, and by our law he ought to die, because he made himself the Son of God." (Jn. 19:4-7)

John the Baptist had once introduced Jesus as, *"Behold the lamb" (Jn. 1:29)*. Pilate now says, *"Behold the man"*. Perhaps the Apostle Paul would later have both statements in mind when he wrote:

"For there is one God, and one mediator between God and men, the man Christ Jesus." (1 Tim. 2:5)

5. Pilate and Jesus (Second encounter)

"When Pilate therefore heard that saying, he was the more afraid; And went again into the judgment hall, and saith unto Jesus, Whence art thou? But Jesus gave him no answer. Then saith Pilate unto him, Speakest thou not unto me? knowest thou not that I have power to crucify thee, and have power to release thee? Jesus answered, Thou couldest have no power at all against me, except it were given thee from above: therefore he that delivered me unto thee hath the greater sin." (Jn. 19:8-11)

6. Pilate and the Jewish leaders (Third encounter)

"When Pilate saw that he could prevail nothing, but that rather a tumult was made, he took water, and washed his hands before the multitude, saying, I am innocent of the blood of this just person: see ye to it. Then answered all the people, and said, His blood be on us, and on our children." (Mt. 27:24-25)

"When Pilate therefore heard that saying, he brought Jesus forth, and sat down in the judgment seat in a place that is called the Pavement, but in the Hebrew, Gabbatha. And it was the preparation of the passover, and about the sixth hour: and he saith unto the Jews, Behold your King! But they cried out, Away with him, away with him, crucify him. Pilate saith unto them, Shall I crucify your King? The chief priests answered, We have no king but Caesar. Then delivered he him therefore unto them to be crucified. And they took Jesus, and led him away." (Jn. 19:13-16)

■ Jesus suffers His seventh unfair trial (before the Roman soldiers)

"Then the soldiers of the governor took Jesus into the common hall, and gathered unto him the whole band of soldiers. And they stripped him, and put on him a scarlet robe. And when they had platted a crown of thorns, they put it upon his head, and a reed in his right hand: and they bowed the knee before him, and mocked him, saying, Hail, King of the Jews!" (Mt. 27:27-29)

"And they smote him on the head with a reed, and did spit upon him, and bowing their knees worshipped him." (Mk. 15:19)

1. According to John's Gospel, both the sixth and seventh trials of Jesus occurred *"in a place that is called the Pavement, but in the Hebrew, Gabbatha" (Jn. 19:13b)*. In New Testament times there was a strong fortress situated on the north side of the temple area known as the Tower of Antonia. That area is now occupied by the Covenant of the Sisters of Zion. Recent excavations beneath this building have revealed a courtyard paved with flagstones called in the Greek *lithostrotos* ("paved"), and in the Aramaic *Gabbatha* ("raised"). This was the place of which John spoke.

2. Here Pilate had Jesus scourged and condemned to be crucified. After a futile attempt to wash away his guilt, the governor turned Jesus over to the Roman soldiers. Carved in that flagstone pavement can be seen the letter B with a rough, prickly crown at the top and a sword at the bottom. The B represented the word Basilicus, which means "the Game of the King," a very popular game among the legion troops. It consisted chiefly in choosing a burlesque king, in loading him down with ludicrous honors, in giving him liberty to satisfy his vices, and then cruelly putting him to death. There is strong evidence in the Gospel accounts that Jesus was the victim of this game.

■ Jesus is led to Calvary

　1. The man of Cyrene, lifting up the cross

　　"And when they had mocked him, they took off the purple from him, and put his own clothes on him, and led him out to crucify him. And they compel one Simon a Cyrenian, who passed by, coming out of the country, the father of Alexander and Rufus, to bear his cross." (Mk. 15:20-21)

　2. The maidens of Jerusalem, lamenting over the cross

　　"And there followed him a great company of people, and of women, which also bewailed and lamented him. But Jesus turning unto them said, Daughters of Jerusalem, weep not for me, but weep for yourselves, and for your children. For, behold, the days are coming, in the which they shall say, Blessed are the barren, and the wombs that never bare, and the paps which never gave suck. Then shall they begin to say to the mountains, Fall on us; and to the hills, Cover us." (Lk. 23:27-30)

THE CRUCIFIXION OF JESUS

Most Christians are aware of Isaiah chapter 53, where the prophet predicts the awful sufferings of Jesus some seven centuries before Bethlehem in graphic fashion, writing:

> *"He is despised and rejected of men; a man of sorrows, and acquainted with grief: and we hid as it were our faces from him; he was despised, and we esteemed him not. Surely he hath borne our griefs, and carried our sorrows: yet we did esteem him stricken, smitten of God, and afflicted. But he was wounded for our transgressions, he was bruised for our iniquities: the chastisement of our peace was upon him; and with his stripes we are healed. All we like sheep have gone astray; we have turned every one to his own way; and the LORD hath laid on him the iniquity of us all. He was oppressed, and he was afflicted, yet he opened not his mouth: he is brought as a lamb to the slaughter, and as a sheep before her shearers is dumb, so he openeth not his mouth. He was taken from prison and from judgment: and who shall declare his generation? for he was cut off out of the land of the living: for the transgression of my people was he stricken." (Isa. 53:3-8)*

In fact the prophet describes the Savior's terrible ordeal in even more brutal fashion at the end of chapter 52:

> *"Many were amazed when they saw him – beaten and bloodied, so disfigured one would scarcely know he was a person" (52:14, taken from the New Living translation).*

■ For scourging, the man was stripped of his clothing and his hands were tied to an upright post. The back, buttocks and legs were flogged either by two soldiers (lictors) or by one who alternated positions. The severity of the scourging depended on the disposition of the lictors and was intended to weaken the victim to a state just short of collapse or death.

   After the scourging, the soldiers often taunted their victim. As the Roman soldiers repeatedly struck the victim's back with full force, the iron balls would cause deep contusions, and the leather thongs and sheep bones would cut into the skin and subcutaneous tissues.

   As the flogging continued, the lacerations would tear into the underlying skeletal muscles and produce quivering ribbons of bleeding flesh. Pain and blood loss generally set the stage for circulatory shock. The extent of blood loss may well have determined how long the victim would survive on the cross.

   At the Praetorium, Jesus was severely whipped. (Although the severity of the scourging is not discussed in the four gospel accounts, it is implied in one of the epistles [1 Pet. 2:24]. A detailed word study of the ancient Greek text for this verse indicates that the scourging of Jesus was particularly harsh.)

It is not known whether the number of lashes was limited to 39, in accordance with Jewish law. When it was determined by the centurion in charge that the prisoner was near death, the beating was finally stopped. The half-fainting Jesus was then untied and allowed to slump to the stone pavement, wet with His own blood.

- The Roman soldiers saw a great joke in this provincial Jew claiming to be a king. They threw a robe across His shoulders and placed a stick in His hand for a scepter. They still needed a crown to make their travesty complete. A small bundle of flexible branches covered with long thorns (commonly used for firewood) was plaited into the shape of a crown and was pressed into His scalp. Again, there was copious bleeding (the scalp being one of the most vascular areas of the body).

  After mocking Him and striking Him across the face, the soldiers took the stick from His hand and struck Him across the head, driving the thorns deeper into His scalp.

  Finally, they tired of their sadistic sport and the robe was torn from His back. This had already become adherent to the clots of blood and serum in the wounds, and its removal, just as in the careless removal of a surgical bandage, caused excruciating pain ... almost as though He were again being whipped—and the wounds again began to bleed. In deference to Jewish custom, the Romans returned His garments.

- The heavy horizontal beam of the cross was tied across His shoulders, and the procession of the condemned Christ, two thieves and the execution party walked along the Via Dolorosa.

  In spite of His efforts to walk erect, the weight of the heavy wooden beam, together with the shock produced by copious blood loss, was too much. He stumbled and fell. The rough wood of the beam gouged into the lacerated skin and muscles of His shoulders. He tried to rise, but His muscles had been pushed beyond their endurance.

  The centurion, anxious to get on with the crucifixion, selected a Stalwart North African onlooker, Simon of Cyrene, to carry the cross. Jesus followed, still bleeding and sweating the cold clammy sweat of shock. The 650-yard journey from the fortress Antonia to Golgotha was finally completed. Jesus was once again stripped of His clothes—except for a loincloth which was allowed.

- Jesus was offered wine mixed with myrrh, a mild analgesic mixture. He refused to drink. Simon was ordered to place the cross beam on the ground, and Jesus was quickly thrown backward with His shoulders against the wood. The legionnaire felt for the depression at the front of the wrist. He drove a heavy, square, wrought-iron nail through His wrist and deep into the wood.

  Quickly, He moved to the other side and repeated the action, being careful not to pull the arms too tightly, but to allow some flexion and movement. The beam was then lifted in place at the top of the vertical beam with the title reading, *"Jesus of Nazareth, King of the Jews"*, and nailed in place. *"And when they were come to the place, which is called Calvary, there they crucified him, and the malefactors, one on the right hand, and the other on the left." (Lk. 23:33)*

- Although the Romans did not invent crucifixion, they perfected it as a form of torture and capital punishment that was designed to produce a slow death, with maximum pain and suffering. It was one of the most disgraceful and cruel methods of execution and usually was reserved for slaves, foreigners, revolutionaries, and the vilest of criminals. Roman law usually protected Roman citizens from crucifixion.

  It was customary for the condemned man to carry his own cross from the logging post to the site of crucifixion outside the city walls. He was usually naked, unless this was prohibited by local customs. Since the weight of the entire cross was probably well over 300 lbs., only the cross bar was carried. The patibulum, weighing 75 to 125 pounds was placed across the nape of the victim's neck and balanced along both shoulders. Usually, the outstretched arms then were tied to the crossbar.

- The processional to the site of the crucifixion was led by a complete Roman military guard, headed by a centurion. One of the soldiers carried a sign (titulus) on which the condemned man's name and crime were displayed. Later, the titulus would be attached to the top of the cross. The Roman guard would not leave the victim until they were sure of his death. Outside the city walls was permanently located the heavy upright wooden stipes, on which the patibulum would be secured.

- To prolong the crucifixion process, a horizontal wooden block or plank, serving as a crude seat (sedile or sedulum), often was attached midway down the stipes. At the site of execution, by law, the victim was given a bitter drink of wine mixed with myrrh (gall) as a mild analgesic.

    The criminal was then thrown to the ground on his back, with his arms outstretched along the patibulum. The hands could be nailed or tied to the crossbar, but nailing apparently was preferred by the Romans.

- Furthermore, ossuary finds, and the Shroud of Turin have documented that the nails commonly were driven through the wrists rather than the palms. Although scriptural references are made to nails in the hands, these are not at odds with the archaeological evidence of wrist wounds, since the ancients customarily considered the wrist to be a part of the hand.

- After both arms were fixed to the crossbar, the patibulum and the victim, together, were lifted onto the stipes. Next, the feet were fixed to the cross, either by nails or ropes. Ossuary findings and the Shroud of Turin suggest that nailing was the preferred Roman practice. Although the feet could be fixed to the sides of the stipes or to a wooden footrest (supped-aneum), they were nailed directly to the front of the stipes. To accomplish this, flexion of the knees may have been quite prominent, and the bent legs may have been rotated laterally.

    Having now reviewed some of the terrible suffering of Jesus we turn our attention to those 16 events associated with the cross and the seven statements spoken from the cross.

I. The 16 Events

- Jesus is placed on the cross at 9:00 a.m. (Mk. 15:25) between two thieves (Mt. 27:38; Lk. 23;32; Jn. 19:18).

- A sign is positioned above the cross which read, *"This is Jesus of Nazareth, King of the Jews"* (Mt. 27:37; Mk. 15:26; Lk. 23:38; Jn. 19:19). It is ironic to note the following:
  1. At Jesus' birth some wise man asked, *"Where is he that is born King of the Jews?"* (Mt. 2:2)
  2. At Jesus' death, some wicked men announced, *"This is ... the King of the Jews."*

- The Jewish leaders complain about the sign to Pilate but he refuses to change it. (Jn. 19:20-22)

- Jesus is ridiculed by many:
  1. The sarcastic (who they were)
     a. The people (Lk. 23:35)
     b. The chief priests and scribes (Mt. 27:41)

  c. The soldiers (Lk. 23:36)

  d. The thieves (Mt. 27:44)

2. The sarcasm (what they said)

  a. *"And they that passed by railed on him, wagging their heads, and saying, Ah, thou that destroyest the temple, and buildest it in three days, Save thyself, and come down from the cross." (Mk. 15:29-30)*

    To wag or shake one's head was a familiar gesture of derision.

    God had once warned through Jeremiah that he would cause the pagan Babylonians and other heathen nations to look upon the city of Jerusalem because of the sin of its people. *"To make their land desolate, and a perpetual hissing; every one that passeth thereby shall be astonished, and wag his head" (Jer. 18:16).* The weeping prophet would later with broken heart testify to the terrible accuracy of this prediction. *"All that pass by clap their hands at thee; they hiss and wag their head at the daughter of Jerusalem, saying, Is this the city that men call The perfection of beauty, The joy of the whole earth?" (Lam. 2:15)* David had predicted this Calvary head-wagging on two occasions (see Psa. 22:7; 109:25).

  b. *"Likewise also the chief priests mocking said among themselves with the scribes, He saved others; himself he cannot save. Let Christ the King of Israel descend now from the cross, that we may see and believe. And they that were crucified with him reviled him." (Mk. 15:31-32)*

    This crude and cruel statement, "He saved others; himself he cannot save," although uttered with ridicule and hatred, nevertheless voiced a precious and profound truth. Our Lord had already wrestled with this in Gethsemane. The divine decision was made. He could not and would not escape the cup. He must and would indeed die to save others.

  c. *"He trusted in God; let him deliver him now, if he will have him: for he said, I am the Son of God." (Mk. 27:43)*

  d. *"And the soldiers also mocked him, coming to him, and offering him vinegar, and saying, If thou be the king of the Jews, save thyself." (Lk. 23:36-37)*

  e. *"And one of the malefactors which were hanged railed on him, saying, If thou be Christ, save thyself and us." (Lk. 23:39)*

■ The soldiers divide Jesus' clothes into four shares and cast lots for His seamless garment (Jn. 19:23-24).

  This garment, doubtless stained with sweat and blood will someday be replaced by a glorious one!

  "And in the midst of the seven candlesticks one like unto the Son of man, clothed with a garment down to the foot, and girt about the paps with a golden girdle." (Rev. 1:13)

■ Jesus is offered wine mixed with myrrh but refuses it (Mt. 27:34; Mk. 15:23). Here is the first of four cups offered to Christ at Calvary:

1. This was the cup of charity. At the site of execution, by law, the victim was given a bitter drink of wine mixed with myrrh (gall) as a mild narcotic or opiate.

2. The second was the cup of mockery. *"And the soldiers also mocked him, coming to him, and offering him vinegar." (Lk. 23:36)*

3. The third was the cup of sympathy. "Now there was set a vessel full of vinegar: and they filled a sponge with vinegar, and put it upon hyssop, and put it to his mouth" (Jn. 19:29). Jesus had refused the first cup at the beginning of his suffering, but now accepted this one at the end of his agony.

4. The fourth was the cup of iniquity. Our Lord himself had spoken of this while in the Garden of Gethsemane. *"Then said Jesus unto Peter, Put up thy sword into the sheath: the cup which my Father hath given me, shall I not drink it?" (Jn. 18:11)*

A verse found in one of the Psalms sung by Christ and his disciples in the Upper Room (Mt. 26:30) in reality summarized all four cups: *"I will take the cup of salvation, and call upon the name of the Lord." (Psa. 116:13)*

■ At noon a strange darkness settled over the area, lasting until His death at 3:00 p.m. (Mt. 27:45; Mk. 15:33; Lk. 23:44). Isaac Watts' great hymn, At The Cross, speaks of this:

"Well might the sun in darkness hide and shut his glories in, When Christ, the mighty Maker died for man, the creature's sin."

Thus, the created sun refused to shine upon the crucifixion of the Creator Son!

■ Just prior to His death Jesus receives some wine vinegar (Mt. 27:48; Mk. 15:36; Jn. 19:29).

■ At the moment of Jesus' death the centurion (officiating Roman soldier) gives dramatic testimony regarding the person of the Savior.
1. The Roman centurion at Calvary affirmed both the royalty and righteousness of Jesus.
   a. His testimony as recorded by Matthew: "Truly, this was the Son of God."
   b. His testimony as recorded by Luke: "Certainly, this was a righteous man." (Lk. 23:47)
2. He thus became the final of five individuals who attested to the sinlessness of Jesus during those horrible hours before and at the time of the crucifixion. The first four were:
   a. Pilate (Jn. 19:4)
   b. Pilate's wife (Mt. 27:19)
   c. Judas (Mt. 27:4)
   d. The dying thief (Lk. 23:41)

■ After His death the following supernatural phenomenon occurs:
1. The temple veil is torn from top to bottom (Mt. 27:51a; Mk. 15:38; Lk. 23:45).

This veil divided the holy place from the holy of holies, into which only the High Priest might enter on the Day of Atonement (see Ex. 26:31). Thus, the tearing of that veil, which was a type of Christ's human body introduced something new and thrilling, as explained by the author of Hebrews:

"Having therefore, brethren, boldness to enter into the holiest by the blood of Jesus, By a new and living way, which he hath consecrated for us, through the veil, that is to say, his flesh; And having an high priest over the house of God; Let us draw near with a true heart in full assurance of faith, having our hearts sprinkled from an evil conscience, and our bodies washed with pure water." (Heb. 10:19-22)
2. The earth shook and the rocks split (Mt. 27:51b).
3. Some well-known individuals were raised from the dead.

"And the graves were opened; and many bodies of the saints which slept arose, And came out of the graves after his resurrection, and went into the holy city, and appeared unto many." (Mt. 27: 52-53)

There are two theories concerning the exact nature of this resurrection.
   a. These "saints" (probably well-known citizens of Jerusalem) were raised from the dead, as was Lazarus (though he eventually died again).
   b. These saints actually received glorified bodies, never again to die.

Question: Why all these miraculous events at this particular time?

Answer: It would appear through all this, including the 3-hour darkness that God the Father was attempting to capture the attention of sinful Israel. If so, His message would be:

"Look, Listen, Hear! Something great and glorious has just happened! Israel's promised Messiah, the Savior of Gentiles, and my beloved Son has just paid the full price for the sins of all men everywhere!"

■ The confused and somewhat fearful crowd disperses.

"And all the people that came together to that sight, beholding the things which were done, smote their breasts, and returned. And all his acquaintance, and the women that followed him from Galilee, stood afar off, beholding these things." (Lk. 23:48-49)

■ At the request of the Jewish leaders, Pilate sends soldiers to Golgotha with orders to kill the three men and remove their bodies (Jn. 19:31).

■ The soldiers execute the two thieves by breaking their legs but discover Jesus already dead. Making sure of this, they pierce His side with a spear (Jn. 19:32-37).

"For these things were done, that the scripture should be fulfilled, A bone of him shall not be broken. And again another scripture saith, They shall look on him whom they pierced." (Jn. 19:36-37)

■ Joseph of Arimathea and Nicodemus request and receive from Pilate the lifeless body of Jesus (Mt. 27:57-58; Mk. 15:42-45; Lk. 23:50-52; Jn. 19:38-39a).

■ Both men quickly prepare His body for burial and placed it in Joseph's new tomb (Mt. 27:59-60; Mk. 15:46-47; Lk. 23:53-54; Jn. 19:39b-56).

■ Mary, Mother of Jesus, Mary Magdalene, and some other women sit near His tomb, viewing it in silent sorrow (Mt. 27:61; Mk. 15:47; Lk. 23:55-56).

These then are the 16 events. We now consider:

II. The Seven Statements

A. **ONE**: *"Father, forgive them; for they know not what they do." (Lk. 23:34)*

■ We note He did not pray, "forgive me," but *"forgive them."*

Our Lord would thus suffer not as a martyr (one who dies for his faith) but rather as a Savior (one who redeems sinners)!

■ This prayer has bothered some, as it seems to be a blanket pardon for all involved in Jesus' crucifixion. Of course, we know this is not the case. Forgiveness can come only through faith (Eph. 2:8-9). It has been pointed out by some that the word "forgive" here can also mean "to allow," and is actually translated thereby on at least thirteen other occasions in the New Testament. If this should be the case here, Christ then would pray, "Father, allow them to crucify me." Thus the prayer would be a plea to stay the wrath of a righteous Father as he viewed his beloved Son being murdered by sinful and wicked men (see Mt. 3:15; 19:14; Mk. 1:34). However, most Bible students would accept the word "forgive" at face value and interpret his prayer as a request for God not to add this horrible crime of regicide (the killing of one's own king) to the personal accounts of those individuals who killed him. Peter and Paul would amplify this point in later sermons (Acts 3:14-15, 17); *"But ye denied the Holy One and the Just, and desired a murderer to be granted unto you; And killed the Prince of life, whom God hath raised from the dead; whereof we are witnesses ..And now, brethren, I wot that through ignorance ye did it, as did also your rulers."*

See also 1 Cor. 2:8: *"Which none of the princes of this world knew: for had they known it, they would not have crucified the Lord of glory."*

The sinlessness of our Savior is again proven here, for he did not pray, "Father, forgive me." He needed no forgiveness, for he knew no sin. In summary, the first cross utterance did not mean that men are excusable, but rather forgivable. (Contrast Rom. 2:1 with 1 Tim. 1:13.)

■ His prayer here would later serve as an example for Stephen in the hour of His death:

"Then they cried out with a loud voice, and stopped their ears, and ran upon him with one accord, And cast him out of the city, and stoned him; and the witnesses laid down their clothes at a young mans feet, whose name was Saul. And they stoned Stephen, calling upon God, and saying, Lord Jesus, receive my spirit. And he kneeled down, and cried with a loud voice, Lord, lay not this sin to their charge. And when he had said this, he fell asleep." (Acts 7:57-60)

■ The Greek here employs the imperfect verb indicating continuous action in past time. Thus the statement should read, "Father," Jesus kept on saying, "Forgive them..."

Russell Bradley Jones asks:

"Can you reconstruct the picture?"

"Arriving at the place of the skull, Jesus looked about and prayed, 'Father, forgive them; for they know not what they do.' As the centurion crushed Him to the ground and tied His arms to the crossbeam, He prayed, 'Father, forgive them; for they know not what they do.' When the blunt spikes tore through each quivering palm, He prayed, 'Father, forgive them; for they know not what they do.' When the soldiers parted His garments and gambled for the seamless robe, He prayed, 'Father, forgive them; for they know not what they do.' How many times that prayer pierced Heaven's blue that day no one knows. It was not an ejaculatory petition shot into Heaven in a moment of mercy. Rather the Surety was storming the Throne of Grace with a barrage of burning appeal. Jesus kept saying, 'Father, forgive them...'" (*Gold from Golgotha*. Moody Press, 1945, pages. 17, 18)

■ Jones continues:

"If the prayer had not been uttered, the clear inference is that immediate doom would have destroyed those who nailed Him to the cross. Like a flash of lightning, the thunderbolts of God's wrath would have cleared the earth of those perpetrators of sin. Then and there Satan and his hosts would have been 'cast into the lake of fire' to suffer forever. The winds of God's wrath would have scorched the earth with the fires of justice. No man would have had a chance at salvation, because no man deserved a chance.

"But, thank God, Jesus prayed, 'Hold the winds of wrath back until the elect are sealed. There are some among these at the cross who will turn when the significance of their crime dawns upon them. Father, postpone the day of judgment. Give them a chance.' And because of that prayer, the gospel has been proclaimed and many an unworthy sinner has been saved." (ibid, pages 24,25)

■ It can be seen through this first statement that Jesus was, among other things, simply putting in practice that which He had once preached:

"Ye have heard that it hath been said, Thou shalt love thy neighbour, and hate thine enemy. But I say unto you, Love your enemies, bless them that curse you, do good to them that hate you, and pray for them which despitefully use you, and persecute you." (Mt. 5:43-44)

■ One final question. Did the Father answer this request? An answer may be seen by the testimony of the officiating Roman military commander at the cross some six hours later:

"And when the centurion, which stood over against him, saw that he so cried out, and gave up the ghost, he said, Truly this man was the Son of God. There were also women looking on afar off: among whom was Mary Magdalene, and Mary the mother of James the less and of Joses, and Salome." (Mk. 15:39-40)

B. **TWO**: *"Verily, I say unto thee, today shalt thou be with me in paradise." (Lk. 23:43)*

■ At first, both thieves were reviling Jesus, along with the crowd. (Mt. 27:44; Mk. 15:32) Note especially the language of the unrepentant thief:

"And one of the malefactors which were hanged railed on him, saying, If thou be Christ, save thyself and us." (Lk. 23:39)

■ Particularly significant are the words, "Come down from the cross." Thus,
1. Satan had once worked through an apostle attempting to prevent Jesus from going to the cross:

"From that time forth began Jesus to shew unto his disciples, how that he must go unto Jerusalem, and suffer many things of the elders and chief priests and scribes, and be killed, and be raised again the third day. Then Peter took him, and began to rebuke him, saying, Be it far from thee, Lord: this shall not be unto thee. But he turned, and said unto Peter, Get thee behind me, Satan: thou art an offence unto me: for thou savourest not the things that be of God, but those that be of men." (Mt. 16:21-23)

2. He now, working through this thing, attempts to prevent Jesus from dying on the cross!

■ The second statement emphasizes several facts concerning the subject of salvation:
1. That salvation is offered to anyone, anywhere. Are deathbed conversions valid? They are indeed, for there is one noted here. But we quickly note:
   a. There is one deathbed conversion in the Bible, so no dying man will despair.
   b. There is only one, so no living man will presume. D. L. Moody once said: "Did ever the new birth take place in so strange a cradle?" Observe the contrast here:
      (1) In the morning the thief we nailed to a cross. In the evening he was a friend of God.
      (2) In the morning he was an enemy of Caesar. In the evening he was a friend of God.
      (3) In the morning he was spurned by men. In the evening he was fellowshipping with angels.
      (4) In the morning he died as a criminal on earth. In the evening he lived as a citizen of heaven.
2. That salvation is by grace through faith alone. This conversion refutes:
   a. The doctrine of sacramentalism. He was saved apart from confirmation, sprinkling, Holy Communion, and church membership.
   b. The doctrine of baptismal regeneration.
   c. The doctrine of purgatory.

d. The doctrine of universalism. Only one thief was saved.

3. That salvation will be rejected by some in spite of everything God can do. The other thief died, eternally lost. Here we see three men:

   a. One was dying for sin (the Savior)

   b. One was dying from sin (the repentant thief).

   c. One was dying in sin (the lost thief).

   All classes of humanity were represented at the cross. There were the indifferent *("the people stood beholding," Lk. 23:35)*; the religious *("the rulers derided him," Lk 23:35)*; the materialistic *("the soldiers parted his raiment and cast lots," Lk. 23:34)*; and the earnest seeker *("Lord, remember me," Lk. 23:42)*. The Cross is indeed the judgment of this world (see John 12:31).

■ Why, it may be asked, was this thief saved? Russell B. Jones suggests:

"For one thing, the thief was willing to be saved, not necessarily from his cross, but from his sin. That must have appealed tremendously to Jesus. So many who come to Him are like the other thief; they want to avoid crosses, but they are not concerned about their sin. Some who come down the aisles of our churches professing to confess His name have gone no further than the first thief; they want to escape any and all discomfort and pain; they are not particularly interested in Him for His own sake. To the advantage of the other bandit, let it be said that he was interested in Kingdom issues and privileges. And whether or not he understood the nature of Christ's Kingdom, he wanted the good will of the King and was willing to yield his allegiance. That pleased Jesus.

"Further, this thief was persistent. We have another imperfect verb in the Greek original, 'He kept saying, Jesus, remember me when Thou comest into Thy kingdom.' His appeal was not an arrow shot at random. It was a storm. It kept pounding on the ear of the Savior: 'Jesus, remember me . . . Jesus, when Thou comest into Thy kingdom ... Jesus, . . . Jesus, remember me ... Jesus.' Above the din of the mocking and the reviling, these words kept pounding at the heart of the Savior." (ibid, pages 35, 36)

■ Finally, it may be concluded that during his time of agony the dying thief observed Jesus in a four-fold light.

1. He saw Jesus the submissive. The man in the middle did not lash out against the hostility coming from the foot of the cross or the criticism coming from either side.

2. He saw Jesus the sinless. *"And one of the malefactors which were hanged railed on him, saying, If thou be Christ, save thyself and us. But the other answering rebuked him, saying, Dost not thou fear God, seeing thou art in the same condemnation? And we indeed justly; for we receive the due reward of our deeds: but this man hath done nothing amiss." (Lk. 23:39-41)*

3. He saw Jesus the Savior. *"And he said unto Jesus, Lord, remember me". (Lk. 23:42a)*

4. He saw Jesus the Sovereign. *"When thou comest into thy kingdom". (Lk. 23:42b)*

■ But suppose the penitent thief had doubted or delayed? A minister was once faithfully warning the people of the danger of procrastination when a man shouted out from the audience, "What about the thief on the cross?" Quickly the preacher asked, "Which thief?" It is dangerous to delay.

One saved—the Lord makes room
For contrite souls above;
One lost—let none presume
On His exceeding love.
— Edith E. Trusted

■ Regarding Mary:

As this heart-broken mother stood weeping at the cross, the strange words by an old prophet spoken some 33 years ago may well have suddenly flashed through her mind:

"And, behold, there was a man in Jerusalem, whose name was Simeon; and the same man was just and devout, waiting for the consolation of Israel: and the Holy Ghost was upon him. And it was revealed unto him by the Holy Ghost, that he should not see death, before he had seen the Lord's Christ. And he came by the Spirit into the temple: and when the parents brought in the child Jesus, to do for him after the custom of the law, Then took he him up in his arms, and blessed God, and said, Lord, now lettest thou thy servant depart in peace, according to thy word: For mine eyes have seen thy salvation, Which thou hast prepared before the face of all people; A light to lighten the Gentiles, and the glory of thy people Israel. And Joseph and his mother marvelled at those things which were spoken of him. And Simeon blessed them, and said unto Mary his mother, Behold, this child is set for the fall and rising again of many in Israel; and for a sign which shall be spoken against; (Yea, a sword shall pierce through thy own soul also,) that the thoughts of many hearts may be revealed." (Lk. 2:25-35)

> *Beside the cross in tears*
> *The woeful mother stood,*
> *Bent 'neath the weight of years,*
> *And viewed His flowing blood;*
> *Her mind with grief was torn,*
> *Her strength was ebbing fast,*
> *And through her heart forlorn*
> *The sword of anguish passed.*

■ Regarding John:

"And from that hour that disciple took her unto his own home" (Jn. 19:27b). The following assumptions may be made from this statement—

1. That Joseph had previously died. This is strongly indicated by two passages:

> *"While he yet talked to the people, behold, his mother and his brethren stood without, desiring to speak with him. Then one said unto him, Behold, thy mother and thy brethren stand without, desiring to speak with thee." (Mt. 12:46-47)*

> *"And when he was come into his own country, he taught them in their synagogue, insomuch that they were astonished, and said, Whence hath this man this wisdom, and these mighty works? Is not this the carpenter's son? is not his mother called Mary? and his brethren, James, and Joses, and Simon, and Judas? And his sisters, are they not all with us? Whence then hath this man all these things?" (Mt. 13:54-56)*

2. That Mary was living in Jerusalem

3. That, for some reason, her unbelieving sons and daughters living in Nazareth were either unable or unwilling to care for her (see Jn. 7:1-5).

D. **FOUR**: *"My God, my God, why hast thou forsaken me?" (Mt. 27:46)*

■ This prayer is deeper in its mystery and higher in its meaning than any other single prayer in the Bible. God forsaken by God! Who can understand that? The wisest and most profound believer feels utterly inadequate as he approaches it. It can never be mastered by the mortal mind, even though that mind has experienced new birth. Eternity alone will exegete this. Elisabeth Clephane has so well phrased it:

> *"But none of the ransomed ever knew,*
> *How deep were the waters crossed;*
> *Nor how dark was the night,*
> *That the Lord passed through,*
> *Ere he found his sheep that was lost."*

Three words in this question deserve careful consideration:

■ "Why"?

1. There are so many unexplained "whys" raised here.
   a. Why did the Father turn His back upon the Son?
   b. Why did not even the Son know the reason?
   c. Why did innocent blood have to be shed for forgiveness of sin?

2. The first and third of these questions are partially answered in Heb. 9:22; 1 Pet. 2:24; 3:18; and Isa. 53. But what of the second question? Did not Christ know? According to Phil. 2:5-8, Christ voluntarily abstained from employing some of His divine attributes while upon this earth. Thus:
   a. He abstained from using His omnipresence for a period (Jn. 11:15).
   b. He abstained from using His omnipotence for a period (Jn. 5:19).
   c. He abstained from using His omniscience for a period (Lk. 8:45; Mk. 13:32). (See also Lk. 2:40.)

3. Why then did the Father forsake His son? The answer is two-fold:
   a. Jesus became our sin bearer!

   > *"All we like sheep have gone astray; we have turned every one to his own way; and the LORD hath laid on him the iniquity of us all." (Isa. 53:6)*

   > *"For he hath made him to be sin for us, who knew no sin; that we might be made the righteousness of God in him" (2 Cor. 5:21). "Who his own self bare our sins in his own body on the tree, that we, being dead to sins, should live unto righteousness: by whose stripes ye were healed." (1 Peter 2:24)*

   b. God cannot look upon sin without judging it!

   > *"For the wrath of God is revealed from heaven against all ungodliness and unrighteousness of men, who hold the truth in unrighteousness." (Rom. 1:18)*

■ "Forsaken"?

Jesus had previously been forsaken by His friends (Mk. 14:50-52). He will now be forsaken by His Father. Forsaken is the saddest word in any language. In the Greek, it is made up of three words: to leave meaning to abandon; down, suggesting defeat and helplessness; and in, referring to place or circumstance. "The total meaning of the word is that of forsaking someone in a state of defeat or helplessness in the midst of hostile circumstances" (*Bypaths in the Greek New Testament*, by Kenneth S. Wuest, p. 87).

■ "Me"?

Why Jesus? Why could not the sin bearer be a mighty angel or a godly human? Paul quickly answers this – *"For there is one God, and one mediator between God and men, the man Christ Jesus." (1 Tim. 2:5)*

■ Thus, He who began His ministry by suffering intense hunger (Mt. 4:2), will now end it by experiencing terrible thirst. And yet, the amazing truth remains:

1. The hungry one was and is the eternal Bread of life.
2. The thirsty one was and is the eternal Water of life.

F. **SIX**: *"It is finished" (Jn. 19:30)*

■ The sixth statement of Jesus is actually one word in the original Greek. It is tetelestai, meaning: "It was finished, and as a result it is forever done." This phrase was a farmer's word. When into his herd there was born an animal so beautiful and shapely that it seemed absolutely destitute of faults and defects, the farmer gazed upon the creature with proud, delighted eyes. "Tetelestai!" he said.

It was also an artist's word. When the painter or the sculptor had put the last finishing touches to the vivid landscape or the marble bust, he would stand back a few feet to admire his masterpiece, and, seeing in it nothing that called for correction or improvement, would murmur fondly, "Tetelestai! Tetelestai!"

■ Our Lord cries out, *"It is finished!"* There are three important places where Scripture employs this word "finish."

It is used in Gen. 2:1, referring to the creation of God's works. It is used here in Jn. 19:30, referring to the salvation of His works (see also Jn. 4:34; 5:36; 17:4). It is used in Rev. 10:7 and 16:17, referring to the completion of His works.

■ With gladness we note that He did not say, "I am finished," for He was just beginning.

As the poet has written:
"Lifted up was he to die,
'It is finished,' was his cry;
Now in heaven exalted high;
Hallelujah! What a Savior!

Nothing in my hand I bring,
Simply to thy cross I cling."

G. **SEVEN**: *"Father, into thy hands I commend my spirit" (Lk. 23:46)*

■ This marks the final of many occasions where Jesus prays to His Father. He did this:

1. Upon hearing the report of the returning 70
   "In that hour Jesus rejoiced in spirit, and said, I thank thee, O Father, Lord of heaven and earth, that thou hast hid these things from the wise and prudent, and hast revealed them unto babes: even so, Father; for so it seemed good in thy sight." (Lk. 10:21)
2. Prior to raising Lazarus
   "Then they took away the stone from the place where the dead was laid. And Jesus lifted up his eyes, and said, Father, I thank thee that thou hast heard me. And I knew that thou hearest me always: but because of the people which stand by I said it, that they may believe that thou hast sent me." (Jn. 11:41-42)

3. After some Greeks sought a meeting with Him

   "Now is my soul troubled; and what shall I say? Father, save me from this hour: but for this cause came I unto this hour. Father, glorify thy name. Then came there a voice from heaven, saying, I have both glorified it, and will glorify it again." (Jn. 12:27-28)

4. During His great High Priestly Prayer (Jn. 17:1, 5, 11, 21, 24, 25)

5. In Gethsemane

   "And he went a little farther, and fell on his face, and prayed, saying, O my Father, if it be possible, let this cup pass from me: nevertheless not as I will, but as thou wilt." (Mt. 26:39)

6. Immediately after being placed on the cross (Lk. 23:34)

■ It can be seen that not only was His birth and resurrection supernatural events (see Lk. 1:34-35; Rom. 1:4; Eph. 1:19-21), but also that of His death. In other words, Jesus died by the sheer act of His will—He dismissed His spirit!

■ He thus (it has been observed) gave up His life because He willed it, when and where He willed it, and as He willed it.

■ All four Gospel accounts record the death of Christ. But one wonders how such a thing could happen? Was not Christ God incarnate? Indeed he was! How, then, could God have actually died on the cross? To explain this, we must return briefly to the book of Genesis. Here we are told of Adam's creation and of his tragic sin. God had warned him that disobedience would result in death, and so it did. In fact, it brought down upon the head of mankind two kinds of death: physical and spiritual.

Both kinds of death here can be defined by one word: separation. That is the biblical and theological meaning of the word death. Physical death is separation, the parting of the soul from the body. Spiritual death is likewise separation, the parting of the unsaved person from God. This is sometimes called the second death (see Rev. 20:6, 14; 21:8).

So then, these two hellish enemies, physical and spiritual death, let loose by Adam, continued to curse and terrorize the human race for over forty centuries. Then, in the fullness of time, God sent his beloved Son to our world. The Father referred to his Son as the last Adam (among other names) in 1 Cor. 15:45. Why this title? Because He had come to undo what the first Adam had previously done; that is, He came to rid mankind of those two evil enemies, physical and spiritual death. This He did, while on the cross, where He died spiritually, being separated from God; and He died physically as He accomplished both tasks.

Spiritual death was immediately given the death blow. Paul later assures us that nothing can now separate the believer from the love of God (Rom. 8:35-39). But what about physical death? Paul answers this question in I Cor. 15:51-55:

"Behold, I shew you a mystery; We shall not all sleep, but we shall all be changed, In a moment, in the twinkling of an eye, at the last trump: for the trumpet shall sound, and the dead shall be raised incorruptible, and we shall be changed. For this corruptible must put on incorruption, and this mortal must put on immortality. So when this corruptible shall have put on incorruption, and this mortal shall have put on immortality, then shall be brought to pass the saying that is written, Death is swallowed up in victory. O death, where is thy sting? O grave, where is thy victory?"

H. Grand conclusion regarding the seven last statements:

■ "Who needeth not daily, as those high priests, to offer up sacrifice, first for his own sins, and then for the people's: for this he did once, when he offered up himself. " (Heb. 7:27)

Author Ray Stedman writes: "As a priest, Jesus Christ could find no unblemished sacrifice that He could offer except Himself, so He offered Himself as a sacrifice; there was found no other priest worthy of offering such a sacrifice, so Christ became both Priest and Victim" (What More Can God Say? p. 115).

This dual arrangement can be seen by listening to his seven final sentences while on the cross. The first three demonstrate his priestly ministry while the final four speak of his sacrificial role.

1. His priestly ministry:

    a. "Father, forgive them; for they know not what they do" (Lk. 23:34).

    b. "Verily, I say unto thee, today shalt thou be with me in paradise" (Lk. 23:43).

    c. "Woman, behold thy son!...Behold thy mother." (Jn. 19:26-27)

2. His sacrificial ministry:

    a. "My God, my God, why hast thou forsaken me?" (Mt. 27:46)

    b. "I thirst" (Jn. 19:28).

    c. "It is finished" (Jn. 19:30).

    d. "Father, into thy hands I commend my spirit" (Lk. 23:46).

Saturday

■ *"Now the next day, that followed the day of the preparation, the chief priests and Pharisees came together unto Pilate, Saying, Sir, we remember that that deceiver said, while he was yet alive, After three days I will rise again. Command therefore that the sepulchre be made sure until the third day, lest his disciples come by night, and steal him away, and say unto the people, He is risen from the dead, so the last error shall be worse than the first. Pilate said unto them, Ye have a watch: go your way, make it as sure as ye can. So they went, and made the sepulchre sure, sealing the stone, and setting a watch." (Mt. 27:62-66)*

How tragic to realize that the only group to remember the oft-repeated prophecies of Jesus concerning his resurrection consisted of his enemies and not his friends. They simply forgot (see Lk. 24:5-8; Jn. 20:9).

THE RESURRECTION APPEARANCES OF JESUS

THE RESURRECTION OF JESUS

"For I delivered unto you first of all that which I also received, how that Christ died for our sins according to the scriptures; And that he was buried, and that he rose again the third day according to the scriptures." (1 Cor. 15:3-4)

Foster writes: "A French philosopher decided to create a new religion for France following the wild excesses of the French Revolution which severed most of the nation from Christianity. He approached the great French statesman Tallyrand for advice on how to proceed. Tallyrand replied sarcastically that it should be a very simple task for the philosopher to create a substitute for Christianity: all he needed to do would be to have himself crucified and then raised from the dead!" (Studies in the Life of Christ, R. C. Foster, Baker Books, Grand Rapids, Mich., 1979)

We will overview this all important historical fact and theological truth in four-fold fashion:

I. PART ONE: The CLASSIFICATION of the Resurrection (the Second Work)

To explain, consider the following: Every work that God has ever done, is doing now, or ever will do, can be correctly arranged (classified) under one of two main categories, namely, His work in creation and His work in redemption! Furthermore, God has chosen two special days of the week to serve as a reminder concerning these all-important accomplishments.

- SATURDAY, celebrating His first great work, that of creation (Gen. 2:1-3; Ex. 20:8-11).

- SUNDAY, celebrating His second great work, that of redemption. This is why the resurrection occurred on Sunday, and why the early Christians observed the first day of the week as their official day of worship (Mt. 28:1; Acts 20:7; 1 Cor. 16:2).

II. PART TWO: The PROCLAMATION of the Resurrection (the Empty Tomb)

- The trips to the tomb
  1. By the woman
     "In the end of the Sabbath, as it began to dawn toward the first day of the week, came Mary Magdalene and the other Mary to see the sepulchre." (Mt. 28:1) "And when the Sabbath was past, Mary Magdalene, and Mary the mother of James, and Salome, had bought sweet spices, that they might come and anoint him." (Mk. 16:1)

2. By the disciples

"The first day of the week cometh Mary Magdalene early, when it was yet dark, unto the sepulchre, and seeth the stone taken away from the sepulchre. Then she runneth, and cometh to Simon Peter, and to the other disciple, whom Jesus loved, and saith unto them, They have taken away the LORD out of the sepulchre, and we know not where they have laid him. Peter therefore went forth, and that other disciple, and came to the sepulchre. So they ran both together: and the other disciple did outrun Peter, and came first to the sepulchre. And he stooping down, and looking in, saw the linen clothes lying; yet went he not in. Then cometh Simon Peter following him, and went into the sepulchre, and seeth the linen clothes lie, And the napkin, that was about his head, not lying with the linen clothes, but wrapped together in a place by itself. Then went in also that other disciple, which came first to the sepulchre, and he saw, and believed. For as yet they knew not the scripture, that he must rise again from the dead. Then the disciples went away again unto their own home". (Jn. 20:1-10)

a. Note the arrangement of the neatly folded grave clothes suggesting Jesus' resurrection was an orderly event, carefully planned, and unhurried to say the least.

b. We are told that John "saw and believed." Just what though did he believe? Was it that Jesus had indeed risen from the dead, or simply that something mysterious and supernatural had occurred? The immediate events following this would suggest the latter, for John seemed to be as shocked as the other disciples when the Savior later appeared to them in the Upper Room (Lk. 24:36-43).

■ The terror at the tomb

"And for fear of him the keepers did shake, and became as dead men... Now when they were going, behold, some of the watch came into the city, and shewed unto the chief priests all the things that were done. And when they were assembled with the elders, and had taken counsel, they gave large money unto the soldiers, Saying, Say ye, His disciples came by night, and stole him away while we slept. And if this come to the governors ears, we will persuade him, and secure you. So they took the money, and did as they were taught: and this saying is commonly reported among the Jews until this day." (Mt. 28:4, 11-15)

1. The splendor and glory of angels is almost inconceivable. Note two other references to their brightness: *"And I saw another mighty angel come down from heaven, clothed with a cloud: and a rainbow was upon his head, and his face was as it were the sun, and his feet as pillars of fire." (Rev. 10:1) "And after these things I saw another angel come down from heaven, having great power; and the earth was lightened with his glory." (Rev. 18:1)*

2. There are at least two glaring flaws in this "official explanation concerning the empty tomb."

a. In the first place the soldiers were to say they had fallen asleep. But if so, how could they have known that "his disciples came... and stole him away"?

b. In the second place, if it were true, why were they not put to death for sleeping on duty? (See Acts 12:19.)

■ The transaction in the tomb

"And very early in the morning the first day of the week, they came unto the sepulchre at the rising of the sun. And they said among themselves, Who shall roll us away the stone from the door of the sepulchre? And when they looked, they saw that the stone was rolled away: for it was very great. And entering into the sepulchre, they saw a young man sitting on the right side, clothed in a long white garment; and they were affrighted. And he saith unto them, Be not affrighted: Ye seek Jesus of Nazareth, which was crucified: he is risen; he is not here: behold the place where they laid him. But go your way, tell his disciples and Peter that he goeth before you into Galilee: there shall ye see him, as he said unto you." (Mk. 16:2-7)

■ The testimony from the tomb

> "And they departed quickly from the sepulchre with fear and great joy; and did run to bring his disciples word." (Mt. 28:8)

■ The talk about the tomb

> "It was Mary Magdalene and Joanna, and Mary the mother of James, and other women that were with them, which told these things unto the apostles And their words seemed to them as idle tales, and they believed them not. Then arose Peter, and ran unto the sepulchre; and stooping down, he beheld the linen clothes laid by themselves, and departed, wondering in himself at that which was come to pass." (Lk. 24:10-12)

III. PART THREE: The VALIDATIONS of the Resurrection (the Risen Lord)

Following His resurrection, Jesus would appear on ten separate occasions. Five of these appearances transpired on the first Easter Sunday, and the final five during the remaining 39 days before His ascension. (Acts 1:3)

A. First Resurrection Appearance — **Before Mary Magdalene**

"Now when Jesus was risen early the first day of the week, he appeared first to Mary Magdalene, out of whom he had cast seven devils. And she went and told them that had been with him, as they mourned and wept. And they, when they had heard that he was alive, and had been seen of her, believed not." (Mk. 16:9-11)

"But Mary stood without at the sepulchre weeping: and as she wept, she stooped down, and looked into the sepulchre, And seeth two angels in white sitting, the one at the head, and the other at the feet, where the body of Jesus had lain. And they say unto her, Woman, why weepest thou? She saith unto them, Because they have taken away my LORD, and I know not where they have laid him. And when she had thus said, she turned herself back, and saw Jesus standing, and knew not that it was Jesus. Jesus saith unto her, Woman, why weepest thou? whom seekest thou? She, supposing him to be the gardener, saith unto him, Sir, if thou have borne him hence, tell me where thou hast laid him, and I will take him away. Jesus saith unto her, Mary. She turned herself, and saith unto him, Rabboni; which is to say, Master Jesus saith unto her, Touch me not; for I am not yet ascended to my father but go to my brethren, and say unto them, I ascend unto my Father, and your Father; and to my God, and your God. Mary Magdalene came and told the disciples that she had seen the LORD, and that he had spoken these things unto her." (Jn. 20:11-18)

■ This was undoubtedly one of the two most dramatic "recognition meetings" in all the Bible. The first involved Joseph revealing himself to his brothers in Egypt (see Gen. 45:1-3). It was a Samaritan woman to whom Christ first revealed his messiahship (see Jn. 4:25-26). It is now to another woman, Mary Magdalene, that Christ first appears in his resurrection body. Both were formerly women of questionable moral background (see Mk. 16:9).

■ Why did Mary fail to recognize Jesus? Probably for several reasons:
1. Her eyes were blinded with tears.
2. The early morning light was still too dim.
3. She was not expecting to see him.

■ Their encounter with the angels of God

"Now upon the first day of the week, very early in the morning, they came unto the sepulchre, bringing the spices which they had prepared, and certain others with them. And they found the stone rolled away from the sepulchre. And they entered in, and found not the body of the Lord Jesus And it came to pass, as they were much perplexed thereabout, behold, two men stood by them in shining garments: And as they were afraid, and bowed down their faces to the earth, they said unto them, Why seek ye the living among the dead? He is not here, but is risen: remember how he spake unto you when he was yet in Galilee, Saying, The Son of man must be delivered into the hands of sinful men, and be crucified, and the third day rise again. And they remembered his words." (Lk. 24:1-8)

"But go your way, tell his disciples and Peter that he goeth before you into Galilee: there shall ye see him, as he said unto you." (Mk. 16:7)

■ Their encounter with the Son of God

"And as they went to tell his disciples, behold, Jesus met them, saying, All hail. And they came and held him by the feet, and worshipped him. Then said Jesus unto them, Be not afraid: go tell my brethren that they go into Galilee, and there shall they see me." (Mt. 28:9-10)

1. Note His phrase, *"Go to my brethren."* There is a progressive intimacy between Jesus and his disciples. He calls them servants (Jn. 13:13), friends (Jn. 15:15), and here, brethren. Note also the phrase, *"I ascend unto my Father."* Some hold that Christ ascended that very first Easter Sunday to sprinkle His blood as the ultimate sacrifice within the heavenly sanctuary.

2. In fact, this occasion marks the third time women have been instructed to relate the glorious news of the resurrection to men (Jn. 20:17; Mk. 16:7; Mt. 28:10)! One reason for this is the fact that only one disciple (John) was present at the crucifixion, but many faithful women were there from start to finish!

C. Third Resurrection Appearance — **Before Simon Peter**

"Saying, The Lord is risen indeed, and hath appeared to Simon." (Lk. 24:34)

"And that he was seen of Cephas, then of the twelve." (1 Cor. 15:5)

■ What a meeting this must have been. The last time these two saw each other, the one was bitterly cursing and denying the other.

D. Fourth Resurrection Appearance — **Before Two Disciples En Route to Emmaus**

"After that he appeared in another form unto two of them, as they walked, and went into the country. And they went and told it unto the residue: neither believed they them." (Mk. 16:12-13)

"And, behold, two of them went that same day to a village called Emmaus, which was from Jerusalem about threescore furlongs. And they talked together of all these things which had happened. And it came to pass, that, while they communed together and reasoned, Jesus himself drew near, and went with them. But their eyes were holders that they should not know

him. And he said unto them, What manner of communications are these that ye have one to another, as ye walk, and are sad? And the one of them, whose name was Cleopas, answering said unto him, Art thou only a stranger in Jerusalem, and hast not known the things which are come to pass there in these days? And he said unto them, What things? And they said unto him, Concerning Jesus of Nazareth, which was a prophet mighty in deed and word before God and all the people: And how the chief priests and our rulers delivered him to be condemned to death, and have crucified him. But we trusted that it had been he which should have redeemed Israel: and beside all this, to day is the third day since these things were done. Yea, and certain women also of our company made us astonished, which were early at the sepulchre; And when they found not his body, they came, saying, that they had also seen a vision of angels, which said that he was alive. And certain of them which were with us went to the sepulchre, and found it even so as the women had said: but him they saw not. Then he said unto them, O fools, and slow of heart to believe all that the prophets have spoken: Ought not Christ to have suffered these things, and to enter into his glory? And beginning at Moses and all the prophets, he expounded unto them in all the scriptures the things concerning himself. And they drew nigh unto the village, whither they went: and he made as though he would have gone further. But they constrained him, saying, Abide with us: for it is toward evening, and the day is far spent. And he went in to tarry with them. And it came to pass, as he sat at meat with them, he took bread, and blessed it, and brake, and gave to them. And their eyes were opened, and they knew him; and he vanished out of their sight. And they said one to another, Did not our heart burn within us, while he talked with us by the way, and while he opened to us the scriptures? And they rose up the same hour, and returned to Jerusalem, and found the eleven gathered together, and them that were with them, Saying, The Lord is risen indeed, and hath appeared to Simon. And they told what things were done in the way, and how he was known of them in breaking of bread." (Lk. 24:13-35)

There are at least four phrases that are worthy of our attention in this passage:

■ *"Today is the third day"* (Lk. 24:21)

    The phrase *"today is the third day since these things were done"* may have been a reference to the Jewish belief that after the third day the soul left the body for good. In other words, the situation was now hopeless.

■ *"Beginning at Moses"* (Lk. 24:27)

    During the 8 mile walk between Jerusalem and Emmaus, our Lord, in essence, provides for these two saddened believers the ultimate "walk thru" summary of the Hebrews Old Testament scriptures!

    He no doubt spoke of the following Old Testament events, objects, feasts, etc.

1. The protoevangelium verse (Gen. 3:15), or "first gospel" verse, which promises the eventual victory of the Messiah over Satan (see also Gal. 4:4; Rom. 16:20; Isa. 53:5).
2. His virgin birth in Bethlehem (Isa. 7:14; Micah 5:2).
3. His work as a prophet and priest (Deut. 18:15; Gen. 14:18-20).
4. His Triumphal Entry into Jerusalem (Zech. 9:9).
5. His rejection by Israel (Isa. 53:3).
6. His betrayal for 30 pieces of silver (Zech. 11:12-13).
7. His work as the Passover Lamb and smitten Rock (Ex. 12:12-13, 17:6-7).
8. His suffering and death (Psa. 22).
9. His resurrection (Psa. 16:10).

■ *"The day is far spent"* (Lk. 24:29)

The two disciples reminded their unrecognized friend that *"The day is far spent"*. Spiritually speaking, however, it was just the opposite. The terrible night of Calvary was far spent. The glorious morning of the resurrection was now at hand. *"The night is far spent, the day is at hand: let us therefore cast off the works of darkness, and let us put on the armour of light." (Rom. 13:12)*

■ *"Did not our heart burn within us...?" (Lk. 24:32)*

The Old Testament prophet Jeremiah could certainly have identified with this statement: *"Then I said, I will not make mention of him, nor speak anymore in his name. But his word was in mine heart as a burning fire shut up in my bones, and I was weary with forbearing, and I could not stay." (Jer. 20:9)*

E. Fifth Resurrection Appearance — **Before the Ten Apostles in the Upper Room**

"Then the same day at evening, being the first day of the week, when the doors were shut where the disciples were assembled for fear of the Jews, came Jesus and stood in the midst, and saith unto them, Peace be unto you." (Jn. 20:19)

"And as they thus spake, Jesus himself stood in the midst of them, and saith unto them, Peace be unto you. But they were terrified and affrighted, and supposed that they had seen a spirit And he said unto them, Why are ye troubled? and why do thoughts arise in your hearts? Behold my hands and my feet, that it is I myself: handle me, and see; for a spirit hath not flesh and bones, as ye see me have. And when he had thus spoken, he shewed them his hands and his feet And while they yet believed not for joy, and wondered, he said unto them, Have ye here any meat? And they gave him a piece of a broiled fish, and of an honeycomb. And he took it, and did eat before them." (Lk. 24:36-43)

"Then said Jesus to them again, Peace be unto you: as my Father hath sent me, even so send I you. And when he had said this, he breathed on them, and saith unto them, Receive ye the Holy Ghost: Whose soever sins ye remit, they are remitted unto them; and whose soever sins ye retain, they are retained." (Jn. 20:21-23)

■ What kind of body did Jesus have after his resurrection? This is of great importance to the Christian, for he or she will someday have a similar body, as testified by both Paul and John (see Phil. 3:21; 1 Jn. 3:1-3).

    1. His new body had flesh and bone (Lk. 24:39-40).

    2. He ate food in the new body (Lk. 24:41-43; Jn. 21:12-13; Acts 10:41).

    3. His new body still bore the marks of his crucifixion (Jn. 20:25-27; Lk. 24:40; Rev. 5:6).

    4. His new body was not subjected to material laws (Jn. 20:19; Lk. 24:31, 36).

■ The disciples thought they had seen a ghost (Lk. 24:37)! They had previously made the same mistake during a life-threatening storm:

    "And in the fourth watch of the night Jesus went unto them, walking on the sea. And when the disciples saw him walking on the sea, they were troubled, saying, It is a spirit; and they cried out for fear. But straightway Jesus spake unto them, saying, Be of good cheer; it is I; be not afraid." (Mt. 14:25-27)

■ The giving of the Holy Spirit here (Jn. 20:22) was apparently a temporary act, awaiting His full and final appearance as recorded in Acts 2:1-4.

F. Sixth Resurrection Appearance — **Before the Eleven Apostles in the Upper Room**

- The reluctance of Thomas

> *"But Thomas, one of the twelve, called Didymus, was not with them when Jesus came. The other disciples therefore said unto him, We have seen the LORD. But he said unto them, Except I shall see in his hands the print of the nails, and put my finger into the print of the nails, and thrust my hand into his side, I will not believe."* (Jn. 20:24-25)

- The revelation to Thomas

> *"And after eight days again his disciples were within, and Thomas with them: then came Jesus, the doors being shut, and stood in the midst, and said, Peace be unto you. Then saith he to Thomas, Reach hither thy finger, and behold my hands; and reach hither thy hand, and thrust it into my side: and be not faithless, but believing. And Thomas answered and said unto him, My LORD and my God. Jesus saith unto him, Thomas, because thou past seen me, thou halt believed: blessed are they that have not seen, and yet have believed."* (Jn. 20:26-29)

During the 1990's a well known American religious leader claimed to have seen the risen Christ on at least 12 separate occasions! Most evangelical Christians would have difficulty with this claim, but even if true, according to Jesus' words here, all those Christians who have believed without seeing exotic visions are far more blessed than those who do! The following passages give strong testimony to this:

> *"(For we walk by faith, not by sight)."* (2 Cor. 5:7)

> *"Whom having not seen, ye love; in whom, though now ye see him not, yet believing, ye rejoice with joy unspeakable and full of glory."* (1 Pet. 1:8)

> *"Now faith is the substance of things hoped for, the evidence of things not seen ... But without faith it is impossible to please him: for he that cometh to God must believe that he is, and that he is a rewarder of them that diligently seek him... By faith Moses, when he was come to years, refused to be called the son of Pharaohs daughter… By faith he forsook Egypt, not fearing the wrath of the king: for he endured, as seeing him who is invisible."* (Heb. 11:1, 6, 24, 27)

G. Seventh Resurrection Appearance — **Before Seven Apostles Beside the Sea of Galilee**

"After these things Jesus shewed himself again to the disciples at the sea of Tiberias; and on this wise shewed he himself There were together Simon Peter, and Thomas called Didymus, and Nathanael of Cana in Galilee, and the sons of Zebedee, and two other of his disciples Simon Peter saith unto them, I go a fishing. They say unto him, We also go with thee. They went forth, and entered into a ship immediately; and that night they caught nothing. But when the morning was now come, Jesus stood on the shore: but the disciples knew not that it was Jesus Then Jesus saith unto them, Children, have ye any meat? They answered him, No. And he said unto them, Cast the net on the right side of the ship, and ye shall find. And They cast therefore, and now they were not able to draw it for the multitude of fishes. Therefore that disciple whom Jesus loved saith unto Peter, It Is the Lord. Now when Simon Peter heard that it was the Lord, he girt his fisher's coat unto him, (for he was naked,) and did cast himself into the sea. And the other disciples came in a little ship; (for they were not far from land, but as it were two hundred cubits,) dragging the net with fishes. As soon then as they were come to land, they saw a fire of coals there, and fish laid thereon, and bread. Jesus saith unto them, Bring of the fish which ye have now caught. Simon Peter went up, and drew the net to land full of great fishes, an hundred and fifty and three: and for all there were so many,

yet was not the net broken. Jesus saith unto them, Come and dine. And none of the disciples durst ask him, Who art thou? knowing that it was the Lord. Jesus then cometh, and taketh bread, and giveth them, and fish likewise. This is now the third time that Jesus shewed himself to his disciples, after that he was risen from the dead. So when they had dined, Jesus saith to Simon Peter, Simon, son of Jonas, lovest thou me more than these? He saith unto him, Yea, Lord; thou knowest that I love thee. He saith unto him, Feed my lambs. He saith to him again the second time, Simon, son of Jonas, lovest thou me? He saith unto him, Yea, Lord; thou knowest that I love thee. He saith unto him, Feed my sheep. He saith unto him the third time, Simon, son of Jonas, lovest thou me? Peter was grieved because he said unto him the third time, Lovest thou me? And he said unto him, Lord, thou knowest all things; thou knowest that I love thee. Jesus saith unto him, Feed my sheep. Verily, verily, I say unto thee, When thou wast young, thou girdest thyself, and walkedst whither thou wouldest: but when thou shalt be old, thou shalt stretch forth thy hands, and another shall gird thee, and carry thee whither thou wouldest not. This spake he, signifying by what death he should glorify God. And when he had spoken this, he saith unto him, Follow me. Then Peter, turning about, seeth the disciple whom Jesus loved following; which also leaned on his breast at supper, and said, Lord, which is he that betrayeth thee? Peter seeing him saith to Jesus, Lord, and what shall this man do? Jesus saith unto him, If I will that he tarry till I come, what is that to thee? follow thou me. Then went this saying abroad among the brethren, that that disciple should not die: yet Jesus said not unto him, He shall not die; but, If I will that he tarry till I come, what is that to thee?" (Jn. 21:1-23)

■ These seven, remembering the thrice repeated divine command (Mt. 26:32; 28:7, 10) to meet the risen Savior in Galilee had all assembled here. Just who the missing four were, where they were, and why they were absent is not recorded.

■ At the conclusion, this appearance, Jesus provides Peter's eventual martyrdom, hinting that it might be by crucifixion. Peter would later recall the Savior's words on this subject:

"Wherefore I will not be negligent to put you always in remembrance of these things, though ye know them, and be established in the present truth. Yea, I think it meet, as long as I am in this tabernacle, to stir you up by putting you in remembrance; Knowing that shortly I must put off this my tabernacle, even as our Lord Jesus Christ hath shewed me." (2 Pet. 1:12-14)

H. Eighth Resurrection Appearance — **Before Eleven Apostles and 500 Disciples**

"After that, he was seen of above five hundred brethren at once; of whom the greater part remain unto this present, but some are fallen asleep." (1 Cor. 15:6)

"Then the eleven disciples went away into Galilee, into a mountain where Jesus had appointed them. And when they saw him, they worshipped him: but some doubted. And Jesus came and spake unto them, saying, All power is given unto me in heaven and in earth. Go ye therefore, and teach all nations, baptizing them in the name of the Father, and of the Son, and of the Holy Ghost: Teaching them to observe all things whatsoever I have commanded you: and, lo, I am with you alway, even unto the end of the world. Amen." (Mt. 28:16-20)

"He that believeth and is baptized shall be saved; but he that believeth not shall be damned. And these signs shall follow them that believe; In my name shall they cast out devils; they shall speak with new tongues; They shall take up serpents; and if they drink any deadly thing, it shall not hurt them; they shall lay hands on the sick, and they shall recover." (Mk. 16:16-18)

■ On this occasion Jesus lists five signs that will accompany them who believe. Of these five, four were fulfilled in the book of Acts.

1. They shall cast out demons (Acts 5:16; 16:16-18; 19:12b)
2. They shall speak with new tongues (Acts 2:1-4; 10:44-46; 19:6)
3. They shall take up serpents (Acts 18:3-6)
4. No poison, if swallowed, would harm them (no record in the New Testament of this happening).
5. They shall heal the sick (Acts 5:15; 19;12a)

I. Ninth Resurrection Appearance — **Before James, His Half-Brother**

"After that, he was seen of James; then of all the apostles." (1 Cor. 15:7)

Until this event James was apparently an unbeliever and highly critical of his older half brother Jesus, as indicated by the following passage:

"After these things Jesus walked in Galilee: for he would not walk in Jewry, because the Jews sought to kill him. Now the Jew's feast of tabernacles was at hand. His brethren therefore said unto him, Depart hence, and go into Judaea, that thy disciples also may see the works that thou doest. For there is no man that doeth any thing in secret, and he himself seeketh to be known openly. If thou do these things, shew thyself to the world. For neither did his brethren believe in him." (Jn. 7:1-5)

J. Tenth Resurrection Appearance — **Before the Eleven Apostles on the Mount of Olives**

"And he said unto them, These are the words which I spake unto you, while I was yet with you, that all things must be fulfilled, which were written in the law of Moses, and in the prophets, and in the psalms, concerning me. Then opened he their understanding, that they might understand the scriptures, And said unto them, Thus it is written, and thus it behooved Christ to suffer, and to rise from the dead the third day: And that repentance and remission of sins should be preached in his name among all nations, beginning at Jerusalem. And ye are witnesses of these things And, behold, I send the promise of my Father upon you: but tarry ye in the city of Jerusalem, until ye be endued with power from on high." (Lk. 24:44-49)

"To whom also he skewed himself alive after his passion by many infallible proofs, being seen of them forty days, and speaking of the things pertaining to the kingdom of God: And, being assembled together with them, commanded them that they should not depart from Jerusalem, but wait for the promise of the Father, which, saith he, ye have heard of me. For John truly baptized with water; but ye shall be baptized with the Holy Ghost not many days hence. When they therefore were come together, they asked of him, saying, Lord, wilt thou at this time restore again the kingdom to Israel? And he said unto them, It is not for you to know the times or the seasons, which the Father hath put in his own power. But ye shall receive power, after that the Holy Ghost is come upon you: and ye shall be witnesses unto me both in Jerusalem, and in all Judaea, and in Samaria, and unto the uttermost part of the earth." (Acts 1:3-8)

■ Jesus speaks regarding the fulfillment of scripture (Lk. 24:44). In essence He was referring to the 40-plus Old Testament messianic prophecies He had already personally fulfilled, beginning with His virgin birth in Bethlehem to His glorious resurrection!

■ In Acts 1:8 Jesus gives the divine program schedule for the preaching of the gospel. This pattern was carefully followed in the book of Acts.

1. Witnessing in Jerusalem (Acts 2-7).
2. Witnessing in Judea and Samaria (Acts 8-12).
3. Witnessing worldwide (Acts 13-28).

IV. PART FOUR: An indication of the Resurrection (the Shroud of Turin)

The following extended passage comes from the pen of Dr. Gary Habermas, considered by many to be the world's foremost scholar on the resurrection of Christ. His work here refers to the Shroud of Turin:

"The Shroud of Turin, Italy, is a linen cloth measuring 14'3" long by 3'7" wide. Historically proclaimed to be the actual burial garment of Jesus, the linen contains a double, head-to-head image of a crucified man reposed in death, that reveals both the obverse and reverse of the body.

If the Shroud of Turin is Jesus' garment, we have highly evidential data for the death and probably even the resurrection of Jesus. Since there is strong evidence against the shroud being a fake, even if it wrapped the body of another victim of crucifixion, it can still provide important and reliable details concerning Jesus' demise. As such, several facts can be learned, most of which, it should be carefully noted, do not depend on the identification of the man buried in the shroud.

1. Once again we learn of the normal wounds associated with crucifixion such as the pre-cross beating, the pierced wrists and feet, as well as lesser details like the knee contusions (presumably from falling) and the shoulder abrasions (perhaps from carrying part of the cross).

2. We also learn of several abnormal points of crucifixion procedure that the man in the shroud had in common with Jesus. Such include: the scalp wounds caused by sharp objects, the absence of broken ankles, the post-mortem chest wound, and the flow of blood plus watery fluid.

3. Afterward, an individual but hasty burial in fine linen for one convicted as a "criminal" is also rather odd.

4. There is strong evidence that the man in the shroud had to move up and down in order to breathe. The blood from each wrist proceeded down each arm and formed a V-shaped blood flow, which is one evidence that suggests that two major bodily positions were taken on the cross.

5. There is evidence that the man buried in the shroud was very possibly raised from the dead, such as the absence of decomposition, an apparent lack of unwrapping the body, and a probably scorch from a dead body. If the man in the shroud is Jesus, as indicated by the similarities in dissimilar areas pointed out in (2), then (4) becomes possible evidence for Jesus' resurrection." (*The Historical Jesus*, College Press Publishing Co., Joplin, MO. 1996, pages 177-186.)

THE ASCENSION OF JESUS

"So then after the Lord had spoken unto them, he was received up into heaven, and sat on the right hand of God. And they went forth, and preached every where, the Lord working with them, and confirming the word with signs following. Amen." (Mk. 16:19-20)

"And he led them out as far as to Bethany, and he lifted up his hands, and blessed them. And it came to pass, while he blessed them, he was parted from them, and carried up into heaven, And they worshipped him, and returned to Jerusalem with great joy: And were continually in the temple, praising and blessing God. Amen." (Lk. 24:50-53)

"And when he had spoken these things, while they beheld, he was taken up; and a cloud received him out of their sight. And while they looked stedfastly toward heaven as he went up, behold, two men stood by them in white apparel; Which also said, Ye men of Galilee, why stand ye gazing up into heaven? this same Jesus, which is taken up from you into heaven, shall so come in like manner as ye have seen him go into heaven." (Acts 1:9-11)

- ■ Jesus had previously predicted His own ascension on several occasions (Jn. 6:22; 16:28; 20:17).

- ■ We are told He ascended to the right hand of God (Mk. 16:19). The dying Stephen, Christianity's first martyr would later see Him there (Acts 7:55). (See also Heb. 8:1; 10:12; 1 Peter 3:22.)

- ■ The heavenly messengers assured the apostles that Jesus would return in similar fashion as He departed. Thus:
  1. The going was personal, and so shall the return be (1 Thess. 4:16).
  2. The going was visible, and so shall the return be (Phil. 3:21).
  3. The going was from the Mount of Olives, and so shall the return be (Zech. 14:4).

- ■ This event marks the seventh of at least nine appearances of God's shekinah glory cloud. Note that it appeared:
  1. To Israel en route to Palestine (Ex. 13:21; 14:19-20)
  2. Over the tabernacle holy of holies (Lev. 16:2)
  3. Over the temple holy of holies (2 Chron. 5:13-14)
  4. In Ezekiel's time (Ezek. 10)
  5. At the birth of Christ (Lk. 2:9-11)
  6. At His transfiguration (Mt. 17:5)
  7. Here at this ascension (Acts 1:9)
  8. It will appear next at the Rapture (1 Thess. 4:17)
  9. It will appear again during His second coming (Mt. 24:30)

Two: TOPICAL

A brief consideration of the following topics:

- ➢ His Miracles

- ➢ His Parables

- ➢ His Sermons

- ➢ His Prayers

- ➢ His Sufferings

- ➢ The Usage of the Old Testament by Jesus

- ➢ The Old Testament Prophecies Fulfilled by Jesus

- ➢ The New Testament Predictions Foretold by Jesus

A LISTING OF JESUS' MIRACLES

1. Turning Water Into Wine . . . .(Jn. 2:1-11)
2. Healing a Nobleman's Son at Cana . . . .(Jn. 4:46-54)
3. Healing a Lame Man at the Pool of Bethesda . . . .(Jn. 4:46-54)
4. First Miraculous Catch of Fish . . . . (Lk. 5:1-11)
5. Delivering a Demoniac in a Capernaum Synagogue . . . . (Mk. 1:23-28; Lk. 4:31-36)
6. Healing Peter's Mother-in-law. . . . .(Mt. 8:14-15; Mk. 1:29-31; Lk. 4:38-39)
7. Cleansing a Leper . . . .(Mt. 8:2-4; Mk. 1:40-45; Lk. 9:12-16)
8. Healing a Paralytic. . . . .(Mt. 9:2-8; Mk. 2:3-12; Lk. 5:18-26)
9. Healing a Man With a Shriveled Hand . . . .(Mt. 12:9-13; Mk. 3:1-5; Lk. 6:6-10)
10. Healing a Centurion's Servant. . . . .(Mt. 8:5-13; Lk. 7:1-10)
11. Raising a Widow's Son . . . . (Lk. 7:11-15)
12. Delivering a Blind and Mute Demoniac . . . . (Mt. 12:22; Lk. 11:14)
13. Stilling a Storm . . . .(Mt. 8:28-34; Mk. 5:1-20; Lk. 8:26-29)
14. Delivering the Maniac of Gadara. . . . .(Mt. 8:28-34; Mk. 5:1-20; Lk. 8:26-39)
15. Healing a Woman With an Issue of Blood . . . .(Mt. 9:20-22; Mk. 5:25-34; Lk. 8:43-48)
16. Raising Jairus' Daughter . . . .(Mt. 9:18-19, 23-26; Mk. 5:22-24, 35-43; Lk. 8:41-42, 49-56)
17. Healing Two Blind Men. . . . . (Mt. 9:27-31)
18. Delivering a Mute Demoniac. . . . . (Mt. 9:32-33)
19. Feeding the 5000 . . . .(Mt. 14:14-21; Mk. 6:34-44; Lk. 9:12-17; Jn. 6:5-13)
20. Walking on the Water. . . . . (Mt. 14:24-33; Mk. 6:45-52; Jn. 6:16-21)
21. Delivering a Syrophenician's Daughter . . . . (Mt. 15:21-28; Mk. 7:24-30)
22. Healing a Deaf Mute Decapoli . . . .(Mk. 7:31-37)
23. Feeding the 4000 . . . . (Mt. 15:32-39; Mk. 8:1-9)
24. Healing a Blind Man at Bethsaida . . . .(Mk. 8:22-26)
25. Delivering a Demon-Possessed Boy . . . .(Mt. 17:14-18; Mk. 9:14-29; Lk. 9:38-42)
26. Finding the Tax Money in a Fish . . . . (Mt. 17:24-27)
27. Healing a Man Born Blind. . . . .(Jn. 9:1-7)
28. Healing a Crippled Woman on the Sabbath . . . . (Lk. 13:10-17)
29. Healing a Man With Dropsy . . . . (Lk. 14:1-6)
30. Raising of Lazarus . . . . (Jn. 11:17-44)
31. Cleansing of Ten Lepers . . . . (Lk. 17:11-19)
32. Healing Blind Bartimaeus . . . .(Mt. 20:29-34; Mk. 10:46-52; Lk. 18:35-43)
33. Cursing the Fig Tree. . . . . (Mt. 21:18-19)
34. Restoring Malchus' Ear . . . . (Lk. 22:49-51)
35. Second Miraculous Catch of Fish . . . .(Jn. 21:1-11)

A Brief Summary of Christ's Miracles

I. The Number of His Miracles

A. General, crowd related miracles. Nine:

1. *"And Jesus went about all Galilee, teaching in their synagogues, and preaching the gospel of the kingdom, and healing all manner of sickness and all manner of disease among the people. And his fame went throughout all Syria: and they brought unto him all sick people that were taken with divers diseases and torments, and those which were possessed with devils, and those which were lunatick, and those that had the palsy; and he healed them."* (Mt. 4:23-24)

2. *"When the even was come, they brought unto him many that were possessed with devils: and he cast out the spirits with his word, and healed all that were sick."* (Mt. 8:16)

3. *"And Jesus went about all the cities and villages, teaching in their synagogues, and preaching the gospel of the kingdom, and healing every sickness and every disease among the people."* (Mt. 9:35)

4. *"But when Jesus knew it, he withdrew himself from thence: and great multitudes followed him, and he healed them all."* (Mt. 12:15)

5. *"And Jesus went forth, and saw a great multitude, and was moved with compassion toward them, and he healed their sick."* (Mt. 14:14)

6. *"And when the men of that place had knowledge of him, they sent out into all that country round about, and brought unto him all that were diseased."* (Mt. 14:35)

7. *"And great multitudes came unto him, having with them those that were lame, blind, dumb, maimed, and many others, and cast them down at Jesus' feet; and he healed them: Insomuch that the multitude wondered, when they saw the dumb to speak, the maimed to be whole, the lame to walk, and the blind to see: and they glorified the God of Israel."* (Mt. 15:30-31)

8. *"And great multitudes followed him; and he healed them there."* (Mt. 19:2)

9. *"And the blind and the lame came to him in the temple; and he healed them."* (Mt. 21:14)

B. Specific, individual related miracles. Thirty-five:

1. Turning water into wine
2. Healing a nobleman's son at Cana
3. Healing a lame man at the pool of Bethesda
4. First miraculous catch of fish
5. Delivering a synagogue demoniac
6. Healing Peter's mother-in-law
7. Cleansing a leper
8. Healing a paralytic
9. Healing a man with a shriveled hand
10. Healing a centurion's servant

11. Raising a widow's son
12. Healing a blind and mute demoniac
13. Stilling a storm
14. Delivering the Gadarene demoniacs
15. Healing a woman with an issue of blood
16. Raising Jairus' daughter
17. Healing two blind men
18. Delivering a mute demon
19. Feeding the 5,000
20. Walking on the water
21. Delivering a Syrophoenician's daughter
22. Healing a deaf mute in Decapolis
23. Feeding 4,000
24. Healing a blind man at Bethsaida
25. Delivering a demon-possessed boy
26. Finding the tax money
27. Healing a man born blind
28. Healing a crippled woman on the Sabbath
29. Healing a man with dropsy
30. Raising of Lazarus
31. Cleansing ten lepers
32. Healing blind Bartimaeus
33. Cursing the fig tree
34. Restoring Malchus' ear
35. Second miraculous catch of fish

II. The Seven-Fold Classification of His Miracles

A. Healing. Sixteen miracles:
1. Lepers (see miracles 7, 31)
2. The blind (17, 24, 27, 32)
3. The deaf (22)
4. The deformed (9)
5. The crippled (3)
6. The fever-ridden (2, 6)
7. The maimed (34)
8. The paralyzed (8, 10)
9. Continuous bleeding (15)
10. Dropsy (29)
B. Casting out of demons. Seven miracles:
1. Man in a synagogue (see miracle 5)
2. A blind and mute demoniac (12)
3. The Gadarene demoniac (14)

4. A mute demoniac (18)

5. Daughter of a Syrophoenician mother (21)

6. A boy at the base of Mt. Hermon (25)

7. Woman in a synagogue (28)

C. Financing. One miracle:

1. Fish with a coin in its mouth (see miracle 26)

D. Feeding. Five miracles:

1. Turning water into wine (see miracle 1)

2. First catch of fish (4)

3. Feeding of the 5000 (19)

4. Feeding of the 4000 (23)

5. Second catch of fish (35)

E. Protecting. Two miracles:

1. Stilling a storm (see miracle 13)

2. Walking on water (20)

F. Resurrecting. Three miracles:

1. Raising a widow's son (see miracle 11)

2. Raising Jairus' daughter (16)

3. Raising of Lazarus (30)

G. Judging. One miracle:

1. Cursing a fig tree (see miracle 33)

III. The Eight-Fold Purpose for His Miracles

A. To fulfill O.T. prophecy

"When the even was come, they brought unto him many that were possessed with devils: and he cast out the spirits with his word, and healed all that were sick: That it might be fulfilled which was spoken by Esaias the prophet, saying, Himself took our infirmities, and bare our sicknesses." (Mt. 8:16-17)

"But though he had done so many miracles before them, yet they believed not on him: That the saying of Esaias the prophet might be fulfilled, which he spake, Lord, who hath believed our report? and to whom hath the arm of the Lord been revealed?" (Jn. 12:37-38)

B. To validate His message

"There was a man of the Pharisees, named Nicodemus, a ruler of the Jews: The same came to Jesus by night, and said unto him, Rabbi, we know that thou art a teacher come from God: for no man can do these miracles that thou doest, except God be with him." (Jn. 3:1-2)

"And a great multitude followed him, because they saw his miracles which he did on them that were diseased." (Jn. 6:2)

C. To reveal His glory

"This beginning of miracles did Jesus in Cana, of Galilee, and manifested forth his glory..." (Jn. 2:11a)

D. To increase the faith of His disciples

"and his disciples believed on him." (Jn. 2:11 b)

"When Jesus then lifted up his eyes, and saw a great company come unto him, he saith unto Philip, Whence shall we buy bread, that these may eat? And this he said to prove him: for he himself knew what he would do." (Jn. 6:5-6)

E. To declare His Messianic claims

"Then those men, when they had seen the miracle that Jesus did, said, This is of a truth that prophet that should come into the world." (Jn. 6:14)

F. To prove His deity

"And when they were come into the ship, the wind ceased. Then they that were in the ship came and worshipped him, saying, Of a truth thou art the Son of God." (Mt. 14:32-33)

G. To demonstrate His compassion

1. Upon the hungry multitudes (Mt. 9:36; 14:14; 15:32)
2. Upon the blind (Mt. 20:34)
3. Upon the lepers (Mk. 1:40-41)
4. Upon the demon-possessed (Mk. 5:18-19)
5. Upon the grief stricken (Lk. 7:12-13)

H. To show His authority to forgive sin

"And when he saw their faith, he said unto him, Man, thy sins are forgiven thee. And the scribes and the Pharisees began to reason, saying, Who is this which speaketh blasphemies? Who can forgive sins, but God alone? But when Jesus perceived their thoughts, he answering said unto them, What reason ye in your hearts? Whether is easier, to say, Thy sins be forgiven thee; or to say, Rise up and walk? But that ye may know that the Son of man hath power upon earth to forgive sins, (he said unto the sick of the palsy,) I say unto thee, Arise, and take up thy couch, and go into thine house." (Lk. 5:20-24)

IV. The Location of His Miracles

A. At a wedding (see miracle 1)
B. At a funeral (11)
C. In graveyards (14, 30)
D. In synagogues (5, 9, 28)
E. In homes (6, 8, 16, 29)
F. By a pool (3, 27)
G. Beside a tree (33)
H. In a garden (34)
I. In a crowd (15)
J. Outside a village (24, 31, 32)
K. On a grassy slope (19, 23)
L. At the base of a mountain (25)
M. On the seashore (4, 35)
N. On the sea (13, 20)
O. Under the sea (26)

THE MIRACLES PERFORMED BY JESUS

I. ONE: Turning Water Into Wine (Jn. 2:1-11)
A. Survey

During a wedding in Cana of Galilee, Jesus, at Mary's request, transforms approximately 120 gallons of water into wine, the quality of which is highly praised by the ruler of the feast.

B. Significance

■ This marks the second of four public encounters Mary had with Jesus. The other three are:
1. In a Jerusalem Temple (Lk. 2:41-52)

   "And when they saw him, they were amazed: and his mother said unto him, Son, why hast thou thus dealt with us? behold, thy father and I have sought thee sorrowing, And he said unto them, How is it that ye sought me? wist ye not that I must be about my fathers business?" (Lk. 2:48, 49)
2. In Capernaum (Mk. 3:31-35)

   "There came then his brethren and his mother, and, standing without, sent unto him, calling him. And the multitude sat about him, and they said unto him, Behold, thy mother and thy brethren without seek for thee." (Mk. 3:31, 32)
3. At Calvary (Jn. 19:26, 27)

■ It is the first of at least five occasions where the word "hour" is used in reference to Calvary ("mine hour is not yet come"). Other references would include:
1. At the feast of tabernacles— *"Then they sought to take him: but no man laid hands on him, because his hour was not yet come." (John 7:30)*
2. In the temple treasury— *"These words spake Jesus in the treasury, as he taught in the temple: and no man laid hands on him, for his hour was not yet come." (John 8:20)*
3. In the Upper Room— *"Now before the feast of the Passover, when Jesus knew that his hour was come that he should depart out of this world unto the Father, having loved his own which were in the world, he loved them unto the end." (John 13:1)*
4. On the Mount of Olives— *"These words spake Jesus, and lifted up his eyes to heaven, and said. Father, the hour is come; glorify thy Son, that thy Son may glorify thee." (John 17:1)*

C. Spiritual Truths

■ Jesus chose a wedding to perform His first miracle, doubtless to emphasize the sanctity of marriage. (See Gen. 2:18-25; Mt. 19:3-8; Eph. 5:22-33; Heb. 13:4.)

- Earthly weddings thus should serve as a reminder of that grand and glorious future wedding between Christ and His Church! (See 2 Cor. 11:2; Rev. 19:7-9.)

- It should be noted Jesus was invited on this occasion. It is always a wonderful thing when He is made welcome in a wedding!

- Jesus used water pots to accomplish his first miracle. He desires to do the same today, but now he uses living, earthly vessels. If we allow him, he fills us with the water of God's Word; and when we pour it out (give it out) it becomes the wine of the Spirit.

- While no Christian of course should pray to Mary, all believers would profit greatly from heeding her advice on this occasion: *"His mother saith unto the servants, Whatsoever he saith unto you, do it." (Jn. 2:5)*

- Jesus thus did this miracle to accomplish a three-fold purpose:
  1. To solve a difficult problem for Mary
  2. To increase the faith of His disciples
  3. To display His glory
     "This beginning of miracles did Jesus in Cana of Galilee, and manifested forth his glory; and his disciples believed on him." (Jn. 2:11)

- Was this real wine? The Greek word used here, oinos, can refer to either grape juice or wine.
  1. Examples in which it means juice:
     a. *"Neither do men put new wine [unfermented grape juice] into old bottles, else the bottles break, and the wine runneth out." (Matt. 9:17)*
     b. *"He treadeth the winepress of the fierceness and wrath of Almighty God." (Rev. 19:15)*
  2. Examples in which it means wine:
     a. *"Be not drunk with wine." (Eph. 5:18)*
     b. *"Drink no longer water, but use a little wine for thy stomachs sake and thine often infirmities." (1 Tim. 5:23)*

- If it was real wine Jesus created, it bore little if any resemblance to the modern product.
  1. In New Testament times wine was first boiled before storage, then diluted with three to ten parts water before serving.
  2. The Old Testament distinguishes between this wine and the strong, coarse, undiluted wine prepared solely to make one intoxicated.
     a. Both Noah and Lot became drunk on this wine (Gen. 9:21; 19:32-34)
     b. Drinking this kind of wine may have caused the death of Aaron's two priestly sons, both killed by God (Lev. 10:1-9)
     c. It was for the sin of national drunkenness that God would destroy Israel (Isa. 28:1-8)
     d. Daniel refused to defile himself by drinking this kind of wine (Dan. 1:8)
     e. The book of Proverbs warns against this kind of wine. *"Wine is a mocker, strong drink is raging, and whosoever is deceived thereby is not wise" (Prov. 20:1). "Look not thou upon the wine when it is red, when It giveth his colour in the cup, when it moveth itself aright. At the last it biteth like a serpent, and stingeth like an adder" (Prov. 23:31-32).*
     f. Habakkuk forbids the giving of this wine to one's neighbor (Hab. 2:14).
     g. Even the pagan Greeks felt only barbarians drank undiluted wine.
     h. The rabbis held that undiluted wine could not be blessed.

- Whatever the meaning of the word wine here in John 2, the sincere believer must carefully consider other Scripture passages even in the practice of social drinking. *"Abstain from all appearance of evil"* (1 Thess. 5:22). *"Whether therefore ye eat, or drink, or whatsoever ye do, do all to the glory of God. Give none offence, neither to the Jews, nor to the Gentiles, nor to the church of God"* (1 Cor. 10:31-32).

II. TWO: Healing a Nobleman's Son at Cana (Jn. 4:46-54)
A. Survey

A royal official in Cana asked Jesus to come and heal his son in Capernaum. The Savior sends him on his way, saying: "You may go. Your son will live."

Upon reaching Capernaum the amazed official discovers the healing had indeed occurred on the previous day at the 7th hour, the exact time Jesus had promised to heal him. This resulted in the father's conversion along with his entire household.

B. Significance

- This is the only recorded miracle which resulted in the spiritual salvation of an entire household.

- It is the first of 5 miracles in which a non-Jewish individual was involved. The other 4 are:
  1. A centurion's servant (Mt. 8:13)
  2. The maniac of Gadara (Mk. 5:8)
  3. A Canaanite girl (Mt. 15:28)
  4. One of the ten lepers (Lk. 17:11)

- It is the first of 3 miracles performed while the recipient was miles away. The other two are:
  1. The centurion's servant (Mt. 8:13)
  2. The Canaanite girl (Mt. 15:28; Mk. 7:30)

C. Spiritual Truths

- The ultimate intended purpose behind Jesus' healing miracles involved the restoration of both bodies and souls.

- This miracle illustrates that all similar prayer requests are instantly heard by and harkened to by God Himself. Various biblical examples record this precious and profound truth:
  1. The nobleman
     "So the father knew that it was at the same hour, in the which Jesus said unto him, Thy son liveth: and himself believed, and his whole house."(Jn. 4:53)
  2. Abraham's servant
     "And he said O LORD God of my master Abraham, I pray thee, send me good speed this day, and shew kindness unto my master Abraham. Behold, I stand here by the well of water; and the daughters of the men of the city come out to draw water; And let it come to pass, that the damsel to whom I shall say, Let down thy pitcher, I pray thee, that I may drink; and she shall say, Drink, and I will give thy camels drink also: let the same be she that thou hast appointed for thy servant Isaac; and thereby shall I know that thou hast shewed kindness unto my master. And it came to pass, before he had done speaking, that, behold, Rebekah came out, who was born to Bethuel, son of Milcah, the wife of Nahor, Abraham s brother, with her pitcher upon her shoulder."(Gen. 24:12-15)

3. Isaiah

> *"And it shall come to pass, that before they call, I will answer; and while they are yet speaking, I will hear."(Isa. 65:24)*

4. Daniel

> *"And, behold, an hand touched me, which set me upon my knees and upon the palms of my hands. And he said unto me, O Daniel, a man greatly beloved, understand the words that I speak unto thee, and stand upright: for unto thee am I now sent. And when he had spoken this word unto me, I stood trembling. Then said he unto me, Fear not, Daniel: for from the first day that thou didst set thine heart to understand, and to chasten thyself before thy God, thy words were heard, and I am come for thy words." (Dan. 10:10-12)*

III. THREE: Healing a Lame Man at the Pool of Bethesda (Jn. 4:46-54)
A. Survey

Jesus heals a man beside this pool near the sheep gate in Jerusalem who had been an invalid for 38 years.

B. Significance

■ This is the first of at least 4 occasions when Jesus was criticized for healing on the Sabbath. For the remaining 3, see miracles 9, 27, and 28.

C. Spiritual Truths

■ The statement, "Sir, I have no man," is profound in its spiritual implications. Both Luke and Paul later write concerning its importance:

1. Luke's testimony— *"And Philip ran thither to him, and heard him read the prophet Esaias, and said, Understandest thou what thou readest? And he said, How can I, except some man should guide me? And he desired Philip that he would come up and sit with him." (Acts 8:30-31)*

2. Paul's testimony— *"How then shall they call on him in whom they have not believed? and how shall they believe in him of whom they have not heard? and how shall they hear without a preacher? And how shall they preach, except they be sent? as it is written, How beautiful are the feet of them that preach the gospel of peace, and bring glad tidings of good things!" (Rom. 10:14-15)*

■ While Scripture is clear that personal suffering is not always a punishment caused by individual sin (Jn. 9:1-3), this case seems to be the exception. Note Jesus' warning to him:

> *"Afterward Jesus findeth him in the temple, and said unto him, Behold, thou art made whole: sin no more, lest a worse thing come unto thee."(Jn. 5:14)*

IV. FOUR: First Miraculous Catch of Fish (Lk. 5:1-11)
A. Survey

Four fishermen (Andrew, Peter, James, and John) had toiled all night without catching one single fish. However, at Jesus' command, Peter rowed out into the deep waters of the Galilean Sea and let down his nets. Immediately they caught so many fish that their nets began to break due to the huge catch, which fish soon filled their boats.

■ This is the first of 4 miracles done upon the Sea of Galilee. For the other 3, see miracles 3, 20, and 26.

■ It is the first of two miracles resulting in a supernatural catch of fish. Note the contrasts and comparisons however:
1. The comparisons
    a. On both occasions they had unsuccessfully fished all night (Lk. 5:5; Jn. 21:3)
    b. On both occasions they obeyed Jesus' command and were successful (Lk. 5:5, 6; Jn. 21:6)
    c. On both occasions Simon Peter was the key figure (Lk. 5:3-8; Jn. 21:7-11)
2. The contrasts
    a. On the first occasion the fishing net broke. On the second it did not (Lk. 5:6; Jn. 21:11)
    b. On the first occasion Jesus instructed Peter to "catch fish," while on the second He would command him to "feed sheep." (Lk. 5:10; Jn. 21:15-17)

C. Spiritual Truths

■ Peter would later fulfill Jesus' two-fold command to catch fish and feed sheep. Thus:
1. He caught fish!
    "Then they that gladly received his word were baptized and the same day there were added unto them about three thousand souls." (Acts 2:41)
2. He fed sheep!
    "As newborn babes, desire the sincere milk of the word, that ye may grow thereby: If so be ye have tasted that the Lord is gracious" (1 Pet. 2:2-3). "The elders which are among you I exhort, who am also an elder, and a witness of the sufferings of Christ, and also a partaker of the glory that shall be revealed: Feed the flock of God which is among you, taking the oversight thereof not by constraint, but willingly; not for filthy lucre, but of a ready mind" (1 Pet. 5:1-2).

■ It should be noted most of Jesus' apostles were busy at work when He called them, as were the God-called O.T. men. Note:
1. Moses and David were tending sheep (Ex. 3:1-2; 1 Sam. 16:11)
2. Gideon was threshing wheat (Judges 6:11-12)
3. Elisha was plowing a field (1 Kings 19:19-21)
4. Amos was herding cattle and picking fruit (Amos 1:1; 7:14-15)
5. Matthew was collecting taxes (Mt. 9:9)
6. Andrew, Peter, James, and John were fishing (Lk. 5:1-11)
7. Saul of Tarsus was arresting Christians in his misguided zeal as a Pharisee (Acts 9:1-6).
    The intended lesson here seems obvious--God's call upon a person is rarely (if ever) dependent upon his (or her) brain capacity, brawn, blue blooded history, or banking achievements, but rather just how busy that individual is at the time!
    Abraham's faithful servant had once given an eloquent testimony to this:
    "And he said, Blessed be the LORD God of my master Abraham, who hath not left destitute my master of his mercy and his truth: I being in the way, the LORD led me to the house of my masters brethren." (Gen. 24:27)

- Finally, it should be noted that these experienced fishermen did exactly what Jesus told them to do, even though it must have seemed unreasonable at the time. King Solomon once wrote:

    "Trust in the LORD with all thine heart; and lean not unto thine own understanding. In all thy ways acknowledge him, and he shall direct thy paths." (Prov. 3:5-6)

V. FIVE: Delivering a Demoniac in a Capernaum Synagogue (Mk. 1:23-28; Lk. 4:31-36)
A. Survey

Jesus was teaching on this occasion when He was suddenly and violently confronted by a demonpossessed man. The evil spirit immediately recognized Jesus as the Son of God, and, at the Savior's command, left his victim.

B. Significance

- This is the first of seven miracles where Jesus casts out evil spirits. For the other instances, see miracles 12, 14, 18, 21, 25, and 28.
- This is the first of at least 3 occasions when evil spirits gave terrified testimony that Jesus was indeed God's Son. Note:

    "And unclean spirits, when they saw him, fell down before him, and cried, saying, Thou art the Son of God." (Mk. 3:11)

    "And devils also came out of many, crying out, and saying, Thou art Christ the Son of God. And he rebuking them suffered them not to speak: for they knew that he was Christ." (Lk 4:41)

    James would later write of this:

    "Thou believest that there is one God; thou doest well: the devils also believe, and tremble." (James 2:19)

- This marks the first miracle performed in a synagogue.

C. Spiritual Truths

- It can be truly said that in the demonic world, unlike the world of sinful men, there are no atheists! These evil spirits knew exactly with whom they were dealing. Note:
  1. The demon called Him "Jesus of Nazareth," acknowledging the Savior's humanity.
  2. The demon called Him, "thou Son of God," acknowledging the Savior's deity.

VI. SIX: Healing Peter's Mother-in-law (Mt. 8:14-15; Mk. 1:29-31; Lk. 4:38-39)
A. Survey

Upon hearing that she was suffering from a high fever, Jesus visits the home of Peter's mother-inlaw and raised her from the bed of affliction. The grateful woman then began to wait upon the Savior and His disciples.

B. Significance

- This is the first of two occasions proving Peter was a married man. For the other, see 1 Cor. 9:5.
- It is the first miracle to be recorded by three gospel writers (Matthew, Mark, and Luke).

■ This miracle is followed by numerous occasions where Jesus performed mass healings. Note:
1. After healing Peter's mother-in-law (Mt. 8:16)
2. After healing a leper (Lk. 5:15)
3. After healing a man with a withered hand (Mt. 12:15)
4. After hearing of John the Baptist's death (Mt. 14:14)
5. After walking on the water (Mt. 14:35)
6. After healing a demon possessed girl (Mt. 15:30)
7. Prior to His sermon on divorce (Mt. 19:2)
8. After His temple cleansing (Mt. 21:14)

C. Spiritual Truths

■ Upon being healed, she immediately began serving Jesus as did the maniac of Gadara (Mk. 5:18). We have been saved to serve! Paul would later link both these together in his epistle to the church in Ephesus:

"For by grace are ye saved through faith; and that not of yourselves: it is the gift of God: Not of works, lest any man should boast. For we are his workmanship, created in Christ Jesus unto good works, which God hath before ordained that we should walk in them." (Eph. 2:8-10)

VII. SEVEN: Cleansing a Leper (Mt. 8:2-4; Mk. 1:40-45; Lk. 9:12-16)
A. Survey

A leper approached Jesus, knelt, and begged to be delivered from his leprosy. Filled with compassion the Savior touched him which resulted in immediate healing.

B. Significance

■ This is the first of at least 6 miracles where Jesus was moved with compassion. For the others, see miracles 11, 14, 19, 23, and 32.

■ It is the first of 5 miracles where Jesus told the recipient not to broadcast what had been done. For the others, see 16, 17, 22, and 24.

■ It is the first of 2 miracles involving a leper. See also miracle 31.

C. Spiritual Truths

■ It is ironic to note:
1. Back then, Jesus commanded these individuals not to spread abroad his fame, but they did.
2. Today he commands us to do this, but we don't (see Mt. 28:19-20).

■ He ordered the cured man to present himself to the priest for the Mosaic cleansing (see Lev. 14:3-4, 10, 22). This excited request from a healed leper doubtless caused much confusion and amazement in the temple among the priests. Up until this point there was no need for the cleansing ceremony, for no Israelite had ever been healed of leprosy until Jesus came (with the single exception of Miriam—see Num. 12:13-15; Naaman, of course, was a Syrian—see 2 Kings 5:1, 14).

VIII. EIGHT: Healing a Paralytic (Mt. 9:2-8; Mk. 2:3-12; Lk. 5:18-26)

A. Survey

Four friends of a paralytic, unable to approach Jesus because of a huge crowd, made an opening in the roof and lowered their companion at Jesus' feet. The Savior immediately both forgave the man of his sins and healed him of his affliction.

B. Significance

- This miracle describes the most unique and innovative way of bringing a person to Jesus.

- It is the first miracle where Jesus forgives the sin of the person, thus announcing His deity, for God alone can forgive sin.

C. Spiritual Truths

- Both Paul and Jude may well have had the four friends of the paralytic when they penned the following words:

    "For though I be free from all men, yet have I made myself servant unto all, that I might gain the more. And unto the Jews I became as a Jew, that I might gain the Jews; to them that are under the law, as under the law, that I might gain them that are under the law; To them that are without law, as without law, (being not without law to God, but under the law to Christ,) that I might gain them that are without law. To the weak became I as weak, that I might gain the weak: I am made all things to all men, that I might by all means save some." (1 Cor. 9:19-22)

    "And of some have compassion, making a difference: And others save with fear, pulling them out of the fire; hating even the garment spotted by the flesh." (Jude 22-23)

- An unknown author has written the following:

    They will not seek, they must be sought,
    They will not come, they must be brought,
    They will not learn, they must be taught.

- J. Vernon McGee writes: "There are many people who are not going to receive the message of salvation unless you lift a corner of their stretcher and carry them to the place where they can hear the word of the Lord. They are paralyzed—immobilized by sin and by many other things the world holds for them. Some are paralyzed by prejudice and others by indifference. They are never going to hear Jesus say to them, 'Son, thy sins be forgiven thee,' unless you take the corner of their stretcher and bring them to Him.' "(Commentary on Luke, p. 74)

IX. NINE: Healing a Man With a Shriveled Hand (Mt. 12:9-13; Mk. 3:1-5; Lk. 6:6-10)

A. Survey

Jesus restores this hand in a synagogue on the Sabbath day. Keenly aware that His action was condemned by the legalistic and wicked Pharisees who were watching His every move, the Savior demanded from them:

"I ask you, which is lawful on the Sabbath: to do good, or to do evil, to save life or to destroy it?"

B. Significance

■ This miracle included the only explicit reference to the anger of Jesus in the 4 gospel accounts. Note Mark's account:

> *"And, when He had looked round about on them with anger..."* (Mk. 3:5)

■ This miracle led to the first plot to kill Jesus. Note:

> *"Then the Pharisees went out, and held a council against him, how they might destroy him."* (Mt. 12:14)

C. Spiritual Truths

■ This episode may well serve as the ultimate illustration of legalism, which places a higher value on a sheep than on a man!

■ Jesus had previously explained the divine purpose of the Sabbath and His relationship to it:

> *"And he said unto them, The sabbath was made for man, and not man for the sabbath: Therefore the Son of man is Lord also of the sabbath."* (Mk. 2:27-28)

X. TEN: Healing a Centurion's Servant (Mt. 8:5-13; Lk. 7:1-10)
A. Survey

This Gentile military officer who loved Israel and had actually built a synagogue for the Jews implored Jesus to heal his dying servant. Jesus agreed to go and heal him. However, the officer replied:

"No need Lord, just say the word and it will be done."

The Savior is amazed at this kind of faith. Upon returning to his home the centurion finds his servant healed!

B. Significance

■ This is the first of two cases involving miracles in which Jesus was amazed at the great amount of faith he found in the one requesting the miracle. Both individuals were Gentiles. The other was the Syro-phoenician mother (Mt. 15:28).

■ How sad to note that he marveled over the unbelief and lack of faith in his own countrymen. *"But Jesus said unto them, A prophet is not without honour, but in his own country, and among his own kin, and in his own house...And he marvelled because of their unbelief. And he went round about the villages, teaching."* (Mk. 6:4, 6)

C. Spiritual Truths

■ Almost all centurions (Roman military commanders of 100 soldiers) in the Bible are presented in a favorable light. Examples:
 1. The one mentioned here
 2. The centurion in charge of Jesus' crucifixion
    > *"And Jesus cried with a loud voice, and gave up the ghost. And when the centurion, which stood over against him, saw that he so cried out, and gave up the ghost, he said, Truly this man was the Son of God."* (Mk. 15:37, 39)
    > *"Now when the centurion saw what was done, he glorified God, saying, Certainly this was a righteous man."* (Lk. 23:47)
 3. The centurion whom Peter led to Christ

"There was a certain man in Caesarea called Cornelius, a centurion of the band called the Italian band, A devout man, and one that feared God with all his house, which gave much alms to the people, and prayed to God alway." (Acts 10:1-2)

4. The centurion who was in charge of Paul's first part of his journey to Rome.

"And when it was determined that we should sail into Italy, they delivered Paul and certain other prisoners unto one named Julius, a centurion of Augustus' band... And the next day we touched at Sidon. And Julius courteously entreated Paul, and gave him liberty to go unto his friends to refresh himself. " (Acts 27:1, 3)

5. The centurion who later saved Paul from death following the storm.

"And the soldiers' counsel was to kill the prisoners, lest any of them should swim out, and escape. But the centurion, willing to save Paul, kept them from their purpose, and commanded that they which could swim should cast themselves first into the sea, and get to land." (Acts 27:42-43)

6. The centurion who allowed Paul to receive visitors during his house arrest in Rome.

"And when we came to Rome, the centurion delivered the prisoners to the captain of the guard but Paul was suffered to dwell by himself with a soldier that kept him." (Acts 28:16)

■ This is in stark contrast to the Jewish rulers who misunderstood their own scriptures and mistreated both Jewish and Gentile believers. Note the following indictments:

1. By Jesus (Mt. 22:29; 23:33)
2. By Stephen (Acts 7:51-53)
3. By Paul (Rom. 9:30-32; 1 Thess. 2:14-16)
4. By John the Baptist (Mt. 3:7-12)
5. By John the Apostle (Rev. 2:8-9)

XI. ELEVEN: Raising a Widow's Son (Lk. 7:11-15)
A. Survey

Jesus meets a funeral procession as He enters the little town of Nain. They were sorrowing over the death of a widow's only son. Approaching the coffin He orders the body to rise, which it does, filling the heart of the grief-stricken mother with joy.

B. Significance

■ This marks the first of three persons raised from the dead by Christ. The other two are Jairus' daughter (Lk. 8:54-56) and Lazarus (Jn. 11:43). The last resurrection had occurred some seven centuries previous to this when the bones of Elisha had restored to life a young man (2 Kings 13:20-22).

■ This is the first recorded instance in which Jesus was recognized by the Jewish crowds as a prophet, although the earliest acknowledgment came from a non-Jewish Samaritan woman (see John 4:19).

1. Jesus called himself a prophet (Mt. 13:57; Jn. 4:44).
2. Herod Antipas suspected it (Mt. 14:5).
3. The crowds on two future occasions would acknowledge it.
   a. During the Feast of Tabernacles (Jn. 7:40)
   b. During the triumphal entry (Mt. 21:11)
4. The 5,000 men Christ fed believed it (Jn. 6:14).
5. A former blind man testified to it (Jn. 9:17).

6. The two disciples en route to Emmaus spoke of it (Lk.24:19).

C. Spiritual Truths

■ It has been rightly observed that Jesus provided no specific instructions to pastors in regards to the proper conducting of funerals, for He simply dismissed the service by raising the deceased!

■ Note the reaction of the amazed crowd:

> "God hath visited his people." (Lk. 7:16)

This was a direct fulfillment of Zacharias' prophecy given during the circumcision ceremony of his infant son, John the Baptist.

> "And his father Zacharias was filled with the Holy Ghost, and prophesied, saying, Blessed be the Lord God of Israel; for he hath visited and redeemed his people... Through the tender mercy of our God; whereby the dayspring from on high hath visited us" (Lk. 1:67-68, 78).

XII. TWELVE: Delivering a Blind and Mute Demoniac (Mt. 12:22; Lk. 11:14)
A. Survey

Jesus delivers this poor wretched man of his demon, and restores both his speech and sight. The wicked Pharisees thereupon accuse Him of doing this miracle through the power of Satan.

B. Significance

■ This is both the shortest and most action-packed of all His miracles!

C. Spiritual Truths

■ Jesus probably did more for the person involved than can be found in any other miracle. It would be difficult to imagine being in a more desperate situation than the one that is described at this point. Here was a blind, deaf, mute, and demon-possessed man. But then Jesus passed by. And the results?
1. The man could see.
2. The man could hear.
3. The man could speak.
4. The man could worship.

■ Thus, in a split second he received sight, sound, speech, and (probably) salvation.

■ The charge by the wicked Pharisees that He had done this miracle through the power of Satan prompted Jesus to warn them in regards to the unpardonable sin.

> "But when the Pharisees heard it, they said, This fellow doth not cast out devils, but by Beelzebub the prince of the devils... Wherefore I "say unto you, All manner of sin and blasphemy shall be forgiven unto men: but the blasphemy against the Holy Ghost shall not be forgiven unto men. And whosoever speaketh a word against the Son of man, it shall be forgiven him: but whosoever speaketh against the Holy Ghost, it shall not be forgiven him, neither in this world, neither in the world to come." (Mt. 12:24, 31-32)

A. Survey

The disciples were caught in a furious storm on the Sea of Galilee which threatened to sink their boat. Awakening Jesus, who had fallen into an exhausted sleep in the ship's stern, the terrified men cried out: "Lord, save us from drowning!" The Savior then stood up and rebuked both the wind and the waves, resulting in a great calm.

B. Significance

■ This is the only recorded reference to Jesus being asleep.

■ It is the first of two occasions where Jesus saved His disciples from drowning. See also miracle 20.

C. Spiritual Truths

■ One of the most famous Old Testament miracles had to do with a sleeping Hebrew prophet in a boat during a storm. One of the most famous New Testament miracles also had to do with a sleeping Hebrew prophet in a boat during a storm. The Old Testament prophet was Jonah. The New Testament prophet was Jesus. The second would later use the experience of the first as a sign to an unbelieving generation: *"For as Jonah was three days and three nights in the whales belly; so shall the Son of man be three days and three nights in the heart of the earth." (Mt. 12:40)*

■ Note the phrase, "they took him even as he was" Our Lord was a real man, with dirt under his fingernails, sweat on his brow, and on this occasion, weariness in his bones.

■ The Greek word here refers to a violent storm, a furious squall of hurricane proportion. The Sea of Galilee, situated in a basin surrounded by mountains, is particularly susceptible to sudden, violent storms. Cool air from the Mediterranean is drawn down through the narrow mountain passes connecting the two bodies of water, and clashes with the hot, humid air lying over the lake. Thus, in a matter of seconds, the quiet Galilean waters can be turned into a howling, lifethreatening watery nightmare for all those sailing upon it.

■ Note the words as recorded by Mark's account:
"And he arose, and rebuked the wind, and said unto the sea, Peace, be still, And the wind ceased, and there was a great calm." (Mk. 4:39)
The language of this verse strongly suggests that the vicious storm may have been caused by satanic activity, perhaps in an attempt to drown Jesus.
1. The Greek word for rebuke is epitimao, a word Jesus used in denouncing both Satan and his demons.
    a. The rebuking of demons (Lk.9:42; Mt. 17:18)
    b. The rebuking of Satan (Mk. 8:33; Jude 1:9)
2. The Greek word for peace, phimoo, used only here and in Mk. 1:25 (where Jesus denounced a demon), mean literally, "be muzzled, be gagged." This action often referred to the muzzling of a wild dog.

■ There are many lessons to be learned today from this miracle. Three questions should be asked when the storms of life beset the Christian.
1. Is this storm one of punishment or purification? That is, am I being chastened for my sin (as was true in the case of Jonah), or is this simply a trial allowed by God to purify me (as was true here with the disciples)?

2. Have I made room for him on board? Am I aware of his presence?

3. What does he want me to do in the time of the storm? In a nutshell, three things:

   a. He wants me to thank him for the storm. *"In every thing give thanks: for this is the will of God in Christ Jesus concerning you." (1 Thess. 5:18)*

   b. He wants me to fellowship with him in the storm. *"Pray without ceasing." (1 Thess. 5:17)*

   c. He wants me to trust him through the storm. *"Trust in the Lord with all thine heart, and lean not unto thine own understanding. In all thy ways acknowledge him, and he shall direct thy paths." (Prov. 3:5-6)*

XIV. FOURTEEN: Delivering the Maniac of Gadara (Mt. 8:28-34; Mk. 5:1-20; Lk. 8:26-39)

A. Survey

Jesus Upon stepping ashore in the land of Gadara, Jesus is confronted by and speaks to the leader of a band of demons who were possessing a violent and uncontrollable maniac. The Savior orders them to leave the victim, and, at their request, permits them to enter a herd of nearby pigs, which results in the death of those animals by drowning as they plunge into the Sea of Galilee.

B. Significance

■ This is perhaps the most graphic and terrifying account of demon possession in all the Bible.
Note the recorded facts regarding this man:

1. His home— *"Who had his dwelling among the tombs" (Mk. 5:3).*

2. His helplessness

   a. He was naked (Lk. 8:27)

   b. He was *"exceeding fierce"* (Mt. 8:28)

   c. He was totally unmanageable (Mk. 5:3-4)

   d. He was constantly crying and cutting himself with stones (Mk. 5:5)

   e. He was seized upon and driven about by a legion of demons (Lk. 8:29; Mk. 5:9). The usage of the word legion here may indicate the man was possessed by as many as 6000 demons.

■ This shows just how many fallen angels there may be if Satan could afford to spare 6000 on a worthless madman!

■ It is the only recorded extended conversation between Jesus and a demon.

■ This is the first of two occasions on which Jesus performed a miracle in a way that had destructive results (the death of the pigs). The other miracle was the withering of the fig tree (Mt. 21:19).

■ This is the only miracle where Jesus instructed the recipient as follows: *"Go home to thy friends and tell them how great things the Lord hath done for thee, and hath had compassion on thee" (Mk. 5:19).* This is in stark contrast as seen in the other healing miracles where Jesus commanded the healed not to tell anyone!

C. Spiritual Truths

■ What a contrast is seen in this wretched demoniac following his glorious conversion: He now is:

1. Sitting, not screaming.

2. Praising, not cursing.

3. Dressed, not naked.
4. In his right mind, not insane.
5. A convert of Christ, not a captive of Satan.

■ This account might well be entitled, "How A Madman Became a Missionary." We have previously observed Jesus' instructions that he should tell others what had been done, which he did.

"*And he departed, and began to publish in Decapolis how great things Jesus had done for him: and all men did marvel.*" *(Mk. 5:20)*

Decapolis (literally, "ten cities") was a league of ten cities characterized by high Greek culture, allied together for purposes of trading. All but one city (Scythopolis) were east of the Galilean Sea and Jordan River. This convert thus became the greatest missionary to Gentiles since the preacher to Nineveh, Jonah the prophet.

■ Why did the demons desire the bodies of pigs? Several reasons have been suggested:
1. To kill Jesus and his disciples. Few animals are more dangerous than angry wild pigs.
2. To turn the community against Jesus by drowning the pigs. If this was the plan, they succeeded.
   Note the tragic reaction of the crowd:

   "*Then they went out to see what was done; and came to Jesus, and found the man, out of whom the devils were departed, sitting at the feet of Jesus, clothed, and in his right mind and they were afraid... Then the whole multitude of the country of the Gadarenes round about besought him to depart from them; for they were taken with great fear: and he went up into the ship, and returned back again.*" *(Lk. 8:35, 37)*

■ These people were more interested in money than in men. They preferred gold to God. They wanted their pigs more than they desired what Christ had to offer. John Oxenham has vividly captured their tragic philosophy in his poem:

Rabbi, begone!

Thy powers bring loss to us and ours; Our ways are not as Thine

Thou lovest men-we swine.

O get Thee gone, O Holy One,

And take these fools of Thine;

Their souls? What care we for their souls?

Since we have lost our swine.

Then Christ went sadly,

He had wrought for them a sign

Of love and tenderness divine

They wanted swine.

Christ stands without your door and gently knocks,

But if your gold or swine the entrance blocks

He forces no man's hold, He will depart,

And leave you to the treasures of your heart.

From "Gadara, A.D. 31"

■ Note the terrible fear exhibited by this horde of demons in the presence of Jesus:
1. They knew him—"*And behold, they cried out, saying, What have we to do with thee, Jesus, thou Son of God?*" *(Mt. 8:29)*

2. They feared him— *"Art thou come hither to torment us before the time?" (Mt. 8:29) "I adjure thee by God, that thou torment me not." (Mk. 5:7b)*

■ They apparently knew about future judgment. Various New Testament writers attest to this judgment of fallen angels.

1. **Paul**: *"Know ye not that we shall judge angels? How much more things that pertain to this life?" (1 Cor. 6:3)*
2. **Peter**: *"For if God spared not the angels that sinned, but cast them down to hell, and delivered them into chains of darkness, to be reserved unto judgment." (2 Pet. 2:4)*
3. **Jude**: *"And the angels which kept not their first estate, but left their own habitation, he hath reserved in everlasting chains under darkness unto the judgment of the great day." (Jude 6)*

   In fact, Jesus said that hell itself was originally created for the devil and his angels, all of which will eventually spend eternity there. *"Then shall he say also unto them on the left hand, Depart from me, ye cursed, into everlasting fire, prepared for the devil and his angels" (Mt. 25:41). "And the devil that deceived them was cast into the lake of fire and brimstone, where the beast and the false prophet are, and shall be tormented day and night for ever and ever." (Rev. 20:10)*

■ The account in Matthew's gospel informs us there were actually two demon possessed men on this occasion (Mt. 8:28). One wonders what happened to the other man. Was he also gloriously delivered? Or, tragically, would he be like the unrepentant thief on the cross? (See Lk. 24:39-43.)

XV. FIFTEEN: Healing a Woman With An Issue of Blood (Mt. 9:20-22; Mk. 5:25-34; Lk. 8:43-48)
A. Survey

A woman who had suffered with internal bleeding for 12 years, being unable to be helped by her physicians, approaches Jesus in a crowd and by faith touches the hem of His garment, resulting in her immediate healing.

B. Significance

■ This is the only miracle where the person in need touched Jesus first.

■ It is the only time where Jesus uses the title "daughter". On a previous occasion He had referred to a paralytic who had been healed as "son" (Mt. 9:2).

C. Spiritual Truths

■ This poor woman's condition carried with it religious and social consequences as well as physical consequences. According to Leviticus 15:19-30, she would have been considered unclean for twelve long years. Note also she had spent all her resources on her problem. Thus, she was pain-wracked, penniless, and prohibited from social gatherings. But then, we read, she ... "heard of Jesus"

■ Luke describes the aftermath of this healing as follows:

   "And Jesus said, Who touched me? When all denied, Peter and they that were with him said, Master, the multitude throng thee and press thee, and sayest thou, Who touched me? And Jesus said, Somebody hath touched me: for I perceive that virtue is gone out of me." (Lk. 8:45-46)

■ The two statements of Jesus here point out two profound insights concerning his earthly ministry.

1. His total dependence upon the Holy Spirit—Note his question, "Who touched me?" Even though Christ retained his divine attributes (his omnipresence, his omnipotence, his omniscience) upon coming to earth, he chose not to use them in an independent way, but depended upon the Holy Spirit to lead, advise, and empower him. In other words, Jesus may not have known at that moment who touched him. A similar example can be seen later when he was asked concerning the date of the second coming.

   His answer was: *"But of that day and that hour knoweth no man, no, not the angels which are in heaven, neither the Son, but the Father" (Mk. 13:32).* (See also Mt. 4:1; Jn. 5:19; Phil. 2:5-8.)

2. The awful demands upon his physical body—Note his statement: "Virtue is gone out of me." The Greek word for virtue here is dunamis, and refers to power or strength. How taxing it must have been upon his body to perform his mighty miracles.

   A hint of this may be seen through a statement made by some Pharisees during a confrontation with Jesus. Note:

   "Your father Abraham rejoiced to see my day: and he saw it, and was glad. Then said the Jews unto him, Thou art not yet fifty years old, and hast thou seen Abraham? Jesus said unto them, Verily, verily, I say unto you, Before Abraham was, I am." (Jn. 8:56-58)

   The point of the above is that Jesus apparently looked to be much older than He really was, being mistaken for nearly fifty (an advanced age back then) when in reality He had yet to celebrate His 33rd birthday! Caring for the sick in the world and, at the same time, carrying the sins of the world was exhausting labor indeed!

XVI. SIXTEEN: Raising Jairus' Daughter (Mt. 9:18-19,23-26; Mk. 5:22-24,35-43; Lk. 8:41-42,49-56)

A. Survey

At Jairus' request, Jesus agrees to minister to his dying daughter, but the father is told en route that she was already dead. Ignoring this bad news Jesus comforts him, and, entering the little girl's room, raises her up!

B. Significance

■ There are three "'firsts" associated with this miracle: It is the first time in human history that a female was raised from the dead.

1. It is the first mention of that special apostolic trio, Peter, James and John. They would be singled out again:
   a. On the Mount of Transfiguration (Mt. 17:1)
   b. In the Garden of Gethsemane (Mk. 14:33)
2. It is the first time the word "sleep" is used to describe the death of a believer. After this, its employment will become very familiar:
   a. Concerning the death of Lazarus—*"These things said he: and after that he saith unto them, Our friend Lazarus sleepeth; but I go, that I may awake him out of sleep" (Jn. 11:11).*
   b. Concerning an event after the death of Chris—*"And the graves were opened; and many bodies of the saints which slept arose" (Mt. 27:52).*
   c. Concerning the martyrdom of Stephen—*"And he kneeled down, and cried with a loud voice, Lord, lay not this sin to their charge. And when he had said this, he fell asleep" (Acts 7:60).*

d. Concerning the bodies of departed believers at the present time—*"For God hath not appointed us to wrath, but to obtain salvation by our Lord Jesus Christ, who died for us, that, whether we wake or sleep, we should live together with him"* (1 Thess. 5:9-10).

e. Concerning the rapture—*"For if we believe that Jesus died and rose again, even so them also which sleep in Jesus will God bring with him"* (1 Thess. 4:14).

C. Spiritual Truths

■ Note the pessimistic statement from the officiating clergyman on that occasion:

"While he yet spake, there came from the ruler of the synagogue's house certain which said, Thy daughter is dead: why troublest thou the Master any further?" (Mk. 5:35)

Wrong. This is precisely the time for a believer to "trouble ... the Master". As the song admonishes:

"Got any rivers you think are uncrossable?
Got any mountains you can't tunnel through?
God specializes in things thought impossible.
What He's done for others, He'll do for you!"

■ This pessimism would later be heard, this time by a crowd at Jericho in regards to the cry of blind Bartimaeus:

"And when he heard that it was Jesus of Nazareth, he began to cry out, and say, Jesus, thou son of David, have mercy on me. And many charged him that he should hold his peace: but he cried the more a great deal, Thou son of David, have mercy on me... And Jesus said unto him, Go thy way; thy faith hath made thee whole. And immediately he received his sight, and followed Jesus in the way." (Mk. 10:47-48, 52)

XVII. SEVENTEEN: Healing Two Blind Men (Mt. 9:27-31)

A. Survey

Hearing the pitiful cries of two sightless men, Jesus asks if they believe He could indeed heal them. Upon their affirmative response, the Savior touches their eyes and restores their sight.

B. Significance

■ This is the first of three occasions where Jesus is referred to as the Son of David by the recipient of a miracle. For the other two, see miracles 21 and 32.

■ This is the first of four miracles where Jesus restored sight to the blind. For the other three, see miracles 24, 27 and 32.

C. Spiritual Truths

■ Note the urgent cry of these two men: *"Have mercy on us."* (Mt. 9:27) It has been said that God will hush every harp in heaven to hear and answer this kind of prayer. This is the first of at least five miracles performed by Christ to answer such a prayer request.

1. The Syrophoenician mother (Mt. 15:22)
2. The father of a demon-possessed son (Mt. 17:15)

3. Ten lepers (Lk. 17:13)

4. Blind Bartimaeus (Lk. 18:38)

■ Jesus' response, "According to your faith, be it unto you" (Mt. 9:29). These words indicate these two men received both physical and spiritual eyesight. Isaiah and David had originally written concerning this two-fold sight:

1. Isaiah spoke in regards to physical eyesight—"Then the eyes of the blind shall be opened." (Isa. 35:5)

2. David spoke in regards to spiritual eyesight—*"Open thou mine eyes, that I may behold wondrous things out of thy law." (Psa. 119:18)*

XVIII. EIGHTEEN: Delivering a Mute Demoniac (Mt. 9:32-33)
A. Survey

Jesus heals this poor man who immediately begins to speak, causing the watching crowd to gasp in amazement.

B. Significance

■ This is the second of two occasions where Jesus was accused of performing His miracles in the energy of Satan. These two are:

1. *"But when the Pharisees heard it, they said, This fellow doth not cast out devils, but by Beelzebub the prince of the devils." (Mt. 12:24)*

2. *"But the Pharisees said, He casteth out devils through the prince of the devils." (Mt. 9:34)*

■ On four other later occasions the wicked Pharisees would accuse Jesus of preaching His messages by the power of the devil.

1. *"The people answered and said, Thou hast a devil: who goeth about to kill thee?" (Jn. 7:20)*

2. *"Then answered the Jews, and said unto him, Say we not well that thou art a Samaritan, and hast a devil?" (Jn. 8:48)*

3. *"Then said the Jews unto him, Now we know that thou hast a devil. Abraham is dead, and the prophets; and thou sayest, If a man keep my saying, he shall never taste of death." (Jn. 8:52)*

4. *"And many of them said, He hath a devil, and is mad; why hear ye him?" (Jn. 10:20)*

C. Spiritual Truths

■ Charles Wesley's great hymn, "O For A Thousand Tongues" beautifully summarizes this miracle. Note the words of stanza number 5:

> *"Hear Him, ye deaf; His praise, ye dumb,*
> *Your loosened tongues employ;*
> *Ye blind, behold your Savior come;*
> *And leap, ye lame, for joy."*

■ Note the testimony of the crowd following this miracle:

"It was never so seen in Israel" (Mt. 9:33).

How true, for there was never such a man so seen in Israel as this man! Note the following testimonies which confirm this fact:

1. Nicodemus

   "The same came to Jesus by night, and said unto him, Rabbi, we know that thou art a teacher come from God: for no man can do these miracles that thou doest, except God be with him." (Jn. 3:2)

2. His hometown people

   "And when he was come into his own country, he taught them in their synagogue, insomuch that they were astonished, and said, Whence hath this man this wisdom, and these mighty works? Is not this the carpenters son? Is not his mother called Mary? and his brethren, James, and Joses, and Simon, and Judas?" (Mt. 13:54-55)

3. Some soldiers in Jerusalem

   "Then came the officers to the chief priests and Pharisees; and they said unto them, Why have ye not brought him? The officers answered, Never man spake like this man." (Jn. 7:45-46)

XIX. NINETEEN: Feeding the 5000 (Mt. 14:14-21; Mk. 6:34-44; Lk. 9:12-17; Jn. 6:5-13)
A. Survey

With but five loaves of bread and two small fishes, donated by a small lad, Jesus feeds 5000 men plus their wives and children. After all had eaten to their satisfaction, there remained twelve basketfuls of food.

B. Significance

■ This is Jesus' only miracle recorded by all four gospel writers.

■ Obviously there were more individuals involved than in any other miracle.

■ It is the only miracle where someone (a small boy) contributed something to the action involved.

■ It marks the only attempt by an Israelite crowd to crown Jesus as King (Jn. 6:14-15).

■ It is the only miracle where He asks His disciples some questions. *"Where shall we buy bread for these people to eat?" (Jn. 6:5), "How many loaves do you have?" (Mk. 6:38)*

■ It is the only miracle where He asks His disciples to serve Him: *"Bring me the five loaves and two fishes" (Mt. 14:17-18), "Have the people sit down." (Lk. 9:14-15)*

C. Spiritual Truths

■ At this time, Jesus fulfilled the prophecies of Ezekiel concerning the ministry of the promised Good Shepherd.

   "For thus saith the Lord God; Behold, I, even I, will both search my sheep, and seek them out. As a shepherd seeketh out his flock in the day that he is among his sheep that are scattered, so will I seek out my sheep, and will deliver them out of all places where they have been scattered in the cloudy and dark day. ...I will feed them in a good pasture, and upon the high mountains of Israel shall their fold be there shall they lie in a good fold, and in a fat pasture shall they feed upon the mountains of Israel." (Ezek. 34:11-12, 14)

■ In John 10 Jesus would later describe His role as the Good Shepherd, but here He will demonstrate it! Note:
   1. He was the sensitive shepherd

a. He knew the needs of the twelve

"And the apostles gathered themselves together unto Jesus, and told him all things, both what they had done, and what they had taught. And he said unto them, Come ye yourselves apart into a desert place, and rest a while: for there were many coming and going, and they had no leisure so much as to eat. And they departed into a desert place by ship privately." (Mk. 6:30-32)

The disciples needed this rest, for they had just learned of John the Baptist's martyrdom. In addition, they were approaching the danger of burnout.

b. He knew the needs of the crowd

"And Jesus, when he came out, saw much people, and was moved with compassion toward them, because they were as sheep not having a shepherd: and he began to teach them many things." (Mk. 6:34)

(1) They needed to be taught

Hosea the prophet had once cried out: *"My people are destroyed for lack of knowledge" (Hos. 4:6)*. To counteract this, our Lord invested a great amount of time during his earthly ministry in teaching the Word of God. *"And they were astonished at his doctrine: for he taught them as one that had authority, and not as the scribes" (Mk. 1:22)*. (See also Mt. 4:23; 5:2; 7:29; 9:35; 11:1; 13:54; Jn. 6:59; 7:14, 28; 8:2, 20; 18:20.)

(2) They needed to be healed

"And he healed them that had need of healing." (Lk. 9:11)

(3) They needed to be fed

It is estimated that it would have required some fifteen tons of food to feed this great multitude.

2. He was the systematic shepherd

"And he commanded them to make all sit down by companies upon the green grass. And they sat down in ranks, by hundreds, and by fifties." (Mk. 6:39-40)

3. He was the sovereign shepherd

"And when he had taken the five loaves and the two fishes, he looked up to heaven, and blessed, and brake the loaves, and gave them to his disciples to set before them; and the two fishes divided he among them all. And they did all eat, and were filled." (Mk. 6:41-42)

4. He was the sufficient shepherd

"When they were filled, he said unto his disciples, Gather up the fragments that remain, that nothing be lost. Therefore they gathered them together, and filled twelve baskets with the fragments of the five barley loaves, which remained over and above unto them that had eaten." (Jn. 6:12-13)

■ There is a note of sorrow at the end of this otherwise fantastic miracle. Rightfully recognizing him as a prophet, the 5,000 men wrongly attempted to make him their king. But both their motive and their method were wrong.

1. Their motive was wrong.

Jesus himself would point this out during his sermon on the following day.

"Jesus answered them and said, Verily, verily, I say unto you, Ye seek me, not because ye saw the miracles, but because ye did eat of the loaves, and were filled. Labour not for the meat which perisheth, but for that meat which endureth unto everlasting fife, which the Son of man shall give unto you: for him hath God the Father sealed." (Jn. 6:26-27)

In a previous incident, another group of men had made the same mistake.

"Now when he was in Jerusalem at the Passover, in the feast day, many believed in his name, when they saw the miracles which he did. But Jesus did not commit himself unto them, because he knew all men, And needed not that any should testify of man: for he knew what was in man." (Jn. 2:23-25)

2. Their method was wrong.

Jesus did not come to be crowned by sinful people, but rather to be crucified for sinful people. The Father alone will someday give the Son his rightful kingdom. *"And the seventh angel sounded; and there were great voices in heaven, saying, The kingdoms of this world are become the kingdoms of our Lord, and of his Christ; and he shall reign for ever and ever" (Rev. 11:15).* (See also Psa. 2:7-12; Dan. 7:13-14; Isa. 6:9-11.)

■ At least five reasons have been suggested concerning why this miracle was performed.

1. To demonstrate Christ's compassion upon people—He was concerned not only with their souls, but also with their bodies.

2. To test his disciples—This undoubtedly strengthened their faith. They would remember it all their lives.

3. To prove his messianic claims—The Jews had a tradition that when the Messiah came, he would feed them with bread as Moses had once done. Note the following dialogue which took place on the next day between the crowd and Jesus: "Our fathers did eat manna in the desert; as it is written, He gave them bread from heaven to eat. Then Jesus said unto them, Verily, verily, I say unto you, Moses gave you not that bread from heaven; but my Father giveth you the true bread from heaven ... And Jesus said unto them, I am the bread of life: he that cometh to me shall never hunger; and he that believeth on me shall never thirst." (Jn. 6:31-32, 35)

4. To show the value of small things when given over to Christ—Especially is this seen by the giving of the loaves, not only in matters of quantity (five loaves), but also in quality (they were barley loaves). Wheat loaves were the normal diet back then. Barley loaves were eaten only by the very poor.

5. To illustrate God's faithfulness—In fact, this miracle was simply an unforgettable illustration of a profound principle Jesus had previously taught during his Sermon on the Mount.

"Therefore take no thought, saying, What shall we eat? or, What shall we drink? or, Wherewithal shall we be clothed? But seek ye first the kingdom of God, and his righteousness; and all these things shall be added unto you." (Mt. 6:31-32)

XX. TWENTY: Walking on the Water (Mt. 14:24-33; Mk. 6:45-52; Jn. 6:16-21)

A. Survey

Obeying the command of Jesus, the disciples begin rowing across the Sea of Galilee where they are suddenly caught in a severe, life-threatening storm. Just at the moment when all hope had gone, they see Jesus walking on the water toward them, fearful at first that He was a ghost. At Peter's request (upon recognizing the Savior), Jesus permits him to join in the watery walk. Soon, however, the apostle begins to sink. He is then rescued and gently rebuked by Jesus who calms the stormy elements, thus allowing both men to safely enter the boat.

B. Significance

■ This marks the first of two instances where the disciples thought that Jesus was a ghost (Mt. 14:26; Mk. 6:49). The other occasion would transpire in the Upper Room following Jesus' glorious resurrection: *"And as they thus spake, Jesus himself stood in the midst of them, and saith unto them, Peace be unto you. But they were terrified and affrighted, and supposed that they had seen a spirit. And he said unto them, Why are ye troubled? and why do thoughts arise in your hearts? Behold my hands and my feet, that it is I myself: handle me, and see; for a spirit hath not flesh and bones, as ye see me have." (Lk. 24:36-39)*

- It records the shortest prayer in the entire New Testament: *"LORD, SAVE ME!" (Mt. 14:30)*

C. Spiritual Truths

- It has been suggested that this miracle serves as a remarkable review of that relationship between Christ and his Church. Note the following comparisons:
    1. In Matthew 14, Christ sent his followers away in a boat on the sea and then ascended a hill to pray. The disciples then ran into a great storm on the Sea of Galilee.
    2. In Acts 1, Christ sends all his followers away and then ascends into heaven to pray. *"But ye shall receive power, after that the Holy Ghost is come upon you: and ye shall be witnesses unto me both in Jerusalem, and in all Judaea, and in Samaria, and unto the uttermost part of the earth. And when he had spoken these things, while they beheld, he was taken up, and a cloud received him out of their sight" (Acts 1:8-9).* As his disciples we often run into great storms on the sea of life.
    3. In Matthew 14, Christ remained on the hill for awhile to pray for his own. In Romans 8, we are told he will remain in heaven for awhile to pray for us. *"Who is he that condemneth? It is Christ that died, yea rather, that is risen again, who is even at the right hand of God, who also maketh intercession for us"(Rom. 8:34).*
    4. In Matthew 14, Christ eventually came for his own. In 1 Thessalonians 4, Christ will eventually come for us. *"For the Lord himself shall descend from heaven with a shout, with the voice of an archangel, and with the trump of God: and the dead in Christ shall rise first: Then we which are alive and remain shall be caught up together with them in the clouds, to meet the Lord in the air: and so shall we ever be with the Lord." (1 Thess. 4:16-17)*
    5. In Matthew 14, he spoke peace to the troubled waters. In Isaiah 2 he will speak peace to the troubled nations. *"And he shall judge among the nations, and shall rebuke many people: and they shall beat their swords into plowshares, and their spears into pruning hooks: nation shall not lift up sword against nation, neither shall they learn war any more." (Isa. 2:4)*

- In light of all of this, there are six all-important facts the Christian must realize in the hour of his or her storm:
    1. Christ allowed me to be here, therefore he knows about the storm.
    2. He is watching over me and praying for me during the storm.
    3. He will come to me at the proper time in the storm.
    4. He will help my faith to grow by the storm.
    5. He will see me safely through the storm.
    6. He will enable me to help others going through a similar storm. *"Blessed be God, even the Father of our Lord Jesus Christ, the Father of mercies, and the God of all comfort; who comforted us in all our tribulation, that we may be able to comfort them which are in any trouble, by the comfort wherewith we ourselves are comforted of God. For as the sufferings of Christ abound in us, so our consolation also aboundeth by Christ." (2 Cor. 1:3-5)*

- It is enlightening indeed to contrast the apostle's reaction following this storm with that of the previous one. Note:
    1. Their reaction following the first storm— *"But the men marvelled, saying, What manner of man is this, that even the winds and the sea obey him!" (Mt. 8:27)*

2. Their reaction following the second storm — *"Then they that were in the ship came and worshipped him, saying, Of a truth thou art the Son of God." (Mt. 14:33)*

   In a nutshell, they were learning!

XXI. TWENTY-ONE: Delivering a Syrophenician's Daughter (Mt. 15:21-28; Mk. 7:24-30)

A. Survey

Jesus begins this miracle by testing the faith of the desperate Gentile mother who begged Him to heal her demon-possessed daughter.

■ **The Messiah**: "It is not right to take the children's bread (a reference to the Jews) and feed it to dogs" (a reference to Gentiles).

The mother: "Yes, Lord, but even the dogs under the table eat the children's crumbs".

Needless to say, she had passed the test with flying colors and her daughter was delivered that very instant.

B. Significance

■ This is the only miracle where Jesus was temporarily silent and non-committal in regards to a miracle for healing.

■ It is the first of two miracles involving a young girl. For the first, see miracle 16.

C. Spiritual Truths

■ Note how Matthew introduces this miracle: *"A Canaanite woman from that vicinity came to him, crying out, Lord... have mercy on me!" (Mt. 15:22)*

W. L. Pettingill writes: "It will not be forgotten that this woman was a Gentile, and not only a Gentile, but a Canaanite, a representative of that race which was under God's peculiar curse. 'Thou shalt drive out the Canaanite—this was the word to Israel upon their entering the land of Canaan; and the promise of Zechariah 14:21, looking forward to the restored land and restored temple worship, says, *'In that day there shall be no more the Canaanite in the house of Jehovah of host.'* But grace is without any limit and overleaps all obstacles. Through Israel's failure, this despised outcast receives the blessing of the Lord that maketh rich. It is at first a most astonishing thing to see the Lord Jesus refusing to respond to this woman's cry of need. It is so unlike him, whose ears are always open to the slightest call upon his name. But he cannot answer her. She is calling upon him as the Son of David; and so he is, but as such,-as Son of David-he has nothing to do with a Canaanite." (*The Gospel of the Kingdom*, Fundamental Truth Publishers, Findlay, Ohio, p. 183.)

■ Usually it was the fickle crowds that kept seekers from Him, but on this occasion and at least one other, it was the disciples themselves! Note:

1. *"But he answered her not a word. And his disciples came and besought him, saying, Send her away; for she crieth after us." (Mt. 15:23)*

2. *"Then were there brought unto him little children, that he should put his hands on them, and pray: and the disciples rebuked them." (Mt. 19:13)*

■ This young girl now joins a number of demon-possessed females to be delivered by Jesus. Note:

1. *"Now when Jesus was risen early the first day of the week, he appeared first to Mary Magdalene, out of whom he had cast seven devils." (Mk. 16:9)*

2. *"And certain women, which had been healed of evil spirits and infirmities, Mary called Magdalene, out of whom went seven devils." (Lk. 8:2)*

XXII. TWENTY-TWO: Healing a Deaf Mute in Decapolis (Mk. 7:31-37)

A. Survey

Jesus placed His fingers in the ears of a deaf-mute, spit, touched the man's tongue, looked up into heaven, and sighed, *Be opened*. Immediately the man could both hear and speak.

B. Significance

- This is the first of three occasions on which Jesus spat when accomplishing a miracle. The other two are:
  1. Upon healing a blind man in Bethsaida (Mk. 8:23)
  2. Upon healing a blind man in Jerusalem (Jn. 9:6)
     It should be noted that all three cases involved blind individuals.

C. Spiritual Truths

- The statement of the amazed crowd, "He hath done all things well" perfectly summarizes the earthly ministry of Jesus perhaps more than any other in the entire New Testament.

- The first stanza of Fanny J. Crosby's beautiful gospel song, All The Way My Savior Leads Me, captures in melody fashion this precious truth:

  "All the way my Savior leads me
  What have I to ask beside?
  Can I doubt His tender mercy,
  Who thru life has been my Guide?
  Heavenly peace, divinest Comfort,
  Here by faith in Him to dwell!
  For I know, what-e'er befall me,
  Jesus doeth all things well."

XXIII. TWENTY-THREE: Feeding the 4000 (Mt. 15:32-39; Mk. 8:1-9)

A. Survey

Jesus feeds a hungry crowd who had not eaten in three days, by supernaturally multiplying seven loaves and a few fish. Following the bountiful meal, seven basketfuls of food were collected by the disciples.

B. Significance

- This is the second of two occasions where Jesus fed the hungry multitudes. See also miracle 19.

■ Some have attempted to show the feeding of the 5000 and that of the 4000 were actually the same event, suggesting that the Gospel writers got their details mixed up. But Jesus himself told us that they were two separate and distinct events. *"When I brake the five loaves among five thousand, how many baskets full of fragments took ye up? They said unto him, Twelve. And when the seven among four thousand, how many baskets full of fragments took ye up? And they said, Seven"* (Mk. 8:19-20).

■ Note the comparisons and contrasts between these two events:
1. Compared with the feeding of the 5000: There are several similarities between these two miracles.
   a. Christ showed compassion toward both groups.
   b. He asked his disciples what should be done.
   c. He had the people sit down in orderly groups.
   d. He supernaturally fed them by multiplying a few fish and loaves.
2. Contrasted with the feeding of the 5000: There are a number of differences between these two miracles.
   a. The size of the crowd: One had 5000 men; the other 4000.
   b. The duration involved: The 5000 men had been with him for one day; the 4000 for three days.
   c. The original food: Christ used five loaves and two fishes to feed the 5000, while using seven loaves and an unspecified number of fish in caring for the 4000.
   d. The remains: Twelve baskets were left over at the feeding of 5000, and seven after the 4000.
   e. The Gospel record: All four Gospel writers record the feeding of the 5000, while only Matthew and Mark speak of the 4000.

XXIV. TWENTY-FOUR: Healing a Blind Man at Bethsaida (Mk. 8:22-26)
A. Survey

Jesus began this miracle by placing His hands on the man and spitting in his eyes.

The Savior: "Do you see anything?"

The sightless: "I see people; they look like trees walking around."

Jesus touched the man's eyes, causing him to now see clearly and completely.

B. Significance

■ This is Jesus' only miracle accomplished in two stages.

C. Spiritual Truths

■ The spiritual application here is crystal clear and sorely needed today. We need that second touch by Jesus, allowing us to see "every man clearly" as God does.

■ As can be seen later, Jesus' disciples would often see men as "trees".
1. Despicable trees

"And sent messengers before his face: and they went, and entered into a village of the Samaritans, to make ready for him. And they did not receive him, because his face was as though he would go to Jerusalem. And when his disciples James and John saw this, they said, Lord, wilt thou that we command fire to come down from heaven, and consume them, even as Elias did? But he turned, and rebuked them, and said, Ye know not what manner of spirit ye are of. For the Son of man is not come to destroy men's lives, but to save them. And they went to another village." (Lk. 9:52-56)

2. Bothersome trees

   "And they brought unto him also infants, that he would touch them: but when his disciples saw it, they rebuked them. But Jesus called them unto him, and said, Suffer little children to come unto me, and forbid them not: for of such is the kingdom of God. Verily I say unto you, Whosoever shall not receive the kingdom of God as a little child shall in no wise enter therein." (Lk. 18:15-17)

3. Competitive trees

   "And John answered him, saying, master, we saw one casting out devils in thy name, and he followeth not us: and we forbad him, because he followeth not us. But Jesus said, Forbid him not: for there is no man which shall do a miracle in my name, that can lightly speak evil of me. For he that is not against us is on our part. For whosoever shall give you a cup of water to drink in my name, because ye belong to Christ, verily I say unto you, he shall not lose his reward. " (Mk. 9:38-41)

4. Sinful trees

   "And as Jesus passed by, he saw a man which was blind from his birth. And his disciples asked him, saying, Master, who did sin, this man, or his parents, that he was born blind? Jesus answered, Neither hath this man sinned, nor his parents: but that the works of God should be made manifest in him." (Jn. 9:1-3)

5. Unclean trees

   "On the morrow, as they went on their journey, and drew nigh unto the city, Peter went up upon the housetop to pray about the sixth hour: And he became very hungry, and would have eaten: but while they made ready, he fell into a trance, And saw heaven opened, and a certain vessel descending upon him, as it had been a great sheet knit at the four corners, and let down to the earth: Wherein were all manner of four footed beasts of the earth, and wild beasts, and creeping things, and fowls of the air. And there came a voice to him, Rise, Peter; kill, and eat. But Peter said, Not so, Lord; for I have never eaten any thing that is common or unclean. And the voice spake unto him again the second time, What God hath cleansed, that call not thou common." (Acts 10:9-15)

■ As can been seen today, Jesus' disciples do often see men as trees. Thus:

1. As a Christian leader, do I view my staff and associates simply as servant trees whose main task is to help me in building my own personal kingdom?

2. As a Christian layperson, do I view my family members and friends merely as enabling trees, existing primarily to meet my needs and enhance my goals?

XXV. TWENTY-FIVE: Delivering a Demon-Possessed Boy (Mt. 17:14-18; Mk. 9:14-29; Lk. 9:38-42)
A. Survey

A desperate father begs Jesus to deliver his tormented son from a cruel and vicious demon who would cause him to fall into fire and water, cast him to the ground, throw him into convulsions, and was slowly killing him. Note the ensuing conversation:

The father: "If you can do anything, please do it."

The Savior: "If you believe, I can do all things."

The father: "Lord, I believe—help thou my unbelief."

With this, Jesus rebuked the evil spirit and freed the son.

B. Significance

- This is the final of three instances in which Jesus would supernaturally minister to an only child.
  1. He raised from the dead the only son of a widow (Lk. 7:12).
  2. He raised from the dead the only daughter of Jairus (Lk. 8:42).

- It is the only miracle showing the utter inability of the disciples to help the person in need.
  1. As testified to by the father
     "And I besought thy disciples to cast him out; and they could not." (Lk. 9:40)
  2. As testified to by the disciples themselves
     "Then came the disciples to Jesus apart, and said, Why could not we cast him out?" (Mt. 17:19)

- This is the second of two of the most frightful and graphic descriptions regarding the horrors of demon possession in the entire Bible! For the first, see miracle 14.

C. Spiritual Truths

- Leaving the Mount of Transfiguration, our Lord enters the valley of disfiguration. On the mountain, the friends of heaven (Moses and Elijah) had comforted Him. In the valley, the foes of hell would challenge Him! In essence, these words serve to summarize Jesus' ministry and mission.

- As His faithful followers we are called upon to do the same. Note Paul's words: *"Blessed be God, even the father of our Lord Jesus Christ, the Father of mercies, and the God of all comfort; Who comforteth us in all our tribulation, that we may be able to comfort them which are in any trouble, by the comfort wherewith we ourselves are comforted of God. For as the sufferings of Christ abound in us, so our consolation also aboundeth by Christ." (2 Cor. 1:3-5)*

  Thus, in church the believer may sing about "The Sweet By and By" but upon leaving, he enters the world of the "Nasty Now and Now".

- Note the Father's struggle for faith: "And straightway the father of the child cried out, and said with tears, Lord, I believe; help thou mine unbelief." (Mk. 9:24)

  This kind of struggling, desperate faith, even though plagued with doubt, will reach the heart of God immediately. The psalmist spoke of this: "Like a father pitieth his children, so the Lord pitieth them that fear him. For he knoweth our frame; he remembereth that we are dust." (Psa. 103:13-14)

  Question: How much faith does it take to please God?

  Response: How much faith do you have?

  Illustration: Let us suppose you face a million-dollar need but only have a 10-dollar bill. God's plan in solving this is both gracious and simple: Give Him your 10 dollars and he will add the remaining $999,990. However small our faith, He wants it all. Our problem, however, is that all too often we shortchange Him on the 10 dollars.

■ Why could not the disciples help this desperate father and his demon possessed son?

On two previous occasions, they had been able to cast out demons. *"And they cast out many devils, and anointed with oil many that were sick, and healed them"* (Mk. 6:13). *"And the seventy returned again with joy, saying, Lord even the devils are subject unto us through thy name"* (Lk. 10:17).

Why then could they not help this heartbroken father? There were at least four reasons:

1. They had too little faith (Mt. 17:20)
2. They had too little self-denial (Mk. 9:29)
3. They had too little prayer (Mk. 9:29)
4. They had too much bickering (Mk. 9:14)

It is so easy to become an Ichabod Christian (meaning *"the glory of the Lord hath departed"*; see 1 Sam. 4:21-22) without even being aware of it until the crisis comes.

The Old Testament strongman Samson serves as a classic and tragic example of this very thing! *"That he told her all his heart, and said unto her, There hath not come a razor upon mine head; for I have been a Nazarite unto God from my mother's womb: if I be shaven, then my strength will go from me, and I shall become weak, and be like any other man. And when Delilah saw that he had told her all his heart, she sent and called for the lords of the Philistines, saying, Come up this once, for he hath shewed me all his heart, Then the lords of the Philistines came up unto her, and brought money in their hand. And she made him sleep upon her knees; and she called for a man, and she caused him to shave off the seven locks of his head; and she began to afflict him, and his strength went from him. And she said, The Philistines be upon thee, Samson. And he awoke out of his sleep, and said, I will go out as at other times before, and shake myself. And he wist not that the LORD was departed from him."* (Judg. 16:17-20)

XXVI. TWENTY-SIX: Finding the Tax Money in a Fish (Mt. 17:24-27)

A. Survey

Simon Peter promises a tax collector that Jesus would pay the imposed temple tax. The following dialogue then occurs:

Jesus: "Peter, from whom do the kings of the earth collect duty and taxes? from their own sons or from others?"

Peter: "From others"

Jesus: "Then the sons are exempt. But so that we might not offend them, go to the lake and throw out your line. Take the first fish you catch, open its mouth and you will find a four-drachma coin. Take it and give it to them for my tax and yours."

B. Significance

■ This is the only miracle involving a brute creature.

■ It is the only miracle resulting in a money coin.

C. Spiritual Truths

■ This temple tax, owed by all Jews from age twenty upward, was two drachma, approximately two days' wages. It was to be used for the temple upkeep and repair. There were three specific occasions recorded in the Old Testament when this tax was collected.

1. During the time of Moses (Ex. 30:13, 38:26)
2. During the time of Joash--This Judean king actually had a special chest built and placed outside by the temple gate to receive the tax (2 Chron. 24:9-14)
3. During the time of Nehemiah (Neh. 10:32)

■ Note Peter's thoughtless response to the tax collector's demand:

They ask: *"Doth not your master pay tribute?"*

He answered: *"Yes."*

Here Peter committed a serious blunder. He committed Jesus to do something without first asking Him. Nathan the prophet once did the same thing when advising King David. It also had to do with the temple. Upon hearing David's desire to construct a temple, Nathan responded: *"Then Nathan said to David, Do all that is in thine heart; for God is with thee" (1 Chron. 17:2)*. But then God stepped in: *"And it came to pass the same night, that the word of God came to Nathan, saying, Go and tell David my servant, Thus saith the Lord, Thou shalt not build me an house to dwell in" (1 Chron. 17:3-4)*. The conclusion of the matter was that God had already determined that Solomon (David's son) would build the temple.

■ Jesus told Peter why he should not have to pay the tax:
1. He owned the temple (Mal. 3:1)
2. He had previously cleansed the temple (Jn. 2:16)
3. He was the eternal Son of God (Mt. 16:16)

■ He then told Peter why he would pay the tax:
1. To maintain a good testimony—*"Notwithstanding, lest we should offend them"*. Here the Savior gave a beautiful example of properly using our Christian liberty, as later echoed by the Apostle Paul in 1 Corinthians 8-10. *"But take heed lest by any means this liberty of yours become a stumblingblock to them that are weak. But when ye sin so against the brethren, and wound their weak conscience, ye sin against Christ. To the weak became I as weak, that I might gain the weak: I am made all things to all men, that I might by all means save some." (1 Cor. 8:9, 12; 9:22)*
2. To increase Peter's faith
3. To illustrate his work as the second Adam—When correctly understood, this amazing miracle serves to illustrate not only the deity of Christ, but even more, his perfect humanity. What was he doing here? In essence, Jesus was fulfilling the very first command in the Bible given to Adam concerning the world of nature: "And God ...said ... subdue it; and have dominion over the fish of the sea, and over the fowl of the air, and over every living thing that moveth upon the earth" (Gen. 1:28). Our Lord thus, in some mysterious manner (lost to us after Adam's sin), was able to communicate and exercise control over a fish swimming in the waters of Galilee.

■ It should be noted here that this fish OBEYED its Creator!
1. As did the ravens near a brook

"And Elijah the Tishbite, who was of the inhabitants of Gilead, said unto Ahab, As the LORD God of Israel liveth, before whom I stand, there shall not be dew nor rain these years, but according to my word. And the word of the LORD came unto him, saying, Get thee hence, and turn thee eastward, and hide thyself by the brook Cherith, that is before Jordan. And it shall be, that thou shalt drink of the brook; and I have commanded the ravens to feed thee there. So he went and did according unto the word of the LORD: for he went and dwelt

by the brook Cherith, that is before Jordan. And the ravens brought him bread and flesh in the morning, and bread and flesh in the evening; and he drank of the brook." (1 Kings 17:1-6)

2. As did the lions in a den

"Then said Daniel unto the king, O king, live for ever My God hath sent his angel, and hath shut the lions' mouths, that they have not hurt me: forasmuch as before him innocency was found in me; and also before thee, O king, have I done no hurt. Then was the king exceedingly glad for him, and commanded that they should take Daniel up out of the den. So Daniel was taken up out of the den, and no manner of hurt was found upon him, because he believed in his God" (Dan. 6:21-23).

Tragically, the only two creatures able to DISOBEY their Creator are ANGELS and HUMAN BEINGS!

XXVII. TWENTY-SEVEN: Healing a Man Born Blind (Jn. 9:1-7)
A. Survey

Jesus began this miracle by spitting on the ground, making mud with the saliva, put it on the man's eyes, and said: *"Go wash in the pool of Siloam."* The blind man obeyed and was immediately able to see!

B. Significance

- This is the only miracle where Jesus commanded the person to be healed to do something.

- This is the final of seven miracles where the parents of the recipient are involved. The other six are miracles 2, 11, 16, 21, and 25.

C. Spiritual Truths

- Notice the insensitivity and callousness shown by the disciples here:

    "And as Jesus passed by, he saw a man which was blind from his birth. And his disciples asked him, saying, Master, who did sin, this man, or his parents, that he was born blind?" (Jn. 9:1-2)

    As it can be seen, there was no desire on their part to help this pitiful man. Rather, his condition served simply as a focal point for an academic, theological discussion!

- At first reading, this seems to be a very silly question, for how could this poor, sightless man be suffering for his sin if he was born blind? However, some rabbis felt a baby could sin in its mother's womb, or that its soul might have sinned in a preexistent state. They also held that terrible punishment from God came upon certain people because of the sin of their parents.

    This grievous error, of course, is totally refuted by both Moses and Ezekiel.

    "The fathers shall not be put to death for the children, neither shall the children be put to death for the fathers: every man shall be put to death for his own sin" (Deut. 24:16). "The soul that sinneth, it shall die. The son shall not bear the iniquity of the father, neither shall the father bear the iniquity of the son: the righteousness of the righteous shall be upon him, and the wicked shall be upon him" (Ezek. 18:20).

- Jesus answered their question as follows:

    "Jesus answered, Neither hath this man sinned, nor his parents: but that the works of God should be made manifest in him." (Jn. 9:3)

Here Jesus corrects that terrible teaching that says that all suffering is a direct result of personal sin. The disciples at this point had made the same false assumption that Job's three "friends" had once made (see Job 4:7-8; 8:20; 20:4-5), and that many modern "faith healers" today still make. However, God himself had severely rebuked the companions of Job for their wicked judgment:

"And it was so, that after the Lord had spoken these words unto Job, the Lord said to Eliphaz the Temanite, My wrath is kindled against thee, and against thy two friends: for ye have not spoken of me the thing that is right, as my servant Job hath" (Job 42:7).

■ After the healing of the blind man the wicked Pharisees interrogated his parents: *"And they asked them, saying, Is this your son, who ye say was born blind? how then doth he now see? His parents answered them and said, We know that this is our son, and that he was born blind." (Jn. 9:19-22).*

How tragic to contemplate the strong possibility that these seeing parents of a sightless son refused the light offered by Christ and probably died still blinded by their sins. Why did this happen? Solomon gives us the sad answer: *"The fear of man bringeth a snare: but whoso putteth his trust in the Lord shall be safe" (Prov. 29:25).* This sad truth is reconfirmed on two additional occasions apart from John 9:

1. *"Nevertheless among the chief rulers also many believed on him; but because of the Pharisees they did not confess him, lest they should be put out of the synagogue: For they loved the praise of men more than the praise of God" (Jn. 12:42-43).*
2. *"But the fearful, and unbelieving, and the abominable, and murderers, and whoremongers, and sorcerers, and idolaters, and all liars, shall have their part in the lake which burneth with fire and brimstone: which is the second death" (Rev. 21:8).*

■ The Pharisees continued their attack on Jesus:

"Therefore said some of the Pharisees, This man is not of God, because he keepeth not the sabbath day. Others said, How can a man that is a sinner do such miracles? And there was a division among them." (Jn. 9:16)

Whenever Jesus enters the scene a division automatically develops. A person might accept his claims or deny them, but he or she cannot ignore them.

"What will you do with Jesus?
Neutral you cannot be!
Someday your heart will be asking,
What will He do with me?"

■ The amazing response by the former blind man to Jesus' critics must surely rank among the most simple yet sublime answers of all time! *"Then again called they the man that was blind, and said unto him, Give God the praise: we know that this man is a sinner. He answered and said, Whether he be a sinner or no, I know not: one thing I know, that, whereas I was blind, now I see." (Jn. 9:24-25)*

■ As a final observation, note the progressive revelation given to this healed blind man by the Holy Spirit regarding the person of Jesus:

In 9:11 he calls Him a man.
In 9:17 he calls Him a prophet.
In 9:32 he calls him a miracle worker.
In 9:33 he calls Him a messenger from God.
In 9:35-38 he worships Him as the Son of God.

XXVIII. TWENTY-EIGHT: Healing a Crippled Woman on the Sabbath (Lk. 13:10-17)

A. Survey

Jesus encountered this woman who had been bent over for 18 long years while He was teaching in a synagogue. Calling her forward, He said:

"Woman, you are set free from your infirmity."

He then laid hands on her and she immediately straightened up and praised God!

B. Significance

■ Jesus uses His sharpest rebuke yet in performing this miracle, saying to the critical synagogue ruler, *"THOU HYPOCRITE!"*

■ It is the third of three miracles where the actual number of years is given in regards to the length of their suffering.
   1. In this case, 18 years (Lk. 13:11)
   2. That of a woman with an issue of blood, 12 years (Mt. 9:20)
   3. That of a crippled man, 38 years (Jn. 5:5)

C. Spiritual Truths

■ This woman was probably a believer. Jesus refers to her as "a daughter of Abraham". In addition, the text indicates that she was a faithful member of the synagogue (Lk. 13:10-11).

■ In spite of this, she had been bound by Satan for nearly two decades. Here it should be said that although Satan (or his fallen angels) cannot possess a believer, he can oppress and physically afflict a child of God. There are two classic examples of this satanic physical affliction in the Scriptures.
   1. The example of Job (Job 1-2)— *"So went Satan forth from the presence of the LORD, and smote Job with sore boils from the sole of his foot unto his crown." (Job 2:7)*
   2. The example of Paul— *"And lest I should be exalted above measure through the abundance of the revelations, there was given to me a thorn in the flesh, the messenger of Satan to buffet me, lest I should be exalted above measure." (2 Cor. 12:7)*

■ During His meeting with Cornelius, Simon Peter would speak of this:
   "How God anointed Jesus of Nazareth with the Holy Ghost and with power: who went about doing good, and healing all that were oppressed of the devil; for God was with him." (Acts 10:38)

XXIX. TWENTY-NINE: Healing a Man with Dropsy (Lk. 14:1-6)

A. Survey

During a Sabbath luncheon in the house of a prominent Pharisee, Jesus encounters a man suffering with dropsy. Turning to the legalistic Pharisees who were present, He asks:

"Is it lawful to heal on the Sabbath?"

Receiving no answer, He touched the man and healed him.

B. Significance

■ This is the only recorded miracle done during a meal in the home of a Pharisee.

C. Spiritual Truths

■ This supper was probably a set-up arranged by the Pharisees to trap Jesus, hoping He would do something unlawful.
   1. It was on the Sabbath.
   2. A very sick man was there who suffered from dropsy. Dropsy was an abnormal accumulation of watery fluid in the body, which caused hideous swelling in the abdomen, legs, and feet. It was symptomatic of cardiac disease. In light of this, it is highly unlikely that this poor, suffering creature would be invited to the home of a Pharisee, especially on the Sabbath. To the contrary, he would have been utterly refused entrance.

■ According to the sacred account Jesus touched this man. This was in stark contrast to the legalistic Pharisees who not only would have refused to touch the leper, the blind, the deaf, the maimed, etc., but would actually hurry home in horror to take a ceremonial bath if their shadow should come into contact with the shadow of those unclean outcasts!

   But not the Savior! He was a "Hands on Healer," as demonstrated by those He personally touched.
   1. A leper (Mt. 8:3)
   2. Peter's mother-in-law (Mt. 8:15)
   3. A deaf mute (Mk. 7:33)
   4. Two blind men (Mt. 20:34)
   5. A man born blind (Jn. 9:6)
   6. Malchus' ear (Lk. 22:51)
   7. Little children (Mk. 10:13)
   8. His frightened disciple (Mt. 17:7)

XXX. THIRTY: Raising of Lazarus (Jn. 11:17-44)
A. Survey

After comforting Lazarus' grieving sisters, Mary and Martha in their hour of sorrow, following Lazarus' death, and expressing His own personal grief, Jesus visits the tomb of the dead man. He then utters four statements:

■ **To Martha**: *"take away the stone"*

■ **To His Father**: *"thank you for hearing me. I do this that those watching may believe that you sent me."*

■ **To Lazarus**: *"Lazarus come out!"*

■ **To those standing by**: *"take off the grave clothes and let him go."*

B. Significance

■ More space is given over to this miracle than to any other of the thirty-five performed by Jesus.

■ More individuals are mentioned by name here than can be found in any other miracle (Lazarus, Mary, Martha, and Thomas).

■ It marks the final of three occasions where Jesus raised someone from the dead. For the first two, see miracles 11 and 16.

■ This is the first of three great cries from the lips of the Savior. All three have to do with the glorious subject of resurrection.

   1. The cry from the cemetery: *"Lazarus, come forth."*

   2. The cry from the cross. *"Jesus when he had cried again with a loud voice, yielded up the ghost And, behold, the vail of the temple was rent in twain from the top to the bottom; and the earth did quake, and the rocks rent; and the graves were opened; and many bodies of the saints which slept arose." (Mt. 27:50-52)*

   3. The cry from the clouds: *"For the Lord himself shall descend from heaven with a shout, with the voice of the archangel, and with the trump of God: and the dead in Christ shall rise first." (1 Thess. 4:16)*

■ Humanly speaking, this miracle would lead to the death of Jesus.

   "Then from that day forth they took counsel together for to put him to death." (Jn. 11:53)

C. Spiritual Truths

■ Lazarus, Mary and Martha lived in Bethany, a little Jewish town two miles east of the Mount of Olives. At least four key events would transpire here in the life of Jesus.

   1. The resurrection of Lazarus (Jn. 11:44)

   2. His anointing by Mary (Mt. 26:6)

   3. The starting point for His triumphal entry (Mk. 11:1)

   4. His final blessing upon the disciples just prior to the ascension (Lk. 24:50)

■ Observe the frequency of the names Lazarus, Mary, and Martha in John 11:

   1. Lazarus is mentioned six times (11:1, 2, 5, 11, 14, 43).

   2. Mary is mentioned seven times (11:1, 2, 19, 20, 28, 31, 32).

   3. Martha is mentioned eight times (11:1, 5, 19, 20, 21, 24, 30, 39).

■ The reason for this can be seen by a statement made during Christ's Good Shepherd sermon, preached just prior to this: *"He calleth his own sheep by name, and leadeth them out." (Jn. 10:3)*

■ John Chapter 11 can be favorably compared with John Chapter 9.

   1. In John 9 Jesus used the tragedy of blindness as an opportunity to manifest the power of God.

     "Jesus answered, Neither hath this man sinned, nor his parents: but that the works of God should be made manifest in him." (Jn. 9:3)

   2. In John 11 Jesus used the tragedy of death as an opportunity to manifest the glory of God.

     "When Jesus heard that, he said, This sickness is not unto death, but for the glory of God, that the Son of God might be glorified thereby." (Jn. 11:4)

   3. Both chapters thus refute that terrible lie which claims all suffering is a result of personal sin.

   4. More information is provided regarding these two miracles than any other of the 35 Jesus performed.

   5. Both miracles would only further harden the hearts of Jesus' enemies. Note:

     "Then again called they the man that was blind, and said unto him, Give God the praise: we know that this man is a sinner." (Jn. 9:24)

"Then gathered the chief priests and the Pharisees a council, and said, What do we? for this man doeth many miracles. If we let him thus alone, all men will believe on him: and the Romans shall come and take away both our place and nation ... Now both the chief priests and the Pharisees had given a commandment, that, if any man knew where he were, he should shew it, that they might take him." (Jn. 11:47-48, 57)

■ Upon hearing of Jesus' decision to attend Lazarus' funeral and raise him from the dead, Thomas expressed grave doubts:

"Then said Thomas, which is called Didymus, unto his fellow disciples, Let us also go, that we may die with him." (Jn. 11:16)

The New Testament relates three incidents between Thomas and Christ. The Gospel of John records all three. In each of them he lives up to his reputation as Doubting Thomas.

1. Here he doubts the power of Christ.
2. In the Upper Room he doubts the promise of Christ. "Thomas saith unto him, Lord we know not whither thou goest; and how can we know the way?" (Jn. 14:5)
3. After the resurrection he at first doubted the very person of Christ. (Jn. 20:24-29)

   "But Thomas, one of the twelve, called Didymus, was not with them when Jesus came. The other disciples therefore said unto him, We have seen the LORD. But he said unto them, Except I shall see in his hands the print of the nails, and put my finger into the print of the nails, and thrust my hand into his side, I will not believe." (Jn. 20:24-25)

■ We note that he waited until Lazarus had been dead for four days. He may have done this because of the superstition among the Jews that after death the spirit hovered over the body for three days, and a resurrection up to that time was at least remotely possible. But after this period, all hope was gone.

■ Martha, and not Mary, is the heroine of this story. (See Lk. 10:38-42 where the opposite was true.)

1. It was Martha who went to meet Jesus while Mary remained in the house. (Jn. 11:20)
2. Martha's great testimony here ranks equally as important as that given by Simon Peter on another occasion.

■ Both contain similar language, but Martha offered hers under far more difficult circumstances:

1. Peter's testimony

   "And Simon Peter answered and said, Thou art the Christ, the Son of the living God." (Mt. 16:16)
2. Martha's testimony

   "Jesus said unto her, I am the resurrection, and the life: he that believeth in me, though he were dead, yet shall he live: And whosoever liveth and believeth in me shall never die. Believest thou this? She saith unto him, Yea, Lord: I believe that thou art the Christ, the Son of God, which should come into the world." (Jn. 11:25-27)

■ Martha's words to Mary here are the most beneficial and blessed ones a believer can give to another believer in the hour of greatest need.

"She went her way, and called Mary her sister secretly, saying, The Master is come, and calleth for thee." (Jn. 11:28)

■ Upon meeting Jesus, Mary said the exact same thing Martha had just said:

"Then said Martha unto Jesus, Lord, if thou hadst been here, my brother had not died...Then when Mary was come where Jesus was, and saw him, she fell down at his feet, saying unto him, Lord, if thou hadst been here, my

brother had not died." (Jn. 11:21, 32) To rephrase the little poem: "The most useless words of tongue or pen, are these four words, 'IT MIGHT HAVE BEEN!'

■ The account tells us of Jesus' sorrow at this time:

> *"When Jesus therefore saw her weeping, and the Jews also weeping which came with her, he groaned in the spirit, and was troubled. And said, Where have ye laid him? They said unto him, Lord, come and see. Jesus wept." (Jn. 11:33-35)*

■ This contains the shortest verse in the English Bible, but in some ways it is the longest. This is the first of at least three occasions on which our Lord wept.

1. He wept over the city of Jerusalem (Lk. 19:41)
2. He wept in Gethsemane— *"Who in the days of his flesh, when he had offered up prayers and supplications with strong crying and tears unto him that was able to save him from death, and was heard in that he feared." (Heb. 5:7)*

■ What caused his tears?

1. He wept because of his true humanity (see Heb. 4:14-16).
2. He wept because of the wicked men he saw around him (see Jn. 11:37, 46).
3. He wept (according to an early Christian tradition) because He was soon to bring Lazarus back from the bliss of paradise to this earthly vale of tears!

■ Twice we read of Jesus groaning (Jn. 11:33, 38). The Greek word here is embrim, suggesting anger. It is translated "indignation" in Mk. 14:5. Thus, the groanings of Christ may have indicated his grief and anger over death itself, a tragic (and unnecessary) result of Adam's sin (see Rom. 5:12).

■ Standing outside the tomb that contained the body of Lazarus, Jesus gives some specific and pointed instructions:

Here we see an example of that desired cooperation God seeks between the Savior and the soul winner in raising dead sinners to newness of life. Jesus issued three commands in accomplishing this miracle. The first and third were directed toward the friends of the corpse, while the second was given to the corpse itself. Note:

1. *"Take ye away the stone" (Jn. 11:39).* The job of the soul winner is to first remove all human barriers so that Christ can come in direct contact with a lost person.
2. *"Lazarus, come forth" (Jn. 11:43).* Only Christ, of course, can do this.
3. *"Loose him, and let him go" (Jn. 11:44).* In a word, this speaks of discipleship, that is, ministering to the new convert.

XXXI. THIRTY-ONE: Cleansing of Ten Lepers (Lk. 17:11-19)
A. Survey

En route to Jerusalem, Jesus encounters ten lepers who call out to Him for mercy and healing. Instantly all ten were cleansed and leave to show themselves to the temple priests as instructed by the Levitical law for ceremonial cleansing. Soon however, one of the ten, a Samaritan returned, fell at the feet of the Savior and began worshipping and thanking Him:

■ Jesus, regarding the thankless nine: *"Were not all ten cleansed? Where are the other nine?"*
■ Jesus, regarding the thankful one: *"Rise and go; your faith has made you whole."*

B. Significance

■ This miracle regards the greatest number of specific (ten) healings than any other as performed by Jesus.

■ It is the only miracle involving a Samaritan.

C. Spiritual Truths

■ This is the second of three miracles demonstrating the tragic fact that the one (or ones) experiencing physical salvation did not apparently experience spiritual salvation. These three cases are:

1. The cripple by the pool of Bethesda (Jn. 5:1-16)— *"Jesus saith unto him, Rise, take up thy bed, and walk. And immediately the man was made whole, and took up his bed, and walked: and on the same day was the sabbath...Afterward Jesus findeth him in the temple, and said unto him, Behold, thou art made whole: sin no more, lest a worse thing come unto thee." (Jn. 5:8-9, 14)*

2. The nine lepers here in Luke 17.

3. The servant of the high priest whose name was Malchus (Jn. 18:10)—There is no evidence that he accepted Christ after having his severed ear restored.

■ The great sin of the nine lepers was that of thanklessness. In some ways this is the ultimate sin, and goes along with pride and self-will, the root of all other sins. Paul says that this transgression in the ancient world caused all mankind to turn from God.

"Because that, when they knew God, they glorified him not as God, neither were thankful; but became vain in their imaginations, and their foolish heart was darkened. Professing themselves to be wise, they became fools, And changed the glory of the uncorruptible God into an image made like to corruptible man, and to birds, and four-footed beasts, and creeping things." (Rom. 1:21-23)

■ In essence, the cure for and solution to pride does not involve pious attempts to practice humility, but rather simply to be thankful. A thankful person is, by definition, a humble person! As someone has observed:

> *"Be careful for nothing,*
> *Be prayerful in everything,*
> *Be thankful for anything!"*

XXXII. THIRTY-TWO: Healing Blind Bartimaeus (Mt. 20:29-34; Mk. 10:46-52; Lk. 18:35-43)

A. Survey

Two blind beggars, one named Bartimaeus, sitting outside of Jericho learn that Jesus was approaching. Both immediately cry out for mercy.

The Savior: "What do you want me to do for you?"

The sightless: "We want to see."

Filled with compassion, Jesus touched their eyes, causing them to instantly reclaim their sight.

B. Significance

■ Of the sixteen healing events, involving some 26 people, only one is named, Bartimaeus.

■ This is also the only New Testament miracle associated with the city of Jericho.

    1. The most famous Old Testament miracle concerning Jericho occurred in Joshua 6:20 (the shouting down of Jericho's walls).

    2. The final Old Testament miracle concerning Jericho is recorded in 2 Kings 2:18-22 (the purifying of some poisoned water).

C. Spiritual Truths

■ This marks Jesus' final visit to Jericho. He will now leave for Jerusalem (see Mt. 20:29). Before this, he had told the story of a man who left Jerusalem for Jericho (the parable of the Good Samaritan--Lk. 10:25-37). But now the original Good Samaritan would reverse the trip, leaving Jericho for Jerusalem, where he would soon "fall among thieves."

■ Note the spiritual insight of the blind beggar:

    1. He asked the right person— *"Jesus, thou Son of David."*

    2. He asked in the right way— *"Have mercy on me."*

       It has been said that God will hush every harp in heaven to hear this kind of prayer!

    3. He asked at the right time— *"And hearing the multitude pass by, he asked what it meant. And they told him, that Jesus of Nazareth passeth by." (Lk. 18:36-37)*

    4. He asked for the right thing— *"that I might regain my sight."*

XXXIII. THIRTY-THREE: Cursing the Fig Tree (Mt. 21:18-19)
A. Survey

One morning, a few days before His crucifixion, en route to Jerusalem from Bethany, Jesus views a fig tree. Being hungry, He approached it, only to find much foliage but no fruit. "May you never bear fruit again," the Savior said to the tree, which immediately withered and dried up!

B. Significance

■ This is the only one of Christ's thirty-five recorded miracles that would cause him great pain and sorrow. It was so important that years later the Apostle Paul took three entire chapters (Rom. 9-11) to expand upon its theological implications.

■ To explain the above, many believe this tree was a symbol of Israel, that divinely favored but utterly fruitless fig tree. Jesus was therefore, if this be true, setting aside the nation due to the absence of fruit. Later, that same day, He made this clear to the Pharisees, those spiritual custodians of the tree:

    "Jesus saith unto them, Did ye never read in the scriptures, The stone which the builders rejected, the same is become the head of the corner: this is the Lord's doing, and it is marvellous in our eyes? Therefore say I unto you, The kingdom of God shall be taken from you, and given to a nation bringing forth the fruits thereof." (Mt. 21:42-43)

■ This particular kind of fig tree found in Israel is different from all other fruit trees in that it bears its fruit before its leaves. This is not the case with apple, pear, cherry, or any other fruit-bearing trees. Even though the tree was apparently blooming earlier than usual, Jesus had the right to see fruit, for the leaves were there.

■ This was the first of two miracles performed by Jesus during the final Passover week. See also miracle 34.

C. Spiritual Truths

■ As has been previously noted, Jesus had every right to find fruit upon the tree of Israel. Its green and massive foliage was impressive indeed, for to it was given the tabernacle, the temple, the Old Testament Scriptures, plus the ministries of godly prophets, priests, and kings. But upon close inspection, it bore no fruit.

■ The overriding lesson from this miracle is painfully obvious—God desires fruit.
  1. His chosen nation failed to bear fruit. *"Israel is an empty vine, he bringeth forth fruit unto himself: according to the multitude of his fruit he hath increased the altars; according to the goodness of his land they have made goodly images." (Hos. 10:1)*
  2. His present plan is for believers to bear fruit. *"Herein is my Father glorified, that ye bear much fruit; so shall ye be my disciples." (Jn. 15:8)*

■ Jesus later would say that He was the true vine and His followers were the branches (Jn. 15:1). The only function therefore of a branch is to bear fruit. Branch wood is never used for firewood or building material! Furthermore it must be realized a branch does not produce fruit (the vine does this), but rather bears it!

XXXIV. THIRTY-FOUR: Restoring Malchus' Ear (Lk. 22:49-51)
A. Survey

While in Gethsemane Jesus restores the ear of Malchus, servant of the High Priest, which ear Simon Peter had foolishly severed with his sword.

B. Significance

■ This was the final miracle performed prior to Calvary.

■ It was also the last of 16 healing miracles.

■ It no doubt saved Simon Peter from certain death.

■ It was the only miracle performed on an enemy.

C. Spiritual Truths

■ It is interesting that although all four gospel writers record the act of Malchus' ear being severed, (Mt. 26:51; Mk. 14:4; Lk. 22:50; Jn. 18:10), only Luke the physician tells us of the restoration by Jesus (Lk. 22:51). Also, of the four, only John's gospel actually identifies the one who cut off the ear, Simon Peter by name (Jn. 18:10).

■ Note Jesus' stern rebuke in regards to this act of violence:
  "Then said Jesus unto him, Put up again thy sword into his place: for all they that take the sword shall perish with the sword. Thinkest thou that I cannot now pray to my Father, and he shall presently give me more than twelve legions of angels?" (Mt. 26:52-53)
  One of Jesus' little known but important roles apparently assigned to Him by the Father was to function as supreme commander of heaven's angelic armies. The O.T. describes this role as being *"captain of the Lord's*

Host" (see Gen. 32:1-2; Josh. 5:13-14; 1 Sam. 17:45). Thus, holding this highest of rank, He could have easily (as was pointed out to Peter) instantly enlisted the aid of 12 legions of heaven's mighty warriors, numbering an elite army some 72,000 strong! BUT HE WOULD NOT! Jesus came to die for sinful men, not destroy them.

XXXV. THIRTY-FIVE: Second Miraculous Catch of Fish (Jn. 21:1-11)

A. Survey

A short time following His resurrection Jesus appears to seven of His disciples who were fishing on the Sea of Galilee.

The Savior: "Have you caught any fish?"

The seven: "No."

The Savior: "Cast your net on the right side of the boat and you will."

In a nutshell, THEY DID AND THEY DID!

B. Significance

■ This was Jesus' final miracle and the only one after His resurrection.

■ John's gospel alone records both His first and final miracle.

C. Spiritual Truths

■ This is the seventh of the ten resurrection appearances made by Christ, and the third before His disciples (Jn. 21:14).

■ It marks the only appearance in which a miracle was involved.

■ Some have wrongly faulted these seven for leaving Jerusalem, accusing them of returning to their old trade of fishing. In fact, nothing could be farther from the truth. On two separate occasions the disciples were instructed to meet Jesus in Galilee after His resurrection!

  1. First occasion:

     "But after I am risen again, I will go before you into Galilee." (Mt. 26:32)

  2. Second occasion:

     "And the angel answered and said unto the women, Fear not ye: for I know that ye seek Jesus, which was crucified. He is not here: for he is risen, as he said. Come, see the place where the Lord lay. And go quickly, and tell his disciples that he is risen from the dead; and, behold, he goeth before you into Galilee; there shall ye see him: lo, I have told you." (Mt. 28:5-7)

     Actually, the backslidden ones were the four who were not there!

■ As has been previously noted, John's Gospel alone records both the first and the final miracle of Christ. His first (Jn. 2) occurred at a wedding. His final miracle (Jn. 21) was on a seashore. Both involved food and fellowship. At the wedding there was wine to drink, and at the seashore fish to eat. Both acts were accomplished to increase the faith of his followers.

     "This beginning of miracles did Jesus in Cana of Galilee, and manifested forth his glory; and his disciples believed on him." (Jn. 2:11)

"And many other signs truly did Jesus in the presence of his disciples, which are not written in this book: But these are written, that ye might believe that Jesus is the Christ, the Son of God; and that believing ye might have life through his name." (Jn 20:30-31)

■ There may have been a double miracle involved here, for Jesus already had fish and bread available even before the disciples had brought in their catch.

■ Following both the miracle and the meal, Jesus asks Peter a question:

"So when they had dined, Jesus saith to Simon Peter, Simon, son of Jonas, lovest thou me more than these? He saith unto him, Yea, Lord; thou knowest that I love thee. He saith unto him, Feed my lambs." (Jn. 21:15)

Jesus' question, "Lovest thou me more than these?" may have referred to at least one of three things. He could have meant:

1. "Do you love me more than you love these men?"
2. "Do you love me more than fishing?"
3. "Do you love me more than these men love me?"

   It would seem that Jesus had the third meaning in mind, based on Mt. 26:33.

   "Peter answered and said unto him, Though all men shall be offended because of thee, yet will I never be offended." (Mt. 26:33)

■ Three times he is asked if he really loves the Savior. Three times he answers in the affirmative. Peter had once denied Christ three times in the presence of the Savior's enemies. Jesus was now giving him the opportunity to affirm his love three times. God is the God of the second chance.

1. As seen in the life of Jonah— *"And the word of the LORD came unto Jonah the second time, saying, Arise, go unto Nineveh, that great city, and preach unto it the preaching that I bid thee." (Jonah 3:1-2)*
2. As seen in the life of John Mark. This young man had once failed God by abandoning Paul and Barnabas during their first missionary journey (see Acts 13:13; 15:36-39). But Mark, like Jonah and Peter, served the God of the second chance. Years later, just prior to his martyrdom in Rome, the Apostle Paul testified of this: *"Only Luke is with me. Take Mark, and bring him with thee: for he is profitable to me for the ministry." (2 Tim. 4:11)*

An Outline of the Parables of Jesus

BASIC FACTS REGARDING JESUS' PARABLES

I. The Definitions Involved (Various Suggestions)

A. The word parable literally means, "a placing alongside of."

B. It is a truth carried in a vehicle.

C. It is an earthly story with a heavenly meaning.

D. It is a narrative which uses earthly elements to teach spiritual truths.

E. It is a true-to-life story to illustrate or illuminate a truth.

II. The Importance Involved

A. One third of Jesus' teachings as recorded in the Gospels was in parabolic form.

B. Nearly one fourth of Jesus' parables were related during the last few weeks of His life.

III. The Purpose Involved

A. To reveal great spiritual truths to the sincere heart

"And the disciples came, and said unto him, why speakest thou unto those in parables?"

"He answered and said unto them, because it is given unto you to know the mysteries of the kingdom of heaven..." (Mt. 13:10, 11)

B. To conceal great spiritual truths from the insincere heart

"Therefore speak I to them in parables: because they seeing see not; and hearing they hear not, neither do they understand. " (Mt. 13:13)

C. To fulfill prophecy

"All these things spake Jesus unto the multitude in parables; and without a parable spake he not unto them: That it might be fulfilled which was spoken by the prophet, saying, I will open my mouth in parables; I will utter things which have been kept secret from the foundation of the world." (Mt. 13:34-35)

D. To emphasize His authority

"And it came to pass, when Jesus had ended these sayings, the people were astonished at his doctrine: For he taught them as one having authority, and not as the scribes." (Mt. 7:28-29)

"The officers answered, Never man spake like this man." (Jn. 7:46)

E. To clarify and illustrate the kingdom of Heaven

Of all the subjects illustrated by Jesus' parables, the kingdom of Heaven was the most frequently referred to by far.

1. Distinguished from the kingdom of God

a. On rare occasions the kingdom of God is used interchangeably for the kingdom of heaven (Millennial meaning). Compare Mk. 1:14-15 with Mt. 3:1-2. (See also Acts 1:3, 6.)

b. The most common meaning, however, is a reference to the new birth. (See Jn. 3:3, 5; Acts 8:12; 19:8; 20:25; 28:23, 31; 1 Cor. 15:50.)

2. Definition of the kingdom of heaven

a. First meaning -- That general rule of the Father from heaven over the affairs of men from creation to the Millennium. Both saved and unsaved belong to this kingdom. (See Dan. 4:17, 32; Mt. 8:12; 22:2, 25:1.)

b. Second meaning -- That specific rule of the Son from Jerusalem over the affairs of men during the Millennium. Only saved people will enter this kingdom. (See Mt. 6:10, 13; 25:34; 26:29.)

A Listing of Jesus' Parables

The Classification and Number Identification of Jesus' Parables

CLASSIFICATION	PARABLE IDENTIFICATION
Baking	16
Building World	5
Business World	32
Compassion	23
Criticism	8
Defilement	21
Demonic World	10, 11
Discernment	27
Discipleship	30
Employee And Employer Relationships	37, 40
Farming	12, 13, 14, 15, 42, 43
Father and Son Relationship	31, 39
Final Judgment	14, 19, 45, 47
Fishing	19
Forgiveness	9, 22
God's Love For The Church	18
God's Love For Israel	17
Good Works, Testimony	1, 2
Hell	25, 33
Kingdom Of Heaven	12-16, 22, 37, 41, 45, 46
Life's Choices	4
Master And Servant Relationships	26, 34, 46
Praying, Persistence	24, 35, 36
Second Coming	26, 43, 44, 45
Shepherding	47
Social World	29
Weddings	6, 28, 41, 45

The Parables of Jesus

I. ONE: Flavored Salt Versus Flawed Salt (Mt. 5:13; Mk. 9:50; Lk. 14:34)

A. Survey

Believers are to be the salt of the earth, but if salt loses its flavor, it is worthless for seasoning or matters of preservation.

B. Significance

This is the first of no less than five parables related by Jesus during His initial formal address to the multitudes. For the remaining four, see parables 2, 3, 4, and 5.

C. Spiritual Truths

- Salt played an important role in the Bible.
    1. All grain offerings under the law of Moses were to be accompanied with salt (Lk. 2:13).
    2. In the future millennium all animal offerings will be accompanied with salt (Ezek. 43:24).
    3. God ratified His covenant with David by salt (2 Chron. 13:5).
    4. Paul commands that our very words *"be always with grace, seasoned with salt, that ye may know how you should answer every man" (Col. 4:6).*

- In the days of Jesus Roman soldiers often received their pay not in gold but in salt.

- As has been observed, Jesus said we are to function as salt. Salt thus:
    1. Flavors
        "Can that which is unsavory be eaten without salt? or is there any taste in the white of an egg?" (Job. 6:6)
    2. Preserves
        It is ironic indeed that those godless individuals who hate and prosecute believers over the very stability and relative health of their society to the restraining and preserving ministry of those same people!
    3. Purifies
        "And he said, Bring me a new cruse, and put salt therein. And they brought it to him. And he went forth unto the spring of the waters, and cast the salt in there, and said, Thus saith the LORD, I have healed these waters; there shall not be from thence any more death or barren land." (2 Kings 2:20-21)

- It has also been suggested that salt serves to make one thirsty, indicating our daily walk should produce a thirst in the lives of unsaved friends, co-workers, relatives, etc.

- Finally, Jesus warned that savorless salt would be *"cast out, and ... be trodden under foot of men" (Mt. 5:13).*
    Perhaps Paul had these words in mind when he would later write concerning the Judgment Seat of Christ.

"For other foundation can no man lay than that is laid, which is Jesus Christ. Now if any man build upon this foundation gold, silver, precious stones, wood, hay, stubble; Every man's work shall be made manifest: for the day shall declare it, because it shall be revealed by fire; and the fire shall try every man's work of what sort it is. If any man's work abide which he hath built thereupon, he shall receive a reward. If any man's work shall be burned, he shall suffer loss: but he himself shall be saved; yet so as by fire." (1 Cor. 3:11-15)

II. TWO: Don't Darken Your Light (Mt. 5:14-16; Mk. 4:21-22; Lk. 8:16-17; 11:33-36)
A. Survey

"Ye are the light of the world. A city that is set on an hill cannot be hid. Neither do men light a candle, and put it under a bushel, but on a candlestick; and it giveth light unto all that are in the house. Let your light so shine before men, that they may see your good works, and glorify your Father which is in heaven." (Mt. 5:14-16)

"Your eye is a lamp for your body. A pure eye lets sunshine into your soul. But an evil eye shuts out the light and plunges you into darkness. Make sure that the light you think you have is not really darkness. If you are filled with light, with no dark corners; then your whole life will be radiant as though a floodlight is shining on you." (Lk. 11:34-36, NLT)

B. Significance

This is but the first of many instances in the New Testament where the nature and function of light is employed to illustrate and describe a believer's testimony.

C. Spiritual Truths

■ As has been observed, Jesus instructs us to function as lights. But in reality we are to serve as light reflectors, for the Savior alone is the only true light!

John's gospel brings this out time and again:

"In him was life; and the life was the light of men. And the light shineth in darkness; and the darkness comprehended it not... Then spake Jesus again unto them, saying, I am the light of the world: he that followeth me shall not walk in darkness, but shall have the light of life ... As long as I am in the world, I am the light of the world...I am come a light into the world, that whosoever believeth on me should not abide in darkness." (Jn. 1:4-5; 8:12; 9:5; 12:46)

■ Here are some elements involved in this light-reflecting ministry:

1. The testimony of John the Baptist was viewed as a light to the Jews (Jn. 5:35).
2. The testimonies of Paul and Barnabas were viewed as lights to the Gentiles (Acts 13:4).
3. We are called the Sons of Light (Lk. 16:8; Jn. 12:36; 1 Thess. 5:5).
4. We are thus to put on the armor of light (Rom. 13:12).
5. We are to walk in the light (Eph. 5:8).
6. We are to shine brightly and blameless in this world of darkness (Phil. 2:13).

III. THREE: The Ultimate Evil Eye: Attempting to Lead or Judge with Impaired Sight (Mt. 7:3-5; Lk. 6:39-42)
A. Survey

Jesus' rule on judging: Be sure you first remove the log from your own eye before attempting to remove a spoke from a friend's eye.

Jesus' rule on leading: One attempting to lead a blind person must himself be able to see.

B. Significance

"Thou hypocrite, first cast out the beam out of thine own eye; and then shalt thou see clearly to cast out the mote out of thy brother's eye." (Mt. 7:5)

- This marks the first of at least 12 occasions where Jesus directly addresses and accuses the Pharisees with gross hypocrisy.

- These instances are recorded in Mt. 16:3; 22:18; 23:13-15, 25-29; Lk. 12:1.

C. Spiritual Truths

- There are two key biblical examples illustrating the tragic results and other hypocrisy of judging falsely:

  1. That of David

     "And it came to pass, after the year was expired, at the time when kings go forth to battle, that David sent Joab, and his servants with him, and all Israel; and they destroyed the children of Ammon, and besieged Rabbah. But David tarried still at Jerusalem. And it came to pass in an eveningtide, that David arose from off his bed, and walked upon the roof of the king's house: and from the roof he saw a woman washing herself; and the woman was very beautiful to look upon. And David sent and enquired after the woman. And one said, Is not this Bathsheba, the daughter of Eliam, the wife of Uriah the Hittite? And David sent messengers, and took her; and she came in unto him, and he lay with her; for she was purified from her uncleanness: and she returned unto her house. And the woman conceived, and sent and told David, and said, I am with child. And David sent to Joab, saying, Send me Uriah the Hittite. And Joab sent Uriah to David. And when Uriah was come unto him, David demanded of him how Joab did, and how the people did, and how the war prospered. And David said to Uriah, Go down to thy house, and wash thy feet. And Uriah departed out of the king's house, and there followed him a mess of meat from the king. But Uriah slept at the door of the king's house with all the servants of his lord, and went not down to his house." (2 Sam. 11:1-9)

  2. That of Judas

     "Then took Mary a pound of ointment of spikenard, very costly, and anointed the feet of Jesus, and wiped his feet with her hair: and the house was filled with the odour of the ointment. Then saith one of his disciples, Judas Iscariot, Simon's son, which should betray him, Why was not this ointment sold for three hundred pence, and given to the poor? This he said, not that he cared for the poor; but because he was a thief, and had the bag, and bare what was put therein." (Jn. 12:3-6)

- Here are some principles that should govern our judging of others:

  1. We must begin by judging ourselves.

     "For if we would judge ourselves, we should not be judged." (1 Cor. 11:31)

  2. We must realize to judge harshly is to be judged harshly (Rom. 2:3).

  3. Restoration, not retaliation should be our goal in judging.

TWO: TOPICAL

> *"Brethren, if a man be overtaken in a fault, ye which are spiritual, restore such an one in the spirit of meekness; considering thyself, lest thou also be tempted. Bear ye one another's burdens, and so fulfil the law of Christ." (Gal. 6:1-2)*

4. We must acknowledge that Jesus alone is the ultimate judge.

> *"For it is written, As I live, saith the Lord, every knee shall bow to me, and every tongue shall confess to God. So then every one of us shall give account of himself to God." (Rom. 14:11-12)*

5. We must never forget all Christians will someday be themselves judged at the Judgment Seat of Christ.

> *"But why dost thou judge thy brother? or why dost thou set at nought thy brother? for we shall all stand before the judgment seat of Christ." (Rom 14:10) "For we must all appear before the judgment seat of Christ; that every one may receive the things done in his body, according to that he hath done, whether it be good or bad." (2 Cor. 5:10)*

6. We are never to judge in non-essential matters.

> *"Let not him that eateth despise him that eateth not; and let not him which eateth not judge him that eateth: for God hath received him. Who art thou that judgest another man's servant? to his own master he standeth or falleth. Yea, he shall be holden up: for God is able to make him stand." (Rom. 14:3-4)*

7. If we are spirit filled, we will never judge wrongly.

> *"But he that is spiritual judgeth all things, yet he himself is judged of no man." (1 Cor. 2:15)*

8. The ones proposing to judge should ask themselves three key questions before proceeding:
   a. Is it valid? Do I really know and understand all the facts involved?
   b. Is it sincere? Will it be performed to help the person out, not to straighten him out?
   c. Is it necessary? Will or can the matter be resolved without my interference?

IV. FOUR: Two Gates, Two Goals (Mt. 7:13-14)
A. Survey

Jesus said only a few will find and travel that narrow highway leading to life, while most will travel the wide, broad one leading to destruction.

B. Significance

■ This marks the first of three instances during His Sermon on the Mount where Jesus contrasts opposing entities:
   1. The narrow gate versus the wide gate
   2. The good trees versus the bad trees (Mt. 7:16-20)
   3. The true disciples versus the false disciples (Mt. 7:21-23)
   4. The wise builder versus the foolish builder (Mt. 7:24-27)

C. Spiritual Truths

"And if it seem evil unto you to serve the LORD, choose you this day whom ye will serve; whether the gods which your fathers served that were on the other side of the food, or the gods of the Amorites, in whose land ye dwell: but as for me and my house, we will serve the LORD." (Josh. 24:15)

■ A number of metaphors can be found in the Bible which vividly describe these two destinies:

1. Right offering versus wrong offering

   "And in process of time it came to pass, that Cain brought of the fruit of the ground an offering unto the LORD. And Abel, he also brought of the firstlings of his flock and of the fat thereof. And the LORD had respect unto Abel and to his offering: But unto Cain and to his offering he had not respect. And Cain was very wroth, and his countenance fell." (Gen. 4:3-5)

2. Life versus death

   "See, I have set before thee this day life and good, and death and evil." (Deut. 30:15)

3. Blessings versus cursings

   a. Blessings (Deut. 28:2-14)

   b. Cursings (Deut. 28:15-68)

4. Fruitful trees versus worthless chaff (Psa. 1)

5. God versus Baal

   "And Elijah came unto all the people, and said, How long halt ye between two opinions? if the LORD be God, follow him: but if Baal, then follow him. And the people answered him not a word." (1 Kings 18:21)

6. Light versus darkness

   "This then is the message which we have heard of him, and declare unto you, that God is light, and in him is no darkness at all. If we say that we have fellowship with him, and walk in darkness, we lie, and do not the truth: But if we walk in the light, as he is in the light, we have fellowship one with another, and the blood of Jesus Christ his Son cleanseth us from all sin." (1 John 1:5-7)

7. Christ versus Antichrist

   "Hereby know ye the Spirit of God: Every spirit that confesseth that Jesus Christ is come in the flesh is of God: And every spirit that confesseth not that Jesus Christ is come in the flesh is not of God: and this is that spirit of antichrist, whereof ye have heard that it should come; and even now already is it in the world." (1 John 4:2-3)

V. FIVE: The Solid Rock Versus the Shifting Sand (Mt. 7:24-27 Lk. 6:46-49)
A. Survey

The house which is built on a rock will survive all storms, but the one built on sand will soon utterly fall.

B. Significance

- This is the last parable Jesus told during His Sermon on the Mount.

- It is the first of two occasions where He refers to Himself as a Rock. *"Therefore whosoever heareth these sayings of mine, and doeth them, I will liken him unto a wise man, which built his house upon a rock." (Mt. 7:24)*

  "Then understood they how that he bade them not beware of the leaven of bread, but of the doctrine of the Pharisees and of the Sadducees." (Mt. 16:12)

C. Spiritual Truths

- In essence this parable is but an extension of the first Psalm. One was wise, the other foolish. Thus:

  1. The wise man described

"Blessed is the man that walketh not in the counsel of the ungodly, nor standeth in the way of sinners, nor sitteth in the seat of the scornful. But his delight is in the law of the LORD; and in his law doth he meditate day and night. And he shall be like a tree planted by the rivers of water, that bringeth forth his fruit in his season; his leaf also shall not wither; and whatsoever he doeth shall prosper." (Psa. 1:1-3)

2. The foolish man described

"The ungodly are not so: but are like the chaff which the wind driveth away. Therefore the ungodly shall not stand in the judgment, nor sinners in the congregation of the righteous. For the LORD knoweth the way of the righteous: but the way of the ungodly shall perish." (Psa. 1:4-6)

■ The New Testament epistles have much to say regarding Jesus as the Rock.

1. He is the smitten Rock to all who will drink (Exod. 17:6; 1 Cor. 10:4; Jn. 4:13-14; 7:37-39).
2. He is the precious Stone to all who have drunk (1 Pet. 2:3, 7).
3. He is the chief Cornerstone to the Church (Eph. 2:20).
4. He is the stumbling Stone to the Jews at his first coming (Rom. 9:32-33; 1 Cor. 1:23).
5. He is the Headstone of the corner to the Jews at His second coming (Zech. 4:7).
6. He is the smiting Stone cut without hands to Gentile world powers at his second coming (Dan. 2:34).
7. He is the crushing Stone of judgment to all unbelievers (Mt. 21:44). Peter says (2:4) this great Stone was "disallowed" by Israel. This word means "to put to a test and then repudiate". After examining Christ for 34 years, Israel rejected Him. He simply was not what they were looking for in a Messiah.

Note, furthermore, the apostle's statement in 2:6: *"Wherefore also it is contained in the scripture, Behold, I lay in Sion a chief cornerstone."* Certainly here is the fulfillment of Christ's promise in Matt. 16:16, 18. Peter was not that foundation; Christ was. Finally (see 2:5), all believers are *"lively stones, built up (into) a spiritual house, an holy priesthood, to offer up spiritual sacrifices, acceptable to God by Jesus Christ."* (See also Rev. 1:6.)

XI. SIX: Facts on Fasting and Feasting (Mt. 9:14-15; Mk. 2:18-20 Lk. 5:33-35)
A. Survey

Jesus was criticized for not always instructing His disciples to observe the various fasts as did the disciples of both John the Baptist and the Pharisees. Jesus defended His action by pointing out wedding guests feast and celebrate when the groom is present with them, and fast and mourn when he is removed from them.

B. Significance

■ This is the first of two occasions where Jesus refers to Himself as a bridegroom (see Mt. 9:15 and 25:1).

■ On a previous occasion John the Baptist had referred to Him as the bridegroom." *Ye yourselves bear me witness, that I said, I am not the Christ, but that I am sent before him. He that hath the bride is the bridegroom: but the friend of the bridegroom, which standeth and heareth him, rejoiceth greatly because of the bridegroom's voice: this my joy therefore is fulfilled." (Jn. 3:28-29)*

■ Paul would later employ this analogy:

"For I am jealous over you with godly jealousy: for I have espoused you to one husband, that I may present you as a chaste virgin to Christ." (2 Cor. 11:2)

"For the husband is the head of the wife, even as Christ is the head of the church: and he is the saviour of the body. Therefore as the church is subject unto Christ, so let the wives be to their own husbands in every thing. Husbands, love your wives, even as Christ also loved the church, and gave himself for it; That he might sanctify and cleanse it with the washing of water by the word, That he might present it to himself a glorious church, not having spot, or wrinkle, or any such thing; but that it should be holy and without blemish." (Eph. 5:23-27)

C. Spiritual Truths

- Jesus was not at this point discouraging fasting.

  1. He himself once fasted for forty days (Mt. 4:2).
  2. He laid down rules for fasting (Mt. 6:16-18).
  3. He indicated that fasting on certain occasions was necessary to experience the power of God (Mt. 17:21).
  4. Following his ascension, his followers would fast (Acts 14:23; 1 Cor. 7:5; 2 Cor. 6:5).

- However, as long as he was with the disciples (right up to the very hour of Calvary), the main priority of the Savior was to teach and train them.

- In reality the Bible presents three kinds of fasting.

  1. Temporary abstinence from food (Acts 14:23)
  2. Temporary abstinence from sleep (2 Cor. 11:27)
  3. Temporary abstinence from sex (1 Cor. 7:5)

XII. SEVEN: Never Put the New On or In the Old (Mt. 9:16-17; Mk. 2:21-22; Lk. 5:36-39)
A. Survey

A new, unshrunk patch placed on an old garment will soon peel away from the old, leaving an even bigger hole than before. Likewise, new wine poured into old wineskins will soon cause the old to burst from the pressure.

B. Significance

This is perhaps the most descriptive of all Jesus' parables illustrating just why His new teaching could not and would not fit into that of the Pharisees.

C. Spiritual Truths

- Jesus may have hinted at this new teaching during His very first miracle. *"When the ruler of the feast had tasted the water that was made wine, and knew not whence it was: (but the servants which drew the water knew;) the governor of the feast called the bridegroom, And saith unto him, Every man at the beginning doth set forth good wine; and when men have well drunk, then that which is worse: but thou hast kept the good wine until now."* (Jn. 2:9-10)

XIII. EIGHT: A Generation of Gripers (Mt. 11:16-19; Lk. 7:29-35)
A. Survey

Jesus likened His generation to a group of spoiled and immature children who complained because their playmates did not always play the game according to their rules.

He then offered an example of this: John the Baptist, who abstained from wine and fasted, was accused of being demon-possessed, while Jesus, who did neither was looked upon as a glutton and drunkard!

B. Significance

"But whereunto shall I liken this generation? It is like unto children sitting in the markets, and calling unto their fellows." (Mt. 11:16)

- This was the first of many occasions where Jesus condemned His generation for their sin and unbelief.

  1. *"But he answered and said unto them, An evil and adulterous generation seeketh after a sign; and there shall no sign be given to it, but the sign of the prophet Jonas: For as Jonas was three days and three nights in the whale's belly; so shall the Son of man be three days and three nights in the heart of the earth." (Mt. 12:39-40)*
  2. *"The men of Nineveh shall rise in judgment with this generation, and shall condemn it: because they repented at the preaching of Jonas; and, behold, a greater than Jonas is here." (Mt. 12:41)*
  3. *"The queen of the south shall rise up in the judgment with this generation, and shall condemn it: for she came from the uttermost parts of the earth to hear the wisdom of Solomon; and, behold, a greater than Solomon is here." (Mt. 12:42)*
  4. *"That the blood of all the prophets, which was shed from the foundation of the world, may be required of this generation; From the blood of Abel unto the blood of Zacharias which perished between the altar and the temple: verily I say unto you, It shall be required of this generation." (Lk. 11:50-51)*
  5. *"But first must he suffer many things, and be rejected of this generation." (Lk. 17:25)*
  6. *"O Jerusalem, Jerusalem, thou that killest the prophets, and stonest them which are sent unto thee, how often would I have gathered thy children together, even as a hen gathereth her chickens under her wings, and ye would not! Behold, your house is left unto you desolate. For I say unto you, Ye shall not see me henceforth, till ye shall say, Blessed is he that cometh in the name of the Lord." (Mt. 23:37-39)*

C. Spiritual Truths

- Perhaps the Holy Spirit had Jesus' generation in mind when he inspired the writing of the following words: *"There is a generation that curseth their father, and doth not bless their mother. There is a generation that are pure in their own eyes, and yet is not washed from their filthiness. There is a generation, O how lofty are their eyes! and their eyelids are lifted up. There is a generation, whose teeth are as swords, and their jaw teeth as knives, to devour the poor from off the earth, and the needy from among men." (Prov. 30:11-14)*

- The ultimate tragedy here was that this generation which began by criticizing the Savior would end by crucifying him. The gripers would become vipers.

- The sin of murmuring and complaining is one of the most serious in all the Bible.

  1. It was the sin that kept Moses' generation out of the Promised Land.

     "Because all those men which have seen my glory, and my miracles, which I did in Egypt and in the wilderness, and have tempted me now these ten times, and have not hearkened to my voice; Surely they

shall not see the land which I sware unto their fathers, neither shall any of them that provoked me see it." (Num. 14:22-23)

"Yea, they despised the pleasant land, they believed not his word: But murmured in their tents, and hearkened not unto the voice of the LORD." (Psa. 106:24-25)

2. It is often the sin that keeps New Testament believers from entering God's spiritual Promised Land, that is, His perfect will.

"Neither murmur ye, as some of them also murmured, and were destroyed of the destroyer." (1 Cor. 10:10)

"So we see that they could not enter in because of unbelief... There remaineth therefore a rest to the people of God... Let us labour therefore to enter into that rest, lest any man fall after the same example of unbelief." (Heb. 3:19; 4:9, 11)

3. It is the sin of godless apostates.

"These are murmurers, complainers, walking after their own lusts; and their mouth speaketh great swelling words, having men's persons in admiration because of advantage." (Jude 16)

4. It is the sin to be avoided at all costs.

"Do all things without murmurings and disputings." (Phil. 2:14)

■ Thus, to complain in regards to our circumstances is not only to deny God's goodness in our lives but to actually question His very motives!

IX. NINE: Little Love, Great Love: Forgiving the 50 and the 500 (Lk. 7:41-50)

A. Survey

Jesus spoke of an individual who loaned 500 pieces of silver to one man and 50 pieces to another. However, upon discovering that neither could repay, he freely forgave both. The Savior then asked: *"Who do you suppose loved him more after that?"* The Pharisee (Simon) to whom Jesus was speaking, replied with the correct answer: *"I suppose the one who had the bigger debt cancelled."*

B. Significance

■ This is the first of at least three parables on the subject of forgiveness. (See also #22 and 31.)

■ It marks the first of two occasions where Jesus was anointed. (Compare Lk. 7:37-38 with Jn. 12:3.)

■ It is the only parable related during a meal.

C. Spiritual Truths

■ Three key concepts make up this parable: Repentance, forgiveness, and affection.

1. Repentance (from sin) leads to forgiveness (from God), resulting in affection (for Christ).
2. No repentance (from sin) leads to no forgiveness (from God), resulting in no affection (for Christ).

■ Here of course Jesus was not saying that God loves an especially wicked but repenting sinner more than one who is less wicked. What He does seem to observe is the first man may have just cause to be more thankful than the second man. Paul could have had all this in mind when he wrote the following:

"But where sin abounded, grace did much more abound." (Rom. 5:20)

"And I thank Christ Jesus our Lord, who hath enabled me, for that he counted me faithful, putting me into the ministry; Who was before a blasphemer, and a persecutor, and injurious: but I obtained mercy, because I did it ignorantly in unbelief. And the grace of our Lord was exceeding abundant with faith and love which is in Christ Jesus." (1 Tim. 1:12-14)

X. TEN: A Kingdom Divided, A Strong Man Subdued (Mt. 12:25-29, Mk. 3.23-30)
A. Survey

- Any kingdom at war against itself, or any city or home divided against itself is doomed.

- One cannot enter a house, rob it, and harm its members without first subduing the strong man of that house.

B. Significance

This parable concludes with the only reference to the unpardonable sin in the entire Bible.

"Wherefore I say unto you, All manner of sin and blasphemy shall be forgiven unto men: but the blasphemy against the Holy Ghost shall not be forgiven unto men. And whosoever speaketh a word against the Son of man, it shall be forgiven him: but whosoever speaketh against the Holy Ghost, it shall not be forgiven him, neither in this world, neither in the world to come." (Mt. 12:31-32)

C. Spiritual Truths

- Jesus offers a three-fold argument to counteract the accusation that He was casting out demons by the power of Satan:

  1. If the devil empowered Him to do this, then he, Satan, would be destroying his own kingdom.
  2. Jesus was successfully doing that which their own Jewish exorcists had claimed to be able to do.
  3. Since He had cast out one of Satan's demons it only stood to reason that He was more powerful than the devil!

- As has been previously observed, Jesus concludes this parable with a somber warning regarding the unpardonable sin. Much ink has been spilled over these words. What is this unforgivable and unpardonable sin? Who can commit it? Can it be done today? Two main views have been offered to explain this sin.

  1. First view—The first view is that the sin can be committed by any unbeliever today and occurs when a sinner rejects the convicting voice of the Holy Spirit once too often. At this point, the Holy Spirit forever ceases to deal with the sinner and he is hopelessly condemned, with no chance of salvation, however he may later desire it. Genesis 6:3 is sometimes offered in support of this theory. *"And the LORD said, My spirit shall not always strive with man, for that he also is flesh: yet his days shall be an hundred and twenty years."*

     However, an examination of the passage shows this meaning is taken completely out of its context. In reality there is no scriptural basis for the first theory.

  2. Second view—The second view is that the sin was dispensational in nature, that it was the sin of ascribing to Satan the earthly miracles performed by our Savior and therefore cannot be committed today. This theory is generally held by the majority of Bible students and the passage context would seem to support its accuracy.

     "Then was brought unto him one possessed with a devil, blind, and dumb: and he healed him, insomuch that the blind and dumb both spake and saw. And all the people were amazed, and said, Is not this the son of

XI. ELEVEN: Seven Spirits and a Swept House (Mt. 12:43-45; Lk. 11:24-26)
A. Survey

A demon left the person it was possessing and eventually returned, finding that person "empty, swept, and clean." The demon then brought seven other demons, each more wicked than it was, all of whom now occupied that person, making his present condition far worse than before.

B. Significance

This is the only parable dealing with the frightful subject of demon possession.

C. Spiritual Truths

■ Here is a case of reformation without regeneration. The man in the parable turned over a new leaf, but not a new life. This can prove to be a very dangerous situation. To illustrate:

1. An unbelieving drunk through sheer human willpower is able to dry out and become a respectable member of society.
2. He then is filled with pride and ridicules the saving grace of God, boasting that human determination is sufficient for all things.
3. In this state he becomes far more valuable to Satan than when he was a poor derelict.

■ In this parable Jesus strongly suggests that there are degrees of evil in the hierarchy of the demonic world. Various Scripture verses seem to support this. Note the diverse actions caused by various demons.

1. Seducing and false spirits—They are associated with false doctrine (2 Cor. 11:4; 1 Tim. 4:1; 1 Jn. 4:1-6).
2. Unclean and evil spirits—They seem to cause physical suffering (Mt. 10:1; Lk. 7:21; Acts 5:16; 8:7).
3. Miracle-working spirits—These may attempt to imitate the work of God (Rev. 16:13-14).
4. Foul spirits—These are linked to sexual immorality (Rev. 18:2-3).
5. Violent spirits (Acts 19:12-16; 1 Sam. 18:10-11).
6. Lying spirits (1 Kings 22:22-23).

■ Jesus may well have had the nation Israel in mind as He related this parable. Plagued with the demon of unbelief since Kadesh-barnea (Num. 13-14; Psa. 78, 106) the nation had, initially at least, favorably responded to the messages of both John the Baptist (Mt. 3:5-6), and Jesus Himself (Jn. 6:14-15). But all too soon the Jewish leaders would officially reject Him (Mt. 27:15-26), thus making *the last state ... worse than the first* (Lk. 11:26).

XII. TWELVE: The Sower, the Seed, and the Soil (Mt. 13:3-9, 18-23; Mk. 4:3-8, 13-20; Lk. 8:5-8, 11-15)
A. Survey

A farmer scattered some seed in a field that consisted of four kinds of soil, all of which yielded different results.

■ Footpath soil: the birds soon came and ate the seed.

- Shallow soil with underlying rock: the plants sprung up quickly, but soon wilted and died for lack of nourishment.
- Thorn infested soil: the tender blades of the plants were quickly choked by these thorns.
- Fertile soil: this area alone produced an abundant crop of 30, 60, and 100-fold return.

B. Significance

This is the first of nine parables explaining and illustrating the Kingdom of Heaven all of which were related by Jesus during an extended lecture given on the banks of the Galilean Sea.

C. Spiritual Truths

- Jesus Himself provided the interpretation regarding these four kinds of soil.
  1. Roadside Soil — A person who receives the Word without really understanding it. Seed soon stolen by both Satan and his false ministers.
  2. Shallow Soil — A person who receives the Word without acting fully upon it. Thus, when persecutions and trials arise, he falls away.
  3. Thorn-infested Soil — A person who receives the Word but attempts to mix it with the pleasures of this life. However, worldly things soon choke it.
  4. Fertile Soil — A person who receives the Word with an honest, sincere, and understanding heart. This one alone will bear fruit.
- The following suggested applications are offered in regard to these four kinds of soil:
  1. Roadside Soil
     a. The apostle John would later in a spiritual sense associate demonic doctrine with unclean birds (Rev. 18:2).
     b. The roadside soil kind of heart refuses to obey God's command as recorded by both Jeremiah and Hosea:
        "For thus saith the LORD to the men of Judah and Jerusalem, Break up your fallow ground, and sow not among thorns." (Jer. 4:3)
        "Sow to yourselves in righteousness, reap in mercy; break up your fallow ground: for it is time to seek the LORD, till he come and rain righteousness upon you." (Hosea 10:12)
     c. These kind of people are seen often during Jesus' earthly ministry.
        "Now when he was in Jerusalem at the passover, in the feast day, many believed in his name, when they saw the miracles which he did. But Jesus did not commit himself unto them, because he knew all men." (Jn. 2:23-24)
        "And this he said to prove him: for he himself knew what he would do." (Jn. 6:6)
  2. Shallow, Rocky Soil — Jesus summarizes this kind of person in two-fold fashion.
     a. They have no root. Both David and Paul speak of this:
        "The ungodly are not so: but are like the chaff which the wind driveth away." (Psa. 1:4)
        "And grieve not the holy Spirit of God, whereby ye are sealed unto the day of redemption." (Eph. 4:30)
     b. They are unable to withstand the storms of life. It has been rightly observed that persecution, pain, travail and tribulation serve as the ultimate tests in revealing the saved from the unsaved, the one having roots from the one without roots.
  3. Thorn Infested Soil. Two factors prevent this soil from producing fruit:

a. The deceitfulness of wealth. The rich young ruler had, sadly enough, allowed this thorn to infest his heart.

"Jesus said unto him, If thou wilt be perfect, go and sell that thou hast, and give to the poor, and thou shalt have treasure in heaven: and come and follow me. But when the young man heard that saying, he went away sorrowful: for he had great possessions" (Mt. 19:21-22). Paul would later warn of this

"For the love of money is the root of all evil: which while some coveted after, they have erred from the faith, and pierced themselves through with many sorrows." (1 Tim. 6:10)

"For Demas hath forsaken me, having loved this present world, and is departed unto Thessalonica; Crescens to Galatia, Titus unto Dalmatia." (2 Tim. 4:10)

b. The desire for and pleasure in worldly things. This would be in direct opposition to that attitude once demonstrated by Moses.

"By faith Moses, when he was come to years, refused to be called the son of Pharaoh's daughter; Choosing rather to suffer affliction with the people of God, than to enjoy the pleasures of sin for a season; Esteeming the reproach of Christ greater riches than the treasures in Egypt: for he had respect unto the recompence of the reward." (Heb. 11:24-26)

4. Fertile Soil — The fertile soil thus receives the Word (unlike the shallow heart), understands it (unlike the hard heart), and holds fast to it (unlike the crowded heart).

Is Jesus indicating here that only one out of four (25%) of those witnessed to will be saved? NO, but He is promising that some will accept Christ. In other words if we sow, we will reap!

In a concluding thought, the 30, 60, and 100-fold harvest produced by the fertile soil seems to tie in with Jesus' vine and branch discourse. Thus:

a. *"Every branch that beareth FRUIT, he purgeth it..." (Jn. 15:1a).* A reference to the 30-fold.

b. *"That it may bring forth MORE FRUIT" (Jn. 15:1b).* A reference to the 60-fold.

c. *"He that abideth in me ... bringeth forth MUCH FRUIT" (Jn. 15:5).* A reference to 100-fold.

XIII. THIRTEEN: The Secret of the Seed (Mk. 4:26-29)

A. Survey

The farmer can sow and harvest the seed, but God alone produces the crop in 3-fold fashion.

<u>First</u>, the leaf blade pushes up through the ground.

<u>Second</u>, the heads of wheat are formed.

<u>Finally</u>, the grain ripens.

B. Significance

This is the first parable to trace the actual spiritual growth of the Kingdom of Heaven.

C. Spiritual Truths

■ As has been already observed, man sows and harvests but only God can grow the seed. Both Paul and James testify to this:

"I have planted, Apollos watered; but God gave the increase. So then neither is he that planteth any thing, neither he that watereth; but God that giveth the increase." (1 Cor. 3:6-7)

"Be patient therefore, brethren, unto the coming of the Lord. Behold, the husbandman waiteth for the precious fruit of the earth, and hath long patience for it, until he receive the early and latter rain." (James 5:7)

■ A spiritual application can be drawn along these lines here from the resurrection of Lazarus. Consider:

  1. Man's part:
     a. The sowing— *"Take away the stone"* (Jn. 11:39).
     b. The reaping— *"Loose him and let him go"* (Jn. 11:44).
  2. God's part:
     a. The growing— *"Lazarus, come forth"* (Jn. 11:43).

■ This parable describes the development of the kingdom of God, that is to say, God's dealings with this world in both the physical and spiritual realms. It is a progressive thing. An analogy here can be seen in the divine progressive revelation of our Bible. God did not reveal all of its truths in the book of Genesis, or even in the Old Testament. Centuries were involved in its writing. But by the time one reaches the book of Revelation, the seed sprout in Genesis has become the fully developed plant.

XIV. FOURTEEN: Satan's Tares in the Savior's Soil (Mt. 13:24-30, 36-43)
A. Survey

A farmer planted good seed in his field only to later discover his enemy had secretly sown poisoned weeds in that same field. When asked by his farm hands if they should pull out the weeds, the man replied:

"No, lest you uproot the wheat also. Let both grow until the harvest, at which time we will sort out both, burning the weeds and storing the wheat."

B. Significance

■ This is the first parable to explain the why, when, who, and what regarding the Kingdom of Heaven.

  1. Why God allows tares in His field of wheat.
  2. When God will remove those tares.
  3. Who God will use in removing the tares.
  4. What will happen to the tares.

C. Spiritual Truths

■ The three questions in regards to this parable.

  1. What are the tares? The Palestinian farmer called them "bearded darnel." In fact, they are a poisonous rye-grass plant, giving every appearance at the beginning to be regular wheat, until both plants reach maturity. Then the tares are easily recognized.
  2. Who (humanly speaking) are the real tares today? It can be said that they are not the ultra-liberals or scoffing agnostics, but rather those religious individuals who know the vocabulary and concepts of salvation, but who have in their hearts totally rejected the Christ of salvation.
  3. Where (humanly speaking) are the real tares today? For the most part they would not be found in the congregations of the cults, or among liberal assemblies. Rather these people have often succeeded in infiltrating the membership of Bible-believing churches.

■ The nine metaphors in this parable:

1. The man is Christ.
2. The enemy is the devil.
3. The field is the world.
4. The wheat is believers.
5. The tares are unbelievers.
6. The harvest is the end of the age.
7. The reapers are angels.
8. The granary is heaven.
9. The furnace is hell.

■ The six New Testament passages testifying to this parable:

1. *"Beware of false prophets, which come to you in sheep's clothing, but inwardly they are ravening wolves."* *(Mt. 7:15)*

2. *"Not every one that saith unto me, Lord, Lord, shall enter into the kingdom of heaven; but he that doeth the will of my Father which is in heaven. Many will say to me in that day, Lord, Lord, have we not prophesied in thy name? and in thy name have cast out devils? and in thy name done many wonderful works? And then will I profess unto them, I never knew you: depart from me, ye that work iniquity."* *(Mt. 7:21-23)*

3. *"Take heed therefore unto yourselves, and to all the flock, over the which the Holy Ghost hath made you overseers, to feed the church of God, which he hath purchased with his own blood. For I know this, that after my departing shall grievous wolves enter in among you, not sparing the flock. Also of your own selves shall men arise, speaking perverse things, to draw away disciples after them."* *(Acts 20:28-30)*

4. *"And many shall follow their pernicious ways; by reason of whom the way of truth shall be evil spoken of."* *(2 Peter 2:2)*

5. *"For there are certain men crept in unawares, who were before of old ordained to this condemnation, ungodly men, turning the grace of our God into lasciviousness, and denying the only Lord God, and our Lord Jesus Christ."* *(Jude 4)*

6. *"I know thy works, and tribulation, and poverty, (but thou art rich) and I know the blasphemy of them which say they are Jews, and are not, but are the synagogue of Satan."* *(Rev. 2:9)*

XV. FIFTEEN: The Mighty Mustard Seed (Mt. 13:31-32; Mk. 4:30-32; Lk. 13:18-19)
A. Survey

Although the mustard seed is one of the smallest of all seeds, it later becomes the largest of garden plants and grows into a tree, where birds can come and find shelter in its branches.

B. Significance

This parable, as no other, stresses the insignificant beginning of the Kingdom of Heaven (in the Upper Room with only 120 - Acts 2) to a world-wide entity. See Col. 1:6.

C. Spiritual Truths

- The mustard seed was indeed the smallest of all seeds sown in the field. It took 750 seeds to weigh a gram. As there are 28 grams in one ounce, and 16 ounces in a pound, it would take 336,000 of these seeds to equal a pound. And yet this tiny seed can, in a very few weeks, grow into a mustard plant 15 feet high.

Jesus compares all of this with the Kingdom of God.

1. Christ's first coming and the kingdom—At that time, it was but a tiny seed. The Roman rulers had ridiculed it, and the Jewish leaders had rejected it. In fact, the last question asked of Christ by his disciples just prior to his ascension had to do with the kingdom. *"When they therefore were come together, they asked of him, saying, Lord, wilt thou at this time restore again the kingdom to Israel?" (Acts 1:6)*

2. Christ's second coming and the kingdom—At that time, it will become as the mighty mustard plant. *"And the seventh angel sounded; and there were great voices in heaven, saying, The kingdoms of this world are become the kingdoms of our Lord, and of his Christ; and he shall reign for ever and ever." (Rev. 11:15)*

- The tree here can be compared with the one described in Daniel 4.

1. As compared: Both trees grew rapidly to a great height, providing refuge for the birds of the air.

2. As contrasted: The tree in Dan. 4 represented Nebuchadnezzar and the Babylonian Empire. The tree in Matt. 13 speaks of Jesus and the Kingdom of Heaven. The Dan. 4 tree was soon cut down. Nebuchadnezzar would be punished with insanity and his kingdom later be given over to the Persians (Dan. 5).

3. The Matt. 13 tree will never fall, but will eventually give way to Jesus' 1000-year reign over all the earth!

XVI. SIXTEEN: The Cook's Leaven and the Kingdom of Heaven (Mt. 13:33)
A. Survey

The Kingdom of Heaven can be likened to yeast as used by a woman in making bread. Even though she uses a large amount of flour, the yeast permeates every part of the dough.

B. Significance

- This is the shortest of all Jesus' parables.

- It is the only one where the word leaven is used.

C. Spiritual Truths

- The key to interpreting this parable is one's understanding of the word "leaven." What does it stand for? There are two main views:

1. It represents the gospel. This is the position of the postmillennialist. He is the one who believes the preaching of the gospel in and by itself will be able to usher in the thousand-year era of peace, at the end of which Christ will return.

2. It represents the presence of evil. This is the position of the premillennialist. He is one who believes that in spite of gospel preaching, the world will become worse and that only the second coming of the King himself

at the beginning of the millennium can usher in that golden era of peace. This seems to be the correct view. In fact, there are three symbols for evil in the Bible. These are:

a. Leprosy (Lev. 13-14; Num. 5:2)

b. The serpent (Gen. 3:1-2, 4, 13-14; Num. 21:8-9; Psa. 58:4; Isa. 27:1; Mt. 23:33; Rev. 12:9; 20:2)

c. Leaven—Leaven, when used in the Old Testament, is always mentioned in an evil sense, and the way the word leaven is used in the New Testament explains its symbolic meaning. (1 Cor. 5:6-8; Mt. 16:12; Mt. 16:6; Mk. 8:15; Mt. 23:14-16, 23-28; Mt. 22:23, 29; Mt. 22:16-21; Mk. 3:6).

■ Thus, this parable predicts the growth of satanic evil until the whole world is affected. It also answers the question of why Christ has not yet come.

1. The postmillennialist says he has not returned because things are not yet good enough.

2. The premillennialist says he has not returned because things are not yet bad enough. (See 1 Tim. 4:1-3; 2 Tim. 3:1-9; 4:1-4; 2 Pet. 3.)

XVII. SEVENTEEN: Finding a Fortune in a Field (Mt. 13:44)

A. Survey

A man discovered a hidden treasure in a field. In his excitement he hid it again and sold everything he owned to get sufficient money to buy the field and thus secure the treasure.

B. Significance

This parable employs the first of (at least) two symbols for the nation Israel. For the second, see parable numbers 42 and 43.

C. Spiritual Truths

■ The treasure here probably represents Israel, and the man is Christ. Often in the Old Testament, God describes that nation as his special treasure. Note: *"Now therefore, if ye will obey my voice indeed, and keep my covenant, then ye shall be a peculiar treasure unto me above all people: for all the earth is mine" (Exod. 19:5). "For thou art an holy people unto the LORD thy God, and the LORD hath chosen thee to be a peculiar people unto himself, above all the nations that are upon the earth" (Deut. 14:2). "For the LORD hath chosen Jacob unto himself, and Israel for his peculiar treasure" (Psa. 135:4). "And they shall be mine, saith the LORD of hosts, in that day when I make up my jewels; and I will spare them, as a man spareth his own son that serveth him." (Mal. 3:17)*

■ Just why God initially chose Israel to be His special people is a mystery indeed. An ancient poem observes:

> *How odd of God to choose the Jews.*
> *Someone however has added the following words to this poem:*
> *But odder still God's plan to see, To use the likes of you and me!*

■ In a key passage Moses explains and describes God's relationship with Israel:

"For thou art an holy people unto the LORD thy God: the LORD thy God hath chosen thee to be a special people unto himself, above all people that are upon the face of the earth. The LORD did not set his love upon you, nor choose you, because ye were more in number than any people; for ye were the fewest of all people: But because the LORD loved you, and because he would keep the oath which he had sworn unto your fathers, hath the LORD brought you out with a mighty hand, and redeemed you out of the house of bondmen, from the hand of Pharaoh king of Egypt." (Deut. 7:6-8)

XVIII. EIGHTEEN: The Price Paid for a Pearl (Mt. 13:45-46)
A. Survey

When a pearl merchant found a pearl of great value, he sold everything he owned and bought it.

B. Significance

Many believe the pearl here is the first allusion to the church in the Bible.

C. Spiritual Truths

- Parables 17 and 18 describe God's two most precious possessions, the nation Israel and the church.
- Both prized possessions are highlighted in the construction of the Holy City, New Jerusalem (Rev. 21:1-2).
    1. The twelve gates in the wall surrounding the city consist of twelve pearls (Rev. 21:21).
        a. Each gate was supervised by a special angel (Rev. 21:12).
        b. Each gate was named after one of the twelve tribes of Israel (Rev. 21:12).
    2. The twelve foundations of the city are named after the twelve apostles of Christ (Rev. 21:14).

XIX. NINETEEN: Sorting Out a Sea Catch (Mt. 13:47-50)
A. Survey

The Kingdom of Heaven is like a fishing net that is thrown into the water and gathers fish of every kind. When the net is full, they drag it onto the shore, sit down, sort out the good fish into crates and throw the bad ones away.

B. Significance

- This parable contains the final of three contrasting entities as used by Jesus in explaining the Kingdom of Heaven in Matthew 13.
    1. Fertile soil versus barren soil (Mt. 13:3-8)
    2. Tares versus wheat (Mt. 13:24-30)
    3. Good fish versus bad fish (Mt. 13:47-50)

C. Spiritual Truths

- Angels are presented in this parable as special agents, assigned by God to eventually separate the saved from the unsaved. This truth is a recurring theme throughout the N.T. Note:

"The enemy that sowed them is the devil; the harvest is the end of the world; and the reapers are the angels. The Son of man shall send forth his angels, and they shall gather out of his kingdom all things that offend, and them which do iniquity." (Mt. 13:39, 41)

"So shall it be at the end of the world: the angels shall come forth, and sever the wicked from among the just." (Mt. 13:49)

"And he shall send his angels with a great sound of a trumpet, and they shall gather together his elect from the four winds, from one end of heaven to the other." (Mt. 24:31)

"When the Son of man shall come in his glory, and all the holy angels with him, then shall he sit upon the throne of his glory: And before him shall be gathered all nations: and he shall separate them one from another, as a shepherd divideth his sheep from the goats." (Mt. 25:31-32)

"And another angel came out of the temple, crying with a loud voice to him that sat on the cloud, Thrust in thy sickle, and reap: for the time is come for thee to reap; for the harvest of the earth is ripe. And he that sat on the cloud thrust in his sickle on the earth; and the earth was reaped. And another angel came out of the temple which is in heaven, he also having a sharp sickle. And another angel came out from the altar, which had power over fire; and cried with a loud cry to him that had the sharp sickle, saying, Thrust in thy sharp sickle, and gather the clusters of the vine of the earth; for her grapes are fully ripe. And the angel thrust in his sickle into the earth, and gathered the vine of the earth, and cast it into the great winepress of the wrath of God. And the winepress was trodden without the city, and blood came out of the winepress, even unto the horse bridles, by the space of a thousand and six hundred furlongs." (Rev. 14:15-20)

XX. TWENTY: A Trained Man and His Treasure (Mt. 13:52)

A. Survey

A disciple in the Kingdom of Heaven is like a person who brings out of the storehouse new teachings as well as old teachings.

B. Significance

This is the final of two parables where Jesus contrasts the old with the new. See parable number 7 for the first.

C. Spiritual Truths

■ Jesus refers to a scribe in this parable.

1. A scribe was one who copied, contemplated, and communicated the Word of God in regard to the people of Israel.
2. Ezra was the most famous of the biblical scribes. *"This Ezra went up from Babylon; and he was a ready scribe in the law of Moses, which the Lord God of Israel had given; and the king granted him all his request, according to the hand of the Lord his God upon him. For Ezra had prepared his heart to seek the law of the Lord, and to do it, and to teach in Israel statutes and judgments" (Ezra 7:6, 10).*
3. What marvelous truths modern-day scribes (diligent Bible students) can still bring from the ultimate treasure, God's Word. *"O the depth of the riches both of the wisdom and knowledge of God! How unsearchable are his judgments, and his ways past finding out!" (Rom. 11:33).*

■ During a conversation on that first Easter Sunday afternoon with two disciples, Jesus would play the role of the Sovereign Scribe, bringing forth both old and new treasures from the Hebrew Bible storehouse. Note: *"And, behold, two of them went that same day to a village called Emmaus, which was from Jerusalem about threescore furlongs. And they talked together of all these things which had happened. And it came to pass, that, while they communed together and reasoned, Jesus himself drew near, and went with them. But their eyes were holden that they should not know him. And he said unto them, What manner of communications are these that ye have one to another, as ye walk, and are sad? And the one of them, whose name was Cleopas, answering said unto him, Art thou only a stranger in Jerusalem, and hast not known the things which are come to pass there in these days? And he said unto them, What things? And they said unto him, Concerning Jesus of Nazareth, which was a prophet mighty in deed and word before God and all the people: And how the chief priests and our rulers delivered him to be condemned to death, and have crucified him. But we trusted that it had been he which should have redeemed Israel: and beside all this, to day is the third day since these things were done. Then he said unto them, O fools, and slow of heart to believe all that the prophets have spoken: Ought not Christ to have suffered these things, and to enter into his glory? And beginning at Moses and all the prophets, he expounded unto them in all the scriptures the things concerning himself."* (Lk. 24:13-21, 25-27)

XXI. TWENTY-ONE: Not the Entrance, but Rather the Exit: A Diagnosis of Defilement (Mt. 15:10-20; Mk. 7:14-23)

A. Survey

Eating food with ceremonially unwashed hands, or from unwashed vessels does not constitute defilement. It is thus not that which enters the mouth and stomach, but rather what comes out of the mouth and heart, such as evil thoughts, murder, adultery, theft, false testimony, etc.

B. Significance

■ This is the final of three parables where, at the request of His disciples, Jesus provided for them its interpretation. These are:

1. The Sower, Seed, and Soil (Mt. 13:3-9, 18-23)
2. The Tares and Wheat (Mt. 13:24-30; 36-43)
3. The Parable on Defilement

C. Spiritual Truths

■ The theme reflected by this parable is the evil of legalism, which can be defined as follows:

1. Emphasizing the outward action to the exclusion of the inward attitude
2. Forcing my personal convictions upon someone else
3. Judging and condemning all those who dare disagree with me regarding even those minor and petty issues
4. Substituting the liberty in Christ with the bondage of the law
5. Living one's life in the flesh and not in the Spirit

■ Note the following passages regarding real defilement:

"Woe unto you, scribes and Pharisees, hypocrites! for ye make clean the outside of the cup and of the platter, but within they are full of extortion and excess. Woe unto you, scribes and Pharisees, hypocrites! for ye are like unto whited sepulchres, which indeed appear beautiful outward, but are within full of dead men's bones, and of all uncleanness" (Mt. 23:25, 27).

"Are ye so foolish? having begun in the Spirit, are ye now made perfect by the flesh? For as many as are of the works of the law are under the curse: for it is written, Cursed is every one that continueth not in all things which are written in the book of the law to do them. But that no man is justified by the law in the sight of God, it is evident: for, The just shall live by faith" (Gal. 3:3, 10, 11). *"For the flesh lusteth against the Spirit, and the Spirit against the flesh: and these are contrary the one to the other: so that ye cannot do the things that ye would"* (5:17). *"For he that soweth to his flesh shall of the flesh reap corruption; but he that soweth to the Spirit shall of the Spirit reap life everlasting"* (6:8).

"For ye, brethren, became followers of the churches of God which in Judaea are in Christ Jesus: for ye also have suffered like things of your own countrymen, even as they have of the Jews: Who both killed the Lord Jesus, and their own prophets, and have persecuted us; and they please not God, and are contrary to all men: Forbidding us to speak to the Gentiles that they might be saved, to fill up their sins always for the wrath is come upon them to the uttermost" (1 Thess. 2:14-16).

■ Paul aptly summarizes all this by one concise verse: *"For the kingdom of God is not meat and drink; but righteousness, and peace, and joy in the Holy Ghost."* (Rom. 14:17)

XXII. TWENTY-TWO: The Forgiven Who Wouldn't Forgive (Mt. 18:23-35)
A. Survey

A king decided to settle accounts with his servants. One of them owed him a vast amount of money but was unable to pay and begged for mercy, pleading that he and his family be not sold into slavery in order to pay on the debt. The king took pity and cancelled his debt. The forgiven servant had a fellow servant who owed him a small amount of money. Like the first servant, he too pled for mercy. However, refusing his plea the forgiven man had him thrown in prison.

Upon hearing of this terrible act of ingratitude the furious king commanded his wicked servant be cast into prison until the entire debt be paid.

B. Significance

■ This parable, perhaps as no other, illustrates in graphic fashion the cruelty, thanklessness, and utter depravity of the unregenerate heart.

C. Spiritual Truths

■ Consider the staggering contrasts concerning both the amounts owed and the attitudes displayed in this parable.

1. The amount owed to the king—It amounted to 10,000 talents. The servant here was no doubt a tax-collecting governor of sorts, entrusted by the king to rule over a city or province. He had apparently either embezzled or misappropriated vast sums of money collected for the king.
   a. One talent would purchase a slave.

    b. One talent represented 20 years' wages for the average workman.

    c. The total annual tax bill for all of Palestine was less than 1,000 talents. Yet the gracious king forgave all this.

  2. The amount owed to the servant—It was only 100 pence, which amounted to approximately four months' wages (1/60 of a talent). Yet the greedy servant refused to forgive.

■ This great principle of the importance for the forgiven to forgive is brought out time and again in the New Testament.

"And lead us not into temptation, but deliver us from evil: For thine is the kingdom, and the power, and the glory, for ever. Amen. For if ye forgive men their trespasses, your heavenly Father will also forgive you." (Mt. 6:13-14)

"And be ye kind one to another, tenderhearted, forgiving one another, even as God for Christ's sake hath forgiven you." (Eph. 4:32)

■ Jesus would begin to end His ministry by voicing that wonderful word FORGIVENESS—

  1. During His Sermon on the Mount

"And forgive us our debts, as we forgive our debtors." (Mt. 6:12)

  2. During His sufferings on the cross

"Then said Jesus, Father, forgive them; for they know not what they do. And they parted his raiment, and cast lots." (Lk. 23:34)

XXIII. TWENTY-THREE: How to Know Your Neighbor (Lk. 10:30-37)
A. Survey

A man en route from Jerusalem to Jericho was attacked, robbed, beaten and left half dead by some bandits.

Soon a priest and then a Levite, traveling that same road, saw the man but quickly walked on, refusing to help.

Finally a Samaritan stopped, bandaged his wounds, placed him on his donkey, took him to a nearby inn and paid the innkeeper to nurse him back to health.

B. Significance

■ This is the only parable where a Samaritan was involved.

■ There is also only one miracle where a Samaritan was involved (Lk. 17:11-19)

■ Both Samaritans were presented in a very positive way. Thus we see:
  1. The gentleness as exhibited in the parable.
  2. The gratitude as exhibited in the miracle.

C. Spiritual Truths

■ There is a two-fold irony and surprise in this parable:
  1. Concerning the two who should have helped the victim but did not
    a. The priest—He might have just come from the temple after presenting the sacrifices to God.
    b. The Levite—He might have just come from the temple after proclaiming the Scriptures. But neither would lift a finger to help a fellow human being.

2. Concerning the one who should not have helped the victim, but did.

He was a Samaritan and a member of a race hated by the Jews (Lk. 10:33).

■ Jesus related this parable to answer a question posed by a lawyer. The question was, "Who is my neighbor?" The answer, of course, is that my neighbor is anyone I can help.

■ Some have accused Jesus of borrowing His words as found in the Golden Rule verse from Confucius, who preached the same message over 500 years prior to Bethlehem. But a quick comparison between these two statements reveal a vast difference. Example:

1. The Golden Rule as attributed to Confucius—"Don't do to others that which you would not have them do unto you."

2. The Golden Rule as attributed to Jesus— *"Therefore all things whatsoever ye would that men should do to you, do ye even so to them: for this is the law and the prophets."* (Mt. 7:12)

■ With this background in mind, consider the reaction of the three men who encountered the wounded traveler:

1. It can be seen that both the priest and Levite followed Confucius' advice in that they did not beat, rob, and leave the victim to die for neither would have wanted this to be done to them.

2. The Samaritan alone however followed Jesus' advice. He not only did not inflict additional harm upon the victim (Confucius' advice) but then did that which he would have desired someone to do for him, namely, to care for his terrible wounds (Jesus' advice).

■ As a final observation, note the three different attitudes seen here:

1. That of the robbers— *"What is thine is mine."*

2. That of the priest and Levite— *"What is mine is mine."*

3. That of the Samaritan— *"What is mine is thine."*

Thus, the first attitude is devilish, the second, fleshly, but the third divine.

XXIV. TWENTY-FOUR: Secrets for Success—Asking, Seeking, Knocking (Lk. 11:5-10)
A. Survey

Jesus spoke of a man who paid a midnight visit to a friend.

The man: "I need to borrow three loaves of bread to set before a guest in my home who has just arrived."

The friend: "I can't help you. The door is locked and we're all in bed here."

Jesus concluded this parable by saying that if the man continued to knock and request, his persistence would eventually be rewarded.

B. Significance

■ This is the first of three parables of Jesus which emphasizes the importance of prayer. For the other two, see parables #35 and #36.

C. Spiritual Truths

■ Negative:

This parable does not teach we must constantly and persistently beg a reluctant God to answer our requests. In fact, to the contrary. Note Peter's words:

"For the eyes of the Lord are over the righteous, and his ears are open unto their prayers: but the face of the Lord is against them that do evil." (1 Pet. 3:12)

■ Positive:

What the parable does teach is that if even an unwilling human friend can be moved by persistent intercession, how much more will God be moved by the requests of His people?

The following verses testify to this:

"If ye then, being evil, know how to give good gifts unto your children, how much more shall your Father which is in heaven give good things to them that ask him?" (Mt. 7:11)

" For we have not an high priest which cannot be touched with the feeling of our infirmities; but was in all points tempted like as we are, yet without sin. Let us therefore come boldly unto the throne of grace, that we may obtain mercy, and find grace to help in time of need." (Heb. 4:15-16)

■ In reality, some Christians do not receive simply because they either do not ask, or if they do, make their requests with impure motives!

"If any of you lack wisdom, let him ask of God, that giveth to all men liberally, and upbraideth not; and it shall be given him. But let him ask in faith, nothing wavering. For he that wavereth is like a wave of the sea driven with the wind and tossed. For let not that man think that he shall receive any thing of the Lord." (Jas 1:5-7)

" Ye lust, and have not: ye kill, and desire to have, and cannot obtain: ye fight and war, yet ye have not, because ye ask not. Ye ask, and receive not, because ye ask amiss, that ye may consume it upon your lusts." (Jas 4:2-3)

■ The truths stressed here are re-emphasized by Jesus in a later parable, dealing with a persistent widow and an uncaring judge. See parable 35.

XXV. TWENTY-FIVE: A Fool In a Fix (Lk. 12:16-21)

A. Survey

The farm of a rich man had yielded such a bumper harvest one year that his barns could not contain. This foolish and materialistic farmer, assuming he would live many years, decided to build bigger barns and spend the rest of his life in luxury and total self-indulgence.

However, that very night God demanded from him his immortal soul!

B. Significance

■ This parable records the only occasion in the Bible in which God Himself personally calls a man a fool.

C. Spiritual Truths

■ Jesus related this parable to warn a listener concerning the sin of covetousness (Lk. 12:13-15). Warren Wiersbe writes:

"Covetousness is a desire for things and it can be the beginning of all kinds of sin. Eve coveted being like God and took the forbidden fruit. Lot's wife coveted Sodom and was killed on the spot. Achan coveted some spoils of war and destroyed himself and his family. David coveted his neighbor's wife and plunged himself, his family, and his nation into trouble. The last of the Ten Commandments is, *'Thou shalt not covet'*. By coveting, we can break all the other nine commandments." (*Meet Yourself in the Parables*, Victor Books, Wheaton, IL., 1979, p. 115.) In the New Testament, Paul confessed that this command, more than any other, caused him to realize his own wretched, sinful condition (Rom. 7:7-9).

■ A pastor once visited a stingy and bitter old man whose great wealth had apparently not brought him the slightest joy or peace. During the conversation as the miser complained about his lot in life, the pastor suddenly asked him to look out the window of his room.

> **Pastor:** "Tell me, what did you see?"

> **Man:** "Well I saw little children playing, mothers laughing, and men going about their daily work."

> The minister then handed the old man a mirror and asked him to gaze into it. Pastor: "Now, what do you see?"

> **Man:** "I see myself."

> After a moment of silent contemplation the pastor quietly observed:

> "You have just looked at two glasses. The first allowed you to see happy and productive people, the second, only yourself? But why this difference? Simply this—The second glass was coated by a thin layer of silver!"

■ Why was the rich man called a fool by God?

1. Because he thought he could satisfy his eternal soul with materialistic goods—Note this statement, *"And I will say to my soul, Soul, thou hast much goods laid up" (12:19)*. (See Jesus' statement in Mt. 4:4; 16:26.) The only real soul food is the Word of God. Our Lord had warned concerning this on two previous occasions: *"But he answered and said, It is written, Man shall not live by bread alone, but by every word that proceedeth out of the mouth of God" (Mt. 4:4)*. *"For what is a man profited, if he shall gain the whole world, and lose his own soul? or what shall a man give in exchange for his soul?" (Mt. 16:26)*

2. Because he smugly assumed he would naturally live to a ripe old age—Again, observe his misplaced confidence: *"Thou has much goods laid up for many years." (See Prov. 27:1; 29:1; Psa. 9:12; James 4:13-15.)*

3. Because he was totally self-centered—The personal pronouns "me, mine, and I" are to be found twelve times in this short account.

XXVI. TWENTY-SIX: On Being Ready for the Returning Redeemer (Lk. 12:35-48)

A. Survey

The Master will deal with two kinds of servants at His return.
1. The wise and watchful servant will be greatly rewarded.
2. The wicked and careless servant will be severely punished.

B. Significance

This marks the first of five parables referring to Jesus' second coming. For the other four, see parables 26, 43, 44, and 46.

C. Spiritual Truths

■ Many students of Bible prophecy believe the future return of Christ will be two-fold:

1. First, He comes in the clouds to receive all Christians

    "But I would not have you to be ignorant, brethren, concerning them which are asleep, that ye sorrow not, even as others which have no hope. For if we believe that Jesus died and rose again, even so them also which sleep in Jesus will God bring with him. For this we say unto you by the word of the Lord, that we which are alive and remain unto the coming of the Lord shall not prevent them which are asleep. For the Lord himself shall descend from heaven with a shout, with the voice of the archangel, and with the trump of God: and the dead in Christ shall rise first: Then we which are alive and remain shall be caught up together with them in the clouds, to meet the Lord in the air: and so shall we ever be with the Lord." (1 Thess. 4:13-17)

2. Finally, He comes to the earth to rule over all nations

    "And the seventh angel sounded; and there were great voices in heaven, saying, The kingdoms of this world are become the kingdoms of our Lord, and of his Christ; and he shall reign for ever and ever." (Rev. 11:15)

    "And I saw heaven opened, and behold a white horse; and he that sat upon him was called Faithful and True, and in righteousness he doth judge and make war. His eyes were as a flame of fire, and on his head were many crowns; and he had a name written, that no man knew, but he himself. And he was clothed with a vesture dipped in blood: and his name is called The Word of God. And the armies which were in heaven followed him upon white horses, clothed in fine linen, white and clean. And out of his mouth goeth a sharp sword, that with it he should smite the nations: and he shall rule them with a rod of iron: and he treadeth the winepress of the fierceness and wrath of Almighty God. And he hath on his vesture and on his thigh a name written, KING OF KINGS, AND LORD OF LORDS." (Rev. 19:11-16)

■ If this view be correct, Jesus is here describing the final appearance.

■ Jesus associates watchfulness with rewards during this parable and in a later one *"Blessed are those servants, whom the lord when he cometh shall find watching: verily I say unto you, that he shall gird himself, and make them to sit down to meat, and will come forth and serve them. And if he shall come in the second watch, or come in the third watch, and find them so, blessed are those servants" (Lk. 12:37-38). "Blessed is that servant, whom his lord when he cometh shall find so doing. Verily I say unto you, That he shall make him ruler over all his goods." (Mt. 24:46-47)*

XXVII. TWENTY-SEVEN: On Knowing the Divine Weather Forecast (Mt. 16:1-3; Lk. 12:54-56)

A. Survey

Jesus is tested by the godless Pharisees.

1. Their request: *"If you are the Messiah, show us a sign."*
2. His response: *"You hypocrites, who boast of your ability to read the weather signs, can't you pick up and understand the spiritual signs? Your Messiah is standing before you!"*

B. Significance

This is the only parable where Jesus compared the signs of the weather with the signs of the times.

C. Spiritual Truths

■ During Peter's sermon at Pentecost he briefly overviewed the earthly ministry of Jesus by the following words:

"Ye men of Israel, hear these words; Jesus of Nazareth, a man approved of God among you by miracles and wonders and signs, which God did by him in the midst of you, as ye yourselves also know." (Acts 2:22)

■ Furthermore, while the Savior was still on earth Nicodemus testified to this: *"There was a man of the Pharisees, named Nicodemus, a ruler of the Jews: The same came to Jesus by night, and said unto him, Rabbi, we know that thou art a teacher come from God: for no man can do these miracles that thou doest, except God be with him." (Jn. 3:1-2)*

■ In fact the gospel accounts record no less than 35 miracles performed by Jesus. These would include healing the sick, transforming the handicapped, feeding the hungry, delivering the possessed, raising the dead, etc. But in spite of all this, the wicked Pharisees were still demanding more signs and wonders from Him. In fact, they had done this on no less than five different occasions! (See Jn. 2:18; 6:30; Mt. 12:38; 16:1; Lk. 11:16.)

■ The Apostle Paul would later give sad testimony to this: *"For the Jews require a sign, and the Greeks seek after wisdom." (1 Cor. 1:22)*

XXVIII. TWENTY-EIGHT: On Being a Winner at the Banquet Dinner (Lk. 14:7-14)
A. Survey

Jesus gives advice to both guest and host in regards to a banquet dinner.

■ To the guest

1. Negative:

    "And he put forth a parable to those which were bidden, when he marked how they chose out the chief rooms; saying unto them. When thou art bidden of any man to a wedding, sit not down in the highest room; lest a more honourable man than thou be bidden of him; And he that bade thee and him come and say to thee, Give this man place; and thou begin with shame to take the lowest room." (Lk. 14:7-9)

2. Positive:

    "But when thou art bidden, go and sit down in the lowest room; that when he that bade thee cometh, he may say unto thee, Friend, go up higher: then shalt thou have worship in the presence of them that sit at meat with thee. For whosoever exalteth himself shall be abased; and he that humbleth himself shall be exalted." (Lk. 14:10-11)

■ To the host

1. Negative:

    "Then said he also to him that bade him, When thou makest a dinner or a supper, call not thy friends, nor thy brethren, neither thy kinsmen, nor thy rich neighbours; lest they also bid thee again, and a recompence be made thee." (Lk. 14:12)

2. Positive:

    "But when thou makest a feast, call the poor, the maimed, the lame, the blind: And thou shalt be blessed; for they cannot recompense thee: for thou shalt be recompensed at the resurrection of the just." (Lk. 14:13-14)

B. Significance

This is the second of two parables which followed a miracle Jesus had just performed. For the first, see #10.

■ Warren Wiersbe writes: "Jesus had watched the guests assemble and fight for the best seats. The Pharisees always wanted the best seats at the feasts (Mt. 23:6), and their guests followed their bad example. We laugh at this, but the same mad scramble goes on today. There are more status seekers and pyramid climbers in churches and other Christian organizations than we care to admit." (*Meet Yourself in the Parables*, Victor Books, Wheaton, Ill., 1979, pp. 93-94)

■ Both James and Peter would write concerning this very thing: "*But he giveth more grace. Wherefore he saith, God resisteth the proud, but giveth grace unto the humble ... Humble yourselves in the sight of the Lord, and he shall lift you up*" (James 4:6, 10). "*Likewise, ye younger, submit yourselves unto the elder. Yea, all of you be subject one to another, and be clothed with humility: for God resisteth the proud, and giveth grace to the humble. Humble yourselves therefore under the mighty hand of God, that he may exalt you in due time.*" (1 Pet. 5:5-6)

■ Two of Jesus' disciples once fell victim of this "scramble - for - supper - seats" syndrome as seen by the following passage:

"*And James and John, the sons of Zebedee, come unto him, saying, Master, we would that thou shouldest do for us whatsoever we shall desire. And he said unto them, What would ye that I should do for you? They said unto him, Grant unto us that we may sit, one on thy right hand, and the other on thy left hand, in thy glory. But Jesus said unto them, Ye know not what ye ask: can ye drink of the cup that I drink of? and be baptized with the baptism that I am baptized with? And they said unto him, We can. And Jesus said unto them, Ye shall indeed drink of the cup that I drink of; and with the baptism that I am baptized withal shall ye be baptized: But to sit on my right hand and on my left hand is not mine to give; but it shall be given to them for whom it is prepared.*" (Mk. 10:35-40)

■ According to John the Apostle, Diotrephes was guilty of this: "*I wrote unto the church: but Diotrephes, who loveth to have the preeminence among them, receiveth us not.*" (3 John 9)

XXIX. TWENTY-NINE: The Three Who Requested to Come, The Many Who Rejoiced to Come (Lk. 14:15-24)
A. Survey

This parable concerns itself with two kinds of guests who were invited to a lavish supper. Details are as follows:

■ The invitation—First guest list (14:15-17)

A man prepares a great feast and sends out many invitations.

The invited (14:18)—All the guests, however, make excuses why they cannot come.

1. First excuse (14:18)—One person has just bought a field and must inspect it.
2. Second excuse (14:19)—One person has just bought some oxen and must try them out.
3. Third excuse (14:20)—One person has just been married.

■ The invitation—Second guest list (14:21-24)

1. The new guests (14:21-23)—They consist of suffering and poor people everywhere, who gladly come.
2. The old guests (14:24)—They don't even receive the smallest taste of what had been prepared for them!

B. Significance

This parable contains what must be three of the most miserable excuses on record for not attending a banquet.

■ Someone has aptly described these three unresponsive individuals as two fools and a henpecked husband. Note each of their pitiful excuses:

1. First: Only a fool would buy a field without seeing it.

2. Second: Only a fool would purchase oxen without trying them.

3. Third: No comment necessary.

■ Note the features of this gracious invitation as recorded in Luke 14:17:

1. Its urgency—"Come!"

2. Its sufficiency—"All things "

3. Its availability—"are now ready."

■ This is but one of many such invitations issued by God to man. Note but a few:

"Come now, and let us reason together, saith the LORD: though your sins be as scarlet, they shall be as white as snow; though they be red like crimson, they shall be as wool. Ho, every one that thirsteth, come ye to the waters, and he that hath no money; come ye, buy, and eat; yea, come, buy wine and milk without money and without price. Wherefore do ye spend money for that which is not bread? and your labour for that which satisfieth not? hearken diligently unto me, and eat ye that which is good, and let your soul delight itself in fatness." (Isa. 1:18; 55:1-2)

"Come unto me, all ye that labour and are heavy laden, and I will give you rest. Take my yoke upon you, and learn of me, for I am meek and lowly in heart: and ye shall find rest unto your souls. For my yoke is easy, and my burden is light. Again, he sent forth other servants, saying, Tell them which are bidden, Behold, I have prepared my dinner: my oxen and my fatlings are killed, and all things are ready come unto the marriage." (Mt. 11:28-30; 22:4)

"And the Spirit and the bride say, Come. And let him that heareth say, Come. And let him that is athirst come. And whosoever will, let him take the water of life freely." (Rev. 3:20)

XXX. THIRTY: Whether a Building or a Battle—Count the Cost (Lk. 14:28-33)
A. Survey

This parable consists of two divine "don'ts":

1. Don't begin construction unless and until you know sufficient funds are available to complete it, lest you suffer derision and ridicule.

2. Don't initiate a battle unless and until you are assured you can muster more troops than the enemy, lest you suffer defeat and ruin.

B. Significance

This is perhaps the key parable dealing with the cost of discipleship.

C. Spiritual Truths

■ It is a tragic thing to begin something but not be able to complete it. It is a tremendous thing to begin something and to successfully complete.

1. A scriptural example of the first Belshazzar the king:

   "In the same hour came forth fingers of a man's hand, and wrote over against the candlestick upon the plaster of the wall of the kings palace: and the king saw the part of the hand that wrote. And this is the writing that was written, MENE, MENE, TEKEL, UPHARSIN. This is the interpretation of the thing: MENE; God path numbered thy kingdom, and finished it. TEKEL; Thou art weighed in the balances, and art found wanting. PERES; Thy kingdom is divided, and given to the Medes and Persians." (Dan. 5:5, 25-28)

2. A scriptural example of the second—Paul the apostle:

   "For I am now ready to be offered, and the time of my departure is at hand. I have fought a good fight, I have finished my course, I have kept the faith: Henceforth there is laid up for me a crown of righteousness, which the Lord, the righteous judge, shall give me at that day: and not to me only, but unto all them also that love his appearing." (2 Tim. 4:6-8)

■ Before declaring war on an enemy, four things must be carefully considered:

1. What are the strengths of my foe?
2. What are my strengths?
3. What are the weaknesses of my foe?
4. What are my weaknesses?

■ Three would-be-followers of Jesus failed the test of discipleship during our Lord's earthly ministry.

1. First candidate: *"And it came to pass, that, as they went in the way, a certain man said unto him, Lord, I will follow thee whithersoever thou goest. And Jesus said unto him, Foxes have holes, and birds of the air have nests; but the Son of man hath not where to lay his head." (Lk. 9:57-58)*

2. Second candidate: *"And he said unto another, follow me. But he said, Lord, suffer me first to go and bury my father. Jesus said unto him, Let the dead bury their dead: but go thou and preach the kingdom of God." (Lk. 9:59-60)*

3. Third candidate: *"And another also said, Lord, I will follow thee; but let me first go bid them farewell which are at home at my house. And Jesus said unto him, No man, having put his hand to the plough, and looking back, is fit for the kingdom of God." (Lk. 9:61-62)*

XXXI. THIRTY-ONE: The Missing Sheep, The Misplaced Silver, and The Miserable Son (Lk. 15:1-32)

A. Survey

■ This is, in reality, a three-fold parable.

1. A shepherd, having 100 sheep, seeks and finds one that has strayed from the fold.
2. A woman, having 10 coins, seeks and finds a misplaced one.
3. A father, having two sons, waits for and welcomes back a returning wayward one.

■ There is great rejoicing on each occasion following the recovery of the sheep and coin, and the return of the son.

B. Significance

■ This is Jesus' most lengthy parable.

■ It features the word rejoicing more than any other parable.

■ It is the only parable that seems to highlight the role of the entire Trinity in the work of salvation.

C. Spiritual Truths

■ Observations regarding the first part of the parable—the missing sheep. J. Dwight Pentecost writes:

"In introducing the first parable—that of the searching shepherd—Christ did not begin, as was often His custom in parables, by referring to a certain man, which would have made the parable impersonal; instead, He personalized the parable by saying, *'Suppose one of you has a hundred sheep and loses one of them'* (*Lk. 15:4*). In this way the Lord caused each of His hearers to immediately take personal interest in what was of value to the one who had suffered a loss." (*The Parables of Jesus.* Zondervan Publishing House, Grand Rapids, Michigan. 1982. Pages 100, 101)

Perhaps the most graphic and glorious song ever composed regarding this seeking shepherd is Elisabeth Clephane's great musical masterpiece, *The Ninety and Nine:*

There were ninety and nine that safely lay

In the shelter of the fold.

But one was out on the hills away,

Far off from the gates of gold,

Away on the mountains wild and bare.

Away from the tender Shepherd's care.

Away from the tender Shepherd's care.

"Lord, Thou hast here Thy ninety and nine;

Are they not enough for Thee?"

"This of mine has wandered away from Me;

And although the road be rough and steep,

I go to the desert to find My sheep,

I go to the desert to find My sheep."

But none of the ransomed ever knew

How deep were the waters crossed;

Nor how dark was the night that the Lord passed thro'

Ere He found His sheep that was lost.

Out in the desert He heard its cry,

Sick and helpless, and ready to die;

Sick and helpless, and ready to die.

"Lord, whence are those blood drops all the way

That mark out the mountains track?"

"They were shed for one who had gone astray

Ere the Shepherd could bring him back."

"Lord whence are thy hands so rent and torn?"

"They're pierced tonight by many a thorn;
They're pierced tonight by many a thorn."

But all thro' the mountains, thunder riv'n,
And up from the rocky steep,
There arose a glad cry to the gate of heav'n,
"Rejoice! I have found my sheep!"
And the angels echoed around the throne;
"Rejoice for the Lord brings back His own!
Rejoice for the Lord brings back His own!"

■ Observations regarding the second part of the parable--the misplaced silver coin. Again, consider the words of J. Dwight Pentecost:

"To teach the lesson a second time, Christ used the figure of a woman who had ten silver coins. The coins may have been the bride's dowry that she had been given at her wedding. Such coins were normally mounted on a headband and were worn on the forehead to be publicly seen. The loss of one of the coins would suggest unfaithfulness on the part of the bride to her husband. The coins not only had a monetary value but an emotional value as well, for they signified the bond between the bride and the bridegroom and the faithfulness that such a bond entailed."

■ Observations regarding the third part of the parable—the miserable son.

The account here concerns a father who has two sons. The following outline will prove helpful:

■ The younger son (15:11-24)

His Rebellion
1. The foolishness he exhibits (15:11-13)
   a. In seeking his inheritance (15:11-12): Soon he has wasted his share of his father's estate.
   b. In squandering his inheritance (15:13): Soon he has wasted all his money in wild living and finds himself penniless in a foreign country.
2. The famine he endures (15:14-16)
   Eventually he is forced to eat the food of the pigs he feeds.

His Return
1. The realization of the younger son
   "And when he came to himself, he said, how many hired servants of my father's have bread enough and to spare, and I perish with hunger!" (Lk. 5:17)
2. The repentance of the younger son
   "I will arise and go to my father, and will say unto him, Father, I have sinned against heaven, and before thee, and am no more worthy to be called thy son: make me as one of thy hired servants" (Lk. 15:18-19).
   a. This boy is one of at least eight individuals in the Bible to utter those three difficult words, "I have sinned". The others were:
   (1) Pharaoh (Ex. 9:27; 10:16)

(2) Balaam (Num. 22:34)

(3) Achan (Josh. 7:20)

(4) Saul (1 Sam. 26:21)

(5) David (2 Sam. 12:13; 24:10)

(6) Job (Job 7:20)

(7) Judas (Mt. 27:4)

b. As the context indicates, however, only three of these were genuinely sorrowful for their sin. These were: David, Job, and the prodigal son.

3. The receiving of the younger son

"And he arose, and came to his father. But when he was yet a great way off, his father saw him, and had compassion, and ran, and fell on his neck, and kissed him. And the son said unto him, Father, I have sinned against heaven, and in thy sight, and am no more worthy to be called thy son. But the father said to his servants, Bring forth the best robe, and put it on him; and put a ring on his hand, and shoes on his feet. And bring hither the fatted calf, and kill it; and let us eat, and be merry: For this my son was dead, and is alive again; he was lost, and is found. And they began to be merry" (Lk. 15:20-24).

■ The older son (Lk. 15:15-32)

"And he went and joined himself to a citizen of that country; and he sent him into his fields to feed swine. And he would fain have filled his belly with the husks that the swine did eat: and no man gave unto him. And when he came to himself, he said, How many hired servants of my father's have bread enough and to spare, and I perish with hunger! I will arise and go to my father, and will say unto him, Father, I have sinned against heaven, and before thee, And am no more worthy to be called thy son: make me as one of thy hired servants. And he arose, and came to his father. But when he was yet a great way off, his father saw him, and had compassion, and ran, and fell on his neck, and kissed him. And the son said unto him, Father, I have sinned against heaven, and in thy sight, and am no more worthy to be called thy son. But the father said to his servants, Bring forth the best robe, and put it on him; and put a ring on his hand, and shoes on his feet: And bring hither the fatted calf, and kill it; and let us eat, and be merry: For this my son was dead, and is alive again; he was lost, and is found. And they began to be merry. Now his elder son was in the field: and as he came and drew nigh to the house, he heard music and dancing. And he called one of the servants, and asked what these things meant. And he said unto him, Thy brother is come; and thy father hath killed the fatted calf, because he hath received him safe and sound. And he was angry, and would not go in: therefore came his father out, and intreated him. And he answering said to his father, Lo, these many years do I serve thee, neither transgressed I at any time thy commandment: and yet thou never gavest me a kid, that I might make merry with my friends: But as soon as this thy son was come, which hath devoured thy living with harlots, thou hast killed for him the fatted calf. And he said unto him, Son, thou art ever with me, and all that I have is thine. It was meet that we should make merry, and be glad: for this thy brother was dead, and is alive again; and was lost, and is found." (Lk. 15:15-32)

■ At least four questions may be asked concerning this threefold parable:

1. What is its intended lesson? Here three positions may be seen.

a. It speaks of the redemption of a lost sinner.

b. It speaks of the restoration of a backslidden believer.

c. It speaks of both.

2. What is the key word found in this threefold parable? It is the word "rejoice," appearing in various forms some seven times (Lk. 15:6-8, 10, 24, 29, 32).

3. What is the reason for this rejoicing? In all cases it results from the recovery of something that was lost.

4. Who does the rejoicing which Jesus said occurs in heaven when the lost is found? There are three suggestions:

   a. The angels are the ones rejoicing.

      (1) Because they are said to be present at the creation and redemption of this world (see Job 38:4-7; Lk. 2:8-14).

      (2) Because they are interested in knowing as much as possible about the subject of salvation (1 Pet. 1:12).

      (3) Because they are said to be ministers to the heirs of salvation (Heb. 1:13-14).

   b. The Savior Himself is the one who rejoices.

      Note: *"Looking unto Jesus the author and finisher of our faith; who for the joy that was set before him endured the cross, despising the shame, and is set down at the right hand of the throne of God" (Heb. 12:2). "Now unto him that is able to keep you from falling, and to present you faultless before the presence of his glory with exceeding joy" (Jude 1:24).*

   c. The redeemed saints in heaven are the ones rejoicing.

      "Wherefore seeing we also are compassed about with so great a cloud of witnesses, let us lay aside every weight, and the sin which doth so easily beset us, and let us run with patience the race that is set before us" (Heb. 12:1).

XXXII. THIRTY-TWO: What the Godless Can Teach the Godly (Lk. 16:1-13)
A. Survey

The following outline will help to survey this parable:

■ The crisis (16:1-2)

   1. The dishonesty of a manager (16:1)

      He is accused of wasting his master's possessions.

   2. The dismissal of the manager (16:2)

      He is fired.

■ The concern (16:3)

   The dishonest manager is worried about the future.

■ The craftiness (16:4-7)

   1. The resolve of the manager (16:4)

      He devises a plan to secure his future with some of his master's debtors.

   2. The reductions by the manager (16:5-7)

      He reduces their debts by as much as 50 percent.

■ The commendation (16:8)

   His master grudgingly admits the shrewdness of the dishonest manager.

■ The caution (16:9-12)

   Jesus warns believers to be faithful even in little matters so that they can be trusted in larger matters.

■ The choice (16:13)

  One must choose between God and money!

B. Significance

This has been often considered as being one of the most difficult of all Jesus' parables to understand, for at first glance it seems to be commending gross dishonesty!

C. Spiritual Truths

■ "The point Jesus was emphasizing was that this world should be used in such a way as to advance eternal benefits. The steward could always live with these people whom he had befriended. Jesus was saying money here on earth should be used in such a way that it will bring benefits in heaven. When a person is through with this world and gets to heaven, there will be eternal rewards from the use made of situations in this world. No matter how many may be surprised to note Jesus' seeming approval of the actions of an unjust man, no one ever misses the lesson as to how one could use money for spiritual advantages."

  (Manford Gutzke. *Plain Talk on Luke*. Zondervan Publishing, 1970. Pages 106, 107)

■ The thrust of this parable seems to be threefold:

  1. Realize that we are but stewards, controlling things (our time, talents, treasure), but owning nothing.
  2. Realize that someday our Master will check our bookkeeping.
  3. In light of this, we are to plan ahead, make friends, but be honest in all of our dealings.

XXXIII. THIRTY-THREE: When Hades Petitioned Paradise (Lk. 16:19-31)
A. Survey

This is the account of the life and afterlife of two men.

■ Their lives

  1. First man: A rich and totally self-indulgent person who lived in the greatest possible luxury.
  2. Second man: A beggar named Lazarus, living in terrible poverty who longed for the scraps of food which fell from the rich man's table.

■ Their afterlife

  1. The beggar: Upon death, he was carried by the angels to be with Abraham in paradise.
  2. The rich man: Upon death, he awakens in the flames of hell and earnestly begs two favors from Abraham, neither of which could be granted
     a. That Lazarus be sent to comfort him in his misery
     b. That Abraham send Lazarus back to earth and warn the rich man's brothers, lest they also awaken in hell

---

B. Significance

■ This is, by far, Jesus' most extended parable on the horrors of hell.

■ Is this only a parable or was it rooted in an historical event? The answer is probably both! A well known rich man may have recently died. If Lazarus had been at his gate for many years the people would have also been acquainted with him. On occasion Jesus would use current events as a spring board to launch spiritual truths. For another example, see the following:

"There were present at that season some that told him of the Galileans, whose blood Pilate had mingled with their sacrifices. And Jesus answering said unto them, Suppose ye that these Galileans were sinners above all the Galileans, because they suffered such things? I tell you, Nay: but, except ye repent, ye shall all likewise perish. Or those eighteen, upon whom the tower in Siloam fell, and slew them, think ye that they were sinners above all men that dwelt in Jerusalem? I tell you, Nay: but, except ye repent, ye shall all likewise perish." (Lk. 13:1-5)

■ Wealth itself is never presented as a vice in the Bible, nor is poverty looked upon as a virtue. God evaluates people by their attitudes and actions, not by their financial assets. The rich man went to hell because he was lost, and not because he was wealthy. The beggar went to heaven because he was saved, not because he was poor.

Observe that Lazarus was assisted by angels. This is in keeping with their assigned duties as seen in Hebrews: *"Are they not all ministering spirits, sent forth to minister for them who shall be heirs of salvation?" (Heb. 1:14)*

Observe also the phrase, "Abraham's bosom".

1. It is held by a number of Bible students that before Jesus died, the souls of all men descended into an abode located somewhere in the earth, known as Hades in the New Testament, and Sheol in the Old Testament.

2. Originally, there were two sections of Hades, one for the saved and one for the lost. The saved section is sometimes called "paradise" (Lk. 23:43), and the other times referred to as "Abraham's bosom"(See Lk. 16:22). There is no name given for the unsaved section apart from the general designation of Hades.

3. In Luke 16:19-31 the Savior relates the account of a poor believer who died and went to the saved part of Hades, and of a rich believer who died and went to the unsaved section. However, many believe that all this changed after Christ had made full payment for the believer's sins on Calvary. The Scofield Bible suggests that during the time of his death and resurrection, our Lord descended into Hades, depopulated Paradise, and led a spiritual triumphal entry into the heavenlies with all the saved up to that time. Ephesians 4:8-10 is offered as proof of this.

4. In his book, *Revelation*, the late Dr. Donald Grey Barnhouse wrote: "When he ascended on High (Eph. 4:8) he emptied Hell of Paradise and took it straight to the presence of God. Captivity was taken captive ... from that moment onward there was to be no separation whatsoever for those who believe in Christ. The gates of hell would never more prevail against any believer (Mt. 16:18). But what of the lost? The state of the unsaved dead remained (and remains) unchanged after the cross. They remain in Hades awaiting the final Great White Judgment Throne (Rev. 20:11-15). But a glorious change has occurred concerning the state of those who fall asleep in Jesus."

Note the following Scripture verses: *"For to me to live is Christ and to die is gain. For I am in a strait betwixt two, having a desire to depart, and to be with Christ; which is far better" (Phil. 1:21, 23). "To be absent from the body [is to be] present with the Lord" (2 Cor. 5:8).*

■ Note the rich man's prayer:

"Strive to enter in at the strait gate: for many, I say unto you, will seek to enter in, and shall not be able" (Lk. 16:24).

At least three facts may be concluded from this statement concerning the state of the dead:

1. They are not annihilated. God does not destroy the wicked.
2. They are not unconscious. The doctrine of soul sleep is unscriptural.
3. They may be given temporary bodies, awaiting their final ones. If this is the case, it applies to both the saved and the lost (see Mt. 17:1-3; 2 Cor. 5:1; Rev. 6:9-11).

■ As has been previously observed, the rich man desires that Lazarus be sent back to warn his unsaved brothers:

And he said, Nay, father Abraham: but if one went unto them from the dead, they will repent. And he said unto him, If they hear not Moses and the prophets, neither will they be persuaded, though one rose from the dead (Lk. 16:30-31).

1. Concerning the words of the rich man—This statement has a prophetic ring to it, for a few months later Jesus would perform his greatest single miracle, the resurrection of a decaying corpse - the body of Lazarus (Jn. 11:43-44). But what was the result of this mighty miracle? Did it result in hundreds of conversions? To the contrary—the foes of Christ became even more vicious in their hatred and opposition.
   a. They determined to kill Christ (Jn. 11:53).
   b. They debated the possibility of killing Lazarus (Jn. 12:10). This is the reason why God does not do mighty miracles today. God's will is accomplished through faith and not through signs. After the rapture many miracles and signs will occur during the tribulation, but sinful people will not believe (see Rev. 9:20-21)
2. Concerning the words of Abraham—This verse (Lk. 16:31) indirectly answers a question asked by many, and that is, "Do the departed saints in glory know what is happening back on earth?" Apparently, up to a point, they do, for here Abraham speaks of a man (Moses) who would not even be born until some six centuries after the "father of the faithful" had departed this earth.

XXXIV. THIRTY-FOUR: When Our Best is But the Least (Lk. 17:7-10)
A. Survey

Here Jesus points out that no servant should expect or demand either praise or reward for performing his duty with the utmost efficiency, for a servant is expected to do just that, namely, to serve!

B. Significance

This parable, as no other, summarizes just what is required from a servant of God.

C. Spiritual Truths

■ John the Baptist had once rebuked some proud Pharisees as follows: *"Bring forth therefore fruits meet for repentance: And think not to say within yourselves, We have Abraham to our Father: for I say unto you, that God is able of these stones to raise up children unto Abraham"* (Mt. 3:8-9). The unvarnished (and unsettling) truth as gleaned from this parable and John's statement is sobering indeed—God simply does not need us.

■ However, while Jesus indeed rightfully expects us to serve him, he condescends to serve us also.

Note the following Scripture verses: *After that he poureth water into a bason, and began to wash the disciples feet, and to wipe them with the towel wherewith he was girded (Jn. 13:5). Henceforth, I call you not servants, for the servant knoweth not what his lord doeth; but I have called you friends; for all things that I have heard of my Father I have made known unto you (Jn. 15:15). Blessed are those servants, whom the lord when he cometh shall find watching: verily I say unto you, that he shall gird himself, and make them to sit down to meat, and will come forth and serve them (Lk. 12:37).*

XXXV. THIRTY-FIVE: A Widow and a Weary Judge (Lk. 18:1-8)
A. Survey

A widow appealed to a callous and godless judge for justice against someone who had harmed her. He ignored her for awhile but eventually the widow's persistence and continuous pleas wore him out, causing him to rule in her favor.

B. Significance

This is the final of two parables emphasizing the importance of persistence in prayer. For the first, see parable 24.

C. Spiritual Truths

■ In this parable Jesus both contrasts and compares two judges--an earthly, uncaring, finite judge with the heavenly, all-caring, infinite Judge.

1. The contrast
   a. The earthly judge responded to a request that he might rid himself of a bothersome woman.
   b. The heavenly Judge responds to our requests so that he might receive us and bless us.
2. The comparison
   Both judges respond to persistence.

■ Note what this parable does not teach, and what it does teach!

1. It does not teach we must badger God, as it were, with our prayers until He finally answers them to get rid of us! To the contrary, note the following words:

   "For we have not an high priest which cannot be touched with the feeling of our infirmities; but was in all points tempted like as we are, yet without sin. Let us therefore come boldly unto the throne of grace, that we may obtain mercy, and find grace to help in time of need." (Heb. 4:15-16)

2. It does teach that persistence in prayer pays off!

   "If any of you lack wisdom, let him ask of God, that giveth to all men liberally, and upbraideth not; and it shall be given him. Confess your faults one to another, and pray one for another, that ye may be healed. The effectual fervent prayer of a righteous man availeth much." (Jas. 1:5; 5:16)

XXXVI. THIRTY-SIX: A Haughty Pharisee and a Humble Publican (Lk. 18:10-14)
A. Survey

Jesus describes two men who entered the temple to pray.

- Their spiritual condition upon arriving at the temple

   1. The Pharisee

      He was arrogant and totally self-centered, as illustrated by his prayer:

      "I thank you God, that I am not a sinner like everyone else."

   2. The Publican

      He was humble and sorrowful, as illustrated by his prayer:

      "O God, be merciful to me, a sinner"

- Their spiritual condition upon departing from the temple

   1. The Pharisee—He left unchanged and unforgiven.

   2. The Publican—He left changed and forgiven.

B. Significance

This parable marks the final of three concerning the subject of prayer. For the first two, see parables 24 and 25.

C. Spiritual Truths

- The temple in Jerusalem served as a place where one could offer up both animal sacrifices and personal prayer to God. Both were of equal importance. Jesus Himself had emphasized the prayer aspect: *"And said unto them, It is written, My house shall be called the house of prayer; but ye have made it a den of thieves" (Mt. 21:13).* Here our Lord quotes from both the Old Testament prophets Isaiah (56:7) and Jeremiah (7:11).

   There are various instances of temple prayers in the New Testament:

   1. As offered up by Simeon (Lk. 2:25-32)

   2. As offered up by Anna (Lk. 2:36-38)

   3. As offered up by Peter and John (Acts 3:1)

- The Mosaic Law ordered a fast on one day out of the year—the Day of Atonement (Lev. 23:26-32). Later, to commemorate various national calamities, other fasts were observed (Zech. 8:19). The Pharisees, however, had gone beyond the Law by fasting twice a week on Monday and Thursday. These days were established by tradition because Moses was supposed to have ascended Mount Sinai on a Thursday and descended on a Monday.

   Note that the Pharisee compared himself with the worst kind of people, the extortioners, the unjust, the sexually impure, and the hated tax collectors, "this publican." Paul later warned about this: *"For we dare not make ourselves of the number, or compare ourselves with some that commend themselves: but they measuring themselves by themselves, and comparing themselves among themselves, are not wise" (2 Cor. 10:12).* In a real sense, the Pharisee was not even praying. He was rather talking to himself about himself. The true and only standard for the believer is not another saint, or a sinner, but the Savior. (See Heb. 12:2-3; 1 Pet. 2:21.)

- The publicans (greedy tax collectors) usually come across badly in the New Testament (see Mt. 5:46; 11:19; 18:17; 21:31). But there were at least two notable exceptions: Matthew (Mt. 10:3), and Zacchaeus (Lk. 19:2). In fact, on occasion, publicans responded favorably to Jesus: *"And all the people that heard him, and the publicans, justified God, being baptized with the baptism of John" (Lk. 7:29).* (See also Luke 15:1-2.)

The publican correctly responded concerning his own unworthiness before God, as once did Isaiah and Simon Peter. *"Then said I, Woe is me! For I am undone; because I am a man of unclean lips, and I dwell in the midst of a people of unclean lips: for mine eyes have seen the King, the Lord of hosts"* (Isa. 6:5). *"When Simon Peter saw it, he fell down at Jesus' knees, saying, Depart from me: for I am a sinful man, O Lord."* This is surely a prayer that God hears and responds to in love.

■ Thus, the Pharisee's prayer was rejected and the publican's prayer received based on the following verses:

1. The rejected prayer

   "Ye ask, and receive not, because ye ask amiss, that ye may consume it upon your lusts;" (Jas. 4:3)

2. The received prayer

   "I acknowledge my sin unto thee, and mine iniquity have I not hid. I said, I will confess my transgressions unto the LORD; and thou forgavest the iniquity of my sin. Selah." (Psa. 32:5)

XXXVII. THIRTY-SEVEN: Hourly Workers and Daily Wages (Mt. 20:1-16)
A. Survey

A landowner hired certain men to work in his vineyard, securing their services at different times of the day, but agreeing to pay the wages for each man. As it turned out, some would labor 12 hours, and the final group but one hour. However, at the end of the day those who had toiled 12 hours complained bitterly upon receiving the exact wages of those who had worked but one hour.

However, the owner's defense was he had paid all exactly what they had been promised and that as owner, he could do exactly as he wanted!

B. Significance

In this parable Jesus makes one statement He has previously said and will later repeat.

"And about the eleventh hour he went out, and found others standing idle, and saith unto them, Why stand ye here all the day idle?" (Mt. 20:16)

For the other two occasions, see Mt. 19:30; 22:14.

C. Spiritual Truths

■ The interpretation of this parable
  1. Negative considerations
     a. It has nothing to do with the subjects of salvation or rewards.
     b. It was not related to describe the ideal working arrangements between management and labor.
  2. Positive considerations
     It may have served as an object lesson to illustrate both the sovereignty and the fairness of God. If so, Jesus was referring to that divine plan for Jews and Gentiles.
     a. The first workers hired would represent Israel. They began "working" in God's vineyard as early as 2000 B.C. in the time of Abraham.

b. The last workers to be hired would represent the Gentiles. As a group, they did not "clock in" until the advent of the Apostle Paul, some twenty centuries later. And yet, in the fullest sense, both groups will share equally in the glorious millennium, God's ultimate payday.

■ The applications of this parable
1. We are not to question or criticize God's dealings, either with us or with other believers. To do so leads to either pride or envy.
   a. Jesus rebuked the Apostle Peter. Our Lord had just predicted the eventual martyrdom of Peter. We read: *"Then Peter, turning about, seeth the disciple whom Jesus loved following; which also leaned on his breast at supper, and said, Lord, which is he that betrayeth thee? Peter seeing him saith to Jesus, Lord, and what shall this man do? Jesus saith unto him, If I will that he tarry till I come, what is that to thee? Follow thou me"* (Jn. 21:20-22).
   b. Paul rebukes the Roman church. *"Who are thou that judgest another man's servant? To his own master he standeth or falleth. Yea, he shall be holden up: for God is able to make him stand... But why dost thou judge thy brother? Or why dost thou set at nought thy brother? For we shall all stand before the judgment seat of Christ"* (Rom. 14:4, 10).

XXXVIII. THIRTY-EIGHT: Two Invested Wisely, One Wickedly (Lk. 19:11-29)
A. Survey

Prior to his departure to be crowned as king of a foreign land, a nobleman called together ten of his servants and entrusted to each a pound of silver. Upon his return the king discovered:

■ One servant reported a ten-fold gain of the original account. He was rewarded by being appointed as governor over ten cities.

■ Another servant showed a five-fold gain and became governor over five cities.

■ A third servant, however, acting out of fear simply hid his pound, thus showing no increase whatsoever. An angry king thereupon took his pound and gave it to the one with the ten-fold increase.

B. Significance

This parable is the first of two that promises rewards for faithful usage of our gifts and opportunities but warns of punishment for not doing so. For the other parable, see #45.

C. Spiritual Truths

■ Jesus related this parable to explain both the what and the when of the kingdom of heaven. *"And as they heard these things, he added and spake a parable, because he was nigh to Jerusalem and because they thought that the kingdom of God should immediately appear"* (Lk. 19:11).

■ In fact the final question His disciples asked Him referred to this very thing. *" When they therefore were come together, they asked of him, saying, Lord, wilt thou at this time restore again the kingdom to Israel? And he said unto them, it is not for you to know the times or the seasons, which the Father hath put in his own power. But ye shall receive power, after that the Holy Ghost is come upon you: and ye shall be witnesses unto me both in Jerusalem, and in all Judaea, and in Samaria, and unto the uttermost part of the earth. And when he had spoken these things, while they beheld, he was taken up; and a cloud received him out of their sight." (Acts 1:6-9)*

■ What is the difference between the pound parable here in Luke 19 and the talent parable related shortly after this in Matthew 25? It has been suggested that the difference is as follows:

1. The pounds represent the opportunities of life.
2. The talents speak of the different gifts God imparts to us.

■ Whatever the case, both the pound and the talent parables stress three all-important themes:

1. My abilities and opportunities from God in the past
2. My dependability for God at the present
3. My accountability to God in the future

XXXIX. THIRTY-NINE: Two Sons: One Said "No," But Did, The Other "Yes," But Didn't (Mt. 2:28-32)
A. Survey

A father instructed his two sons to go out and work in the vineyard.

■ The first son initially refused but later changed his mind and obeyed.

■ The second son initially agreed, but later changed his mind and disobeyed.

B. Significance

This is the final of two parables involving a father and son relationship. For the first, see parable 31.

C. Spiritual Truths

■ Who are the true believers? Will the real sons of God please stand? The ultimate test of ownership is obedience. One's sonship is demonstrated by one's submission. Both Old Testament and New Testament Israel failed this test. Their words were correct, but their works were corrupt. They said, "I go, sir;" and went not.

1. Old Testament Israel
   a. Their words— *"And all the people answered together, and said, All that the Lord hath spoken we will do. And Moses returned the words of the people unto the Lord" (Ex. 19:8).*
   b. Their works— *"Wherefore the Lord said, forasmuch as this people draw near me with their mouth, and with their lips do honour me, but have removed their heart far from me, and their fear toward me is taught by the precept of men" (Isa. 29:13).*
2. New Testament Israel
   a. Their words— *"We are Abraham's seed" (John 8:33). "Abraham is our father" (John 8:39a).*
   b. Their works— *"Jesus saith unto them, If ye were Abraham's children, ye would do the works of Abraham" (John 8:39b). Later, when advising the disciples concerning the Pharisees, our Lord concluded sadly: "All therefore whatsoever they bid you observe, that observe and do; but do not ye after their works: for they say, and do not" (Mt. 23:3).*

- Who then are the true believers? Upon being told that his mother and brothers were waiting to speak to him, Jesus once replied: *"But he answered and said unto him that told him, Who is my mother? And who are my brethren? And he stretched forth his hand toward his disciples, and said, Behold my mother and my brethren! For whosoever shall do the will of my Father which is in heaven, the same is my brother, and sister, and mother"* (Mt. 12:48-50).

- There is no single concept in the Christian life most important than that of obedience.

  1. The earthly ministry of Jesus served as a perfect role model in matters of obedience. *"And being found in fashion as a man, he humbled himself, and became obedient unto death, even the death of the cross"* (Phil. 2:8). *"Though he were a Son, yet learned he obedience by the things which he suffered"* (Heb. 5:8).

  2. The apostle Paul's amazing accomplishments and Christian testimony can be aptly summarized by that one word—obedience.

     "Whereupon, O king Agrippa, I was not disobedient unto the heavenly vision" (Acts 26:19).

XL. FORTY: Some Vicious Vine Keepers (Mt. 21:33-45; Mk. 12:1-12; Lk. 20:9-16)
A. Survey

A landlord rented his fertile vineyard to some tenants and went away on a journey. When harvest time approached, he sent his servants to collect his fruit. However, the wicked tenants refused his rightful request, beating some of the servants, stoning others, and actually killing a few. In a final attempt, the owner sent his own son, assuming they would surely respect him. But to the contrary, the godless tenants murdered the son and took control of the vineyard. Responding in righteous indignation the furious owner descended upon the vineyard, killed those murderers and entrusted his vineyard to others.

B. Significance

This is the only parable which seems to predict the following three events:

  1. The rejection of both the Father and Son by Israel
  2. The killing of the Son by Israel
  3. The wrath of God (destruction of Jerusalem by Titus in 70 A.D.?) upon Israel

C. Spiritual Truths

As the context indicates, Jesus deals with the nation Israel in this parable. It contains a historical, prophetical, and spiritual element.

- The historical element

  1. The divine Householder did plant a special vineyard—Israel (Isa. 5:1-7).
  2. In the fullness of time he did send forth his servants to obtain fruit, but they were badly treated (see Acts 7:51-52).
     a. Zechariah the high priest was stoned to death (2 Chron. 24:20-21).
     b. Isaiah the prophet was (probably) sawn asunder (Heb. 11:37).
     c. Elijah and Elisha were mocked.
     d. Jeremiah was beaten and imprisoned.
     e. Amos was rejected by the religious leaders (Amos 7).
  3. Finally, the divine Householder did send his beloved Son (Gal. 4:4).

- The prophetical element
    1. The Son would be killed by crucifixion.
    2. The city of the wicked workers would be destroyed (Titus the Roman general burned Jerusalem in A.D. 70).

- The spiritual element

    The Father did not do what the crowd suggested in the parable, namely, to "miserably destroy those wicked men." To the contrary, the divine plan called not for destruction resulting from wrath, but rather for redemption resulting from grace.

    "Simeon hath declared how God at the first did visit the Gentiles, to take out of them a people for his name. And to this agree the words of the prophets, as it is written, After this I will return, and will build again the tabernacle of David, which is fallen down; and I will build again the ruins thereof and I will set it up; That the residue of men might seek after the Lord, and all the Gentiles, upon whom my name is called, saith the Lord, who doeth all these things. Known unto God are all his works from the beginning of the world." (Acts 15:14-18)

    "And so all Israel shall be saved: as it is written, There shall come out of Sion the Deliverer, and shall turn away ungodliness from Jacob: For this is my covenant unto them, when I shall take away their sins." (Rom. 11:26-27)

XLI. FORTY-ONE: The Wedding Guest With No Wedding Garment (Mt. 22:1-14)

A. Survey

A king prepared a wedding banquet for his son and set forth his servants, carrying special invitations to certain selected guests. But they all refused, ignoring the royal messengers, mistreating them, and actually killing some. The enraged king thereupon destroyed them and invited any and all, rich or poor, bond or free to attend, thus filling up the banquet hall.

However, during the celebration the king was insulted by a rebellious guest who had refused to wear the proper wedding garment which had been freely issued to all guests. This disrespectful person was quickly seized and imprisoned.

B. Significance

This parable records the first of two occasions where God refers to a disloyal person as "friend". Compare Mt. 22:12 with Jesus' reference to Judas Iscariot in Gethsemane (Mt. 26:50).

C. Spiritual Truths

- In this parable, the millennial kingdom of heaven is likened to a royal wedding prepared by the king for his son. The entire kingdom is invited to attend. As we have already seen, many refused to come.

- There were three separate stages in a mideastern wedding:
    1. The betrothal stage
        This consisted of the selection of the bride and the payment of the dowry. This step often occurred when both bride and groom were still children. They were then considered engaged.
    2. The presentation stage
        When the couple was old enough, the bride was brought to the house of the groom's father, where the wedding service took place.

3. The celebration stage

Following the private marriage ceremony, the public marriage supper would begin.

■ It was during this joyous stage when the king saw an invited wedding guest not wearing a wedding garment.

1. The anger of the king

Often at royal weddings each guest would be provided with his or her own wedding garment which bore the imprint of both the king and his son. To refuse to wear this garment was looked upon as a terrible insult directed toward the groom himself.

2. The silence of the guest

We are told "and he was speechless". In reality, what could he have said?

a. He could not have pled ignorance, for he knew exactly what was expected of him.

b. He could not have pled poverty, for the garments were given out at no charge.

■ This necessary but free royal robe pictured here may serve to illustrate the divine robe of righteousness, freely given to all repenting sinners. Paul testifies of this: *"But what things were gain to me, those I counted loss for Christ. Yea doubtless, and I count all things but loss for the excellency of the knowledge of Christ Jesus my Lord: for whom I have suffered the loss of all things, and do count them but dung, that I may win Christ, And be found in him, not having mine own righteousness, which is of the law, but that which is through the faith of Christ, the righteousness which is of God by faith."* (Phil. 3:7-9)

XLII. FORTY-TWO: The Fruitless Fig Tree (Lk. 13:6-8)

A. Survey

A fig tree bore no fruit for three years, resulting in the owner's decision to cut it down. However, the gardener requested it be given another year.

B. Significance

This is the first of two parables where Israel seems to be symbolized as a fig tree. For the other, see parable 43.

C. Spiritual Truths

■ This 42nd parable may be directly associated with the 33rd miracle, namely, the supernatural withering of a fig tree.

"Now in the morning as he returned into the city, he hungered. And when he saw a fig tree in the way, he came to it, and found nothing thereon, but leaves only, and said unto it, Let no fruit grow on thee henceforward for ever. And presently the fig tree withered away. Jesus saith unto them, Did ye never read in the scriptures, The stone which the builders rejected, the same is become the head of the corner: this is the Lord's doing, and it is marvellous in our eyes? Therefore say I unto you, The kingdom of God shall be taken from you, and given to a nation bringing forth the fruits thereof. And whosoever shall fall on this stone shall be broken: but on whomsoever it shall fall, it will grind him to powder. And when the chief priests and Pharisees had heard his parables, they perceived that he spake of them" (Mt. 21:18-19, 42-45).

■ At any rate, the parable marks the tragic fulfillment of both Isaiah's and Hosea's sad predictions regarding Israel.

"Now will I sing to my well-beloved a song of my beloved touching his vineyard. My well beloved hath a vineyard in a very fruitful hill: And he fenced it, and gathered out the stones thereof, and planted it with the choicest vine, and built a tower in the midst of it, and also made a winepress therein: and he looked that it should bring forth grapes, and it brought forth wild grapes" (Isa. 5:1-2).

"Israel is an empty vine, he bringeth forth fruit unto himself: according to the multitude of his fruit he hath increased the altars; according to the goodness of his land they have made goodly images" (Hos. 10:1).

XLIII. FORTY-THREE: The Fig Tree and the Future (Mt. 24:32-35; Mk. 13:28-31; Lk. 21:29-33)
A. Survey

This parable records a question and an answer:

1. The disciples' question:

"Tell us, what will be the sign of your coming and the end of the age?" (Mt. 24:3)

2. The Savior's answer:

"Now learn a parable of the fig tree; When his branch is yet tender, and putteth forth leaves, ye know that summer is nigh: So likewise ye, when ye shall see all these things, know that it is near, even at the doors. Verily I say unto you, This generation shall not pass, till all these things be fulfilled." (Mt. 24:32-34)

B. Significance

Many hold this parable offers Scripture's most significant and clearest sign regarding Jesus' second coming, namely, the rebirth of the nation Israel.

C. Spiritual Truths

■ Jesus related this parable during His Mt. Olivet Discourse which He began with a startling prediction: *"And Jesus went out, and departed from the temple: and his disciples came to him for to shew him the buildings of the temple. And Jesus said unto them, See ye not all these things? verily I say unto you, There shall not be left here one stone upon another, that shall not be thrown down."* (Mt. 24:1-2)

■ This probably no doubt referred to the destruction of Jerusalem by the Roman soldiers led by Titus in 70 A.D. From that point on for centuries Israel as a nation would cease to exist.

■ The suggested interpretation of the parable

1. The fig tree is Israel.
2. The other trees represent those Gentile nations, such as Russia, which play a vital role in the final days.
3. The leaf-bearing event may refer to Israel's modern return to the land.
4. The generation that would not pass away may speak of that generation born in 1948.
5. The "things to be accomplished" phrase could speak of Christ's second coming.

XLIV. FORTY-FOUR: Watch and Work, for We Know Not When (Mt. 24:42-44; Mk. 13:32-37)
A. Survey

"Watch therefore: for ye know not what hour your Lord doth come. But know this, that if the goodman of the house had known in what watch the thief would come, he would have watched, and would not have suffered his house to be broken up. Therefore be ye also ready: for in such an hour as ye think not the Son of man cometh." (Mt. 24:42-44)

B. Significance

The phrases be on guard, be alert, and watch are found four times in this short parable, more often than in any other one.

C. Spiritual Truths

■ Both Paul and Peter may have had this parable in mind when they wrote the following: *"For yourselves know perfectly that the day of the Lord so cometh as a thief in the night. For when they shall say, Peace and safety; then sudden destruction cometh upon them, as travail upon a woman with child; and they shall not escape" (1 Thess. 5:2-3). "But the day of the Lord will come as a thief in the night; in the which the heavens shall pass away with a great noise, and the elements shall melt with fervent heat, the earth also and the works that are therein shall be burned up" (1 Pet. 3:10).*

XLV. FORTY-FIVE: Virgins, Vessels, and Vigilance (Mt. 25:1-13)
A. Survey

Ten virgins took their lamps and went out to meet the bridegroom. Five were foolish because they carried no oil with them while five were wise because they did. Upon learning of the bridegroom's impending arrival, the ten virgins reacted as follows:
1. The five foolish ones hurried out to buy more oil, but upon their return found the door of the banquet hall shut.
2. The five wise ones quickly trimmed their lamps and entered into the joy of the wedding celebration.

B. Significance

This parable is unique in that it seems to suggest the unsaved will unsuccessfully attempt to seek the aid of the saved at the second coming of Christ, as seen by their request:
"And the foolish said unto the wise, Give us of your oil; for our lamps are gone out." (Mt. 25:8)

C. Spiritual Truths

■ The following interpretation is suggested for this parable:
1. The chronology of the parable
   When does the action in the parable take place? It occurs during the coming great tribulation, perhaps at the very end.
2. The characters in the parable
   a. The bridegroom is Christ.
   b. The bride is the Church.
   c. The ten virgins represent Israel, awaiting the coming of their Messiah.

(1) The five foolish ones had not experienced the new birth.

(2) The five wise ones had experienced the new birth.

■ As has been noted, the wise virgins possessed oil. Oil is a recognized symbol for the Holy Spirit. Oil indicates light, healing and anointing for service as the following passages testify to:

"The Spirit of the Lord is upon me, because he hath anointed me to preach the gospel to the poor; he hath sent me to heal the brokenhearted, to preach deliverance to the captives, and recovering of sight to the blind, to set at liberty them that are bruised" (Lk. 4:18). "But in every nation he that feareth him, and worketh righteousness, is accepted with him" (Acts 10:38).

■ The Holy Spirit will thus play an important role in the coming Great Tribulation. He is spoken of on at least three occasions:

"And after three days and an half the spirit of life from God entered into them, and they stood upon their feet; and great fear fell upon them which saw them; And I heard a voice from heaven saying unto me, Write, Blessed are the dead which die in the Lord from henceforth: Yea, saith the Spirit, that they may rest from their labours, and their works do follow them. So he carried me away in the spirit into the wilderness: and I saw a woman sit upon a scarlet coloured beast, full of names of blasphemy, having seven heads and ten horns." (Rev. 11:11; 14:13; 17:3)

■ It will be no doubt the Holy Spirit who will seal and anoint for service the 144,000 Jewish evangelists in Rev. 7 *"And I saw another angel ascending from the east, having the seal of the living God: and he cried with a loud voice to the four angels, to whom it was given to hurt the earth and the sea, Saying, Hurt not the earth, neither the sea, nor the trees, till we have sealed the servants of our God in their foreheads. And I heard the number of them which were sealed: and there were sealed an hundred and forty and four thousand of all the tribes of the children of Israel." (Rev. 7:2-4)*

XLVI. FORTY-SIX: A Traveler, Three Stewards and Eight Talents (Mt. 25:14-30)
A. Survey

Prior to his departure on an important mission a nobleman entrusted to his three chief servants eight talents, giving five to the first servant, two to the second, and one to the third. Upon his return, be discovered:

1. The servant who had received five talents had doubled this and was generously rewarded:

    "His lord said unto him, Well done, thou good and faithful servant: thou hast been faithful over a few things, I will make thee ruler over many things: enter thou into the joy of thy lord" (Mt. 25:21).

2. The servant who had received two talents had also doubled his money and likewise rewarded as had been the first servant.

3. The servant who had received one talent had done absolutely nothing and was severely punished.

    "His lord answered and said unto him, Thou wicked and slothful servant, thou knewest that I reap where I sowed not, and gather where I have not strawed: Thou oughtest therefore to have put my money to the exchangers, and then at my coming I should have received mine own with usury. Take therefore the talent from him, and give it unto him which hath ten talents. For unto everyone that hath shall be given, and he shall have abundance: but from him that hath not shall be taken away even that which he hath. And cast ye the unprofitable servant into outer darkness: there shall be weeping and gnashing of teeth." (Mt. 25:26-30)

B. Significance

This parable is the final of five describing the relationships and responsibilities between a master and his servants. For the previous four, see parables 26, 34, 38, 43.

> C. Spiritual Truths

■ Note both the similarities and contrasts between the talent parable (number 45) and the pound parable (number 38).

1. Similarities between the talent parable and the pound parable

    a. Both parables describe the stewardship arrangements between a departing master and his servants.

    b. Both relate the accounting episode upon the master's return.

    c. Both record faithfulness on the part of at least two servants who are subsequently rewarded.

    d. Both record the unfaithfulness on the part of one servant who is subsequently punished.

2. Contrast between the talent and pound parable

    a. The master of the servants—He is a nobleman in Luke 19 and a traveler in Matthew 25.

    b. The number of servants—There are ten in the pound parable and three in the talent parable.

    c. The responsibility of the servants—In Luke 19 each servant receives the same, approximately $5000, the value of a pound. In Matthew 25 the first servant is entrusted with five talents ($1.5 million), the second servant two talents ($600,000), and the third servant one talent ($300,000).

    d. The accomplishments of the faithful servants—In Luke 19 the first servant increased his pound 1,000 percent. In Matthew 25 the first two servants doubled their original sum.

    e. The punishment of the unfaithful servants—In Luke 19 the man lost the original pound, but in Matthew 25 the man not only had the talent taken from him, but was then cast into outer darkness.

■ Here it may prove helpful to repeat the following differences between these two parables as were previously observed under parable 38:

1. What is the difference between the pound parable here in Luke 19 and the talent parable related shortly after this in Matthew 25? It has been suggested that the difference is as follows:

    a. The pounds represent the opportunities of life.

    b. The talents speak of the different gifts God imparts to us.

2. Whatever the case, both the pound and the talent parables stress three all-important themes:

    a. My abilities and opportunities from God in the past

    b. My dependability for God at the present

    c. My accountability to God in the future

XLVII. FORTY-SEVEN: Separating the Sheep from the Goats (Mt. 25:1-46)

> A. Survey

Jesus compares the final judgment to a shepherd's separating sheep from goats.

■ The separator (25:31). The Savior himself will occupy this role.

■ The separation (25:32-33). The goats (lost people) will be placed on his left hand, and the sheep (saved people) on his right hand.

■ The separated (25:34-46)

1. The sheep (25:34-40)

   They will be rewarded!

   a. The contents (25:34)

      They will receive the Father's Kingdom, prepared for them from the foundation of the world.

   b. The cause (25:35-36)

      It is due to their loving ministry in feeding, clothing, caring for, and even assisting Jesus in prison!

   c. The confusion (25:37-39)

      The saved ask when all this takes place.

   d. The clarification (25:40)

      Jesus says that when they ministered to others, they ministered to Him!

2. The goats (25:41-46)

   They will be punished!

   a. The contents (25:41)

      Eternal hell

   b. The cause (25:42-43)

      They did not minister to Jesus!

   c. The confusion (25:44)

      The unsaved ask when it was that they did not minister to Jesus.

   d. The clarification (25:45-46)

      Jesus says because they did not minister to others, they did not minister to him!

B. Significance

■ This parable is the most well-known in regards to the Second Coming.

■ It is the final of four parables contrasting the saved with the unsaved in regards to the Second Coming of Christ.

   1. The wheat and the tares (Parable 14)
   2. The good fish and the bad fish (Parable 19)
   3. The wise virgins and the foolish virgins (Parable 45)
   4. The sheep and the goats (Parable 47)

C. Spiritual Truths

■ At first reading this parable seems to teach that salvation can be earned by good works, which of course, is totally refuted by a host of Scripture verses (Eph. 2:8-9; Titus 3:5, etc.). At least five questions need to be answered in rightly interpreting this parable.

   1. When does this judgment take place? The context clearly indicates that it occurs at the end of the tribulation.
   2. Who is being judged here? According to 25:32 it will be the Gentiles.
   3. What is the basis of this judgment? It is based on how they have treated or mistreated a certain group during the tribulation.
   4. Who is this group? Christ calls them *"my brethren" (25:40);* thus they are Jewish people.
   5. Why would some Gentiles risk their lives during the reign of the antichrist to help persecuted and suffering Jews? The new birth experience would offer the only logical explanation for such behavior. Thus, the good works spoken of here are not the basis for salvation, but rather the proof of salvation.

■ This parable tells us one of the six activities of God the Father before He created man.

1. He was fellowshipping with His Son (Prov. 8:22-30; Jn. 17:5, 24)
2. He was preparing for Calvary (1 Pet. 1:18-20; Rev. 13:8)
3. He was creating the stars and angels (Job 38:4, 7)
4. He was choosing the elect (Eph. 1:4; 2 Tim. 1:9)
5. He was planning for the Church (Eph. 3:8, 9)
6. He was preparing a kingdom

    "Then shall the King say unto them on his right hand, Come, ye blessed of my Father, inherit the kingdom prepared for you from the foundation of the world" (Mt. 25:34).

■ Jesus prophesied condemnation of the wicked unsaved here is sobering indeed: *"Then shall he say also unto them on the left hand, Depart from me, ye cursed, into everlasting fire, prepared for the devil and his angels" (Mt. 25:41).*

Especially observe three frightening phrases:

1. *"Depart from me"*

    This is in stark contrast to His previous gracious invitation, also recorded by Matthew: *"Come unto me, all ye that labour and are heavy laden, and I will give you rest. Take my yoke upon you, and learn of me; for I am meek and lowly in heart: and ye shall find rest unto your souls. For my yoke is easy, and my burden is light." (Mt. 11:28-30)*

2. *"into everlasting fire "*

    There are some today who would deny the concept of unending punishment, but here Jesus warns of it on two occasions! *"And these shall go away into everlasting punishment: but the righteous into life eternal." (Mt. 25:46)*

3. *"prepared for the devil and his angels"*

    One of the saddest aspects about hell is that it was originally prepared for Satan, not for man! In fact, heaven is said to be the prepared place!

    "In my fathers house are many mansions: if it were not so, I would have told you. I go to prepare a place for you." (Jn. 14:2)

    "But now they desire a better country, that is, an heavenly: wherefore God is not ashamed to be called their God: for he hath prepared for them a city." (Heb. 11:16)

    Tragically, though, when men refuse the prepared place, they are forever banished to the unprepared place!

THE SERMONS OF JESUS

An Overview of Jesus' Sermons

A. Title of Sermon

- One: The Scroll of Isaiah's Sermon in Nazareth (Luke 4:16-30)
- Two: The Sermon on the Mount (Matt. 5-7; Luke 6:17-49)
- Three: The Source of Life Sermon (John 5:12-47)
- Four: The Bread of Life Sermon (John 6:22-71)
- Five: The Feast of Tabernacles Sermon (John 7:1-53)
- Six: The Temple Treasury Sermon (John 8:12-59)
- Seven: The Good Shepherd Sermon (John 10:1-39)
- Eight: The Mount of Olives Sermon (Matt. 24:1-31; Mark 13:1-27; Luke 21:5-28)
- Nine: The Thursday Night Passover Sermon (John 14-16)

B. Location of Sermon

- In a Nazareth synagogue (# One)
- On a hillside near the Sea of Galilee (# Two)
- Beside the pool of Bethesda in Jerusalem (# Three)
- In Capernaum of Galilee (# Four)
- In Jerusalem during the Feast of Tabernacles (# Five)
- In the Jerusalem Temple (# Six)
- In Jerusalem during the Feast of Dedication (# Seven)
- On the Mount of Olives (# Eight)
- In the Upper Room and en route to Gethsemane (# Nine)

C. Purpose of Sermon

- To announce that He was the Jewish Messiah as prophesied in Isa. 61 (# One)
- To instruct believers in their day to live by these kingdom principles which will become universal during the Millennium (# Two)

- To explain His unique relationship with the Father (# Three)
- To proclaim that He was the true Bread of Life (# Four)
- To proclaim that He was the Water of Life (# Five)
- To proclaim that He was the Light of the World (# Six)
- To proclaim that He was the only true Shepherd (# Seven)
- To describe conditions which will prevail during the coming Great Tribulation (# Eight)
- To identify Himself as the True Vine (# Nine)

D. Unique Features in the Various Sermons

- The longest: 111 verses(# Two)
- The shortest: 15 verses (# One)
- The most prophetical (# Eight)
- The final one prior to His death (# Nine)
- The most controversial (# Five)
- The most rejected (# One)
- The most misunderstood (# Two)
- The most references to prayer and fasting (# Two)
- The most personal (# Nine)
- The most confrontational (# Six)
- The most references to the Holy Spirit (# Nine)
- The most comforting (# Nine)

E. Those Who Heard the Sermon

- A local synagogue congregation (# One)
- A great Galilee crowd (# Two)
- The 12 apostles (# Eight)
- The 11 apostles (# Nine)
- A large crowd of sick people and some legalistic Jews (# Three)
- Many of the 5000 men Jesus had fed on the previous day (# Four)
- Those attending the Feast of Tabernacles in Jerusalem (# Five)
- A group of confrontational Pharisees in Jerusalem (# Seven)
- A crowd in the temple area (# Six)

F. Results from the Sermon

■ His hometown people attempted to throw Him off a cliff (# One)

■ The crowds were amazed at the nature of His teaching and the authority behind it (# Two)

■ The crowd attempted to kill Him (# Three)

■ The crowd attempted to crown Him as their King (# Four)

■ The Pharisees attempted to arrest Him (# Five)

■ The crowd attempted to stone Him (# Six)

■ The crowd attempted to kill Him (# Seven)

■ Reaction not recorded (# Eight)

■ They were reassured that He was indeed sent from God (# Nine)

The Sermons of Jesus

ONE: *The Scroll of Isaiah Sermon in Nazareth (Luke 4:16-30)*

■ **The occasion for the sermon**— *"And he came to Nazareth, where he had been brought up: and, as his custom was, he went into the synagogue on the sabbath day, and stood up for to read" (Luke 4:16).*

   1. Note the phrase, "as his custom was." Our Lord had faithfully attended the synagogue services each Sabbath day while growing up in Nazareth. He had already fulfilled that admonition later written in the book of Hebrews: *"Not forsaking the assembling of ourselves together, as the manner of some is; but exhorting one another: and so much the more, as ye see the day approaching" (Heb. 10:25).*

■ **The text of the sermon** (taken from Isa. 61:1-3)— *"And there was delivered unto him the book of the prophet Esaias. And when he had opened the book, he found the place where it was written, The Spirit of the Lord is upon me, because he hath anointed me to preach the gospel to the poor; he hath sent me to heal the brokenhearted, to preach deliverance to the captives, and recovering of sight to the blind, to set at liberty them that are bruised, To preach the acceptable year of the Lord" (Luke 4:17-19).*

   In an amazing demonstration of *"rightly dividing the word of truth" (2 Tim. 2:15)*, Jesus stopped his reading with the words, *"the acceptable year of the Lord,"* and did not finish the last half of the sentence in Isa. 61:2 which declares: *"and the day of vengeance of our God."* He did this because:

   The *"acceptable year"* belonged to his first coming.

   The *"day of vengeance"* spoke of his second coming.

■ **The interest in the sermon**— *"And he closed the book, and he gave it again to the minister, and sat down. And the eyes of all them that were in the synagogue were fastened on him" (Luke 4:20).*

■ **The announcement in the sermon**— *"And he began to say unto them, This day is this scripture fulfilled in your ears" (Luke 4:21).*

■ **The power of the sermon**— *"And all bare him witness, and wondered at the gracious words which proceeded out of his mouth. And they said, Is not this Joseph's son?" (Luke 4:22).*

- **The application of the sermon** — *"And he said unto them, Ye will surely say unto me this proverb, physician, heal thyself: whatsoever we have heard done in Capernaum, do also here in thy country. And he said, Verily I say unto you, No prophet is accepted in his own country" (Luke 4:23-24).*

1. As illustrated by Elijah and a starving widow — *"But I tell you of a truth, many widows were in Israel in the days of Elias, when the heaven was shut up three years and six months, when great famine was throughout all the land; But unto none of them was Elias sent, save unto Sarepta, a city of Sidon, unto a woman that was a widow" (Luke 4:25-26).*

2. As illustrated by Elisha and a suffering warrior — *"And many lepers were in Israel in the time of Elisha the prophet; and none of them was cleansed, saving Naaman the Syrian" (Luke 4:27).*

   He refers to a widow and a soldier in an attempt to convince his hometown people of their unbelief.

   Both were Gentiles.

   The widow was a Phoenician.

   The soldier was a Syrian.

   Each was ministered to by one of the two most famous Old Testament prophets.

   Elijah ministered to the widow.

   Elisha ministered to the soldier.

   Both the widow and the soldier experienced a unique miracle.

   The widow saw her dead son raised. This had never before happened in human history (1 Kings 17:9-16).

   The soldier was healed of leprosy. He was the only man in the Old Testament to be delivered from this terrible disease (2 Kings 5:1-14).

- **The reaction to the sermon**

1. The anger against him — *"And all they in the synagogue, when they heard these things, were filled with wrath" (Luke 4:28).*

2. The attempt against him — *"And rose up, and thrust him out of the city, and led him unto the brow of the hill whereon their city was built, that they might cast him down headlong. But he passing through the midst of them went his way" (Luke 29-30).*

   a. This marks the first of at least seven attempts to kill Jesus by the Jewish religious leaders prior to his death at Calvary. These incidents occurred:

      In Jerusalem after he had healed a cripple on the Sabbath (John 5:15-18)

      In Jerusalem during the Feast of Tabernacles (John 7:30)

      In Jerusalem after he claimed to be greater than Abraham (John 8:59)

      In Jerusalem after he claimed to be equal with the Father (John 10:31-33).

   b. (Note: Humanly speaking, the Jewish leaders did not crucify Christ because he claimed to be the Messiah. In truth, following the feeding of the 5,000, a number of them had recognized him as the Christ and attempted to crown him king on the spot—see John 6:14-15. The fact is, they turned against him because he said he was the Son of God himself.)

      In Jerusalem after the resurrection of Lazarus (John 11:53)

      In Jerusalem following his Mount Olivet Discourse (Matt. 26:3-4)

Introduction:

- Probably no other sermon in all of history has been more misunderstood and misinterpreted than the Sermon on the Mount.

    1. Liberal theologians, although blatantly denying the deity of Christ and the inerrancy of scripture, have for centuries used and misused Christ's words here, twisting them to fit their own humanistic and unbiblical social gospel. One false claim along this line is that a person can be saved by keeping the concepts of the Sermon on the Mount (as if this were possible for a non-Christian).

    2. Others, however, who do accept the Bible as God's Word, have also erred, concluding that Jesus' lofty message here does not in the least apply to us today, but refers to a totally different dispensation. Thus, while the first group misuses it, this group ignores it.

- Both views are soundly refuted by the Apostle Paul: *"All scripture is given by inspiration of God, and is profitable for doctrine, for reproof, for correction, for instruction in righteousness: That the man of God may be perfect, throughly furnished unto all good works"* (2 Tim. 3:16, 17).

- The following outline is based on the interpretation that in the Sermon on the Mount Jesus was instructing and encouraging born-again believers in their day (in spite of opposition) to live by those kingdom principles which will become universal during the millennium.

- A number of people believe that the sermon may have been delivered on one of the twin peaks on the Horns of Hattin, located about four miles west of the Sea of Galilee and some eight miles southwest of Capernaum. It was in this exact area on July 15, A.D. 1187, that a very famous battle was fought. At that time the brilliant Moslem military leader Saladin met and utterly crushed an army of European Crusaders. Saladin would later that same year, on October 12, capture the city of Jerusalem.

- We will survey this sermon in a five-fold manner, all dealing with the subject of the Kingdom:
    —the Believer and the Kingdom
    —Law and the Kingdom
    —Old Testament and the Kingdom
    —Worship and the Kingdom
    —Entrance to the Kingdom

I. The Believer and the Kingdom (Matt. 5:1-16; Luke 6:24-26)

A. Positive characteristics: Things to achieve

  1. Those who are poor in spirit: *"Blessed are the poor in spirit: for theirs is the kingdom of heaven"* (Matt. 5:3).

- Why are the "poor in spirit" happy? Because they recognize their own spiritual poverty and are qualified to be filled by the riches of his grace. There are two local churches described in the book of Revelation which vividly illustrate this concept. One recognized its true condition; the other did not.

    Smyrna, the happy church— *"I know thy works, and tribulation, and poverty, (but thou art rich) and I know the blasphemy of them which say they are Jews, and are not, but are the synagogue of Satan"* (Rev. 2:9).

    Laodicea, the wretched church—*"I know thy works, that thou art neither cold nor hot: I would thou wert cold or hot. So then because thou are lukewarm, and neither cold nor hot, I will spue thee out of my mouth. Because thou sayest, I am rich, and increased with goods, and have need of nothing; and knowest not that thou art wretched, and miserable, and poor, and blind, and naked" (Rev. 3:15-17).*

---

2. Those who mourn: *"Blessed are they that mourn: for they shall be comforted" (Matt. 5:4).*

■ J. Dwight Pentecost wrote: Our Lord did not promise, 'Blessed are they that moan, for they shall be comforted,' but, *'Blessed are they that mourn.'* When we carry some burden that brings tears, our natural response is to complain, to moan, to question God's wisdom and benevolence, God's right to do this to us. He did not say, 'Those who moan will be comforted,' but *'those who mourn.'* (*The Sermon on the Mount*, Multnomah Press, Portland, Ore., 1980, pp. 31-32)

■ There are four classic examples in the Old Testament where men of God mourned over their own sins and the sins of Israel:

> Daniel (9:3-19)
>
> Isaiah (6:5)
>
> Ezra (9:5-15)
>
> Nehemiah (1:4-11)

---

3. Those who are meek: *"Blessed are the meek: for they shall inherit the earth" (Matt. 5:5).*

■ It should be immediately understood that meekness is not weakness. To the contrary, one of the most fearless and courageous individuals in the entire Word of God was Moses. Consider his amazing life: At age eighty he confronted the mightiest monarch of his day, the Egyptian pharaoh. Ignoring the king's threats, Moses thundered down ten terrible plagues upon the land. He then led his people across the surging waters of the Red Sea, through a burning desert up to the very borders of the promised land. He was hardly a coward. And how did God describe this champion of courage? *"Now the man Moses was very meek, above all the men which were upon the face of the earth" (Num. 12:3).*

■ In light of all this, biblical meekness may be defined as subdued strength. Moses never used this divine strength for his own selfish interests. Although he was constantly slandered by his own people, he refused to retaliate. Like the Savior, who could have instantly marshaled twelve legions of angels to protect him in Gethsemane, Moses chose instead to pray for, rather than destroy his enemies.

---

4. Those who hunger and thirst after righteousness: *"Blessed are they which do hunger and thirst after righteousness: for they shall be filled" (Matt. 5:6).*

■ Jesus is saying here that the secret of spiritual growth is a spiritual appetite. In other words, those who eat little will grow a little; those who eat much will grow much.

One of the greatest books ever written on the person of God is entitled, *The Pursuit of God*, by the late A. W. Tozer. In this book, Dr. Tozer wrote:

In this hour of all but universal darkness, one cheering gleam appears. Within the fold of conservative Christianity, there are to be found increasing numbers of persons whose religious lives are marked by a growing hunger after God himself. They are eager for spiritual realities, and will not be put off with words, nor will they

---

be content with correct 'interpretations' of truth. They are athirst for God, and they will not be satisfied until they have drunk deep at the fountain of living water. (Christian Publications, Inc., Harrisburg, Penn., p. 7)

> 5. Those who are merciful: *"Blessed are the merciful: for they shall obtain mercy" (Matt. 5:7).*

- The Romans spoke of four cardinal virtues—wisdom, justice, temperance, and courage. But mercy was not among them. Both divine mercy and grace can be thought of as opposite sides of the same coin.

  > God's mercy is not receiving what we deserve; that is, hell.

  > God's grace is receiving what we do not deserve; that is, heaven.

- Thus the merciful person is one who both sees and serves another human being in Jesus' stead.

> 6. Those that are pure in heart: *"Blessed are the pure in heart: for they shall see God" (Matt. 5:8).*

- The word "pure" here is the Greek word *katharos*, which can also be translated by the English words, "clean and clear." *Katharos* is an important word in the book of Revelation, referring to:

  > The garb worn by angels (Rev. 15:6)

  > The heavenly city (Rev. 21:18)

  > The river of life— *"And he shewed me a pure river of life, clear as crystal, proceeding out of the throne of God and of the Lamb" (Rev. 22:1).*

> 7. Those that are peacemakers: *"Blessed are the peacemakers: for they shall be called the children of God" (Matt. 5:9).*

- The role of the peacemakers is later described by Paul:

  > Their leader is the God of peace (1 Cor. 14:33)

  > They aspire after peace with all people (Rom. 12:18)

  > They proclaim the gospel of peace (Eph. 6:15)

> 8. Those that are persecuted for righteousness' sake: *"Blessed are they which are persecuted for righteousness' sake: for theirs is the kingdom of heaven. Blessed are ye, when men shall revile you, and persecute you, and shall say all manner of evil against you falsely, for my sake. Rejoice, and be exceeding glad: for great is your reward in heaven: for so persecuted they the prophets which were before you" (Matt. 5:10-12).*

- What is to be the reaction of those who are persecuted for righteousness' sake? In a word, they are to rejoice. Two reasons are given for this:

  > Because of the relationship down here—To suffer in this manner is a great privilege, for it associates one with the godly prophets of the past who were also persecuted.

  > Because of the rewards up there— *"For great is your reward in heaven" (Matt. 5:12).*

- Note—the promises given to believers:

  > a. To possess the kingdom of heaven (Matt. 5:3)

b. To be comforted (Matt. 5:4)

c. To inherit the earth (Matt. 5:5)

d. To be filled (Matt. 5:6)

e. To obtain mercy (Matt. 5:7)

f. To see God (Matt. 5:8)

g. To be called the sons of God (Matt. 5:9)

h. To possess the kingdom of heaven (Matt. 5:10)

■ Note—the duties assigned to believers:

a. They are to function as the salt of the earth: *"Ye are the salt of the earth: but if the salt have lost his savour, wherewith shall it be salted? it is thenceforth good for nothing, but to be cast out, and to be trodden under foot of men" (Matt. 5:13).*

(1) In the ancient world, on occasion, salt was considered to be more valuable than gold. It was certainly more practical. Roman soldiers were paid in salt. If one were derelict in his duty, he was said to be "not worth his salt." Salt prevents, provides, and promotes.

It prevents:

Corruption

Dehydration

It provides flavor.

It promotes thirst.

(2) In a spiritual sense, the salt of the believer's testimony can accomplish all three functions.

b. They are to function as the light of the world: *"Ye are the light of the world. A city that is set on an hill cannot be hid" (Matt. 5:14).*

(1) The believer receives this divine light from Christ (John 1:9) so that he might reflect it for Christ. *"Do all things without murmurings and disputings: That ye may be blameless and harmless, the sons of God, without rebuke, in the midst of a crooked and perverse nation, among whom ye shine as lights in the world" (Phil. 2:14-15).*

B. Negative characteristics—Things that should be avoided

■ Money seeking— *"No man can serve two masters: for either he will hate the one, and love the other; or else he will hold to the one, and despise the other. Ye cannot serve God and mammon. Therefore I say unto you, Take no thought for your life, what ye shall eat, or what ye shall drink; nor yet for your body, what ye shall put on. Is not the life more than meat, and the body than raiment?" (Matt. 6:24-25).*

■ The word *"mammon"* is an Aramaic word, pointing to wealth or riches. The word "despise" here refers to the act of placing a low value on something or someone. Jesus is not saying here that one must hate money in order to serve God. He is saying that possessions must be placed on the lowest rung of our priority ladder.

■ An Islamic proverb says: "He that seeks after this world is like one that drinks sea water. The more he drinks the thirstier he becomes, until it slays him."

Men pleasing— *"Behold the fowls of the air: for they sow not, neither do they reap, nor gather into barns; yet your heavenly Father feedeth them. Are ye not much better than they?" (Matt. 6:26).*

II. The Law and the Kingdom (Matt. 5:17-20; 7:12)

A. The divine fulfiller of the Law—*"Think not that I am come to destroy the law; or the prophets: I am not come to destroy, but to fulfill. For verily I say unto you, Till heaven and earth pass, one jot or one tittle shall in no wise pass from the law, till all be fulfilled" (Matt. 5:17-18).*

B. The divine fulfilling of the Law—*"Therefore all things whatsoever ye would that men should do to you, do ye even so to them: for this is the law and the prophets" (Matt. 7:12).*

■ This famous command, known by millions as the Golden Rule, is in reality the Gracious Rule, for one must experience the saving grace of God to fully practice its teaching.

■ Some have accused Christ of plagiarism here, claiming that he simply repeated what the Chinese philosopher Confucius and others had already said centuries before. Note, though, the words attributed to them: "Do not do unto others that which you would not have them do unto you." A quick comparison shows that there is a tremendous difference between these two statements. One is negative, the other positive. An example of the usage of both concepts can be seen in the parable of the Good Samaritan.

The negative usage, as demonstrated by the priest and Levite. They did not in the slightest either harm or harass the poor bleeding and half-dead victim. In essence, they simply did not do to him that which they would not desire for him to do to them in the same situation. But they left him to die.

The positive usage was demonstrated by the Good Samaritan. He *"bound up his wounds, pouring in oil and wine, and set him on his own beast, and brought him to an inn, and took care of him" (Luke 10:34).* Why did he do this? Because the Good Samaritan would have desired the same treatment if the situation had been reversed. The difference between Confucius' words and those of Jesus is the difference between death and life.

III. The Old Testament and the Kingdom (Matt. 5:21-48)

A. In relation to murder (Matt. 5:21-26)

1. The basic concept—*"Ye have heard that it was said by them of old time, Thou shalt not kill; and whosoever shall kill shall be in danger of the judgment" (Matt. 5:21).*

■ Jesus here refers to the Sixth Commandment, *"Thou shalt not kill" (Exod. 20:13).* The word "kill" literally means "murder," that is, the unlawful taking of a human life.

■ The judgment mentioned here has in view the common local courts, arranged according to Deut. 16:18, consisting of seven judges and two assistant Levites.

2. The broadened concept—*"But I say unto you, That whosoever is angry with his brother without a cause shall be in danger of the judgment and whosoever shall say to his brother, Raca, shall be in danger of the council: but whosoever shall say, Thou fool, shall be in danger of hell fire" (Matt. 5:22).*

■ Jesus equates anger and hatred with murder. He is saying that a devilish attitude is as serious as a devilish act. Finally, he warns that to hate and harass one's brother may result (unless, of course, repented of) in both human and divine retribution. John the apostle later amplified upon this: *"Whosoever hateth his brother is a murderer: and ye know that no murderer hath eternal life abiding in him" (1 John 3:15).*

B. In relationship to adultery (5:27-30)

    1. The basic concept— *"Ye have heard that it was said by them of old time, Thou shalt not commit adultery" (Matt. 5:27).*

    2. The broadened concept— *"But I say unto you, That whosoever looketh on a woman to lust after her hath committed adultery with her already in his heart" (Matt. 5:28).*

■ Our Lord treats the Seventh Commandment, *"Thou shalt not commit adultery" (Exod. 20:14),* as he did the Sixth Commandment. Evil acts are the result of evil attitudes. As Solomon once observed: *"For as a man thinketh in his heart, so is he" (Prov. 23:7).* The Apostle Paul was attempting to drive home this concept when he addressed his peers, the Jewish leaders, in the following manner: *"Thou that sayest a man should not commit adultery, dost thou commit adultery?" (Rom. 2:22).*

C. In relationship to divorce (Matt. 5:31-32)

    1. The basic concept— *"It hath been said, Whosoever shall put away his wife, let him give her a writing of divorcement" (Matt. 5:31).*

    2. The broadened concept— *"But I say unto you, That whosoever shall put away his wife, saving for the cause of fornication, causeth her to commit adultery: and whosoever shall marry her that is divorced committeth adultery" (Matt. 5:32).*

D. In relationship to oath taking (Matt. 5:33-37)

    1. The basic concept— *"Again, ye have heard that it hath been said by them of old time, Thou shalt not forswear thyself, but shalt perform unto the Lord thine oaths" (Matt. 5:33).*

    2. The broadened concept

        Negative— *"But I say unto you, Swear not at all; neither by heaven; for it is God's throne: Nor by the earth; for it is his footstool: neither by Jerusalem; for it is the city of the great King. Neither shalt thou swear by thy head, because thou canst not make one hair white or black" (Matt. 5:34-36).*

        Positive— *"But let your communication be, Yea, yea; Nay, nay; for whatsoever is more than these cometh of evil" (Matt. 5:37).*

■ The Pharisees knew that they would be held accountable if they swore by God's name and broke their oath (see Lev. 19:12; Num. 30:2; Deut. 23:21). In light of this, they had invented four lesser oaths. Thus, one might swear by heaven, earth, Jerusalem, or his own head. But Jesus here points out that these oaths were just as binding. He then concluded:

        Don't swear by heaven, for it is God's throne.

        Don't swear by the earth, for it is God's footstool.

        Don't swear by your own head, for it is God's creation.

E. In relationship to retaliation (Matt. 5:38-42)

    1. The basic concept— *"Ye have heard that it hath been said, An eye for an eye, and a tooth for a tooth" (Matt. 5:38).*

    2. The broadened concept— *"But I say unto you, That ye resist not evil: but whosoever shall smite thee on thy right cheek, turn to him the other also. And if any man will sue thee at the law, and take away thy coat, let*

> *him have thy cloak also. And whosoever shall compel thee to go a mile, go with him twain. Give to him that asketh thee, and from him that would borrow of thee turn not thou away" (Matt. 5:39-42).*
>
> F. In relationship to love (Matt. 5:43-48)
>
>   1. The basic concept— *"Ye have heard that it hath been said, Thou shalt love thy neighbour, and hate thine enemy" (Matt. 5:43).*

■ This statement cannot be found in the Old Testament. It was no doubt one of the common (but incorrect) teachings of the rabbis. In fact, to the contrary, the Old Testament teaches just the opposite. Note: *"If thou meet thine enemy's ox or his ass going astray, thou shalt surely bring it back to him again. If thou see the ass of him that hateth thee lying under his burden, and wouldest forbear to help him, thou shalt surely help with him" (Exod. 23:4-5). "If thine enemy be hungry, give him bread to eat; and if he be thirsty, give him water to drink" (Prov. 25:21).*

> 2. The broadened concept— *"But I say unto you, Love your enemies, bless them that curse you, do good to them that hate you, and pray for them which despitefully use you, and persecute you"(Matt. 5:44).*

IV. Worship and the Kingdom (Matt. 6:1-7:11)

A. Giving (Matt. 6:1-4; Luke 6:38)

  1. The rules

   a. Fruitless giving— *"Take heed that ye do not your alms before men, to be seen of them: otherwise ye have no reward of your Father which is in heaven. Therefore when thou doest thine alms, do not sound a trumpet before thee, as the hypocrites do in the synagogues and in the streets, that they may have glory of men. Verily I say unto you, They have their reward" (Matt. 6:1-2).*

   b. Fruitful giving— *"But when thou doest alms, let not thy left hand know what thy right hand doeth"* *(Matt. 6:3).*

  2. The rewards— *"That thine alms may be in secret: and thy Father which seeth in secret himself shall reward thee openly" (Matt. 6:4). "Give, and it shall be given unto you; good measure, pressed down, and shaken together, and running over, shall men give into your bosom. For with the same measure that ye mete withal it shall be measured to you again" (Luke 6:38).*

B. Praying (Matt. 6:5-15; 6:7-11)

  1. Essentials in prayer

   a. Those prayers God rejects— *"And when thou prayest, thou shalt not be as the hypocrites are: for they love to pray standing in the synagogues and in the corners of the streets, that they may be seen of men. Verily I say unto you, They have their reward ... But when ye pray, use not vain repetitions, as the heathen do: for they think that they shall be heard for their much speaking" (Matt. 6:5, 7).*

   b. Those prayers God receives— *"But thou, when thou prayest, enter into thy closet, and when thou hast shut thy door, pray to thy Father which is in secret; and thy Father which seeth in secret shall reward thee openly" (Matt. 6:6). "For your Father knoweth what things ye have need of, before ye ask him" (6:8b).*

  2. Elements in prayer

     "After this manner therefore pray ye: Our Father which art in heaven, Hallowed be thy name. Thy kingdom come. Thy will be done in earth, as it is in heaven. Give us this day our daily bread. And forgive us our debts, as we forgive our debtors. And lead us not into temptation, but deliver us from evil: For thine is the kingdom, and the power, and the glory, for ever. Amen" (Matt. 6:9-13).

- This prayer, the most well known and oft quoted in the entire Bible, has been greatly misunderstood concerning both its name and nature.

   Its name—It is not the Lord's Prayer, but the Disciples' Prayer. The Lord's Prayer is found in John 17.

   Its nature—Some have overused it, memorizing and reciting it, feeling there is a magical blessing attached to it.

   Others have underused it, concluding that it belongs to another dispensational age.

- These positions are, of course, in error. In essence, what is referred to as the Lord's Prayer is a model prayer, given by the Savior to his own, serving as a guideline to help them pray more fruitfully.

- Luke provides the background which led to this prayer. *"And it came to pass, that, as he was praying in a certain place, when he ceased, one of his disciples said unto him, Lord, teach us to pray, as John also taught his disciples" (Luke 11:1).* It is extremely significant to observe that on no occasion is it ever recorded that the disciples ask: "Lord, teach us to preach," or, "Lord, teach us to work miracles." But they did ask him to instruct them in prayer. The implications are staggering, for this indicates that the prayer life of Christ had more influence on them than the sermons he preached or the miracles he performed.

- Note the various elements listed in this prayer:

   a. FAITH! *"Our Father, who art in heaven" (6:9a)*

      (1) The first two words here serve as a reminder concerning my *horizontal* responsibility ("our") and my *vertical* responsibility ("Father").

   b. WORSHIP! *"Hallowed be thy name" (6:9b)*

      (1) David felt this part of prayer to be so important that he appointed a select group of men who did nothing else in the temple but praise and worship God. (See 1 Chron. 23:5; 25:1, 7.) In the book of Revelation John sees four special angels who exist solely to worship God and who *"rest not day and night, saying Holy, holy, holy, Lord God Almighty, which was, and is, and is to come" (Rev. 4:8).* See also Christ's statement to the Samaritan woman (John 4:23-24).

   c. EXPECTATION! *"Thy kingdom come" (6:10)*

      (1) This kingdom is that blessed millennial kingdom spoken of so much in the Old Testament (see Isa. 2:2-4; 25:8; 35:1, 8, 10; 65:20, 25) and later previewed by John in the New Testament (Rev. 20:1-6).

   d. SUBMISSION! *"Thy will be done in earth as it is in heaven" (6:10b)*

      (1) Jesus would later give the finest example of this element in Gethsemane (see Matt. 26:39).

   e. PETITION! *"Give us this day our daily bread" (6:11)*

      (1) This suggests our praying should be as regular and often as our eating—namely, daily!

   f. CONFESSION! *"And forgive us our debts" (6:12)*

      (1) The blood of Christ will forgive us of every sin, but not of one excuse. Only confessed sin can be forgiven (see 1 John 1:9).

   g. COMPASSION! *"As we forgive our debtors" (6:12b)*

   h. DEPENDENCE! *"And lead us not into temptation but deliver us from evil" (6:13)*

      (1) It should be understood that while God has never promised to keep us from temptation, he has promised to preserve us in and through temptation. (See 1 Cor. 10:13.)

   i. ACKNOWLEDGMENT! *"For thine is the kingdom, and the power, and the glory, forever, Amen" (6:13b)*

(1) Some ten centuries prior to this, one of Israel's earliest kings had prayed in a similar fashion: *"Wherefore David blessed the Lord before all the congregation: and David said, Blessed be thou, Lord God of Israel our father, for ever and ever. Thine, O Lord is the greatness, and the power, and the glory, and the victory, and the majesty: for all that is in the heaven and in the earth is thine; thine is the kingdom, O Lord, and thou art exalted as head above all"* (1 Chron. 29:10-11). Now, 1,000 years later, Israel's ultimate King, the son of David, appears upon the scene, *"exalted as head above all."*

(2) Someone has pointed out the extraordinary collection of relationships which emerge in this prayer:

That of father and child (Our Father)

That of God and worshiper (Hallowed be thy name)

That of king and subject (Thy kingdom come)

That of master and servant (Thy will be done)

That of benefactor and suppliant (Give us this day our daily bread)

That of creditor and debtor (Forgive us our debts)

That of guide and pilgrim (Lead us not into temptation)

That of Redeemer and redeemed (Deliver us from the evil one)

3. Encouragements in prayer (Matt. 7:7-11)

The rewards involved—*"Ask, and it shall be given you; seek, and ye shall find; knock, and it shall be opened unto you: For every one that asketh receiveth; and he that seeketh findeth; and to him that knocketh it shall be opened. Or what man is there of you, whom if his son ask bread, will he give him a stone? Or if he ask a fish, will he give him a serpent?"* (Matt. 7:7-10).

The rationale involved—*"If ye then, being evil, know how to give good gifts unto your children, how much more shall your Father which is in heaven give good things to them that ask him?"* (Matt. 7:11).

C. Fasting (Matt. 6:16-18)

1. As practiced by the hypocrites—*"Moreover when ye fast, be not, as the hypocrites, of a sad countenance: for they disfigure their faces, that they may appear unto men to fast. Verily I say unto you, They have their reward"* (Matt. 6:16).

2. As practiced by the humble—*"But thou, when thou fastest, anoint thine head, and wash thy face; that thou appear not unto men to fast, but unto thy Father which is in secret: and thy Father, which seeth in secret, shall reward thee openly"* (Matt 6:17-18).

D. Earning (Matt. 6:19-23)

1. Earthly treasure is insecure and corruptible—*"Lay not up for yourselves treasures upon earth, where moth and rust doth corrupt, and where thieves break through and steal"* (Matt. 6:19).

2. Eternal treasure is secure and incorruptible—*"But lay up for yourselves treasure in heaven, where neither moth nor rust doth corrupt, and where thieves do not break through nor steal: for where your treasure is, there will your heart be also"* (Matt. 6:20-21).

E. Serving (Matt. 6:24)—*"No man can serve two masters: for either he will hate the one, and love the other; or else he will hold to the one, and despise the other. Ye cannot serve God and mammon"* (Matt. 6:24).

F. Trusting (Matt. 6:25-34)

1. The illustrations

   a. The fowls of the air— *"Behold the fowls of the air: for they sow not, neither do they reap, nor gather into barns; yet your heavenly Father feedeth them. Are ye not much better than they?" (Matt. 6:26).*

   b. The lilies of the field— *"And why take ye thought for raiment? Consider the lilies of the field, how they grow; they toil not, neither do they spin: and yet I say unto you, That even Solomon in all his glory was not arrayed like one of these. Wherefore, if God so clothe the grass of the field, which to day is, and to morrow is cast into the oven, shall he not much more clothe you, O ye of little faith?" (Matt. 6:28-30).*

2. The invitation— *"Therefore take no thought, saying, What shall we eat? Or, What shall we drink? Or, Wherewithal shall we be clothed? (For after all these things do the Gentiles seek:) for your heavenly Father knoweth that ye have need of all these things. But seek ye first the kingdom of God, and his righteousness; and all these things shall be added unto you. Take therefore no thought for the morrow: for the morrow shall take thought for the things of itself. Sufficient unto the day is the evil thereof" (Matt. 6:31-34).*

G. Judging (Matt. 7:1-5) *"Judge not, that ye be not judged. For with what judgment ye judge, ye shall be judged: and with what measure ye mete, it shall be measured to you again. And why beholdest thou the mote that is in thy brother's eye, but considerest not the beam that is in thine own eye? Or how wilt thou say to thy brother, Let me pull out the mote out of thine eye; and, behold, a beam is in thine own eye? Thou hypocrite, first cast out the beam out of thine own eye; and then shalt thou see clearly to cast out the mote out of thy brother's eye" (Matt. 7:1-5).*

   1. Jesus here lists three reasons against passing judgment upon another:

      The one judging will himself be judged,

      The one judging will be judged by the same measuring stick he uses to measure others,

      The one judging is often more corrupted by the same sin he condemns others for. Consider the utter hypocrisy as described by Jesus

      Here is a man blinded by a huge "wooden" sin the size of a building beam.

      Here is another man bothered by a small "wooden" sin the size of a mote. And the result? The first tries to condemn the second!

   2. Honest and critical evaluation on the part of one believer toward another is sometimes necessary. This should only be done, however, if the person evaluating is not guilty of the same sin and if three rules are carefully observed:

      a. Is my criticism unkind? (Prov. 18:8)

      b. Is my criticism untrue? (Exod. 23:1)

      c. Is my criticism unnecessary? (Prov. 11:13)

H. Witnessing (Matt. 7:6)— *"Give not that which is holy unto the dogs, neither cast ye your pearls before swine, lest they trample them under their feet, and turn again and rend you" (Matt. 7:6).*

   1. The hogs and dogs probably refer to apostate religious teachers (see 2 Peter 2:22).

V. The Entrance to the Kingdom (Matt. 7:13-27)

A. The way (Matt. 7:13-14)

   1. The gate to hell— *"Enter ye in at the strait gate: for wide is the gate, and broad is the way, that leadeth to destruction, and many there be which go in thereat" (Matt. 7:13).*

2. The gate to heaven—*"Because strait is the gate, and narrow is the way, which leadeth unto life, and few there be that find it" (Matt. 7:14).*

B. The warning (Matt. 7:15-23)

1. Concerning false prophets

   a. Their deceit—*"Beware of false prophets, which come to you in sheep's clothing, but inwardly they are ravening wolves" (Matt. 7:15).*

      (1) Various Old Testament prophets had warned Israel concerning the danger of false shepherds. *"Son of man, prophesy, and say unto them, Thus saith the Lord God unto the shepherds; Woe be to the shepherds of Israel that do feed themselves! Should not the shepherds feed the flocks? Ye eat the fat, and ye clothe you with the wool, ye kill them that are fed; but ye feed not the flock. The diseased have ye not strengthened, neither have ye healed that which was sick, neither have ye bound up that which was broken, neither have ye brought again that which was driven away, neither have ye sought that which was lost: but with force and with cruelty have ye ruled them" (Ezek. 34:2-4). "For, lo, I will raise up a shepherd in the land, which shall not visit those that be cut off, neither shall seek the young one, nor heal that that is broken, nor feed that that standeth still: but he shall eat the flesh of the fat, and tear their claws in pieces. Woe to the idle shepherd that leaveth the flock! the sword shall be upon his arm, and upon his right eye: his arm shall be clean dried up, and his right eye shall be utterly darkened" (Zech. 11:16-17).*

   b. Their description—*"Ye shall know them by their fruits. Do men gather grapes of thorns, or figs of thistles? Even so every good tree bringeth forth good fruit; but a corrupt tree bringeth forth evil fruit. A good tree cannot bring forth evil fruit, neither can a corrupt tree bring forth good fruit" (Matt. 7:16-18).*

   c. Their destruction—*"Every tree that bringeth not forth good fruit is hewn down, and cast into the fire" (Matt. 7:19).*

2. Concerning false profession

   a. The caution—*"Not every one that saith unto me, Lord, Lord, shall enter into the kingdom of heaven; but he that doeth the will of my Father which is in heaven" (Matt. 7:21).*

   b. The claim—*"Many will say to me in that day, Lord, Lord, have we not prophesied in thy name? and in thy name have cast out devils? And in thy name done many wonderful works?" (Matt. 7:22).*

   c. The condemnation—*"And then will I profess unto them, I never knew you: depart from me, ye that work iniquity" (Matt. 7:23).*

■ Note the terrible two-fold deception described here:

1. Religious deceivers deceive others.

2. Religious deceivers deceive themselves.

■ It is tragically possible to mouth the words of God, to imitate the works of God, but never personally to know the true witness from God, that is, Jesus Christ.

■ The wisdom (7:24-27)

1. Its abundance as seen by the first builder— *"Therefore whosoever heareth these sayings of mine, and doeth them, I will liken him unto a wise man, which built his house upon a rock and the rain descended, and the floods came, and the winds blew, and beat upon that house: and it fell not: for it was founded upon a rock"(Matt. 7:24-25).*

2. Its absence as seen by the second builder— *"And every one that heareth these sayings of mine, and doeth them not, shall be likened unto a foolish man, which built his house upon the sand: and the rain descended, and the floods came, and the winds blew, and beat upon that house; and it fell: and great was the fall of it"* (Matt. 7:26-27).

THREE: The Source of Life Sermon (John 5:12-47)

"For as the Father hath life in himself; so hath he given to the Son to have life in himself" (John 5:26).

I. The Oneness Enjoyed by Christ:

A. His equality with the Father— *"Therefore the Jews sought the more to kill him, because he not only had broken the Sabbath, but said also that God was his Father, making himself equal with God"* (John 5:18).

Humanly speaking, the reason the Jewish religious leaders attempted to kill Christ was not because he claimed to be the Messiah, but because he made himself equal with God. This same incident occurred at a later date. *"The Jews answered him, saying, For a good work we stone thee not; but for blasphemy; and because that thou, being a man, makest thyself God"* (John 10:33).

B. His dependence upon the Father— *"Then answered Jesus and said unto them, Verily,verily, I say unto you, The Son can do nothing of himself, but what he seeth the Father do: for what things soever he doeth, these also doeth the Son likewise"* (John 5:19).

This verse is associated closely with one found in the epistles in which Paul writes concerning Christ: *"But made himself of no reputation, and took upon him the form of a servant, and was made in the likeness of men"* (Phil. 2:7). The *"made himself of no reputation"* is a translation of the Greek work *kenos*, which means "to make empty."

Question: Of what did Christ empty himself?

Answer: He did not give up (empty) his divine attributes (his omnipotence, omniscience, etc.) when coming to earth: but he did agree not to use them, depending totally upon the Father and the Holy Spirit.

C. His responsibilities from the Father

1. Concerning future resurrection— *"For as the Father raiseth up the dead, and quickeneth them; even so the Son quickeneth whom he will"* (John 5:21).

2. Concerning future judgment— *"For the Father judgeth no man, but hath committed all judgment unto the Son"* (John 5:22).

Jesus later referred again to this profound truth, as does the Apostle Paul: *"When the Son of man shall come in his glory, and all the holy angels with him, then shall he sit upon the throne of his glory: and before him shall be gathered all nations: and he shall separate them one from another as a shepherd divideth his sheep from the goats"* (Matt. 25:31-32). *"And the times of this ignorance God winked at; but now commandeth all men every where to repent: because he hath appointed a day, in the which he will judge the world in righteousness by that man whom he hath ordained; whereof he hath given assurance unto all men, in that he hath raised him from the dead"* (Acts 17:30-31).

D. His esteem by the Father

    1. He is loved — *"For the Father loveth the Son, and sheweth him all things that himself doeth: and he will shew him greater works than these, that ye may marvel"* (John 5:20).

    2. He is honored — *"That all men should honour the Son, even as they honour the Father. He that honoureth not the Son honoureth not the Father which hath sent him"* (John 5:23).

E. His submission to the Father — *"I can of mine own self do nothing: as I hear, I judge; and my judgment is just; because I seek not mine own will, but the will of the Father which hath sent me"* (John 5:30).

F. His authority from the Father — *"I am come in my Father's name, and ye receive me not if another shall come in his own name, him ye will receive"* (John 5:43).

    They will, indeed, and the one they receive will be the antichrist. *"And all that dwell upon the earth shall worship him, whose names are not written in the book of life of the Lamb slain from the foundation of the world"* (Rev. 13:8).

II. The Two Resurrections Accomplished by Christ

A. The resurrection of the saved

    1. Present-day spiritual resurrection — *"Verily, verily, I say unto you, He that heareth my word, and believeth on him that sent me, hath everlasting life, and shall not come into condemnation: but is passed from death unto life"* (John 5:24).

    2. Future-day physical resurrection — *"Verily, verily, I say unto you, The hour is coming, and now is, when the dead shall hear the voice of the Son of God: and they that hear shall live ... Marvel not at this: for the hour is coming in the which all that are in the graves shall hear his voice"* (John 5:25, 28). *"And shall come forth; they that have done good, unto the resurrection of life"* (John 5:29a).

B. The resurrection of the unsaved — *"And hath given him authority to execute judgment also, because he is the Son of man"* (John 5:27). *"And they that have done evil, unto the resurrection of damnation"* (John 5:29b).

This two-fold resurrection seems to refer to those occurring just prior to and following the Millennium, as described by both Daniel the prophet and John the apostle. *"And many of them that sleep in the dust of the earth shall awake, some to everlasting life, and some to shame and everlasting contempt"* (Dan. 12:2). *"And I saw thrones, and they sat upon them, and judgment was given unto them: and I saw the souls of them that were beheaded for the witness of Jesus, and for the word of God, and which had not worshipped the beast, neither his image, neither had received his mark upon their foreheads, or in their hands; and they lived and reigned with Christ a thousand years. But the rest of the dead lived not again until the thousand years were finished. This is the first resurrection"* (Rev. 20:4-5).

III. The Four Witnesses Concerning Christ

A. Witnessed to by John the Baptist (John 5:33-35) *"Ye sent unto John, and he bare witness unto the truth"* (John 5:33).

B. Witnessed to by his own works — *"But I have greater witness than that of John: for the works which the Father hath given me to finish, the same works that I do, bear witness of me, that the Father hath sent me"* (John 5:36).

C. Witnessed to by the Father — *"And the Father himself, which hath sent me, hath borne witness of me. Ye have neither heard his voice at any time, nor seen his shape. And ye have not his word abiding in you: for whom he hath sent, him ye believe not"* (John 5:37-38).

D. Witnessed to by the Scriptures (John 5:39-47)—*"Search the scriptures; for in them ye think ye have eternal life: and they are they which testify of me ...Do not think that I will accuse you to the Father: there is one that accuseth you, even Moses, in whom ye trust. For had ye believed Moses, ye would have believed me: for he wrote of me. But if ye believe not his writings, how shall ye believe my words?" (John 5:39, 45-47).*

Where and when did Moses (author of the first five Old Testament books) refer to Christ? He wrote of him as follows:

1. The Seed of the woman (Gen. 3:15)
2. The giver of peace (Gen. 49:10)
3. The Passover Lamb (Exod. 12:3-13
4. The slaughtered goat and the scapegoat (Lev. 16:7-10)
5. The red heifer (Num. 19:2)
6. The brazen serpent (Num. 21:8-9)
7. The great Prophet of God (Deut. 18:15)
8. The Angel of the Lord—as appearing to:
   a. Hagar (Gen. 16:7)
   b. Abraham (Gen. 22:11-18)
   c. Jacob (Gen. 48:16)
   d. Moses (Exod. 3:2)

FOUR: The Bread of Life Sermon (John 6:22-71)

"And Jesus said unto them, I am the bread of life: he that cometh to me shall never hunger; and he that believeth on me shall never thirst ... I am that bread of life" (John 6:35, 48).

■ This is the first of at least seven great "I am" statements uttered by Christ, as recorded in the Gospel of John:

I am the Bread of life (6:35)

I am the Light of the world (8:12; 9:5)

I am the Door (10:9)

I am the Good Shepherd (10:11)

I am the Resurrection and the Life (11:25)

I am the Way and the Truth (14:6)

I am the true Vine (15:1)

I. Christ and the Crowd (John 6:22-40)

A. He speaks about God's salvation

1. Their confusion

   a. They sought him only for physical bread (John 6:26).

   b. They were ignorant about pleasing God—*"Then said they unto him, What shall we do, that we might work the works of God?" (John 6:28).*

   c. They assumed the Old Testament manna came from Moses—*"Our fathers did eat manna in the desert; as it is written, He gave them bread from heaven to eat" (John 6:31).*

---

2. His correction

    a. They were to seek him for that living bread— *"And Jesus said unto them, I am the bread of life: he that cometh to me shall never hunger; and he that believeth on me shall never thirst" (John 6:35).*

    b. They would please God by believing on his Son— *"Jesus answered and said unto them, This is the work of God, that ye believe on him whom he hath sent" (John 6:29).*

    c. The Old Testament manna came from God and was a type of himself— *"Then Jesus said unto them, Verily, verily, I say unto you, Moses gave you not that bread from heaven; but my Father giveth you the true bread from heaven. For the bread of God is he which cometh down from heaven, and giveth life unto the world" (John 6:32-33).*

B. He speaks about God's sovereignty

  1. This guarantees that all the elect would come to Christ— *"All that the Father giveth me shall come to me; and him that cometh to me I will in no wise cast out" (John 6:37).*

  2. This guarantees that all the elect would continue in Christ— *"And this is the Father's will which hath sent me, that of all which he hath given me I should lose nothing, but should raise it up again at the last day. And this is the will of him that sent me, that every one which seeth the Son, and believeth on him, may have everlasting life: and I will raise him up at the last day" (John 6:39-40).*

    a. This great truth, *"That all which he hath given me I should lose nothing,"* is amplified by the Apostle Jude: *"Now unto him that is able to keep you from falling, and to present you faultless before the presence of his glory with exceeding joy, to the only wise God our Saviour, be glory and majesty, dominion and power, both now and ever. Amen" (Jude 1:24-25).*

II. Christ and the Clergy (John 6:41-59)

A. They were ignorant concerning his origin— *"And they said, Is not this Jesus, the son of Joseph, whose father and mother we know? How is it then that he saith, I came down from heaven" (John 6:42).*

B. They were ignorant concerning his offer— *"I am the living bread which came down from heaven: if any man eat of this bread, he shall live for ever: and the bread that I will give is my flesh, which I will give for the life of the world. The Jews therefore strove among themselves, saying, How can this man give us his flesh to eat?" (John 6:51, 52).*

  1. Our Lord continued here by saying that one must "eat" of his flesh and "drink" of his blood to be saved. (See John 6:53-55.) Much controversy has surrounded these verses.

■ The fiction involved:

    In the past, the political world of Rome associated these words with cannibalism. In fact, the early church was falsely accused of this very thing.

    At the present, the religious world of Rome associates them with the doctrine of transubstantiation. This is the belief that at Communion the wafer and wine actually become the body and blood of Christ.

■ The facts involved:

    Both of the above positions are refuted by Jesus in John 6:63. *"It is the spirit that quickeneth; the flesh profiteth nothing: the words that I speak unto you, they are spirit, and they are life."*

  2. Thus, to "eat his body and drink his blood" is simply to accept his sacrifice on the cross. To refuse his body and blood is to reject his sacrifice on the cross.

III. Christ and the Carnal (John 6:59-66)

A. Many now decide against Christ—*"These things said he in the synagogue, as he taught in Capernaum. Many therefore of his disciples, when they had heard this, said, This is an hard saying; who can hear it?"* (John 6:59-60).

B. Many now depart from Christ—*"From that time many of his disciples went back, and walked no more with him"* (John 6:66).

1. It should be noted that there is a difference between an apostle and a disciple. A disciple literally means "a learner." There were many such disciples who joined Christ for a while, but would leave when the going became difficult.

2. An apostle literally means "one sent forth." There were only twelve apostles during the earthly ministry of Jesus.

IV. Christ and the Chosen (John 6:67-71)

A. Jesus and the eleven apostles—*"Then said Jesus unto the twelve, Will ye also go away? Then Simon Peter answered him, Lord, to whom shall we go? thou hast the words of eternal life. And we believe and are sure that thou art that Christ, the Son of the living God"* (John 6:67-69).

B. Jesus and the evil apostle

1. The nature of this apostle—*"Jesus answered them, Have not I chosen you twelve, and one of you is a devil?"* (John 6:70).

Note: Some believe that Judas will be the future antichrist because of this passage and others which refer to him.

■ In Luke 22:3 and John 13:27, it is recorded that Satan entered Judas. This is never said of any other individual in the Bible.

■ There are two instances in the New Testament where the title "Son of Perdition" is used. In the first instance, Jesus used it to refer to Judas (John 17:12); and on the second occasion, Paul referred to the antichrist (2 Thess. 2:3).

2. The name of this apostle—*"He spake of Judas Iscariot the son of Simon: for he it was that should betray him, being one of the twelve"* (John 6:71).

■ Iscariot means "a man from Kerioth." This was a Judean city. Thus, Judas was the only non-Galilean apostle, and, on the surface, the least probable to betray Christ.

FIVE: *The Feast of Tabernacles Sermon (John 7:1-53)*

I. The Disbelief of the Brethren of Christ (John 7:1-9)

A. Their ridicule—*"His brethren therefore said unto him, Depart hence, and go into Judaea, that thy disciples also may see the works that thou doest. For there is no man that doeth any thing in secret, and he himself seeketh to be known openly. If thou do these things, shew thyself to the world. For neither did his brethren believe in him"* (John 7:3-5).

The names of Jesus' younger half brothers are recorded for us by Matthew, as is the fact that he had some younger half sisters: *"Is not this the carpenter's son? Is not his mother called Mary? And his brethren, James and Joses, and Simon, and Judas? And his sisters, are they not all with us? Whence then hath this man all these things?"* (Matt. 13:55-56).

The "time" in mind here, of course, is his crucifixion. He was always acutely aware of this time and hour. Note:

"Jesus saith unto her" [his mother at the marriage feast in Cana], *"Woman, what have I to do with thee? Mine hour is not yet come" (John 2:4).*

"Then they" [a murderous crowd in Jerusalem] *"sought to take him; but no man laid hands on him, because his hour was not yet come" (John 7:30).*

"And Jesus answered them" [some Greeks who wanted to see him] *"saying, The hour is come, that the Son of man should be glorified" (John 12:23). (See also 12:27.)*

"Now before the feast of the passover ... Jesus knew that his hour was come that he should depart out of this world unto the Father" (John 13:1).

2. Especially important to note are the statements found in John 7:30 and 8:20. These verses teach that the servant of God is indestructible until the will of God has been accomplished in his life. (See also Rev. 11:7.)

II. The Division of the Temple Crowds (John 7:10-30, 40-43)

A. Some thought he was a good man (John 7:12).

B. Some thought he was a deceiver (John 7:12).

C. Some thought he was a demoniac (John 7:20).

D. Some thought he was an ordinary man (John 7:27).

E. Some thought he was a prophet (John 7:40).

F. Some thought he was the Messiah (John 7:31, 41).

III. The Disdain of the Pharisees

A. They attempted to detain him, but were frustrated by their own officers— *"The Pharisees heard that the people murmured such things concerning him; and the Pharisees and the chief priests sent officers to take him ... And some of them would have taken him; but no man laid hands on him. Then came the officers to the chief priests and Pharisees; and they said unto them, Why have ye not brought him? The officers answered, Never man spake like this man. Then answered them the Pharisees, Are ye also deceived?" (John 7:32, 44-47).*

B. They attempted to denounce him, but were frustrated by one of their own members— *"Nicodemus saith unto them, (he that came to Jesus by night, being one of them,) Doth our law judge any man, before it hear him, and know what he doeth? They answered and said unto him, Art thou also of Galilee? Search, and look: for out of Galilee ariseth no prophet" (John 7:50-52).*

IV. The Decision of the Thirsty

A. The invitation— *"In the last day, that great day of the feast, Jesus stood and cried, saying, If any man thirst, let him come unto me, and drink. He that believeth on me, as the scripture hath said, out of his belly shall flow rivers of living water. (But this spake he of the Spirit, which they that believe on him should receive: for the Holy Ghost was not yet given; because that Jesus was not yet glorified)" (John 7:37-39).*

■ The feast referred to here was the Feast of Tabernacles. It was one of the three great Jewish feasts. Josephus called it their holiest and greatest feast (The Antiquities of the Jews 8. 4. 1). This feast, also called the Feast of Ingathering, was a time of thanksgiving for harvest. It was a happy time; devout Jews lived outdoors in booths made of tree branches for seven days as a reminder of God's provision in the desert during their forefathers' wanderings. The feast also signified that God dwells with his people.

■ Dr. Homer Kent of Grace Seminary suggested the following:

The custom had developed of having the priests bring a vessel of water daily during the festival from the Pool of Siloam and come with it in procession to the Temple. Here the water would be poured on the altar of burnt offering as a reminder of how God supplied Israel's need in the wilderness. On the eighth day the ceremony was omitted, signifying Israel's presence in the land. If this event occurred on the eighth day, Christ's invitation to men to come to him for living water was especially dramatic as he claimed to be the fulfillment of the typology carried out at the feast. He was the supplier of the spiritual living. (See also John 4:10 and 1 Cor. 10:4.)

B. The determination— *"And many of the people believed on him"* (John 7:31).

SIX: *The Temple Treasury Sermon (John 8:12-59)*

"These words spake Jesus in the treasury, as he taught in the temple: and no man laid hands on him; for his hour was not yet come" (John 8:20).

I. The Conflict with Some Unbelieving Jews
A. Their question
  1. They wanted to know who he was (John 8:25)
  2. They wanted to know who his father was (John 8:19)
  3. They wanted to know if he claimed to be greater than their father Abraham (John 8:53)
B. His answers
  1. Concerning himself
    a. He was the light of the world (John 8:12).
      (1) His temple treasury sermon (also known as the Light of the World Discourse) was probably the second of two preached during the Feast of Tabernacles. Here Jesus claims to be the Light of the world.
    b. He came to bring light and life to all (John 8:12)
    c. He was the Messiah (John 8:24, 28)
    d. He was sinless (John 8:6)
    e. He was from above (John 8:23)
    f. He would become the Lamb (John 8:28)
  2. Concerning his Father
    a. He came from the Father (John 8:18, 42)
    b. He was the son of the Father (John 8:19)
    c. He was taught by the Father (John 8:28)
    d. He was honored by the Father (John 8:54)

e. He spoke for the Father (John 8:26)

f. He would ascend back to the Father (John 8:21)

3. Concerning Abraham

a. He was greater than Abraham, for he preceded Abraham — *"Then said the Jews unto him, Thou are not yet fifty years old, and hast thou seen Abraham? Jesus said unto them, Verily, verily, I say unto you, Before Abraham was, I am" (John 8:57-58).*

(1) Their statement here gives us an insight concerning the awesome pressure and burden carried by our Lord. Here he is, barely thirty-three, and yet mistaken for nearly fifty. We note that Jesus did not say, "I was," but rather, "I am." Here he was simply replying as he once did to Moses: *"And God said unto Moses, I AM THAT I AM: and he said, Thus shalt thou say unto the children of Israel, I AM hath sent me unto you" (Exod. 3:14).*

b. He was greater than Abraham, for he ministered to Abraham — *"Your father Abraham rejoiced to see my day: and he saw it, and was glad" (John 8:56).*

(1) When did this happen in the life of Abraham? It was probably a reference to the offering up of Isaac. Compare Gen. 22:1-14 with Heb. 11:17-19.

C. Their accusation

1. That he alone bore witness of himself (John 8:13)

2. That he was threatening suicide (John 8:22)

3. That he was born of fornication (John 8:41)

a. Note their sneering insinuation, *"We be not born of fornication" (8:41).* This is but one of several occasions on which the Jews made snide remarks questioning the unusual circumstances surrounding Christ's birth. When our Lord later healed a blind man, the Pharisees refused to believe it, telling the cured man to *"Give God the praise. We know that this man [Jesus] is a sinner" (John 9:24).*

4. That he was a demon-possessed Samaritan (John 8:48, 52)

D. His defense — *"Jesus answered and said unto them, Though I bear record of myself, yet my record is true; for I know whence I came, and whither I go; but ye cannot tell whence I come, and whither I go ... It is also written in your law, that the testimony of two men is true. I am one that bear witness of myself, and the Father that sent me beareth witness of me ... Jesus answered, I have not a devil; but I honour my Father, and ye do dishonour me. And I seek not mine own glory: there is one that seeketh and judgeth" (John 8:14, 17-18, 49-50).*

E. Their errors

1. That they had never been in bondage (John 8:33)

2. That they were the true seed of Abraham (John 8:33, 39)

F. His correction — *"Jesus answered them, Verily, verily, I say unto you, Whosoever committeth sin is the servant of sin ... They answered and said unto him, Abraham is our father. Jesus saith unto them, If ye were Abraham's children, ye would do the works of Abraham. But now ye seek to kill me, a man that hath told you the truth, which I have heard of God: this did not Abraham ... Ye are of your father the devil, and the lusts of your father ye will do. He was a murderer from the beginning, and abode not in the truth, because there is no truth in him. When he speaketh a lie, he speaketh of his own: for he is a liar, and the father of it" (John 8:34, 39-40, 44).*

G. Their rejection — *"Then took they up stones to cast at him: but Jesus hid himself, and went out of the temple, going through the midst of them, and so passed by" (John 8:59).*

> H. His condemnation—*"I said therefore unto you, that ye shall die in your sins: for if ye believe not that I am he, ye shall die in your sins" (John 8:24).*
>
> **II. The conversion of some believing Jews**—*"As he spake these words, many believed on him. Then said Jesus to those Jews which believed on him, If ye continue in my word, then are ye my disciples indeed; And ye shall know the truth, and the truth shall make you free ... If the Son therefore shall make you free, ye shall be free indeed ... Verily, verily, I say unto you, If a man keep my saying, he shall never see death" (John 8:30-32, 36, 51).*

SEVEN: The Good Shepherd Sermon (John 10:1-39)

Introduction:

On three occasions in the New Testament Jesus is described as a shepherd:

The author of Hebrews calls him the Great Shepherd (Heb. 13:20). This corresponds to Psalm 22.

The Apostle Peter refers to him as the Chief Shepherd (1 Peter 5:4). This corresponds to Psalm 24.

The Savior in this sermon describes himself as the Good Shepherd. This corresponds to Psalm 23.

We are told in John 10:22 that Jesus preached this sermon during the Feast of Dedication, also called the Feast of Lights. This was not an Old Testament feast. It came to be observed after the close of the Old Testament Canon. It commemorated the purifying of the temple after its defilement by the Syrians under Antiochus Epiphanes. The feast began on the 25th of Chisleu, which in A.D. 29 was the same as our December 20. It lasted for eight days, the length of time Judas Maccabaeus, the deliverer of the city, took in purifying it. It came to be called the Feast of Lights because the city of Jerusalem was brightly illuminated for its observance.

In this sermon we have described for us the characteristics of the following individuals or groups:
- Characteristics of the shepherd
- Characteristics of the sheep
- Characteristics of thieves and robbers
- Characteristics of the hierarchy
- Characteristics of goats

> ### I. Characteristics of the Shepherd
> A. He does things the right way—*"But he that entereth in by the door is the shepherd of the sheep" (John 10:2).*
> B. He is recognized by the porter—*"To him the porter openeth" (John 10:3).* (Note: The porter referred to here may possibly be the Holy Spirit.)
> C. He knows his sheep (John 10:3, 14, 27)—*"He calleth his own sheep by name" (John 10:3).*

Paul the apostle amplified upon this in a later epistle: *"Nevertheless the foundation of God standeth sure, having this seal, the Lord knoweth them that are his. And, let every one that nameth the name of Christ depart from iniquity" (2 Tim. 2:19).*

> D. He is known by his sheep (John 10:4, 14, 27) *"The sheep follow him: for they know his voice" (John 10:4).*
> E. He leads his sheep (John 10:3).
> F. He is the only true Shepherd—*"All that ever came before me are thieves and robbers: but the sheep did not hear them" (John 10:8).*

G. He lays down his life for the sheep (John 10:17-18)— *"I am the good shepherd: the good shepherd giveth his life for the sheep"* (John 10:11).

In the Old Testament the sheep died for the shepherd. In the New Testament the Shepherd will die for the sheep. Homer Kent wrote:

Many shepherds died while defending their flocks. There were knives and clubs of robbers to be faced, as well as the attacks of wild animals. In their cases, however, death was always unintended. Christ, on the other hand, was also to die for his sheep in order to save them, but he was going to do so voluntarily. He would "give his life." His sheep were in danger of the greatest kind. *"All we like sheep have gone astray"* (Isa. 53:6). Jesus was thus predicting his own death, which would occur the following spring. (*Light in the Darkness*, p. 140)

H. He takes up his life for the sheep (John 10:17-18)— *"No man taketh it from me, but I lay it down of myself. I have power to lay it down, and I have power to take it again. This commandment have I received of my Father"* (John 10:18).

I. He imparts life to the sheep (John 10:9-10)— *"I am the door: by me if any man enter in, he shall be saved, and shall go in and out, and find pasture"* (John 10:9). *"I am come that they might have life"* (John 10:10).

J. He imparts abundant life to the sheep— *"And that they might have it more abundantly"* (John 10:10).

K. He imparts eternal life to the sheep— *"And I give unto them eternal life; and they shall never perish, neither shall any man pluck them out of my hand. My Father, which gave them me, is greater than all; and no man is able to pluck them out of my Father's hand"* (John 10:28-29).

Note the "life" and "abundant life" phrases here:

1. The first (life) speaks of that peace with God in Rom. 5:1.

2. The second (abundant life) refers to that peace of God in Phil. 4:7.

The phrase "no man" is not found in the Greek text. It reads rather, "No thing." In other words, not even the believer himself can remove himself from the Father's hand. Paul later built a marvelous case for this. (See Rom. 8:33-39.)

L. He is approved by the Father (John 10:15).

M. He is loved by the Father (John 10:17).

N. He is authorized by the Father (John 10:18).

O. He is one with the Father (John 10:30, 38).

P. He is the son of the Father (John 10:36).

II. Characteristics of the Sheep

A. They will not follow strangers (John 10:5, 8)— *"And a stranger will they not follow; but will flee from him: for they know not the voice of strangers"* (John 10:5).

B. They are totally dependent upon the shepherd (John 10:12). They share the same fold with other sheep— *"And other sheep I have, which are not of this fold: them also I must bring, and they shall hear my voice; and there shall be one fold, and one shepherd"* (John 10:16).

Here is a reference to the Church. Our Lord had already promised it and would soon pray for it.

1. The promise—*"And I say also unto thee, That thou art Peter, and upon this rock I will build my church; and the gates of hell shall not prevail against it"* (Matt. 16:18).

2. The prayer—*"Neither pray I for these alone, but for them also which shall believe on me through their word; that they all may be one; as thou, Father, art in me, and I in thee, that they also may be one in us: that the world may believe that thou hast sent me"* (John 17:20-21).

III. Characteristics of Thieves and Robbers (John 10:1, 8, 10)

A. Their words are evil—*"All that ever came before me are thieves and robbers: but the sheep did not hear them"* (John 10:8).

B. Their works are evil—*"Verily, verily, I say unto you, He that entereth not by the door into the sheepfold, but climbeth up some other way, the same is a thief and a robber. The thief cometh not, but for to steal, and to kill, and to destroy: I am come that they might have life, and that they might have it more abundantly"* (John 10:1, 10).

It was at the dawn of human history when the first thief (Cain) killed the first sheep (Abel).

IV. Characteristics of the Hireling (John 10:12-13)

A. He is unconcerned.

B. He is unprotective—*"But he that is an hireling, and not the shepherd, whose own the sheep are not, seeth the wolf coming, and leaveth the sheep, and fleeth: and the wolf catcheth them, and scattereth the sheep. The hireling fleeth, because he is an hireling, and careth not for the sheep"* (John 10:12-13).

V. Characteristics of the Goats (John 10:19-20, 31-39)

A. They deny the claims of the Shepherd (John 10:38)—*"The Jews answered him, saying, For a good work we stone thee not; but for blasphemy; and because that thou, being a man, makest thyself God"* (John 10:33).

B. They accuse the Shepherd of demon possession—*"And many of them said, He hath a devil, and is mad; why hear ye him?"* (John 10:20).

C. They accuse the Shepherd of blasphemy (John 10:33, 36).

D. They attempt to kill him—*"Then the Jews took up stones again to stone him . . . Therefore they sought again to take him: but he escaped out of their hand"* (John 10:31, 39).

EIGHT: The Mount of Olivet Discourse Sermon (Matt. 24:1-31; Mark 13:1-27; Luke 21:5-28)

I. Christ's Remarks Concerning the Temple Destruction

A. The place involved—*"And as he sat upon the Mount of Olives"* (Mark 13:3a).

1. The Mount of Olives is directly east of the City of Jerusalem. It rises to a height of 2,743 feet above sea level, some 300 feet higher than the temple mount area.

B. The purpose involved—*"And Jesus went out, and departed from the temple: and his disciples came to him for to shew him the buildings of the temple"* (Matt. 24:1).

C. The prophecy involved

1. The what of the matter—*"And as some spake of the temple, how it was adorned with goodly stones and gifts, he said, As for these things which ye behold, the days will come, in the which there shall not be left one stone upon another, that shall not be thrown down"* (Luke 21:5-6).

■ This prophecy doubtless shocked the disciples, if for no other reason than because of the casting down of those massive temple blocks. Since 1967 the Ministry of Religious Affairs, in cooperation with the Department of Antiquities, has cleared out an ancient passage in Jerusalem which they named the Rabbinical Tunnel. Undoubtedly it dates back to the time of Christ. The tunnel runs north along the Western Wall and is more than 600 feet long. Meir Kusnetz, an American-born civil engineer, has been in charge of the project. Since 1967, more than 17,000 cubic meters of fill have been excavated. The tunnel stops just short of the northwest corner of the Temple Mount. Its starting point is in the hall under Wilson's Arch, which is directly left of the present-day men's prayer section of the Western Wall. The finished stones inside the tunnel are still beautifully preserved, and some are of unbelievable size. For example, near the beginning of the tunnel is a gigantic chiseled limestone rock 46 feet long, 10 feet wide, and 10 feet high, weighing more than 415 tons. By comparison, the largest megalith at Stonehenge, England, is a mere 40 tons, and the rocks used by the Egyptians to build the pyramids were only 15 tons. Other similar stones weighing more than 300 tons have been uncovered in the tunnel. The amazing thing is that all those massive rocks are so well cut that although there is no mortar holding them together, even a thin knife blade cannot fit between their joints. (*Israel at Forty*, Willmington & Pritz, Tyndale House Publishers, Wheaton, Ill., 1987, p. 63)

---

2. The who of the matter— *"Peter and James and John and Andrew asked him privately"* (Mark 13:3b).

3. The when of the matter— *"Tell us, when shall these things be? And what shall be the sign when all these things shall be fulfilled"* (Mark 13:4). *"And when ye shall see Jerusalem compassed with armies, then know that the desolation thereof is nigh"* (Luke 21:20)

D. The program involved. Note: It appears Christ actually had two temple destructions in mind here.

1. The destruction of the second temple (Herod's temple) by Titus the Roman general in 70 A. D.

2. The destruction of the third temple (tribulation temple) by the coming antichrist in the future.

■ Facts concerning the second temple:

The temple proper—It was the most beautiful building in the world. Herod had trained 1,000 priests in building arts and had employed 10,000 skilled masons. He then secured 1,000 wagons to haul stones from the quarries. The temple was made of beautiful marble and gold—so gleaming that it appeared from afar as a mountain of snow glittering in the sun. It could easily hold 120,000 worshippers.

The temple personnel—

The high priest

The chief priests (200 highborn Jews who could trace their descent back to Zadok). They had charge of the weekly temple services, temple treasury, and maintenance of the sacred vessels.

The regular priests (7,200 in number). They were divided into twenty-four priestly clans, each serving a week at a time. Their job was lighting the altar fires, burning incense, baking the unleavened bread, and sacrificing the animals.

Levites (9,600 in number). They also served one week at a time, as guards, policemen, doorkeepers, singers, musicians, and servants.

The daily temple ritual required the services of 1,000 chief priests and Levites. During the three great feast days (Passover, Weeks, Booths) all clans were required to attend; thus, there were some 18,000 priests on hand.

The temple prophecy—As predicted by our Lord, the temple was destroyed by the Roman armies in A.D. 70 when Titus burned the city of Jerusalem. The soldiers pried apart those massive stones to collect the gold leaf that had melted from the fiery heat.

■ Facts concerning the third temple—

It will (probably) be constructed by the nation Israel (Rev. 11:1).

It will be corrupted by the antichrist (Dan. 9:27; Matt. 24:15; 2 Thess. 2:3-4; Rev. 13:11-18).

II. Christ's Remarks Concerning the Tribulation Destruction

A. Those events to transpire during the first three-and-a-half years of the tribulation— *"All these are the beginning of sorrows" (Matt. 24:8).*

   1. The wrath of God

      a. Disturbances from the cosmic and natural world.

■ Cosmic world— *"And fearful sights and great signs shall there be from heaven" (Luke 21:11).* *"And there shall be signs in the sun, and in the moon, and in the stars" (Luke 21:25).* *"For the powers of heaven shall be shaken" (Luke 21:26).*

■ Natural world: Great sea storms— *"the sea and the waves roaring" (Luke 21:25);* *"famines, pestilences; and earthquakes" (Matt. 24:7).*

---

      b. Deception from the religious world

■ False prophets— *"And many false prophets shall rise, and shall deceive many" (Matt. 24:11).*

■ False Christs— *"For there shall arise false Christs, and false prophets, and shall shew great signs and wonders; insomuch that, if it were possible, they shall deceive the very elect" (Matt. 24:24).* *"For many shall come in my name, saying, I am Christ; and shall deceive many" (Matt. 24:5).*

---

      c. Destruction from the military world— *"And ye shall hear of wars and rumours of wars: see that ye be not troubled: for all these things must come to pass, but the end is not yet" (Matt. 24:6).* *"For nation shall rise against nation, and kingdom against kingdom: and there shall be famines, and pestilences, and earthquakes, in divers places" (Matt. 24:7).*

   2. The witnesses of God

      a. To be abused grievously by the devil

■ Arrested by the authorities— *"But take heed to yourselves: for they shall deliver you up to councils; and in the synagogues ye shall be beaten: and ye shall be brought before rulers and kings for my sake, for a testimony against them" (Mark 13:9).*

■ Betrayed by their families— *"And ye shall be betrayed both by parents, and brethren, and kinsfolks, and friends; and some of you shall they cause to be put to death" (Luke 21:16).*

■ Hated by all— *"And ye shall be hated of all men for my name's sake" (Luke 21:17).*

---

      b. To be used greatly by the Lord

- In ministering the wisdom of God — *"But when they shall lead you, and deliver you up, take no thought beforehand what ye shall speak, neither do ye premediate: but whatsoever shall be given you in that hour, that speak ye: for it is not ye that speak, but the Holy Ghost" (Mark 13:11).* *"For I will give you a mouth and wisdom, which all your adversaries shall not be able to gainsay nor resist" (Luke 21:15).*

- In ministering the Word of God — *"And this gospel of the kingdom shall be preached in all the world for a witness unto all nations; and then shall the end come" (Matt. 24:14).* Many believe this task will be accomplished by the 144,000 Jewish evangelists. See. Rev. 7:1-8.

B. Those events to transpire during the last three-and-a-half years of the tribulation — *"For then shall be great tribulation, such as was not since the beginning of the world to this time, no, nor ever shall be. And except those days should be shortened, there should no flesh be saved: but for the elect's sake those days shall be shortened" (Matt. 24:21-22).*

   1. The defiling of the temple of God — *"When ye therefore shall see the abomination of desolation, spoken of by Daniel the prophet, stand in the holy place, (whoso readeth, let him understand)" (Matt. 24:15).*

Here Jesus seems to refer to both a historic and a prophetic event, both having to do with the defiling of the Jewish temple.

- The historic event — Daniel the prophet, writing six centuries before Christ, predicted the desolation of the second temple (Dan. 9:27; 11:31; 12:11). Some 400 years later this happened at the hands of a godless Syrian warrior known as Antiochus Epiphanes, after he captured the city of Jerusalem. On December 15, 168 B.C., his temple desecration reached its ultimate low, for on that day this Nero of the Old Testament sacrificed a giant sow on an idol altar he had made in the Jewish temple. He forced the priests to swallow its flesh, and also made a broth of it and sprinkled it all throughout the temple. He finally carried off the golden candlesticks, table of shewbread, altar of incense, and various other vessels, and destroyed the sacred books of the law. A large image of Jupiter was placed in the Holy of Holies. All this was known by the horrified Jews as "the abomination of desolation," and is referred to by Jesus in Matt. 24:15 as a springboard to describe the activities of the future antichrist.

- The prophetic event — John the apostle describes the desolation of the third temple (tribulational temple) in Scripture's final book. It has to do with the image and mark of the antichrist. (See Rev. 13:11-18.)

   2. The destroying of the city of God — *"And when ye shall see Jerusalem compassed with armies, then know that the desolation thereof is nigh. And they shall fall by the edge of the sword, and shall be led away captive into all nations: and Jerusalem shall be trodden down of the Gentiles, until the times of the Gentiles be fulfilled" (Luke 21:20, 24).*

   3. The directing of the elect of God — *"Then let them which be in Judaea flee into the mountains: Let him which is on the housetop not come down to take any thing out of his house: Neither let him which is in the field return back to take his clothes. And woe unto them that are with child, and to them that give suck in those days! But pray ye that your flight be not in the winter, neither on the Sabbath day ... Wherefore if they shall say unto you, Behold, he is in the desert; go not forth: behold, he is in the secret chambers; believe it not. For as the lightning cometh out of the east, shineth even unto the west; so shall also the coming of the Son of man be" (Matt. 24:16-20, 26-27).*

   4. The darkening of the skies of God — *"Immediately after the tribulation of those days shall the sun be darkened, and the moon shall not give her light, and the stars shall fall from heaven, and the powers of the heavens shall be shaken" (Matt. 24:29).*

5. The descending of the Son of God—*"And then shall appear the sign of the Son of man in heaven: and then shall all the tribes of the earth mourn, and they shall see the Son of man coming in the clouds of heaven with power and great glory. And he shall send his angels with a great sound of trumpet, and they shall gather together his elect from the four winds, from one end of heaven to the other"* (Matt. 24:30-31).

NINE: The Thursday Night Passover Sermon (John 14-16)

Introduction:

Assuming that Jesus was crucified at 9:00 A.M. on Friday, this sermon was given piecemeal at various locations over an extended period. It was begun in the Upper Room (John 14) and completed during a midnight walk through the deserted streets of Jerusalem en route to Gethsemane (John 15-16).

I. Reasons for the Sermon—*"These things have I spoken unto you, being yet present with you"* (John 14:25).

A. That the believer might experience joy—*"These things have I spoken unto you, that my joy might remain in you, and that your joy might be full"* (John 15:11).

B. That we might not stumble—*"These things have I spoken unto you, that ye should not be offended"* (John 16:1).

C. That we might not forget his words—*"But these things have I told you, that when the time shall come, ye may remember that I told you of them. And these things I said not unto you at the beginning, because I was with you"* (John 16:4).

D. That we might experience peace—*"These things I have spoken unto you, that in me ye might have peace. In the world ye shall have tribulation: but be of good cheer; I have overcome the world"* (John 16:33).

II. Relationships in the Sermon

A. Those relationships involving the Savior

1. Christ and the Father

    a. He declares him (John 14:7-9)—*"Philip saith unto him, Lord, shew us the Father, and it sufficeth us. Jesus saith unto him, Have I been so long time with you, and yet hast thou not known me, Philip? He that hath seen me hath seen the Father; and how sayest thou then, Shew us the Father?"* (John 14:8-9).

    b. He is inseparably linked to him (John 14:10-11)—*"Believest thou not that I am in the Father, and the Father in me? The words that I speak unto you I speak not of myself: but the Father that dwelleth in me, he doeth the works"* (John 14:10).

    c. He glorifies him (John 14:13).

    d. He goes to him (John 14:2, 12, 28; 16:10, 16, 28)—*"I came forth from the Father, and am come into the world: again, I leave the world, and go to the Father"* (John 16:28).

Here in one verse Jesus summarizes his entire ministry.

- His incarnation—*"I came forth from the Father."*
- His earthly life—*"And am come into the world."*
- His ascension (following the crucifixion and resurrection)—*"Again, I leave the world."*
- His great high priestly work—*"And go to the Father."*

2. Christ and the Holy Spirit

    a. He comes at Christ's prayer request— *"And I will pray the Father, and he shall give you another Comforter, that he may abide with you for ever" (John 14:16).*

    b. He comes to honor and bear witness to Christ (John 15:26, 16:13-15)— *"But when the Comforter is come, whom I will send unto you from the Father, even the Spirit of truth, which proceedeth from the Father, he shall testify of me" (John 15:26).* *"Howbeit when he, the Spirit of truth, is come, he will guide you into all truth: for he shall not speak of himself; but whatsoever he shall hear, that shall he speak: and he will shew you things to come. He shall glorify me: for he shall receive of mine, and shall shew it unto you" (John 16:13-14).*

    c. He comes to perform a three-fold work for Christ (John 16:7-11).

        (1) To reprove the world of sin (John 16:8)— *"Of sin, because they believe not on me" (John 16:9).*

        (2) To reprove the world of righteousness (John 16:8)— *"Of righteousness, because I go to my Father, and ye see me no more" (John 16:10).*

        (3) To reprove the world of judgment (John 16:8)— *"Of judgment, because the prince of this world is judged" (John 16:11).*

Note that Jesus says "sin" and not "sins." The only sin the Holy Spirit will rebuke sinners of is the sin of rejecting Christ. The reason is that this is the only sin which will eventually send a person to hell.

3. Christ and believers

    a. He will come for them— *"In my Father's house are many mansions: if it were not so, I would have told you. I go to prepare a place for you. And if I go and prepare a place for you, I will come again, and receive you unto myself; that where I am, there ye may be also" (John 14:2-3).*

Note the phrase, *"I will come again, and receive you unto myself."* This is the only reference to the rapture in the four Gospels, and the first time in Scripture that God promises to take people from the earth.

    b. He will dwell in them— *"At that day ye shall know that I am in my Father, and ye in me, and I in you" (John 14:20).*

    c. He will attach to them (John 14:20).

    d. He will work through them in producing fruit and more fruit (John 15:2); in producing much fruit (John 15:5).

Note the progression of this: Fruit, more fruit, and much fruit (15:1-5). This fruit can signify converts (Rom. 1:13), Christian character (Gal. 5:22-23), or conduct (Phil. 1:11; Rom. 6:21-22). Jesus then promises that this fruit will remain (see John 15:16).

B. Those relationships involving the saint

   1. The believer and the Father

    a. Indwelled by the Father— *"Jesus answered and said unto him, If a man love me, he will keep my words: and my Father will love him, and we will come unto him, and make our abode with him" (John 14:23).*

Here is an amazing revelation:

In Col. 1:27 we are told that the Son indwells the believer.

In 1 Cor. 6:19 we learn that the Holy Spirit indwells the believer. Here in John 14:23 we hear Jesus saying the Father himself also indwells the believer.

Note also an additional truth:

In Gal. 2:20 we are told that the Son loves us.

In 2 Cor. 13:14 we learn that the Holy Spirit loves us.'

Here in John 14:23 (see also 16:27) we read that the Father loves us.

> b. Loved by the Father (John 14:21; 16:27) — *"For the Father himself loveth you, because ye have loved me, and have believed that I came out from God" (John 16:27).*
>
> c. Empowered by the Father — *"Verily, verily, I say unto you, He that believeth on me, the works that I do shall he do also; and greater works than these shall he do; because I go unto my Father" (John 14:12).*

He meant "greater works" in a quantitative way and not a qualitative sense. Examples:

The establishment of local churches.

The spread of the gospel to the ends of the earth.

> 2. The believer and the Holy Spirit
>
> a. To be taught by the Holy Spirit — *"But the Comforter, which is the Holy Ghost, whom the Father will send in my name, he shall teach you all things, and bring all things to your remembrance, whatsoever I have said unto you" (John 14:26).*

These words would later have great significance for three of those disciples in the Upper Room. They were Matthew, John, and Peter, all of whom were inspired by the Holy Spirit to write a portion of the Word of God.

> b. To be permanently indwelled by the Holy Spirit — *"And I will pray the Father, and he shall give you another Comforter, that he may abide with you for ever" (John 14:16).*

This is a startling new revelation, for it promises the permanent indwelling of the Holy Spirit in the believer. This concept was unknown in the Old Testament.

> 3. The believer and other believers — *"This is my commandment. That ye love one another, as I have loved you. Greater love hath no man than this, that a man lay down his life for his friends. Ye are my friends, if ye do whatsoever I command you" (John 15:12-14).*
>
> 4. The believer and persecutions
>
> a. To expect many persecutions — *"If the world hate you, ye know that it hated me before it hated you. If ye were of the world, the world would love his own: but because ye are not of the world, but I have chosen you out of the world, therefore the world hateth you. Remember the word that I said unto you, The servant is not greater than his lord. If they have persecuted me, they will also persecute you: if they have kept my saying, they will keep yours also. But all these things will they do unto you for my name's sake,*

because they know not him that sent me" (John 15:18-21). "These things have I spoken unto you, that ye should not be offended. They shall put you out of the synagogues: yea, the time cometh, that whosoever killeth you will think that he doeth God service. And these things will they do unto you, because they have not known the Father, nor me" (John 16:1-3).

    b. To rejoice in all persecutions— "Let not your heart be troubled: ye believe in God, believe also in me ... Peace I leave with you, my peace I give unto you: not as the world giveth, give I unto you. Let not your heart be troubled, neither let it be afraid" (John 14:1, 27). "A woman when she is in travail hath sorrow; because her hour is come: but as soon as she is delivered of the child, she remembereth no more the anguish, for joy that a man is born into the world. And ye now therefore have sorrow: but I will see you again, and your heart shall rejoice, and your joy no man taketh from you ... These things I have spoken unto you, that in me ye might have peace. In the world ye shall have tribulation: but be of good cheer; I have overcome the world" (John 16:21-23, 33).

5. The believer and fruit bearing

    a. The source involved— "I am the true vine, and my Father is the husbandman" (John 15:1).

    b. The steps involved

        (1) <u>Abide in Christ</u>— "Abide in me, and I in you. As the branch cannot bear fruit of itself, except it abide in the vine; no more can ye, except ye abide in me. I am the vine, ye are the branches: He that abideth in me, and I in him, the same bringeth forth much fruit: for without me ye can do nothing" (John 15:4-5).

Various explanations have been offered as to why Christ used the vine and branch analogy concerning the relationship between himself and his followers. He may have seen a vine growing over the door of the Upper Room house as they were leaving. He may have called attention to the small fires on the horizon caused by the burning of dead branches.

        (2) <u>Study the Word</u>— "Now ye are clean through the word which I have spoken unto you" (John 15:3).

        (3) <u>Submit to pruning</u>— "Every branch in me that beareth not fruit he taketh away: and every branch that beareth fruit, he purgeth it, that it may bring forth more fruit ... If a man abide not in me, he is cast forth as a branch, and is withered; and men gather them, and cast them into the fire, and they are burned" (John 15:2, 6).

If a branch fails to bear fruit, it is rejected and cast aside (15:6). There is a problem concerning these fruitless branches that are removed from the vine (15:2, 6). Three theories are offered at this point.

—That the removed branches represent Christians who lose their salvation—This theory is totally refuted by various Scripture verses.

—That they are Christians who commit the sin unto death as described in Acts 5:1-11; 1 Cor. 11:27-34; 1 John 5:16

—The burning, according to this theory, would be their works, as seen in 1 Cor. 3:11-15.

—That they represent mere professing Christians (religious people) who are finally severed from their superficial connection with Christ—This had already happened with Judas. (See John 13:27-30; 17:12.)

    c. The success involved— "If ye abide in me, and my words abide in you, ye shall ask what ye will, and it shall be done unto you. Herein is my Father glorified, that ye bear much fruit; so shall ye be my disciples" (John 15:7-8).

> d. The stability involved— *"Ye have not chosen me, but I have chosen you, and ordained you, that ye should go and bring forth fruit, and that your fruit should remain: that whatsoever ye shall ask of the Father in my name, he may give it you" (John 15:16).*

Note the phrase, *"I have chosen you."* In Jesus' day the disciple would normally select his own rabbi. But this is not the case with the believer. The author of Hebrews makes this very clear: *"And no man taketh this honour unto himself, but he that is called of God, as was Aaron" (Heb. 5:4).*

Note also the role that the Father plays in all this. Here we are told that a fruitbearing son or daughter will enjoy a prayer-answering Father. We usually reverse the formula, assuming prayers must precede fruit.

We are the branches and Christ is the vine. The only function of a branch is to bear fruit. Branch wood makes poor firewood. No builder would think of using branch wood to construct a ship, or a house, or a piece of furniture.

A LISTING OF JESUS' PRAYERS

PRAYER	OCCASION	REQUEST
1ˢᵗ Prayer	At his baptism (Lk. 3:21)	Probably for strength to endure Satan's temptations in the wilderness (Lk. 4:1-13)
2ⁿᵈ Prayer	Before his first preaching tour of Galilee (Mk. 1:35; Lk. 4:42)	He no doubt asked for the Father's anointing and power upon his mission to preach in all the town throughout Galilee (Mk. 1:36-39; Lk. 4:43-44)
3ʳᵈ Prayer	After healing a leper (Lk. 5:16)	For continued power to heal and forgive sins (Lk. 5:18-26)
4ᵗʰ Prayer	Before choosing his twelve disciples (Lk. 6:12)	For wisdom in their selection (see also Jn. 6:70)
5ᵗʰ Prayer	During the feeding of the 5000 (Mt. 14:19; Mk. 6:41; Lk. 9:16; Jn. 6:11)	That the Father would supernaturally feed the hungry multitude (Mt. 14:20-21; Mk. 6:42-44; Lk. 9:17; Jn. 6:12-13)
6ᵗʰ Prayer	After the feeding of the 5000 (Mt. 14:23; Mk. 6:46; Jn. 6:15)	In regards to the deliverance of his disciples who were battling a storm on the Sea of Galilee (Mt. 14:24-25; Mk. 6:47-48; Jn. 6:16 18)
7ᵗʰ Prayer	Before hearing Peter's great confession (Lk. 9:18)	That the Father would reveal to Peter concerning the Deity of the Son (Mt. 16:17)
8ᵗʰ Prayer	During the Transfiguration (Lk. 9:28)	In regards to his soon death on the cross (Lk. 9:31)
9ᵗʰ Prayer	Upon hearing the report of the returning seventy (Mt. 11:25)	On this occasion he thanks the Father for two things: (1) For revealing great spiritual truths to the disciples (Mt. 11:25) (2) For allowing him to reveal the Father to his disciples (Mt. 11:27)
10ᵗʰ Prayer	After visiting Mary and Martha (Lk. 11:1)	That the Father would give his wisdom in instructing his disciples how to pray (Lk. 11:2-4). See also (Mt. 6:9-15)
11ᵗʰ Prayer	Upon receiving some little children (Mt. 19:13; Mk. 10:13; Lk. 8:15)	That they might be converted and enter the kingdom of God (Mt. 18:1-3; 19:14-15; Mk. 10:14-16; Lk. 18:16-17)
12ᵗʰ Prayer	Before raising Lazarus (Jn. 11:41-42)	That Lazarus be raised to prove the Father had indeed sent his Son (Jn. 11:4)
13ᵗʰ Prayer	When some Greeks desired to see him (Jn. 12:20-26)	*Now is my soul troubled; and what shall I say? Father, save me from this hour: but for this cause came I unto this hour. Father, glorify thy name. Then came there a voice from heaven, saying, I have both glorified it, and will glorify it again.* (Jn. 12:27-28)
14ᵗʰ Prayer	In the upper room prior to his crucifixion (Mt. 26:26; Mk. 14:22; Lk. 22:17, 19, 20; 1 Cor. 11:24-26)	Probably that the disciples might understand the true significance of the bread and wine (Mt. 26:27-29; Mk. 14:23-25; Lk. 22:14-16, 18)

PRAYER	OCCASION	REQUEST
15ᵗʰ Prayer	After leaving the upper room (Jn. 17:1)	Here he offers up a three-fold prayer: **(1)** Praying for himself (Jn. 17:1-5) **(2)** Praying for his disciples (Jn. 17:6-19) **(3)** Praying for all believers (Jn. 17:20-26)
16ᵗʰ Prayer	En route to Gethsemane (Lk. 22:31-32)	*"And the Lord said, Simon, Simon, behold, Satan hath desired to have you, that he may sift you as wheat: But I have prayed for thee, that thy faith fail not; and when thou art converted, strengthen thy brethren." (Lk. 22:31-32)*
17ᵗʰ Prayer	In the Garden of Gethsemane– first prayer (Mt. 26:39; Mk. 14:35; Lk. 22:41-42)	That his Father's will be done
18ᵗʰ Prayer	In the Garden of Gethsemane– second prayer (Mt. 26:42; Mk. 14:39; Lk. 22:44)	That his Father's will be done
19ᵗʰ Prayer	In the Garden of Gethsemane– third prayer (Mt. 26:44; Mk. 14:41)	That his Father's will be done
20ᵗʰ Prayer	Probably sometime either before or after his Gethsemane ordeal	*"Who in the days of his flesh, when he had offered up prayers and supplications with strong crying and tears unto him that was able to save him from death, and was heard in that he feared." (Heb. 5:7)*
21ˢᵗ Prayer	While on the cross–first prayer (Lk. 23:34)	*"Then said Jesus, Father forgive them; for they know not what they do. And they parted his raiment, and cast lots." (Lk. 23:34)*
22ⁿᵈ Prayer	While on the cross–second prayer (Mt. 27:46; Mk. 15:34)	*"And at the ninth hour Jesus cried with a loud voice, saying, Eloi, Eloi, lama sabachthani? which is, being interpreted, My God, my God, why has thou forsaken me?" (Mk. 15:34)*
23ʳᵈ Prayer	While on the cross–third prayer (Lk. 23:46)	*"And when Jesus had cried with a loud voice, he said, Father, into thy hands I commend my spirit and having said thus, he gave up the ghost." (Lk. 23:46)*
24ᵗʰ Prayer	While eating a meal in an Emmaus home (Lk. 24:30)	Probably that the two disciples would recognize him as the resurrected Christ (Lk. 24:31-32)
25ᵗʰ Prayer	On the Mount of Olives just prior to his ascension (Lk.24:50-51)	That the Father would encourage his disciples to remain in Jerusalem for the coming of the Holy Spirit (Lk. 24:49)

The Sufferings Endured by Jesus Christ

REJECTED	• By his nation (Jn. 1:11) • By his hometown (Lk. 4:28-29) • By his friends (Mk. 3:21) • By his family (Jn. 7:5)
TEMPTED	• By Satan (Lk. 4:1-2, 13; 22:28)
RIDICULED	• Because of his hometown (Jn. 1:46; 7:52) • Because of his background (Jn. 8:41; 9:24, 29)

THREATENED	• By Herod (Mt. 2:16)
	• By his hometown (Lk. 4:29)
	• By the Jews
	  ◇ Because he healed on the Sabbath (Jn. 5:16; Lk. 6:10-11)
	  ◇ Because of his claims (Jn. 8:58-59; 10:30-33)
	  ◇ Because of his sermons (Jn. 8:40; Lk. 11:53-54; Mk. 12:12; Mt. 26:1-4)
	  ◇ Because of his miracles (Jn. 11:53; see also Jn. 12:10)
	• By the devil (Mt. 26:37-38; Mk. 14:33-34; Lk. 22:44)

HOMELESS	• (Mt. 8:20)
BETRAYED	• By a follower (Jn. 13:21)
DENIED	• By a friend (Mt. 26:58, 69-75; Mk. 14:54, 66-72; Lk. 22:54-62; Jn. 18:15-18, 25-27)
MISUNDERSTOOD	• By his disciples (Mt. 15:16; 17:6-11; Mk. 6:52; Jn. 10:6; 12:16)
FORSAKEN	• By all (Mt. 26:56)
MISQUOTED	• (Mt. 26:61)

TRIED	• Illegally seven times:
	  ◇ First trial, before Annas (Jn. 18:12-14, 19-24)
	  ◇ Second trial, before Caiaphas (Mt. 26:57-68; Mk. 14:53-65)
	  ◇ Third trial, before the Sanhedrin (Mt. 27:1-2; Mk. 15:1; Lk. 22:66-23:1)
	  ◇ Fourth trial, before Pilate (Jn. 18:28-38; Mt. 27:2, 11-14; Mk. 15:1-5; Lk. 23:13-25)
	  ◇ Fifth trial, before Herod (Lk. 23:7-12)
	  ◇ Sixth trial, before Pilate (Jn. 18:39-19:16; Mt. 27:15-26; Mk. 15:6-15; Lk. 23:13-25)
	  ◇ Seventh trial, before the Roman soldiers (Mt. 27:27-31; Mk. 15:16-20)

INDICTED	• On false charges (Lk. 23:1-2)
MOCKED	• By Roman soldiers (Lk. 23:36-37; Mk. 15:16-20) • By the watching crowd (Lk. 23:35) • By the chief priests (Mk. 15:31) • By the two thieves (Mk. 15:32; Mt. 27:44)

TORTURED	• Slapped (Jn. 18:22) • Blindfolded (Lk. 22:64) • Spit upon (Mt. 26:67) • Buffeted (Mt. 26:67) • Scourged (Mt. 27:26) • Pierced with thorns (Mt. 27:29) • Struck upon the head (Mt. 27:30)
CRUCIFIED	• (Matt. 27; Mk. 15; Luke 23; John 19)

THE USAGE OF THE OLD TESTAMENT BY JESUS CHRIST

The Events and Individuals He Referred To

- The creation of Adam and Eve (Gen. 1:27; 2:24; Mk. 10:6-8)

- The murder of Abel (Gen. 4:10; Lk. 11:51)

- The corruption of Noah's day and the flood (Gen. 6-7; Lk. 17:26-27)

- The corruption of Lot's day and the fire (Gen. 19; Lk. 17:28-29)

- The worldliness of Lot's wife (Gen. 19:26; Lk. 17:32)

- The faith of Abraham, Isaac, and Jacob (Mt. 22:32)

- Moses and the burning bush (Ex. 3; Mk. 12:26)

- Moses and the heavenly manna (Ex. 16:15; Jn. 6:31)

- Moses and the brazen serpent (Num. 21:18; Jn. 3:14)

- David and some shewbread (1 Sam. 21:6; Mt. 12:3-4)

- Solomon and the Queen of Sheba (1 Kings 10:1; Mt. 12:42)

- Elijah, a widow, and the famine (1 Kings 17:1, 9; Lk. 4:25-26)

- Naaman and his leprosy (2 Kings 5; Lk. 4:27)

- The murder of Zechariah (2 Chron. 24:20-21; Lk. 11:51)

- Daniel and the abomination of desolation (Dan. 9:27; 11:31; 12:11; Mt. 24:15)

- Jonah and the fish (Jon. 1:17; Mt. 12:40; 16:4)

- Jonah and the repentance of the Ninevites (Jon. 3:4-10; Lk. 11:30; Mt. 12:41)

The Passages He Quoted From

- During His temptations
  1. The first temptation (in Mt. 4:4 he quoted Deut. 8:3)
  2. The second temptation (in Mt. 4:7 he quoted Deut. 6:16)
  3. The third temptation (in Mt. 4:10 he quoted Deut. 6:13)

- During His Sermon on the Mount
  1. In Mt. 5:21 he quoted Ex. 20:13, the sixth commandment

2. In Mt. 5:27 he quoted Ex. 20:14, the seventh commandment; (also compare Mt. 5:31 with Deut. 24:1). (Note: He later quoted some of the same commandments during his talk with a rich young ruler. See Mk. 10:19)

■ During his hometown sermon (in Lk. 4:18-19 he quoted Isa. 61:1-2)

■ During various confrontations with Jewish rulers

1. As He defended his associating with sinners (in Mt. 9:13 he quoted Hos. 6:6)
2. As He expounded on marriage (in Mk. 10:7-8 he quoted Gen. 2:24)
3. As He was asked concerning the greatest of the commandments (in Mk. 12:29-30 he quoted Deut. 6:4-5)
4. As He rebuked their vain traditions (in Mt. 15:7-9 he quoted Isa. 29:13)
5. As the Pharisees questioned his authority (in Jn. 8:17 he quoted Deut. 17:6)

■ During His tribute to John the Baptist (in Lk. 7:27 he quoted Malachi 3:1)

■ During His Triumphal Entry Day (in Mt. 21:16 he quoted Psa. 8:2)

■ During His cleansing of the temple (in Lk. 19:46 he quoted Isa. 56:7)

■ During a parable about Israel (in Mt. 21:42, 44 he quoted Psa. 118:22-23; Isa. 8:14-15)

■ During a question session in the temple (in Mk. 12:36 he quoted Psa. 110:1)

■ During his last Passover night—predicting the world would hate the disciples as they hated him (in Jn. 15:25 he quoted Psa. 35:19; 69:4)

■ On the cross

1. His fourth utterance (in Mt. 27:46 he quoted Psa. 22:1)
2. His seventh utterance (in Lk. 23:46 he quoted Psa. 31:5)

In summary, our Lord said the Law would be fulfilled (Mt. 5:18) and the Scriptures could not be broken (Jn. 10:35). It has been estimated that over one-tenth of Jesus' recorded New Testament words were taken from the Old Testament. In the four Gospels, 180 of the 1,800 verses that report his discourses are either Old Testament quotes or Old Testament allusions.

THE OLD TESTAMENT PROPHECIES
FULFILLED BY JESUS CHRIST

In Regard to Jesus' Birth

- Messiah would come! (Gen. 3:15; Lk. 2:6)

- Messiah would be a male! (Gen. 3:15; Lk. 2:7)

- Messiah would be born! (Gen. 3:15; Lk. 2:11)

- Messiah would be born of a woman! (Gen. 3:15; Gal. 4:4)

- Messiah would be born of a virgin woman! (Isa. 7:14; Mt. 1:18; Lk. 1:34)

- Messiah would be born in Bethlehem! (Micah 5:2; Lk. 2:4; Jn. 7:42)

- Messiah would be born before the "69 weeks" of Daniel had ended! (Dan. 9:25-26; Gal. 4:4)

- Messiah would possess a dual nature! (Isa. 9:6; Mt. 1:23; Jn. 1:49; 11:27)

- Messiah would come from the line of Shem! (Gen. 9:26-27; Lk. 3:36)

- Messiah would come from the seed of Abraham! (Gen. 12:2-3; Mt. 1:1; Gal. 3:16)

- Messiah would come from the nation Israel! (Num. 24:17; Jn. 4:22)

- Messiah would come from the tribe of Judah! (Gen. 49:10; Heb. 7:14)

- Messiah would be from the House of David! (2 Sam. 7:16; Mt. 1:1; 22:42; Rom. 1:3)

- Messiah would be worshipped by wise men led by a star! (Isa. 60:3, 6, 9; Num. 24:17; Mt. 2:1-2; 9-11)

- Messiah would be carried into Egypt as an infant! (Hos. 11:1; Mt. 2:15)

- Messiah's birthplace would suffer a blood purge! (Jer. 31:15; Mt. 2:17-18)

In Regard to Jesus' Earthly Ministry

- That He would be called a Nazarene (compare Isa. 11:1 with Mt. 2:23)

- That He would be zealous for the Father (compare Ps. 69:9; 119:139 with Jn. 2:13-17)

- That He would be filled with God's Spirit (compare Isa. 11:2; 61:1-2; Ps. 45:7 with Lk. 4:18-19)

- That He would heal many (compare Isa. 53:4 with Mt. 8:16-17)

- That He would minister as a prophet (Deut. 18:15; Jn. 6:14; 7:40)

- That He would deal gently with the Gentiles (compare Isa. 9:1-2; 42:1-3 with Mt. 12:17-21; 4:13-16)

- That He would speak in parables (compare Isa. 6:9-10; Ps. 78:2 with Mt. 13:10-15)

- That He would be rejected by His own (compare Isa. 53:3; Ps. 69:8 with Jn. 1:11; 7:5)

- That He would make a triumphal entry into Jerusalem (compare Zech. 9:9 with Mt. 21:4-5)

- That He would be praised by little children (compare Ps. 8:2 with Mt. 21:16)
- That He would be the rejected Cornerstone (compare Ps. 118:22-23 with Mt. 21:42)
- That His miracles would not be believed (compare Is. 53:1 with Jn. 12:37-38)

In Regard to Jesus' Crucifixion

- That His friend would betray him for 30 pieces of silver (compare Ps. 41:9; 55:12-14; Zech. 11:12-13 with Mt. 26:14-16; 21-25)
- That He would be a man of sorrows (compare Isa. 53:3 with Mt. 26:37-38)
- That He would be forsaken by His disciples (compare Zech. 13:7 with Mt. 26:31, 56)
- That He would be accused by false witnesses (Ps. 35:11 with Mk. 14:57-58)
- That He would be scourged and spat upon (compare Isa. 50:6 with Mt. 26:67; 27:26)
- That His price money would be used to buy a potter's field (compare Zech. 11:12-13; Jer. 18:1-4; 19:14 with Mt. 27:9-10)
- That He would be crucified between two thieves (compare Isa. 53:12 with Mt. 27:38; Mk. 15:27-28; Lk. 22:37)
- That He would pray for His enemies (Ps. 109:4 with Lk. 23:34)
- That He would be given vinegar to drink (compare Ps. 69:21 with Mt. 27:34, 48; Jn. 19:28-30)
- That He would suffer the piercing of His hands and feet (compare Ps. 22:16, Zech. 12:10 with Mk. 15:25; Jn. 19:34, 37; 20:25-27)
- That His garments would be parted and gambled for (compare Ps. 22:18 with Lk. 23:34; Jn. 19:23-24)
- That He would be surrounded and ridiculed by His enemies (compare Ps. 22:7-8 with Mt. 27:39-44; Mk. 15:29-32)
- That He would thirst (compare Ps. 22:15 with Jn. 19:28)
- That He would commend His spirit to the Father (compare Ps. 31:5 with Lk. 23:46)
- That His bones would not be broken (compare Ps. 34:20; Ex. 12:46; Num. 9:12 with Jn. 19:33-36)
- That He would be stared at in death (compare Zech. 12:10 with Jn. 19:37; Mt. 27:36)
- That He be looked upon as a transgressor (compare Isa. 53:12 with Lk. 22:37)
- That He would be buried with the rich (compare Isa. 53:9 with Mt. 27:57-60)

In Regard to Jesus' Resurrection

- That He be raised from the dead (compare Ps. 16:10 with Mt. 28:2-7)

In Regard to Jesus' Ascension

- That He would ascend into heaven (compare Ps. 24:7-10; 68:18 with Mk. 16:19; Lk. 24:51)

The New Testament Prophecies
Foretold by Jesus Christ

Concerning the Church

- Its symbol (Mt. 13:45)
- Its foundation—Christ himself (Mt. 16:13-19)
- Its ministry (Mt. 28:19-20; Acts 1:8)
- Its field of service (Mt. 28:19; Acts 1:8)
- Its authority (Mt. 16:19; 18:18; Jn. 20:23)
- Its persecution (Mt. 10:16-23, 34; Jn. 15:18-21; 16:1-3, 33)
- Its discipline (Mt. 18:15-17)
- Its removal (Jn. 14:2-3)

Concerning Himself

- His transfiguration (Mt. 16:28)
- His betrayal by Judas
  1. Predicted in Galilee
     a. First occasion (Jn. 6:70-71)
     b. Second occasion (Mt. 17:22)
  2. Predicted in the Upper Room (Mt. 26:21, 25)
- His denial by Peter
  1. Predicted in the Upper Room (Jn. 13:37-38)
  2. Predicted en route to the Mount of Olives and Gethsemane (Mt. 26:30, 34)
- His abandonment by the Twelve (Mt. 26:31)
- His sufferings
  1. Predicted in Caesarea Philippi (Mt. 16:21a)
  2. Predicted on the Mount of Transfiguration (Mt. 17:12b)
- His death
  1. The fact of His death (Jn. 10:11, 15; Mt. 17:23)
  2. The place of His death (Mt. 20:18)
  3. The method of His death (Jn. 3:14; 12:32; Mt. 20:18-19)
- His resurrection

1. The fact of His resurrection (Jn. 10:17-18)
2. The time element in His resurrection (Mt. 12:40; Jn. 2:19)

■ His appearance in Galilee (Mt. 26:32)

■ His ascension (Jn. 7:33; 16:32)

■ His return

1. In the air (Jn. 14:3)
2. On the earth (Mt. 16:27; 24:30; 26:63-64)

Concerning the Resurrection of Lazarus

(John 11:11)

Concerning the Destruction of Jerusalem and the Temple

■ The destruction of Jerusalem (Lk. 19:43-44)

■ The destruction of the temple (Mk. 13:1-2)

Concerning the Death of Peter

(Jn. 21:18-19)

Concerning Pentecost and the Ministry of the Holy Spirit

■ The fact of his ministry (Jn. 7:37-39; Lk. 24:49)

■ The duration of his ministry (Jn. 14:16)

■ The location of his ministry (Jn. 14:17)

■ The nature of his ministry

1. Regarding the Savior (Jn. 15:26; 16:14)
2. Regarding the saved (Jn. 14:26; 16:13)
3. Regarding the sinner (Jn. 16:8)

Concerning the Last Days

(Lk. 17:26-30; Mt. 24:32-34)

Concerning the Nation Israel

■ Its blindness (Mt. 23:37-39)

■ Its rejection (Mt. 21:43)

■ Its regathering (Mt. 24:31)

Concerning the Great Tribulation
(Mt. 24:21, 29; Lk. 21:22-26)

Concerning the Coming of Elijah
(Mt. 17:11)

Concerning the Coming Antichrist
(Jn. 5:43; Mt. 24:15)

Concerning the Battle of Armageddon
(Lk. 17:34-37; Mt. 24:28)

Concerning the Resurrection of the Dead
(Jn. 5:28-29)

Concerning the Future Rewards
(Mt. 10:41-42; 19:29)

Concerning the Millennium
(Mt. 8:11; 13:43; 19:28; 25:34)

Concerning the Great White Throne Judgment
(Mt. 25:31-33)

Concerning Hell
(Mt. 5:28-29; 13:49-50; 18:8-9)

Concerning Heaven
(Jn. 14:2-3)

Three: CHRONOLOGICAL

A listing of the 100 most important or well-known events in the Savior's walk among men, beginning with His arrival in a Bethlehem manger to His ascension from a Jerusalem mountain.

The 100 Most Important or Well-Known Events in the Life of Jesus Christ

Event 1:

The two genealogical records of Jesus

- As recorded by Matthew (Mt. 1:1-17)

- As recorded by Luke (Lk. 3:23-37)

Event 2:

The three predictions preceding the birth of Jesus

- To Zacharias, concerning the birth of John (Lk. 1:5-25)

- To Mary, concerning the birth of Jesus (Lk. 1:26-38)

- To Joseph, concerning the purity of Mary (Mt. 1:18-25)

Event 3:

The three songs of praise anticipating the birth of Jesus

- The praise of Elisabeth to Mary (Lk. 1:41-45)

- The praise of Mary to God (Lk. 1:46-56)

- The praise of Zacharias to God (Lk. 1:57-79)

Event 4:

The birth of Jesus (Lk. 2:1-19)

Event 5:

The worship of Jesus by the shepherds (Lk. 2:8-20)

Event 6:

The circumcision of Jesus (Lk. 2:21-24)

Event 7:

The dedication of Jesus in the temple (Lk. 2:25-38)

Event 8:

The worship of Jesus by the wise men (Mt. 2:1-12)

Event 9:

Jesus' flight into Egypt (Mt. 2:13-23)

Event 10:

Jesus' early years in Nazareth (Lk. 2:39-40, 52)

Event 11:

Jesus' temple visit at age twelve (Lk. 2:41-50)

Event 12:

Jesus' baptism (Mt. 3:13-17; Mk. 1:9-11; Lk. 3:21-22; Jn. 1:32-34)

Event 13:

Jesus' temptation (Mt. 4:1-11; Mk. 1:12-13; Lk. 4:1-13)

Event 14:

The ministry of Jesus' forerunner, John the Baptist

- ■ The maturing of John (Lk. 1:80; 3:1-2)
- ■ The message of John (Mt. 3:1-3; 8-10; Mk. 1:1-2; Lk. 3:4-14; 7:29-30; Jn. 1:29-30, 35-36)

- ■ The mantle of John (Mk. 1:4, 6)
- ■ The ministry of John (Mt. 3:5-6; Mk. 1:4-5; Lk. 3:3; Jn. 1:28)
- ■ The misunderstanding concerning John (Lk. 3:15; Jn. 1:19-26)
- ■ The Messiah of John (Mt. 3:11-12; Mk. 1:7-8; Lk. 3:16-18; Jn. 1:6-18, 27, 30)
- ■ The attempted muzzling of John (Mt. 14:1-5; Mk. 6:14-20)
- ■ The brief misgivings by John (Mt. 11:2-6; Lk. 7:19-23)
- ■ The martyrdom of John (Mt. 14:6-12; Mk. 6:21-29)
- ■ The magnificence of John (Mt. 11:7-15; Lk. 7:24-28)

Event 15:

Jesus turns water into wine (Jn. 2:1-11)

Event 16:

Jesus performs His first temple cleansing (Jn. 2:13-25)

Event 17:

Jesus selects Capernaum as His northern headquarters (Mt. 4:13-16; Jn. 2:12)

Event 18:

Jesus meets with Nicodemus (Jn. 3:1-21)

Event 19:

Jesus meets with the Samaritan woman (Jn. 4:1-42)

Event 20:

Jesus conducts five preaching tours
- ■ First tour (Mt. 4:17; Mk. 1:1415; Lk. 4:14-15)
- ■ Second tour (Mt. 4:23-25; Mk. 1:35-39; Lk. 4:42-44)

- Third tour (Mt. 9:35-38)
- Fourth tour (Mt. 11:1)
- Fifth tour (Lk. 8:1-3)

EVENT 21:

The conversion, choosing, and commissioning of Jesus' disciples

- The conversion of His followers
    1. Andrew and John (Jn. 1:37-40)
    2. Simon Peter (Jn. 1:41-42)
    3. Philip (Jn. 1:43-45)
    4. Nathanael (Jn. 1:46-51)
    5. Matthew (Mt. 9:9; Mk. 2:14; Lk. 5:27-29)
- The choosing of His followers
    1. First call to Peter, Andrew, James and John (Mt. 4:18-22; Mk. 1:16-20; Lk. 5:1-11)
    2. Final call to the twelve (Mt. 10:1-41; Mk. 3:13, 16-19; Lk. 6:12-16)
- The commissioning of His followers
    1. The first followers
        a. The twelve apostles (Mt. 10:5-15; Mk. 3:14-15; 6:7-13; Lk. 9:1-6)
        b. The seventy disciples (Mt. 11:25-27; Lk. 10:1-24)
    2. The future followers (Mt. 10:17-42; Lk. 10:16, 22)

EVENT 22:

Jesus heals a lame man at the pool of Bethesda (Jn. 4:46-54)

Event 23:

Jesus preaches His Sermon on the Mount (Mt. 5-7)

EVENT 24:

Jesus relates the parable of the sower and seed (Mt. 13:1-23)

Event 25:

Jesus preaches from Isa. 61 in a Nazareth synagogue (Lk. 4:16-30)

Event 26:

Jesus heals a paralytic (Mt. 9:2-8; Mk. 2:3-12; Lk. 5:18-26)

Event 27:

Jesus visits with Mary and Martha (Lk. 10:38-42)

Event 28:

Jesus discusses various key topics

- Heaven and hell (Jn. 14:1-3; Mk. 9:42-50)
- Divorce (Mt. 19:3-12; Mk. 10:1-12)
- Discipleship (Mt. 16:24-26; Mk. 8:34-38; Lk. 9:23-26; 14:25-27)
- Last days (Lk. 17:22-37)
- Church discipline (Mt. 18:15-20)

Event 29:

Jesus invites the weary and burdened to come to Him (Mt. 11:28-30)

Event 30:

Jesus stills a storm (Mt. 8:23-27; Mk. 4:36-41; Lk. 8:22-25)

Event 31:

Jesus feeds the 5000 (Mt. 14:15-21; Mk. 6:30-44; Lk. 9:10-17; Jn. 6:1-14)

Event 32:

Jesus walks on the water (Mt. 14:22-32; Mk. 6:45-52; Jn. 6:15-21)

EVENT 33:

Jesus delivers a Syrophenician's daughter (Mt. 15:21-28; Mk. 7:24-30)

EVENT 34:

Jesus hears Peter's great confession and promises to build the church (Mt. 16:13-23)

EVENT 35:

Jesus meets with three would-be disciples

- ■ First candidate: He allows his finances to disqualify him (Mt. 8:19-20; Lk. 9:57-58)
- ■ Second candidate: He allows his family to disqualify him (Mt. 8:21-22; Lk. 9:59-60)
- ■ Third candidate: He allows his friends to disqualify him (Lk. 9:61-62)

EVENT 36:

Jesus denounces key Galilean cities

- ■ Chorazin and Bethsaida (Mt. 11:20-22; Lk. 10:13)
- ■ Capernaum (Mt. 11:23-24; Lk. 10:15)

Event 37:

Jesus is confronted on two occasions by the Pharisees who demand a sign

- ■ First occasion (Mt. 12:38-42; Lk. 11:29-32)
- ■ Second occasion (Mt. 16:14; Mk. 8:10-12; Lk. 12:34-58)

EVENT 38:

Jesus has two encounters with His family

- ■ First encounter (Mt. 12:46-48; Mk. 3:31-35; Lk. 8:19-21)
- ■ Second encounter (Jn. 7:1-10)

EVENT 39:

Jesus meets with the rich young ruler (Mt. 19:16-26; Mk. 10:17-22)

Event 40:

Jesus delivers the maniac of Gadara (Mk. 5:1-20)

EVENT 41:

Jesus heals a woman with an issue of blood (Mt. 9:20-22; Mk. 5:25-34; Lk. 8:43-48)

EVENT 42:

Jesus raises Jairus' daughter (Mt. 9:18-19, 23-26; Mk. 5:22-24, 35-43; Lk. 8:41-42, 49-56)

EVENT 43:

Jesus is transfigured (Mt. 17:1-13; Lk. 9:28-36)

EVENT 44:

Jesus delivers a demonic son (Mt. 17:14-18; Mk. 9:14-29; Lk. 9:38-42)

EVENT 45:

Jesus relates the parable of the Good Samaritan (Lk. 10:30-37)

EVENT 46:

Jesus relates the parable of the lost sheep, coin, and son (Lk. 15:1-32)

EVENT 47:

Jesus relates the parable of the rich man and Lazarus (Lk. 16:19-31)

EVENT 48:

Jesus forgives the woman taken in the act of adultery (Jn. 8:1-11)

EVENT 49:

Jesus preaches His sermon on the Good Shepherd and his sheep (Jn. 10:1-21)

EVENT 50:

Jesus heals the man born blind (Jn. 9)

EVENT 51:

Jesus predicts His sufferings, death, and resurrection on three important occasions

- First occasion: After hearing Peter's confession (Mt. 16:21-23; Mk. 8:31-33; Lk. 9:22)
- Second occasion: After the Transfiguration (Mt. 17:22-23; Mk. 9:30-32; Lk. 9:43-45)
- Third occasion: Just prior to His final week (Mt. 20:17-19; Mk. 10:32-34; Lk. 18:31-34)

EVENT 52:

Jesus raises Lazarus from the dead (Jn. 11:1-44)

EVENT 53:

Jesus cleanses the lepers (Lk. 17:11-19)

EVENT 54:

Jesus rebukes James and John on three occasions

- First occasion, for sectarianism (Mk. 9:38-41; Lk. 9:49-50)
- Second occasion, for barbarism (Lk. 9:51-56)
- Third occasion, for egotism (Mt. 20:20-28; Mk. 10:35-45)

EVENT 55:

Jesus blesses some little children (Mt. 19:13-15; Mk. 10:13-16; Lk. 18:15-17)

Event 56:

Jesus heals blind Bartimaeus (Mt. 20:29-34; Mk. 10:46-52; Lk. 18:35-43)

Event 57:

Jesus calls down Zacchaeus from a sycamore tree (Lk. 19:1-10)

Event 58:

Jesus is anointed by Mary of Bethany (Mt. 26:6-13; Mk. 14:3-9; Jn. 12:1-8)

Event 59:

Jesus' triumphal entry into Jerusalem (Mt. 21:1-11; Mk. 11:1-10; Lk. 19:29-38; Jn. 12:12-19)

Event 60:

Jesus performs His second temple cleansing (Mt. 21:12-17; Mk. 11:15-18; Lk. 19:45-47)

Event 61:

Jesus curses the fig tree (Mt. 21:18-19)

Event 62:

Jesus hears the voice of His Father for the third and final time

- First occasion: At His baptism (Mt. 3:16-17)
- Second occasion: At His transfiguration (Mt. 17:1-5)
- Third occasion: After the request by some Greeks to see Jesus (Jn. 12:20-33)

Event 63:

Jesus is subjected to the final of five confrontations by the wicked Pharisees and Sadducees

- Over His authority (Mt. 21:23-27; Mk. 11:27-33; Lk. 20:3-8)
- Over paying tribute to Caesar (Mt. 22:15-22; Mk. 12:13-17; Lk. 20:19-25)
- Over the doctrine of the resurrection (Mt. 22:23-33; Mk. 12:18-27; Lk. 20:27-40)

- Over the greatest commandment (Mt. 22:34-40; Mk. 12:28-34)
- Over the Messiah (Mt. 22:41-46; Mk. 12:35-37; Lk. 20:41-44)

EVENT 64:

Jesus utterly condemns the wicked Pharisees (Mt. 23:1-36; Mk. 12:38-40; Lk. 20:45-47)

EVENT 65:

Jesus weeps over the city of Jerusalem for the final time
- First occasion (Mt. 23:37-39; Lk. 13:34-35)
- Second occasion (Lk. 19:41-44)

EVENT 66:

Jesus commends a poor widow for her sacrificial gift (Mk. 12:41-44; Lk. 21:1-4)

EVENT 67:

Jesus delivers His Mt. Olivet Discourse (Mt. 2425)

EVENT 68:

Jesus makes preparation for the Passover (Mt. 26:17-19; Mk. 14:12-16; Lk. 21:7-13)

EVENT 69:

Jesus washes the disciples' feet, institutes the Lord's Supper, and announces His betrayal in the Upper Room (Mt. 26:17-39; Mk. 14:12-25; Lk. 22:7-30; Jn. 13-14)

EVENT 70:

Jesus delivers His fruit bearing sermon (Jn. 15-16)

EVENT 71:

Jesus prays His Great High Priestly Prayer (Jn. 17)

EVENT 72:

Jesus offers up three prayers in great agony in Gethsemane (Mt. 26:36-46; Mk. 14:32-42; Lk. 22:39-46; Jn. 18:1-11)

EVENT 73:

Jesus is betrayed by Judas Iscariot

- ■ The bargain—Judas agrees to sell Jesus out for 30 pieces of silver (Mt. 26:14-16; Mk. 14:10-11; Lk. 22:3-6)

- ■ The betrayal—Judas betrays Jesus in Gethsemane (Mt. 26:43-50; Lk. 22:47-48; Jn. 18:1-5)

- ■ The bloody field—Judas returns the money and hangs himself. The 30 pieces are used to purchase a field called the field of blood. (Mt. 27:3-10)

EVENT 74:

Jesus restores a severed ear in Gethsemane (Mt. 26:51-56; Mk. 14:47-49; Lk. 22:50-51; Jn. 18: 10-11)

EVENT 75:

Jesus is arrested in Gethsemane (Jn. 18:10)

EVENT 76:

Jesus is forsaken by all in Gethsemane (Mt. 26:56; Mk. 14:50-52)

EVENT 77:

Jesus suffers His unfair and illegal trials

- ■ The Jewish, religious trials
  1. The three-fold travesty during these trials (denunciation by Annas, Caiaphas, and the Sanhedrin)
     a. Christ stands before Annas (Jn. 18:13-14, 19-23)
     b. Christ stands before Caiaphas (Mt. 26:57, 59-68; Mk. 14:53-65; Lk. 22:54, 63-65; Jn. 18:24)
     c. Christ stands before the entire Sanhedrin (Mt. 27:1; Mk. 15:1)
  2. The two-fold tragedy during those trials (the denials of Peter and death of Judas)
     a. The denials by Peter (Mt. 26:33-35, 69-73, 75; Mk. 14:29-31, 54, 66-70, 72; Lk. 22:31-34, 54-59, 61-62; Jn. 13:36-38; 18:15-17, 25-27)
     b. The death of Judas (Mt. 27:3-10)

- ■ The Roman, political trials
  1. Christ stands before Pilate (for the first time) (Mt. 27:2, 11-14; Mk. 15:25; Lk. 23:1-5; Jn. 18:28-38)
  2. Christ stands before Herod Antipas (Lk. 23:6-12)
  3. Christ stands before Pilate (for the final time) (Mt. 27:15-26; Lk. 15:6-15; 23:13-24; Jn. 18:40; 19:1, 4-5, 7-15)
- ■ The military, mockery trial
  1. Christ stands before the soldiers (Mt. 27:27-31; Mk. 15:16-20; Jn. 19:2-3)

Event 78:

Jesus is brutally scourged (Mt. 27:26; Mk. 15:15)

Event 79:

Jesus is led to Calvary

- ■ The man of Cyrene, lifting up Jesus' cross (Mt. 27:32; Mk. 15:21; Lk. 23:26)
- ■ The maidens of Jerusalem, lamenting over Jesus' cross (Lk. 23:27-31)

Event 80:

Jesus is crucified between two thieves (Mt. 27:32-49; Mk. 15:25; Lk. 23:32; Jn. 19:16-18)

Event 81:

Jesus makes seven statements while on the cross.

- ■ The first three hours (9:00 am till Noon)
  1. First statement from the cross: *"Father, forgive them; for they know not what they do."* (Lk. 23:34)
  2. Second statement from the cross: *"Verily I say unto thee, to day shalt thou be with me in paradise."* (Lk. 23:43)
  3. Third statement from the cross: *"Woman, behold thy son! Behold thy mother."* (Jn. 19:26-27)
- ■ The final three hours (Noon till 3:00 pm)
  4. Fourth statement from the cross: *"My God, my God, why hast thou forsaken me."* (Mt. 27:46)
  5. Fifth statement from the cross: *"I thirst."* (Jn. 19:28)
  6. Sixth statement from the cross: *"It is finished."* (Jn. 19:30)
  7. Seventh statement from the cross: *"Father, into thy hands I commend my spirit."* (Lk. 23:46)

EVENT 82:

Jesus dies on the cross (Mt. 27:50; Mk. 15:37; Lk. 23:46; Jn. 19:30)

EVENT 83:

Jesus' body is pierced (Jn. 19:31-37)

EVENT 84:

Jesus' death is accompanied by a series of miracles

- In regard to the temple: The veil is torn from top to bottom (Mt. 27:51; Mk. 15:38; Lk. 23:45)
- In regard to the terrain: A localized but severe earthquake occurred (Mt. 27:51)
- In regard to the tombs: A number of people were raised from the dead (Mt. 27:52-53)

EVENT 85:

Jesus' body is claimed by and prepared for burial by Joseph of Arimathaea and Nicodemus (Mt. 27:57-59; Mk. 15:42-45; Lk. 23:50-52; Jn. 19:38-40)

EVENT 86:

Jesus' body is placed in Joseph's tomb (Mt. 27:60; Mk. 15:46; Lk. 23:53; Jn. 19:41-42)

EVENT 87:

Jesus' tomb is officially sealed (Mt. 27:62-66)

EVENT 88:

Jesus is raised from the dead (Mt. 28:2-4; Mk. 16:4; Lk. 24:2; Jn. 20:6-7)

EVENT 89:

Jesus appears to Mary Magdalene in the Garden (Mk. 16:9-10; Jn. 20:11-18)

EVENT 90:

Jesus appears to some women returning from the tomb (Mt. 28:5-10)

Event 91:

Jesus appears to two disciples on the Emmaus Road (Lk. 24:13-32; Mk. 16:12-13)

Event 92:

Jesus appears to Peter in Jerusalem (Lk. 24:34; 1 Cor. 15:5)

Event 93:

Jesus appears to ten of His apostles in the Upper Room (Mk. 16:14; Lk. 24:36-43; Jn. 20:19-23)

Event 94 :

Jesus appears to eleven of His apostles in the Upper Room (Jn. 20:19-29)

Event 95:

Jesus appears to seven of His apostles by the Sea of Galilee (Jn. 21:1-23)

Event 96:

Jesus appears to the eleven and 500 believers on Mt. Tabor (Mt. 28:16-20; 1 Cor. 15:6)

Event 97:

Jesus appears to James His half-brother in Jerusalem (1 Cor. 15:7)

Event 98:

Jesus appears to the eleven on Mt. Olivet (Lk. 24:44-50)

Event 99:

Jesus instructs His apostles forty days after His resurrection (Acts 1:3)

Event 100:

Jesus ascends to Heaven from Mt. Olivet (Mk. 16:19; Lk. 24:51; Acts 1:9)

Four: BIOGRAPHICAL

A concise introduction of some 100-plus individuals (both named and unnamed) who are mentioned in the gospel accounts.

NAMED INDIVIDUALS WHO ARE
MENTIONED IN THE GOSPEL ACCOUNTS

Andrew. He was a former fisherman and one of the twelve apostles who brought his brother Peter to Christ (Mk. 1:16; Mt. 10:2; Jn. 1:40-42)

Anna. She was a prophetess and a widow from the tribe of Asher who, like Simeon, recognized the infant Jesus being dedicated in the temple as Israel's Messiah and praised God for this (Lk. 2:36-38)

Annas. He was the former and totally corrupt Jewish High Priest who, along with his son-in-law Caiaphas (current High Priest) treated Jesus in shameful fashion during the Savior's unfair trials (Jn. 18:12-13, 19-24)

Barabbas. He was the anarchist (Mk. 15:7; Lk. 23:19), murderer (Mk. 15:7; Lk. 23:19) and robber (Jn. 18:40), released by Pilate over Jesus who did so at the insistence of the Jewish leaders who preferred a convicted murderer over their own Messiah (Mt. 27:17, 20-21, 26)

Bartimaeus. This blind man, sitting and begging by the highway leading into Jericho, upon hearing that Jesus was passing by, cried out for healing and immediately received his sight (Mk. 10:46-52)

Caiaphas. He was the wicked High Priest who plotted the death of Jesus and who later persecuted the leaders of the early church (Mt. 26:3-5, 62-65; Acts 4:6-7)

Cleopas. The resurrected Savior (at first unrecognized) appears to Cleopas and a fellow disciple en route to Emmaus. After realizing it was Jesus, he quickly returned to the Upper Room in Jerusalem to report the wonderful news to the frightened apostles. Even as he spoke, the Savior appeared in their presence (Lk. 24:13-35)

Elisabeth. She was the wife of Zacharias the Jewish High Priest who supernaturally gave birth to John the Baptist in her old age (Lk. 1:5-7, 57-60)

Herod Antipas. He was the ruling son of Herod the Great who beheaded John the Baptist and later ridiculed Jesus during one of the Savior's unfair trials (Mt. 14:10-11; Lk. 23:10-11)

Herodias. This wicked and vindictive queen arranged for the beheading of John the Baptist who had fearlessly denounced her unlawful marriage to King Herod Antipas (Mk. 6:18-19; Mt. 14:3, 6-11)

Herod the Great. He was a great builder who (for the most part) constructed the second Jewish Temple and later attempted to kill the infant Jesus in Bethlehem (Mt. 2)

Jairus. At the tearful request from this heartbroken and desperate father, Jesus accompanies him to heal his dying 12-year old daughter, only however to find the little girl dead upon their arrival. Jesus thereupon raises her from the dead (Mk. 5:22-24, 35-43; Lk. 8:41-42, 49-56)

James the Apostle. He was a former fisherman, the brother of John, and the first of the twelve apostles to be martyred for Christ (Mt. 4:21; 10:2; Acts 12:1-2)

James the half brother of Jesus. He was an unbeliever prior to Jesus' resurrection but following his conversion became pastor of the church in Jerusalem and would author the New Testament Book of James (Jn. 7:3-5; 1 Cor. 15:7; Acts 15:13-14, 19; 21:17-18; Jas. 1:1)

Joanna. This godly wife, whose husband was King Herod Antipas' steward often helped Jesus financially. She was also present at the empty tomb on the first Easter Sunday (Lk. 8:3; 24:1-7, 10)

John the Apostle. He was a former fisherman, the brother of James, the beloved disciple of Jesus and the author of five New Testament books (the Gospel of John, First, Second and Third John, the Book of Revelation)

John the Baptist. He was the miracle baby of the barren Elisabeth, the Nazarite evangelist who both introduced the Messiah and baptized him, who would later be martyred for his fearless preaching (Lk. 1:5-17; Jn. 1:29; Mt. 3:16-17; 14:1-11)

Joseph of Arimathaea. This wealthy disciple of Jesus, along with Nicodemus, requested and received from Pilate the lifeless body of Jesus and placed it in his own tomb (Mt. 27:57-60; Mk. 15:42-46; Lk. 23:50-54; Jn. 19:38-42)

Joseph, husband of Mary. He was the husband of Mary and the godly, legal (but not physical) father of Jesus (Mt. 1:18-25)

Judas Iscariot. He was the dishonest and demon-possessed apostle of Jesus who betrayed his master for 30 pieces of silver and then committed suicide (Jn. 12:4-5; 6:70-71; Mt. 26:14-15; 27:5)

Lazarus, the beggar. He was the saved beggar carried by the angels into Abraham's bosom (Lk. 16:19-23)

Lazarus, the brother. He was the brother of Mary and Martha whom Christ raised from the dead at Bethany (Jn. 11)

Malchus. He was the servant of the Jewish High Priest whose ear was cut off by Simon Peter in Gethsemane and healed by Jesus (Jn. 18:10; Lk. 22:51)

Martha. She was the sister of Mary who reaffirmed her faith in Jesus during the funeral of her brother Lazarus and then witnessed him being raised from the dead by the Savior (Jn. 11)

Mary Magdalene. She was a demon possessed woman who was delivered by Jesus and later became the first person to see the resurrected Christ (Lk. 8:2; Jn. 20:16)

Mary, mother of James and Joses. This godly mother helped Jesus financially and was present at His crucifixion and resurrection (Mt. 27:56; 28:5-10; Mk. 15:40-41, 47; 16:1-4; Lk. 24:6-11)

Mary, mother of Jesus. She was the virgin wife of Joseph who was chosen to give birth to the Savior of the world (Lk. 1:26-38; 2:7)

Mary, sister of Martha. She worshipped at the feet of Jesus, witnessed Him raising her dead brother Lazarus, and later would anoint the body of the Savior (Lk. 10:39; Jn. 11:43; 12:1-3)

Matthew. He was a former tax collector, called by Jesus to become an apostle, who would later author the book of Matthew (Mt. 9:9; 10:3)

Nathanael. He was also known as Bartholomew, introduced to Christ and later called to become one of the twelve apostles (Jn. 1:45-51; Mt. 10:3)

Nicodemus. He was a well-known Pharisee and teacher, led to Christ during a midnight visit with the Savior and who would later help prepare His crucified body for burial (Jn. 3:1-15; 19:39)

Peter. He was a former fisherman, brought to Christ by his brother Andrew, called to serve as one of the twelve, later denying his Savior on three occasions but after the resurrection becoming His chief spokesman at Pentecost, finally authoring two New Testament epistles (1 and 2 Peter) and dying a martyr's death (Mt. 4:18-19; 10:2; Jn. 1:40-42; Lk. 22:54-62 Acts 2:14-40; 2 Peter 1:13-14)

Philip the Apostle. He led his friend Nathanael to Christ shortly after his own conversion and later was called to serve as one of the twelve apostles (Jn. 1:43-46; Mt. 10:3)

Pilate. He was the Roman governor who was pressured by the wicked Jewish leaders to release the guilty Barabbas and to both scourge and crucify the innocent Jesus (Mt. 27:2; 15-26)

Salome. She contributed financially to the needs of Jesus and was present during His crucifixion and resurrection (Lk. 8:2-3; Mk. 15:40-41; 16:1, 6)

Simeon. The Holy Spirit had promised this godly old man he would live to see the first coming of the Messiah, which promise was realized when Mary brought her infant son Jesus in the Jerusalem temple to be dedicated to the Lord (Lk. 2:25-35)

Simon the Cyrenian. This visiting pilgrim to Jerusalem was ordered by the Roman soldiers to carry the cross of the bruised and beaten Jesus to the hill of Golgotha (Mk. 15:21; Lk. 23:26)

Simon the Leper. This former leper whom Jesus had once healed hosted a supper in Bethany to celebrate the raising of Lazarus, during which meal Mary (sister of Lazarus) anointed the feet of the Savior with a costly ointment (Mt. 26:6-13; Mk. 14:3-9; Jn. 12:1-8)

Simon the Pharisee. During a meal in Simon's home, an immoral but heartbroken woman approached Jesus, who began washing His feet with her tears and drying them with her hair. Knowing her sinful background, Simon secretly condemned Jesus in his thoughts for allowing this but is suddenly rebuked publicly by the Savior for his hypocrisy (Lk. 7:36-50)

Theophilus. Luke addressed both of his New Testament books (Gospel of Luke; Acts of the Apostles) to this man (Lk. 1:1-4; Acts 1:1-5)

Thomas. He had an unnamed twin brother and was known as the doubting apostle as he initially could not believe the glorious reports of Christ's resurrection until the Savior appeared to him personally a week later (Jn. 20:19-29)

Zacchaeus. This dishonest tax collector met Jesus while in a sycamore tree and immediately accepted Him as Savior (Lk. 19:1-10)

Zacharias. He was a priest, visited by the angel Gabriel who predicted his barren wife would present him with a son, John the Baptist (Lk. 1:5-25, 57-80)

Unnamed Individuals in the Gospel Accounts Arranged in Nine Basic Categories

In regard to Jesus' birth:

- The shepherds (Lk. 2:8-18)
- The wise men (Mt. 2:1-12)

In regard to Jesus' miracles:

- A Capernaum demoniac (Mk. 1:23)
- Peter's mother-in-law (Mt. 8:14)
- A Galilean leper (Mk. 1:40)
- A Capernaum paralytic (Mk. 2:3-5, 11-12)
- Man with a withered right hand (Mk. 3:1)
- A Centurion whose servant was sick (Lk. 7:2-3)
- The widow in Nain (Lk. 7:12-13)
- The maniac of Gadara (Mk. 5:1-5)
- A woman with an issue of blood (Mk. 5:25-27)
- Two Galilean blind men (Mt. 9:27)
- Man who had been a cripple for 38 years (Jn. 5:2-5)
- The boy who gave his lunch to Jesus (Jn. 6:8-9)
- Mother of a demon possessed daughter (Mk. 7:32)
- Father of a demon possessed son (Mk. 9:17-29)
- Deaf man with a speech impediment (Mk. 7:32)
- The blind man of Bethsaida (Mk. 8:32)
- The man born blind (Jn. 9:1-2)
- The ten lepers (Lk. 17:12-19)
- Jairus' 12-year old daughter (Mk. 5:35-42)
- The parents of the man born blind (Jn. 9:20)

In regard to Jesus' parables:

- The sinful woman who washed Jesus' feet (Lk. 7:37-38)
- The forgiven servant who wouldn't forgive (Mt. 18:23-34)
- The good Samaritan (Lk. 10:33-35)
- The uncaring priest and Levi who refused to help an injured man (Lk. 10:30-32)
- The rich fool (Lk. 12:16-20)
- The rich man who prepared a great supper (Lk. 14:16-17)
- The king who prepared a marriage feast for his son (Mt. 22:2)
- The guest who attended a wedding feast who refused to wear a wedding garment (Mt. 22:2, 11-13)
- Shepherd who sought and found a lost sheep (Lk. 15:1-7)
- A woman who sought and found a lost coin (Lk. 15:8-10)
- The prodigal son, his father, and his elder brother (Lk. 15:11-30)
- The unjust steward (Lk. 16:1-7)
- The rich man in hell (Lk. 16:19-31)
- The man who hired workers for his vineyard (Mt. 20:1)
- The Nobleman who entrusted his servants with ten pounds (Lk. 19:12-13)
- The businessman who entrusted his servants with seven talents (Mt. 25:14-30)

In regard to Jesus soul-wining activities:

- The Samaritan woman (Jn. 4:7-39)
- The woman taken in the act of adultery (Jn. 8:3-11)
- A sincere scribe (Mk. 12:28-34)

In regard to true discipleship:

- The rich young ruler (Mk. 10:17-22)
- Three would-be disciples (Lk. 9:57-62)

In regard to those whom Jesus commended:

- A man who was casting out demons (Mk. 9:38)
- A little child (Mt. 18:2)

- A widow and her offering (Mk. 12:41)
- A woman who blessed Jesus (Lk. 11:27)

In regard to those whom Jesus rebuked:

- The mother of James and John (Mt. 20:20-21)
- An insincere lawyer (Lk. 10:25-29)

In regard to Jesus' sufferings and crucifixion:

- A young man who abandoned Jesus in Gethsemane (Mk. 14:51)
- Pilate's wife (Mt. 27:19)
- The maid that accused Peter
- The dying saved thief (Lk. 23:39-43)
- The dying lost thief (Mt. 27:44; Mk. 15:32)
- The four soldiers who gambled for Jesus' clothes (Jn. 19:23)
- The centurion in charge at Golgotha (Mt. 27:44; Mk. 15:39; Lk. 23:47)
- The soldier who pierced Jesus' side with his spear (Jn. 19:34)

In regard to Jesus' resurrection:

- The soldiers who were present at Jesus' resurrection but later accepted a bribe to deny it (Mt. 28:11-15)
- The associate of Cleopas en route to Emmaus (Lk. 24:13)

Five: VISUAL

Forty-Five Charts Illustrating The Earthly Life Of Christ

VISUAL CHARTS OVERVIEWING THE EARTHLY MINISTRY OF JESUS

CHART # 1

	SCRIPTURE

MATTHEW, MARK, LUKE, JOHN

	SUBJECT

THE EARTHLY LIFE OF JESUS CHRIST

	SPECIFICS

THE FOURFOLD GOSPEL ACCOUNT

	MATTHEW	MARK	LUKE	JOHN
Portrait Of Christ	King And Lion Like	Servant And Ox Like	Perfect Man And Man Like	Mighty God And Eagle Like
Style Of Writer	Teacher	Preacher	Historian	Theologian
Emphasis By Writer	His Sermons	His Miracles	His Parables	His Doctrines
Culture Of Original Readers	Jews	Romans	Greeks	The World
Place Of Main Action	Capernaum In Galilee	Capernaum In Galilee	Capernaum In Galilee	Jerusalem In Judea
Twofold Division	Synoptic Gospels - Stress The Humanity Of Christ			Fourth Gospel Stresses The Deity Of Christ

	SAINTS AND SINNERS

* Elisabeth
* Herod the Great
* Herod Antipas
* John the Apostle

* John the Baptist
* Joseph
* Judas
* Martha

* Mary
* Mary Magdalene
* Mary, Sister of Martha
* Nicodemus

* Peter
* Pilate
* Thomas
* Zachariah

	SENTENCE SUMMARIES

Old Testament Verse

The LORD thy God will raise up unto thee a Prophet from the midst of thee, of thy brethren, like unto me unto him ye shall hearken (Dt. 18:15).

New Testament Verse

And there are also many other things which Jesus did, the which, if they should be written every one, I suppose that even the world itself could not contain the books that should be written. Amen (Jn. 21:25).

CHART # 2

	SUBJECT

THE FIRST TWELVE YEARS OF JESUS' EARTHLY MINISTRY

	SPECIFICS

Pre-Bethlehem Events

Event 1: The Two Genealogies

* The Genealogy as Recorded by Matthew (Mt. 1:1-17)
* The Genealogy as Recorded by Luke (Lk.3:23-37)

Event 2: The Two Prefaces

* As Recorded by Luke (Lk.1:1-4)
* As Recorded by John (Jn. 1:1-5)

Event 3: The Three Announcements

* To Zacharias, Concerning the Birth of John (Lk.1:5-25)
* To Mary, Concerning the Birth of Jesus (Lk.1:26-38)
* To Joseph, Concerning the Purity of Mary (Mt. 1:18-25)

Event 4: The Three Songs Of Praise

* The Praise of Elisabeth to Mary (Lk.1:41-45)
* The Praise of Mary to God (Lk.1:46-56)
* The Praise of Zacharias to God (Lk.1:57-79)

Bethlehem Events

Jehovah's Son Is Born (Lk.2:1-7)

1. The Decree by Caesar (2:1-5)

   * The law (2:1-3): All are required to return to their ancestral homes because of a census
   * The location (2:4-5): Joseph and Mary must travel to Bethlehem

2. The Delivery by Mary (2:6-7): While in Bethlehem, Mary gives birth to Jesus

Judah's Shepherds Are Briefed (Lk.2:8-12)

* They Watch! (2:8)
* They Wonder! (2:9-14)
* They Worship! (2:15, 16)
* They Witness! (2:17-21)

Post-Bethlehem Events

Temple Dedication

* Testimony of Simeon (Mt. 2:25-35)
* Testimony of Anna (Mt. 2:36-38)

Visit By Wise Men

* The Journey of the Wise Men (Mt. 2:1-8)
* The Joy of the Wise Men (Mt. 2:8-12)

Flight Into Egypt

* Reason for the trip (Mt. 2:13-15)
* Retaliation during the trip (Mt. 2:16-18)

Return To Nazareth

* God tells Joseph in a dream to leave Egypt and settle in Nazareth (Mt. 2:19-23)

Temple Visit At Twelve

* The Missing Son (Lk.2:41-47)
* The Messianic Son (Lk.2:48-49)
* The Misunderstood Son (Lk.2:50)

FIVE: VISUAL

CHART # 3

SUBJECT

THE TWO GENEALOGIES AND THE TWO PREFACES RELATING TO THE BIRTH OF JESUS

SPECIFICS

MATTHEW'S GENEALOGY: (Mt. 1:1-17)

OVERVIEWED

[1]The book of the genealogy of Jesus Christ, the Son of David, the Son of Abraham: [2]Abraham begat Isaac, Isaac begat Jacob, and Jacob begat Judah and his brothers.

- He begins with Abraham and goes forward in time to Joseph
- He gives the royal line of Joseph
- He traces this line through Solomon, David's first son
- His list includes forty-one names, four of which are women

OUTLINED

- From Abraham to David (1:2-6)
- From Solomon to Jehoiakim (Jechonias) (1:7-11)
- From Shealtiel to Jesus (1:12-16)

LUKE'S GENEALOGY: (Lk.3:23-38)

OVERVIEWED

[23]Now Jesus Himself began His ministry at about thirty years of age, being (as was supposed) the son of Joseph, the son of Heli,

- He begins with Joseph and goes backward in time to Adam
- He gives the racial line of Mary
- He traces this line through Nathan, David's second son
- His list includes seventy-four names

OUTLINED

- From Jesus, the legal son of Joseph, to Nathan, the biological son of David (3:23-31)
- From Obed, the son of Boaz, to Adam, the son of God (3:32-38)

THE TWO GENEALOGIES

LUKE'S PREFACE	JOHN'S PREFACE
Luke introduces Jesus as the earthly Son of Man	John introduces Jesus as the eternal Son of God
[1]Inasmuch as many have taken in hand to set in order a narrative of those things which have been fulfilled among us, [2]just as those who from the beginning were eyewitnesses and ministers of the word delivered them to us, [3]it seemed good to me also, having had perfect understanding of all things from the very first, to write to you an orderly account, most excellent Theophilus, [4]that you may know the certainty of those things in which you were instructed. *[5]There was in the days of Herod, the king of Judea, a certain priest named Zacharias, of the division of Abijah. His wife was of the daughters of Aaron, and her name was Elisabeth.*	*[1]In the beginning was the Word, and the Word was with God, and the Word was God. [2]He was in the beginning with God. [3]All things were made through Him, and without Him nothing was made that was made. [4]In Him was life, and the life was the light of men. [5]And the light shines in the darkness, and the darkness did not comprehend it.*

THE TWO PREFACES

CHART # 4

SUBJECT

THE THREE ANNOUNCEMENTS RELATING TO THE BIRTH OF JESUS

SPECIFICS

TO ZACHARIAS, CONCERNING THE BIRTH OF JOHN

HIS SPOUSE	HIS SERVICE	HIS SORROW
[5]*There was in the days of Herod, the king of Judea, a certain priest named Zacharias, of the division of Abijah. His wife was of the daughters of Aaron, and her name was Elisabeth* (Lk.1:5).	[6]*And they were both righteous before God, walking in all the commandments and ordinances of the Lord blameless.* [8]*So it was, that while he was serving as priest before God in the order of his division,* [9]*according to the custom of the priesthood, his lot fell to burn incense when he went into the temple of the Lord* (Lk.1:6, 8, 9).	[7]*But they had no child, because Elisabeth was barren, and they were both well advanced in years* (Lk.1:7).

HIS SURPRISE

1 The Reason Involved	2 The Revelation Involved
[11]*Then an angel of the Lord appeared to him, standing on the right side of the altar of incense* (Lk.1:11).	[12]*And when Zacharias saw him, he was troubled, and fear fell upon him.* [13]*But the angel said to him, "Do not be afraid, Zacharias, for your prayer is heard; and your wife Elisabeth will bear you a son, and you shall call his name John.* [15]*"For he will be great in the sight of the Lord, and shall drink neither wine nor strong drink. He will also be filled with the Holy Spirit, even from his mother's womb".* [17]*"He will also go before Him in the spirit and power of Elijah, 'to turn the hearts of the fathers to the children,' and the disobedient to the wisdom of the just, to make ready a people prepared for the Lord"* (Lk.1:12, 13, 15, 17).

3 The Rebuke Involved	4 The Rejoicing Involved
[18]*And Zacharias said to the angel, "How shall I know this? For I am an old man, and my wife is well advanced in years."* [19]*And the angel answered and said to him, "I am Gabriel, who stands in the presence of God, and was sent to speak to you and bring you these glad tidings.* [20]*"But behold, you will be mute and not able to speak until the day these things take place, because you did not believe my words which will be fulfilled in their own time"* (Lk.1:18-20).	[24]*Now after those days his wife Elisabeth conceived; and she hid herself five months, saying,* [25]*"Thus the Lord has dealt with me, in the days when He looked on me, to take away my reproach among people"* (Lk.1:24-25).

TO MARY, CONCERNING THE BIRTH OF JESUS

THE SALUTATION TO MARY (LK.1:26-37)

- The Message: The angel Gabriel tells her she will give birth to the Messiah
- The Mystery: Mary, a virgin asks how this would occur
- The Method: She is told the Holy Spirit would overshadow her
- The Miracle: Mary is told Elisabeth would soon bear a son

THE SUBMISSION BY MARY

[38]*Then Mary said, "Behold the maidservant of the Lord! Let it be to me according to your word." And the angel departed from her* (Lk.1:38).

TO JOSEPH, CONCERNING THE PURITY OF MARY

JOSEPH'S DISTRESS	JOSEPH'S DECISION	JOSEPH'S DREAM
• He is Heartbroken: He is reassured by the angel that Mary has not been unfaithful (Mt. 1:18).	• Not willing to publicly disgrace her, he plans to break their engagement secretly (Mt. 1:19)	• The Angel of the Lord assures him of Mary's purity, saying her unborn son would be the Jewish Messiah! (Mt. 1:20-25)

THE THREE TESTIMONIES OF PRAISE RELATING TO THE BIRTH OF JESUS

	THE BABE WITHIN ELISABETH	THE BLESSING FROM ELISABETH
THE PRAISE OF ELISABETH TO GOD	*39Now Mary arose in those days and went into the hill country with haste, to a city of Judah, 40and entered the house of Zacharias and greeted Elisabeth. 41And it happened, when Elisabeth heard the greeting of Mary, that the babe leaped in her womb; and Elisabeth was filled with the Holy Spirit* (Lk.1:39-41).	*42Then she spoke out with a loud voice and said, "Blessed are you among women, and blessed is the fruit of your womb!" 43"But why is this granted to me, that the mother of my Lord should come to me?" 44"For indeed, as soon as the voice of your greeting sounded in my ears, the babe leaped in my womb for joy." 45"Blessed is she who believed, for there will be a fulfillment of those things which were told her from the Lord"* (Lk.1:42-45).

	THE TESTIMONY INVOLVED	THE TIME INVOLVED
THE PRAISE OF MARY TO GOD	*46And Mary said: "My soul magnifies the Lord, 47And my spirit has rejoiced in God my Savior. 48For He has regarded the lowly state of His maidservant; For behold, henceforth all generations will call me blessed. 49For He who is mighty has done great things for me, And holy is His name. 54He has helped His servant Israel, In remembrance of His mercy, 55As He spoke to our fathers, To Abraham and to his seed forever"* (Lk.1:46-49, 54, 55).	*56And Mary remained with her about three months, and returned to her house* (Lk.1:56).

	ZECHARIAH THE FATHER	ZECHARIAH THE FORETELLER
THE PRAISE OF ZECHARIAH TO GOD	• He is seen writing: *59So it was, on the eighth day, that they came to circumcise the child; and they would have called him by the name of his father, Zacharias. 60His mother answered and said, "No; he shall be called John." 61But they said to her, "There is no one among your relatives who is called by this name." 62So they made signs to his father—what he would have him called. 63And he asked for a writing tablet, and wrote, saying, "His name is John." So they all marveled* (Lk.1:59-63). • He is seen worshipping: *64Immediately his mouth was opened and his tongue loosed, and he spoke, praising God* (Lk.1:64).	**The Prophecy Concerning His Savior** • Jesus will fulfill the Davidic Covenant (Lk.1:67-72) • Jesus will fulfill the Abrahamic Covenant (Lk.1:73-75) **The Prophecy Concerning His Son** • He will prepare the way of the Lord. (Lk.1:76) • He will prepare the words of the Lord. (Lk.1:77-80)

CHART # 6

	SUBJECT

THE BIRTH OF JESUS: (Lk.2:1-20)

	SPECIFICS

	THE DECREE BY CAESAR	THE DELIVERY BY MARY
JEHOVAH'S SON IS BORN	• **The Command:** *[1]And it came to pass in those days that a decree went out from Caesar Augustus that all the world should be registered. [2]This census first took place while Quirinius was governing Syria. [3]So all went to be registered, everyone to his own city* (Lk.2:1-3). • **The City:** *Joseph also went up from Galilee, out of the city of Nazareth, into Judea, to the city of David, which is called Bethlehem, because he was of the house and lineage of David, to be registered with Mary, his betrothed wife, who was with child* (Lk.2:4, 5).	*[6]So it was, that while they were there, the days were completed for her to be delivered. [7]And she brought forth her firstborn Son, and wrapped Him in swaddling clothes, and laid Him in a manger, because there was no room for them in the inn (Lk.2:6, 7).*

1	WATCHING

[8]Now there were in the same country shepherds living out in the fields, keeping watch over their flock by night (Lk.2:8).

2	WONDERING

• **The reassurance by the angel:** *[9]And behold, an angel of the Lord stood before them, and the glory of the Lord shone around them, and they were greatly afraid. [10]Then the angel said to them, "Do not be afraid, for behold, I bring you good tidings of great joy which will be to all people"* (Lk.2:9, 10).
• **The revelation by the angel:** *[11]"For there is born to you this day in the city of David a Savior, who is Christ the Lord." [12]"And this will be the sign to you: You will find a Babe wrapped in swaddling clothes, lying in a manger"* (Lk.2:11, 12).
• **The rejoicing by the angel:** *[13]And suddenly there was with the angel a multitude of the heavenly host praising God and saying: [14]"Glory to God in the highest, And on earth peace, goodwill toward men!"* (Lk.2:13, 14)

3	WORSHIPPING

• **Their Decision:** *[15]So it was, when the angels had gone away from them into heaven, that the shepherds said to one another, "Let us now go to Bethlehem and see this thing that has come to pass, which the Lord has made known to us"* (Lk.2:15).
• **Their Discovery:** *[16]And they came with haste and found Mary and Joseph, and the Babe lying in a manger* (Lk.2:16).

4	WITNESSING

• **The proclamation by the men:** *[17]Now when they had seen Him, they made widely known the saying which was told them concerning this Child. [18]And all those who heard it marveled at those things which were told them by the shepherds. [20]Then the shepherds returned, glorifying and praising God for all the things that they had heard and seen, as it was told them* (Lk.2:17, 18, 20).
• **The contemplation by the mother:** *[19]But Mary kept all these things and pondered them in her heart* (Lk.2:19).

(Left margin label: JUDAH'S SHEPHERDS ARE BRIEFED)

THE CIRCUMCISION AND DEDICATION OF JESUS

SPECIFICS

HIS CIRCUMCISION IN BETHLEHEM

²¹And when eight days were completed for the circumcision of the Child, His name was called Jesus, the name given by the angel before He was conceived in the womb (Lk.2:21).

HIS DEDICATION IN JERUSALEM

THE TESTIMONY OF SIMEON

* **The Ritual Involved:** *²²Now when the days of her purification according to the law of Moses were completed, they brought Him to Jerusalem to present Him to the Lord ²³(as it is written in the law of the Lord, "Every male who opens the womb shall be called holy to the Lord"), ²⁴and to offer a sacrifice according to what is said in the law of the Lord, "A pair of turtledoves or two young pigeons"* (Lk.2:22-24).

* **The Reassurance Involved:** *²⁵And behold, there was a man in Jerusalem whose name was Simeon, and this man was just and devout, waiting for the Consolation of Israel, and the Holy Spirit was upon him. ²⁶And it had been revealed to him by the Holy Spirit that he would not see death before he had seen the Lord's Christ* (Lk.2:25, 26).

* **The Recognition Involved:** *²⁷So he came by the Spirit into the temple. And when the parents brought in the Child Jesus, to do for Him according to the custom of the law, ²⁸he took Him up in his arms and blessed God and said: ²⁹"Lord, now You are letting Your servant depart in peace, According to Your word; For my eyes have seen Your salvation ³¹Which You have prepared before the face of all peoples, ³²A light to bring revelation to the Gentiles, And the glory of Your people Israel"* (Lk.2:27-32).

* **The Revelation Involved:** *³³And Joseph and His mother marveled at those things which were spoken of Him. ³⁴Then Simeon blessed them, and said to Mary His mother, "Behold, this Child is destined for the fall and rising of many in Israel, and for a sign which will be spoken against ³⁵"(yes, a sword will pierce through your own soul also), that the thoughts of many hearts may be revealed." ³⁶Now there was one, Anna, a prophetess, the daughter of Phanuel, of the tribe of Asher. She was of a great age, and had lived with a husband seven years from her virginity;* (Lk.2:33-36).

THE TESTIMONY OF ANNA

³⁶Now there was one, Anna, a prophetess, the daughter of Phanuel, of the tribe of Asher. She was of a great age, and had lived with a husband seven years from her virginity; ³⁷and this woman was a widow of about eighty-four years, who did not depart from the temple, but served God with fastings and prayers night and day. ³⁸And coming in that instant she gave thanks to the Lord, and spoke of Him to all those who looked for redemption in Jerusalem (Lk.36-38).

CHART # 8

SUBJECT	

THE WORSHIP OF JESUS BY THE WISE MEN

SPECIFICS	

THE JOURNEY OF THE WISE MEN

THE JOURNEY OF THE MAGI

* **Their public meeting with King Herod:** *¹Now after Jesus was born in Bethlehem of Judea in the days of Herod the king, behold, wise men from the East came to Jerusalem, ²saying, "Where is He who has been born King of the Jews? For we have seen His star in the East and have come to worship Him." ³When Herod the king heard this, he was troubled, and all Jerusalem with him. ⁴And when he had gathered all the chief priests and scribes of the people together, he inquired of them where the Christ was to be born. ⁵So they said to him, "In Bethlehem of Judea, for thus it is written by the prophet: ⁶'But you, Bethlehem, in the land of Judah, Are not the least among the rulers of Judah; For out of you shall come a Ruler Who will shepherd My people Israel"* (Mt. 2:1-6).

* **Their private meeting with King Herod:** *⁷Then Herod, when he had secretly called the wise men, determined from them what time the star appeared. ⁸And he sent them to Bethlehem and said, "Go and search carefully for the young Child, and when you have found Him, bring back word to me, that I may come and worship Him also"*
(Mt. 2:7, 8).

THE JOY OF THE WISE MEN

* **The witness of the star:** *⁹When they heard the king, they departed; and behold, the star which they had seen in the East went before them, till it came and stood over where the young Child was* (Mt. 2:9).

* **The worship by the magi:** *¹⁰When they saw the star, they rejoiced with exceedingly great joy. ¹¹And when they had come into the house, they saw the young Child with Mary His mother, and fell down and worshiped Him. And when they had opened their treasures, they presented gifts to Him: gold, frankincense, and myrrh* (Mt. 2:10, 11).

* **The warning from the Lord:** *¹²Then, being divinely warned in a dream that they should not return to Herod, they departed for their own country another way* (Mt. 2:12).

THE JOURNEY OF THE MESSIAH

THE REASON FOR THE TRIP	THE RETALIATION DURING THE TRIP	THE RETURN FROM THE TRIP
To flee the wrath of Herod: *¹³Now when they had departed, behold, an angel of the Lord appeared to Joseph in a dream, saying, "Arise, take the young Child and His mother, flee to Egypt, and stay there until I bring you word; for Herod will seek the young Child to destroy Him." ¹⁴When he arose, he took the young Child and His mother by night and departed for Egypt,* (Mt. 2:13, 14). **To fulfill the words of Hosea:** *¹⁵and was there until the death of Herod, that it might be fulfilled which was spoken by the Lord through the prophet, saying, "Out of Egypt I called My Son"* (Mt. 2:15).	**The purge of Herod:** *¹⁶Then Herod, when he saw that he was deceived by the wise men, was exceedingly angry; and he sent forth and put to death all the male children who were in Bethlehem and in all its districts, from two years old and under, according to the time which he had determined from the wise men* (Mt. 2:16). **The prophecy of Jeremiah:** *¹⁷Then was fulfilled what was spoken by Jeremiah the prophet, saying: ¹⁸"A voice was heard in Ramah, Lamentation, weeping, and great mourning, Rachel weeping for her children, Refusing to be comforted, Because they are no more"* (Mt. 2:17, 18).	**Joseph's first dream:** *¹⁹But when Herod was dead, behold, an angel of the Lord appeared in a dream to Joseph in Egypt, ²⁰saying, "Arise, take the young Child and His mother, and go to the land of Israel, for those who sought the young Child's life are dead." ²¹Then he arose, took the young Child and His mother, and came into the land of Israel* (Mt. 2:19-21). **Joseph's second dream:** *²²But when he heard that Archelaus was reigning over Judea instead of his father Herod, he was afraid to go there. And being warned by God in a dream, he turned aside into the region of Galilee. ²³And he came and dwelt in a city called Nazareth, that it might be fulfilled which was spoken by the prophets, "He shall be called a Nazarene"* (Mt. 2:22, 23).

THE TEMPLE VISIT OF JESUS AT AGE TWELVE AND HIS EARLY YEARS IN NAZARETH

THE MISSING SON

- **The Occasion:** [41]*His parents went to Jerusalem every year at the Feast of the Passover.* [42]*And when He was twelve years old, they went up to Jerusalem according to the custom of the feast* (Lk.2:41, 42).

- **The Oversight:** [43]*When they had finished the days, as they returned, the Boy Jesus lingered behind in Jerusalem. And Joseph and His mother did not know it;* [44]*but supposing Him to have been in the company, they went a day's journey, and sought Him among their relatives and acquaintances.* [45]*So when they did not find Him, they returned to Jerusalem, seeking Him* (Lk.2:43-45).

- **The Outcome:** [46]*Now so it was that after three days they found Him in the temple, sitting in the midst of the teachers, both listening to them and asking them questions.* [47]*And all who heard Him were astonished at His understanding and answers* (Lk.2:46, 47).

THE MESSIANIC SON

- **The Mother's Rebuke:** [48]*So when they saw Him, they were amazed; and His mother said to Him, "Son, why have You done this to us? Look, Your father and I have sought You anxiously"* (Lk.2:48).

- **The Messiah's Reminder:** [49]*And He said to them, "Why did you seek Me? Did you not know that I must be about My Father's business?"* (Lk.2:49).

THE MISUNDERSTOOD SON

[50]*But they did not understand the statement which He spoke to them* (Lk.2:50).

HIS VISIT TO THE TEMPLE IN JERUSALEM

JESUS' RELATIONSHIP TO MARY AND JOSEPH	JESUS' RELATIONSHIP TO GOD AND MAN
[51]*Then He went down with them and came to Nazareth, and was subject to them, but His mother kept all these things in her heart* (Lk.2:51).	[40]*And the Child grew and became strong in spirit, filled with wisdom; and the grace of God was upon Him.* [52]*And Jesus increased in wisdom and stature, and in favor with God and men* (Lk.2:40, 52).

HIS EARLY YEARS IN NAZARETH

CHART # 10

SUBJECT

THE BAPTISM AND TEMPTATION OF JESUS CHRIST

	THE SUMMARY	THE SIGNIFICANCE
HIS BAPTISM (MT. 3:13-17; LK.3:21, 22)	• The appeal by the Son. Jesus asks a reluctant John to baptize Him • The anointing by the Spirit. The Holy Spirit, like a dove comes upon Him • The approval by the Father "*And lo a voice from heaven, saying, This is my beloved Son, in whom I am well pleased.*"	• This is the clearest illustration of the Trinity in all the Bible • It is the first of three occasions where the Father orally approves of His Son • It marks the first recorded example of Jesus' prayer life • It serves as the introduction to His prophetical office
	THE SUMMARY	**THE SIGNIFICANCE**
HIS TEMPTATION (MT. 4:1-11; LK.4:1-13)	<u>**Jesus is attacked**</u> **by the Devil!** • 1st. temptation: "*Turn stones into bread*" • 2nd. Temptation: "*Jump off the Temple*" • 3rd. Temptation: "*Fall down and worship me*" <u>**Jesus is acquitted**</u> **by the Scriptures**! • He counters each temptation by quoting God's Word <u>**Jesus is assisted**</u> **by the angels** • "angels came and ministered to Him"	• The first Adam was tempted in a beautiful garden, the second Adam in a desolate wilderness • Satan defeats the first Adam but was himself defeated by the second Adam • This marks the first occasion where angels aided Christ • It is the only time where Satan quotes Scripture! • The purpose of the temptations was to prove Jesus <u>could not</u> and <u>would not</u> sin!

OVERVIEW: THE LIFE OF JOHN THE BAPTIST - A MAN SENT FROM GOD

SPECIFICS

1	MATURING OF JOHN	2	MESSAGE OF JOHN
[80]And the child grew, and waxed strong in spirit, and was in the deserts till the day of his shewing unto Israel (Lk.1:80).		*[1]In those days came John the Baptist, preaching in the wilderness of Judaea, [2]And saying, Repent ye: for the kingdom of heaven is at hand. [3]For this is he that was spoken of by the prophet Esaias, saying, The voice of one crying in the wilderness, Prepare ye the way of the Lord, make his paths straight (Mt. 3:1-3).*	

3	MINISTRY OF JOHN	4	MANTLE OF JOHN
[4]John did baptize in the wilderness, and preach the baptism of repentance for the remission of sins. [5]And there went out unto him all the land of Judaea, and they of Jerusalem, and were all baptized of him in the river of Jordan, confessing their sins (Mk. 1:4, 5)		*[6]And John was clothed with camel's hair, and with a girdle of a skin about his loins; and he did eat locusts and wild honey (Mk. 1:6).*	

5	MISUNDERSTANDING CONCERNING JOHN	6	MESSIAH OF JOHN
[19]And this is the record of John, when the Jews sent priests and Levites from Jerusalem to ask him, Who art thou? [20]And he confessed, and denied not; but confessed, I am not the Christ. [21]And they asked him, What then? Art thou Elias? And he saith, I am not. Art thou that prophet? And he answered, No. [23]He said, I am the voice of one crying in the wilderness, Make straight the way of the Lord, as said the prophet Esaias (Jn. 1:19-21, 23).		*[17]For the law was given by Moses, but grace and truth came by Jesus Christ. [29]The next day John seeth Jesus coming unto him, and saith, Behold the Lamb of God, which taketh away the sin of the world (Jn. 1:17, 29).*	

7	ATTEMPTED MUZZLING OF JOHN	8	BRIEF MISGIVINGS BY JOHN
[3]For Herod had laid hold on John, and bound him, and put him in prison for Herodias' sake, his brother Philip's wife. [4]For John said unto him, It is not lawful for thee to have her (Mt. 14:3-4).		*[2]Now when John had heard in the prison the works of Christ, he sent two of his disciples, [3]And said unto him, Art thou he that should come, or do we look for another? [4]Jesus answered and said unto them, Go and shew John again those things which ye do hear and see: [5]The blind receive their sight, and the lame walk, the lepers are cleansed, and the deaf hear, the dead are raised up, and the poor have the gospel preached to them (Mt. 11:2-5).*	

9	MARTYRDOM OF JOHN	10	MAGNIFICENCE OF JOHN
[6]But when Herod's birthday was kept, the daughter of Herodias danced before them, and pleased Herod. [7]Whereupon he promised with an oath to give her whatsoever she would ask. [8]And she, being before instructed of her mother, said, Give me here John Baptist's head in a charger. [10]And he sent, and beheaded John in the prison (Mt. 14:6-8, 10).		* John's view of Jesus: *"He must increase, but I must decrease"* (Jn. 3:30). * Jesus' view of John: *"Among them that are born of woman there hath not risen a greater than John the Baptist . . ."* (Mt. 11:11).	

CHART # 12

SUBJECT
THE CONVERSION, CHOOSING, AND COMMISSIONING OF JESUS' EARLY FOLLOWERS

SPECIFICS

THEIR CONVERSION

Andrew and John (Jn. 1:37-40)

These two disciples of John the Baptist leave him to follow Christ

Simon Peter (Jn. 1:41, 43)

Andrew brings his brother Peter to Christ

Philip

[43]*The day following Jesus would go forth into Galilee, and findeth Philip, and saith unto him, Follow me.* [44]*Now Philip was of Bethsaida, the city of Andrew and Peter (Jn. 1:43-44).*

Nathanael (Jn. 1:46-51)

[45]*Philip findeth Nathanael, and saith unto him, We have found him, of whom Moses in the law, and the prophets, did write, Jesus of Nazareth, the son of Joseph (Jn. 1:45).*

Matthew (Mt. 9:9)

[9]*And as Jesus passed forth from thence, he saw a man, named Matthew, sitting at the receipt of custom: and he saith unto him, Follow me. And he arose, and followed him (Mt. 9:9).*

THEIR CHOOSING

First call to Peter, Andrew, James and John

[18]*And Jesus, walking by the sea of Galilee, saw two brethren, Simon called Peter, and Andrew his brother, casting a net into the sea: for they were fishers.* [19]*And he saith unto them, Follow me, and I will make you fishers of men.* [20]*And they straightway left their nets, and followed him.* [21]*And going on from thence, he saw other two brethren, James the son of Zebedee, and John his brother, in a ship with Zebedee their father, mending their nets; and he called them.* [22]*And they immediately left the ship and their father, and followed him (Mt. 4:18-22).*

Final call to the Twelve

[12]*And it came to pass in those days, that he went out into a mountain to pray, and continued all night in prayer to God.* [13]*And when it was day, he called unto him his disciples: and of them he chose twelve, whom also he named apostles (Lk.6:12-13).*

THEIR COMMISSIONING

HIS FIRST FOLLOWERS

The Twelve Apostles

[1]*Then he called his twelve disciples together, and gave them power and authority over all devils, and to cure diseases.* [2]*And he sent them to preach the kingdom of God, and to heal the sick (Lk.9:1-2).*

The Seventy Disciples

[1]*After these things the Lord appointed other seventy also, and sent them two and two before his face into every city and place, whither he himself would come (Lk.10:1).*

HIS FUTURE FOLLOWERS

Some believe Jesus' words in Matthew 10:16-42 may refer to those believers in the Great Tribulation. Note His warning:

[22]*And ye shall be hated of all men for my name's sake: but he that endureth to the end shall be saved.* [23]*But when they persecute you in this city, flee ye into another: for verily I say unto you, Ye shall not have gone over the cities of Israel, till the Son of man be come (Mt. 10:22-23).*

THE TWELVE APOSTLES OF JESUS CHRIST (Part One)

| SPECIFICS |

SIMON PETER

EVENT	REFERENCE
• Brother of Andrew and fishing partner with James and John	Lk.5:10
• A married man	Mk. 1:30; 1 Cor. 9:5
• Brought to Christ by his brother Andrew	Jn. 1:41-42
• Later called into full-time service by Christ	Lk.5:3-11
• Watches Christ heal his mother-in-law	Mt. 8:14-15
• Becomes (along with James and John) one of the "Key Three"	Lk.8:51; Mt. 17:1-4; Mt. 26:36-40
• Walks on water	Mt. 14:28-31
• Gives two great confessions concerning Christ's deity	Jn. 6:68, 69; Mt. 16:16
• Allows Satan to influence him concerning Christ's death	Mt. 16:21-23
• Catches a fish with a coin in its mouth	Mt. 17:27
• Is instructed by Christ concerning forgiveness	Mt. 18:21-22
• Sees the transfiguration of Christ	Mt. 17:1-4
• Is promised a reward for following Christ	Mt. 19:27
• Helps prepare for the final Passover	Lk.22:8
• Is present with Christ in the Upper Room	Jn. 13:6, 24, 36
• Cuts off Malchus' ear in Gethsemane	Jn. 18:10-11
• Follows Christ afar off	Mk. 14:50, 54
• Denies Christ on 3 occasions	Jn. 18:15-18, 25-27
• Bitterly regrets these denials	Lk.22:62
• Visits the empty tomb with John	Lk.24:12; Jn. 20:2-10
• Is himself visited by the resurrected Christ	Lk.24:34; 1 Cor. 15:5
• Is present at Christ's last miracle by the Galilean Sea	Jn. 21:1-23

ANDREW

EVENT	REFERENCE
• The brother of Peter and a fisherman from Bethsaida in Galilee	Jn. 1:44
• An early disciple of John the Baptist	Jn. 1:40
• Accepted Christ and brought his brother to the Saviour	Jn. 1:40
• Was tested by Christ during the feeding of the 5,000	Jn. 6:12-22

CHART # 14

SUBJECT

THE TWELVE APOSTLES OF JESUS CHRIST (Part Two)

SPECIFICS

JOHN

EVENT	REFERENCE
• A fisherman and brother of James	Mt. 4:21
• Was the most prominent Apostle, and a member of the "Key Three"	Mt. 17:1-4
• Was an original disciple of John the Baptist	Jn. 1:35
• Was gently rebuked by Christ for his sectarianism on one occasion	Lk.9:49-50
• Asked Christ for a special place of honor in the millennium	Mk. 10:35
• Demonstrated vindictiveness on one occasion	Lk.9:54
• Helped prepare for the Last Supper	Lk.22:8
• Leaned on the bosom of Christ during the Last Supper	Jn. 13:23
• With Peter, he followed Christ afar off	Jn. 18:26
• Was the only Apostle present at the cross	Jn. 19:26
• Assumed the responsibility of taking care of Mary	Jn. 19:27
• Visited the empty tomb along with Peter	Jn. 20:2, 3
• Was present during the last miracle of Christ	Jn. 21:7, 23

JAMES

EVENT	REFERENCE
• Brother of John, and fishing partners with Peter and Andrew	Mt. 4:21
• Was nicknamed "A Son of Thunder" by Christ	Mk. 3:17
• Was the first Apostle to be martyred	Acts 12:1-2

PHILIP

EVENT	REFERENCE
• Brought Nathanael to Christ	Jn. 1:40-46
• Had his faith tested during the feeding of the 5,000	Jn. 6:5-7
• Was approached by some Greeks who desired to see Jesus	Jn. 12:20-22
• Asked Christ to show him the Father	Jn. 14:8-9

THE TWELVE APOSTLES OF JESUS CHRIST (Part Three)

SPECIFICS

NATHANAEL (also called) BARTHOLOMEW

EVENT	REFERENCE
• Was witnessed to under a fig tree by Philip	Jn. 1:45, 46
• First to call Christ Son of God and King of Israel	Jn. 1:49
• Hears Christ's first prediction (The Ascension)	Jn. 1:51
• Was present during Christ's final miracle	Jn. 21:2

MATTHEW (also called) LEVI

EVENT	REFERENCE
• Was a Publican tax collector	Lk.5:27
• Responds to Christ after a simple "Follow Me" invitation	Mt. 9:9
• Hosted a large feast and shared his new faith	Lk.5:27-29

THADDAEUS (also called) JUDE

EVENT	REFERENCE
• Brother of James the Less	Mk. 15:40
• Asked Christ how he would manifest Himself	Jn. 14:22

JAMES THE LESS

EVENT	REFERENCE
• Title may refer to his size	Mk. 15:40

SIMON THE ZEALOT

EVENT	REFERENCE
• Member of a right-wing political party called the Zealots	Mt. 10:4; Mk. 3:18

CHART # 16

SUBJECT

THE TWELVE APOSTLES OF JESUS CHRIST (Part Four)

SPECIFICS

THOMAS

EVENT	REFERENCE
* Was a twin	Jn. 11:16
* Despaired at Christ's decision to raise Lazarus	Jn. 11:16
* Asked Christ where he was going in Upper Room	Jn. 14:5
* Absent during first resurrection appearance in Upper Room	Jn. 20:24
* Felt he could not believe unless he saw and touched Christ	Jn. 20:25
* Fell at his feet after seeing Christ a week later	Jn. 20:28
* Was present during Christ's final miracle	Jn. 21:2

JUDAS ISCARIOT

EVENT	REFERENCE
* Thought to be only Apostle from Judea	
* Was a treasurer for the group	Jn. 12:6
* Was a heartless thief	Jn. 12:4-6
* Given over to Satan even at beginning of ministry	Jn. 6:70-71
* Agreed to betray Christ for 30 pieces of silver	Mt. 26:15, 16
* Allows Satan to actually enter into him	Lk.22:3; Jn. 13:27
* Dipped the sop with Christ in the Upper Room	Jn. 13:26-30
* Led soldiers to Gethsemane to arrest Christ	Jn. 18:2-4
* Betrayed Saviour with a kiss	Mt. 26:49
* In great remorse he later returned his blood money	Mt. 27:3, 4
* Went out and hanged himself	Mt. 27:5
* Will possibly be the coming Antichrist	Jn. 17:12; 2 Th. 2:3

SOME KEY INDIVIDUALS WHO MET WITH CHRIST (Part One)

SPECIFICS

1	**CREDENTIALS OF NICODEMUS**	**2**	**CONFESSION OF NICODEMUS**

CREDENTIALS OF NICODEMUS

* He was a Pharisee
* He was a member of the Sanhedrin
* He was a respected religious teacher

CONFESSION OF NICODEMUS

²The same came to Jesus by night, and said unto him, Rabbi, we know that thou art a teacher come from God: for no man can do these miracles that thou doest, except God be with him (Jn. 3:2).

3	**COMMAND TO NICODEMUS**	**4**	**CONFUSION OF NICODEMUS**

COMMAND TO NICODEMUS

³Jesus answered and said unto him, Verily, verily, I say unto thee, Except a man be born again, he cannot see the kingdom of God (Jn. 3:3).

CONFUSION OF NICODEMUS

⁴Nicodemus saith unto him, How can a man be born when he is old? can he enter the second time into his mother's womb, and be born? (Jn. 3:4)

5	**CHASTENING OF NICODEMUS**	**6**	**CLARIFICATION FOR NICODEMUS**

CHASTENING OF NICODEMUS

¹⁰Jesus answered and said unto him, Art thou a master of Israel, and knowest not these things? (Jn. 3:10)

CLARIFICATION FOR NICODEMUS

Jesus Employs Illustrations

* A physical illustration (3:5-7)
* A natural illustration (3:8)
* A scriptural illustration (3:14,15)

7	**CONCLUSION FOR NICODEMUS**	**8**	**CONVERSION OF NICODEMUS**

CONCLUSION FOR NICODEMUS

Jesus now speaks both the most important and greatest verse in all the Bible

* It is the most important verse, because it contains the gospel in a nutshell

* It is the greatest verse, because it contains nine of the most profound truths ever recorded

  1. *"For God"* - The greatest Person
  2. *"So loved the world"* - The greatest truth
  3. *"That he gave"* - The greatest act
  4. *"His only begotten Son"* - The greatest gift
  5. *"That whosoever"* - The greatest number
  6. *"Believeth in him"* - The greatest invitation
  7. *"Should not perish"* - The greatest promise
  8. *"But have"* - The greatest certainty
  9. *"Everlasting life"* - The greatest destiny
     (Jn. 3:16)

CONVERSION OF NICODEMUS

Did Nicodemus accept Christ? Two later instances strongly suggest that he did.

* **First Occasion** (Jn. 7:50-51)
  ⁵⁰Nicodemus saith unto them, (he that came to Jesus by night, being one of them,) ⁵¹Doth our law judge any man, before it hear him, and know what he doeth?

* **Second Occasion** (Jn. 19:38-42)
  ³⁸And after this Joseph of Arimathaea, being a disciple of Jesus, but secretly for fear of the Jews, besought Pilate that he might take away the body of Jesus: and Pilate gave him leave. He came therefore, and took the body of Jesus. ³⁹And there came also Nicodemus, which at the first came to Jesus by night, and brought a mixture of myrrh and aloes, about an hundred pound weight. ⁴⁰Then took they the body of Jesus, and wound it in linen clothes with the spices, as the manner of the Jews is to bury. ⁴¹Now in the place where he was crucified there was a garden; and in the garden a new sepulchre, wherein was never man yet laid. ⁴²There laid they Jesus therefore because of the Jews' preparation day; for the sepulchre was nigh at hand.

THE SAVIOR AND NICODEMUS (JN. 3:1-21)

CHART # 18

SOME KEY INDIVIDUALS WHO MET WITH CHRIST (Part Two)

SPECIFICS

THE SAVIOR AND THE SAMARITAN WOMAN (JN. 4:1-42)

1

The Savior At Sychar (4:1-6)
Jesus Leaves Judea For Galilee

- Why he leaves (4:1-3): He departs to avoid a popularity contest between himself and John.
- Where he stops (4:4-6): He rests beside Jacob's well at Sychar, a town in Samaria.

2

The Sinner From Sychar (4:7-27)
A Samaritan Woman Comes To The Well For Water

THE CONTACT

- Jesus' request (4:7-8): He asks her for a drink
- Her response (4:9): She wants to know why he, a Jew, is even talking to her, a Samaritan!

THE CONTRASTS

JESUS CONTRASTS LIQUID WATER WITH LIVING WATER	JESUS CONTRASTS RITUAL WORSHIP WITH REAL WORSHIP
13Jesus answered and said unto her, Whosoever drinketh of this water shall thirst again: 14But whosoever drinketh of the water that I shall give him shall never thirst; but the water that I shall give him shall be in him a well of water springing up into everlasting life (Jn. 4:13-14).	*23But the hour cometh, and now is, when the true worshippers shall worship the Father in spirit and in truth: for the Father seeketh such to worship him. 24God is a Spirit: and they that worship him must worship him in spirit and in truth (Jn. 4:23-24).*

3

The Soul Winner In Sychar (4:28-42)
Note The Faithfulness And Fruitfulness Of The Samaritan Woman

HER FAITHFULNESS	HER FRUITFULNESS
25The woman saith unto him, I know that Messias cometh, which is called Christ: when he is come, he will tell us all things. 26Jesus saith unto her, I that speak unto thee am he. 28The woman then left her waterpot, and went her way into the city, and saith to the men, 29Come, see a man, which told me all things that ever I did: is not this the Christ? (Jn. 4:25-26,28-29)	*39And many of the Samaritans of that city believed on him for the saying of the woman, which testified, He told me all that ever I did (Jn. 4:39).*

CHART # 19

	SUBJECT	

SOME KEY INDIVIDUALS WHO MET WITH CHRIST (Part Three)

	SPECIFICS	

THE SAVIOR, AN ADULTEROUS WOMAN AND TWO SISTERS

THE ADULTEROUS WOMAN (JOHN 8:1-11)

The Connivers
- The accusers (8:3a): A group of Jewish leaders approaches Jesus
- The accused (8:3b-4): They put before him a woman caught in the act of adultery!

The Conniving
- What they say (8:5): *"The law of Moses says to stone her. What do you say?"*
- Why they said it (8:6a): They want him to say something they can use against him

The Convictor
- What Jesus does (8:6b-8): Twice he bends down and writes in the dust
- What Jesus says (8:7): *"Let those who have never sinned throw the first stones!"*

The Convicted
- They all walk away in shame (8:9)

The Cleansed
- No earthly condemnation (8:10): Her accusers have disappeared
- No heavenly condemnation (8:11): Jesus tells her to go and sin no more

THE TWO SISTERS (LK.10:38-42)

Jesus Visits The Home Of Mary And Martha

- The complaint by Martha (10:38-40)

  1. The diligent student (10:38-39): Mary sits at Jesus' feet, listening to everything he says
  2. The dutiful servant (10:41-42): He tells Martha she must first be ministered to by the Savior before she can effectively minister for the Savior

CHART # 20

SUBJECT

SOME KEY INDIVIDUALS WHO MET WITH CHRIST (Part Four)

SPECIFICS

THE SAVIOR, A RICH YOUNG RULER AND A TAX COLLECTOR

THE RICH YOUNG RULER (MT. 19:16-26)

JESUS AND THE RULER

* The seeking ruler (19:16-21)
    1. The ruler's confusion (19:16): "*What good things must I do to have eternal life?*"
    2. The Savior's clarification (19:17): "*Keep the commandments!*"
    3. The ruler's confirmation (19:18-20): "*I've obeyed all these commandments.*"
    4. The Savior's conclusion (19:21): "*If you want to be perfect, go and sell all you have and give the money to the poor.... Then come, follow me*".
* The sorrowing ruler (19:22): He turns away with sadness, not willing to give up his wealth

JESUS AND THE DISCIPLES

* The allegory (19:23-24): Jesus says it is easier for a camel to go through the eye of a needle than for a rich man to enter heaven
* The amazement (19:25): The disciples ask who can possibly be saved
* The assurance (19:26): Jesus says with God all things are possible

THE TAX COLLECTOR (LUKE 19:1-10)

ZACCHAEUS THE SINNER

* He is a wealthy tax collector (19:1, 2)

ZACCHAEUS THE SEEKER

* The source of his problem (19:3): He is too short to see Jesus over the crowds!
* The solution to his problem (19:4): He climbs up into a sycamore tree

ZACCHAEUS THE SOUGHT

* Savior's request (19:5): Jesus sees him and says: "*Quick, come down! For I must be a guest in your home today*"
* The tax collector's response (19:6): He comes down and welcomes Jesus gladly!
* The crowd's reaction (19:7): They complain that Jesus is associating with this notorious sinner

ZACCHAEUS THE SAVED

* As witnessed by his testimony (19:8)
    1. He will give half of his wealth to the poor (19:8a)
    2. He will restore fourfold any money to any person he has cheated (19:8b)
* As witnessed by Jesus' testimony (19:9-10): He says that Zacchaeus is indeed a saved man!

CHART # 21

SUBJECT

THE CONFESSION OF PETER AND THE CHURCH OF CHRIST (Mt. 16:13-23)

SPECIFICS

THE REQUEST INVOLVED

¹³When Jesus came into the coasts of Caesarea Philippi, he asked his disciples, saying, Whom do men say that I the Son of man am? (Mt. 16:13)

THE RUMORS INVOLVED

¹⁴And they said, Some say that thou art John the Baptist: some, Elias; and others, Jeremiah, or one of the prophets (Mt. 16:14).

THE RECOGNITION INVOLVED

¹⁵He saith unto them, But whom say ye that I am? ¹⁶And Simon Peter answered and said, Thou art the Christ, the Son of the living God (Mt. 16:15, 16)

THE REVELATIONS INVOLVED

- **From The Father, Regarding His Christ**
  ¹⁷And Jesus answered and said unto him, Blessed art thou, Simon Barjona: for flesh and blood hath not revealed it unto thee, but my Father which is in heaven (Mt. 16:17).
- **From The Son, Regarding His Church**
  ¹⁸And I say also unto thee, That thou art Peter, and upon this rock I will build my church; and the gates of hell shall not prevail against it. ¹⁹And I will give unto thee the keys of the kingdom of heaven: and whatsoever thou shalt bind on earth shall be bound in heaven: and whatsoever thou shalt loose on earth shall be loosed in heaven (Mt. 16:18-19).

THE RESTRICTION INVOLVED

²⁰Then charged he his disciples that they should tell no man that he was Jesus the Christ (Mt. 16:20).

THE REJECTION AND RESURRECTION INVOLVED

²¹From that time forth began Jesus to shew unto his disciples, how that he must go unto Jerusalem, and suffer many things of the elders and chief priests and scribes, and be killed, and be raised again the third day (Mt. 16:21).

THE REBUKES INVOLVED

- **Peter Rebukes Christ**
  ²²Then Peter took him, and began to rebuke him, saying, Be it far from thee, Lord: this shall not be unto thee. (Mt. 16:22)
- **Christ Rebukes Peter**
  ²³But he turned, and said unto Peter, Get thee behind me, Satan: thou art an offence unto me: for thou savourest not the things that be of God, but those that be of men (Mt. 16:23).

CHART # 22

	SUBJECT

THE TRANSFIGURATION OF CHRIST

	SPECIFICS

ASCENDING THE MOUNTAIN

- **The Anticipation Involved :** [1]*And he said unto them, Verily I say unto you, That there be some of them that stand here, which shall not taste of death, till they have seen the kingdom of God come with power* (Mk. 9:1).
- **The Apostles Involved:** [1]*And after six days Jesus taketh Peter, James, and John his brother, and bringeth them up into an high mountain apart* (Mt. 17:1).

ATOP THE MOUNTAIN

1	WHAT IS SEEN

- **The Transfiguration of The Messiah:** [2]*And was transfigured before them: and his face did shine as the sun, and his raiment was white as the light* (Mt. 17:2).
- **The Visitation of Two Men:** [30]*And, behold, there talked with him two men, which were Moses and Elias: Who appeared in glory, and spake of his decease which he should accomplish at Jerusalem* (Lk.9:30-31)

2	WHAT IS SAID

- [4]*Then answered Peter, and said unto Jesus, Lord, it is good for us to be here: if thou wilt, let us make here three tabernacles; one for thee, and one for Moses, and one for Elias* (Mt. 17:4).

3	WHAT IS HEARD

- [5]*While he yet spake, behold, a bright cloud overshadowed them: and behold a voice out of the cloud, which said, This is my beloved Son, in whom I am well pleased; hear ye him* (Mt. 17:5).

4	WHAT IS FELT

- **The Terror Of Their Hearts:** [6]*And when the disciples heard it, they fell on their face, and were sore afraid* (Mt. 17:6).
- **The Touch Of His Hand:** [7]*And Jesus came and touched them, and said, Arise, and be not afraid.* [8]*And when they had lifted up their eyes, they saw no man, save Jesus only* (Mt. 17:7-8).

DESCENDING THE MOUNTAIN

- **The Command:** [9]*And as they came down from the mountain, Jesus charged them, saying, Tell the vision to no man, until the Son of man be risen again from the dead* (Mt. 17:9).
- **The Confusion:** [10]*And his disciples asked him, saying, Why then say the scribes that Elias must first come?* (Mt. 17:10)
- **The Clarification:** [11]*And Jesus answered and said unto them, Elias truly shall first come, and restore all things.* [12]*But I say unto you, That Elias is come already, and they knew him not, but have done unto him whatsoever they listed. Likewise shall also the Son of man suffer of them* (Mt. 17:11-12).
- **The Comprehension:** [13]*Then the disciples understood that he spake unto them of John the Baptist* (Mt. 17:13).

THE ANOINTING OF JESUS BY MARY AND THE TRIUMPHAL ENTRY

SPECIFICS

SATURDAY: THE ANOINTING

1	THE PLACE

* A dinner in Bethany

5	THE POOR

[6]And Jesus said, Let her alone; why trouble ye her? she hath wrought a good work on me. [7]For ye have the poor with you always, and whensoever ye will ye may do them good: but me ye have not always (Mk. 14:6-7).

2	THE PEOPLE

* Jesus
* Simon the Leper
* Martha
* Lazarus
* Mary
* Judas

6	THE PREPARATION

[8]She hath done what she could: she is come aforehand to anoint my body to the burying (Mk. 14:8).

3	THE PERFUME

[3]Then took Mary a pound of ointment of spikenard, very costly, and anointed the feet of Jesus, and wiped his feet with her hair: and the house was filled with the odour of the ointment (Jn. 12:3).

7	THE PROPHECY

[9]Verily I say unto you, Wheresoever this gospel shall be preached throughout the whole world, this also that she hath done shall be spoken of for a memorial of her (Mk. 14:9).

4	THE PROTEST

[4]Then saith one of his disciples, Judas Iscariot, Simon's son, which should betray him, [5]Why was not this ointment sold for three hundred pence, and given to the poor? [6]This he said, not that he cared for the poor, but because he was a thief, and had the bag, and bare what was put therein (Jn. 12:4-6).

8	THE PLOT

[9]Much people of the Jews therefore knew that he was there: and they came not for Jesus' sake only, but that they might see Lazarus also, whom he had raised from the dead. [10]But the chief priests consulted that they might put Lazarus also to death; [11]Because that by reason of him many of the Jews went away, and believed on Jesus.

SUNDAY: THE TRIUMPHAL ENTRY

1	THE PREPARATION

* **The Men Involved:** [29]And it came to pass, when he was come nigh to Bethphage and Bethany, at the mount called the mount of Olives, he sent two of his disciples (Lk.19:29).
* **The Mission Involved:** [30]Saying, Go ye into the village over against you; in the which at your entering ye shall find a colt tied, whereon yet never man sat: loose him, and bring him hither. [31]And if any man ask you, Why do ye loose him? thus shall ye say unto him, Because the Lord hath need of him. [32]And they that were sent went their way, and found even as he had said unto them. [33]And as they were loosing the colt, the owners thereof said unto them, Why loose ye the colt? [34]And they said, The Lord hath need of him. [35]And they brought him to Jesus: and they cast their garments upon the colt, and they set Jesus thereon (Lk.19:30-35).

3	THE PARADE

[8]And a very great multitude spread their garments in the way; others cut down branches from the trees, and strawed them in the way. [9]And the multitudes that went before, and that followed, cried, saying, Hosanna to the Son of David: Blessed is he that cometh in the name of the Lord; Hosanna in the highest (Mt. 21:8-9).

4	THE PROTEST

[39]And some of the Pharisees from among the multitude said unto him, Master, rebuke thy disciples. [40]And he answered and said unto them, I tell you that, if these should hold their peace, the stones would immediately cry out (Lk.39-40).

5	THE PAIN

[41]And when he was come near, he beheld the city, and wept over it, [42]Saying, If thou hadst known, even thou, at least in this thy day, the things which belong unto thy peace! but now they are hid from thine eyes (Lk.19:41-42).

2	THE PROPHECY

[4]All this was done, that it might be fulfilled which was spoken by the prophet, saying, [5]Tell ye the daughter of Sion, Behold, thy King cometh unto thee, meek, and sitting upon an ass, and a colt the foal of an ass (Mt. 21:4-5).

6	THE PRAISES

[15]And when the chief priests and scribes saw the wonderful things that he did, and the children crying in the temple, and saying, Hosanna to the Son of David; they were sore displeased, [16]And said unto him, Hearest thou what these say? And Jesus saith unto them, Yea; have ye never read, Out of the mouth of babes and sucklings thou hast perfected praise? (Mt. 21:15-16)

CHART # 24

SUBJECT

THE CURSING OF THE FIG TREE AND THE SECOND TEMPLE CLEANSING

SPECIFICS

MONDAY: CURSING OF THE FIG TREE

THE REASON FOR THE FIG TREE VISIT

[18]Now in the morning as he returned into the city, he hungered (Mt. 21:18).

THE REACTION DURING THE FIG TREE VISIT

- **What Jesus Discovered:** *[13]And seeing a fig tree afar off having leaves, he came, if haply he might find any thing thereon: and when he came to it, he found nothing but leaves; for the time of figs was not yet* (Mk. 11:13).
- **What Jesus Did:** *[14]And Jesus answered and said unto it, No man eat fruit of thee hereafter for ever. And his disciples heard it* (Mk. 11:14).

THE RESULTS FROM THE FIG TREE VISIT

- **The Amazement Of The Apostles:** *[20]And when the disciples saw it, they marvelled, saying, How soon is the fig tree withered away!* (Mt. 21:20).
- **The Application By The Savior:** *[21]Jesus answered and said unto them, Verily I say unto you, If ye have faith, and doubt not, ye shall not only do this which is done to the fig tree, but also if ye shall say unto this mountain, Be thou removed, and be thou cast into the sea; it shall be done. [22]And all things, whatsoever ye shall ask in prayer, believing, ye shall receive* (Mt. 21:21-22).

MONDAY: SECOND TEMPLE CLEANSING

JESUS REMOVES THE MONEY TABLES FROM THE TEMPLE	JESUS REBUKES THE MONEY CHANGERS IN THE TEMPLE
- **The Severity Of His Act:** *[12]And Jesus went into the temple of God, and cast out all them that sold and bought in the temple, and overthrew the tables of the moneychangers, and the seats of them that sold doves* (Mt. 21:12). - **The Scope Of His Act:** *[16]And would not suffer that any man should carry any vessel through the temple* (Mk. 11:16).	- **The Prophecy Involved:** *[13]And said unto them, It is written, My house shall be called the house of prayer; but ye have made it a den of thieves* (Mt. 21:13). - **The Plot Involved:** *[18]And the scribes and chief priests heard it, and sought how they might destroy him: for they feared him, because all the people was astonished at his doctrine* (Mk. 11:18).

CHART # 25

MONDAY: THE REQUEST BY SOME GREEKS TO VISIT WITH JESUS

SPECIFICS

1	**JESUS AND TWO APOSTLES**

[20]*And there were certain Greeks among them that came up to worship at the feast:* [21]*The same came therefore to Philip, which was of Bethsaida of Galilee, and desired him, saying, Sir, we would see Jesus.* [22]*Philip cometh and telleth Andrew: and again Andrew and Philip tell Jesus.* [23]*And Jesus answered them, saying, The hour is come, that the Son of man should be glorified.* [24]*Verily, verily, I say unto you, Except a corn of wheat fall into the ground and die, it abideth alone: but if it die, it bringeth forth much fruit.* [25]*He that loveth his life shall lose it; and he that hateth his life in this world shall keep it unto life eternal.* [26]*If any man serve me, let him follow me; and where I am, there shall also my servant be: if any man serve me, him will my Father honour* (Jn. 12:20-26).

2	**JESUS AND HIS FATHER**

[27]*Now is my soul troubled; and what shall I say? Father, save me from this hour but for this cause came I unto this hour.* [28]*Father, glorify thy name. Then came there a voice from heaven, saying, I have both glorified it, and will glorify it again. The people therefore, that stood by, and heard it, said that it thundered: others said, An angel spake to him.* [30]*Jesus answered and said, This voice came not because of me, but for your sakes* (Jn. 12:27-30).

3	**JESUS AND THE DEVIL**

[31]*Now is the judgment of this world: now shall the prince of this world be cast out* (Jn. 12:31).

4	**JESUS AND THE CROSS**

[32]*And I, if I be lifted up from the earth, will draw all men unto me.* [33]*This he said, signifying what death he should die* (Jn. 12:32-33).

5	**JESUS AND THE PASSOVER CROWD**

[34]*The people answered him, We have heard out of the law that Christ abideth for ever- and how sayest thou, The Son of man must be lifted up? who is this Son of man?* [35]*Then Jesus said unto them, Yet a little while is the light with you. Walk while ye have the light, lest darkness come upon you: for he that walketh in darkness knoweth not whither he goeth.* [36]*While ye have light, believe in the light, that ye may be the children of light. These things spake Jesus, and departed, and did hide himself from them* (Jn. 12:34-36).

6	**JESUS AND THE PROPHET ISAIAH**

[37]*But though he had done so many miracles before them, yet they believed not on him:* [38]*That the saying of Esaias the prophet might be fulfilled, which he spake, Lord, who hath believed our report? and to whom hath the arm of the Lord been revealed?* [39]*Therefore they could not believe, because that Esaias said again,* [40]*He hath blinded their eyes, and hardened their heart; that they should not see with their eyes, nor understand with their heart, and be converted, and I should heal them.* [41]*These things said Esaias, when he saw his glory, and spake of him* (Jn. 12:37-41).

7	**JESUS AND SOME JEWISH LEADERS**

[42]*Nevertheless among the chief rulers also many believed on him; but because of the Pharisees they did not confess him, lest they should be put out of the synagogue:* [43]*For they loved the praise of men more than the praise of God* (Jn. 12:42-43).

8	**JESUS AND ALL MEN**

[44]*Jesus cried and said, He that believeth on me, believeth not on me, but on him that sent me.* [45]*And he that seeth me seeth him that sent me.* [46]*I am come a light into the world, that whosoever believeth on me should not abide in darkness.* [47]*And if any man hear my words, and believe not, I judge him not: for I came not to judge the world, but to save the world.* [48]*He that rejecteth me, and receiveth not my words, hath one that judgeth him: the word that I have spoken, the same shall judge him in the last day.* [49]*For I have not spoken of myself; but the Father which sent me, he gave me a commandment, what I should say, and what I should speak.* [50]*And I know that his commandment is life everlasting: whatsoever .I speak therefore, even as the Father said unto me, so I speak* (Jn. 12:44-50).

CHART # 26

TUESDAY: CHRIST'S CONFRONTATIONS WITH
THE PHARISEES AND SADDUCEES (Part One)

SPECIFICS

	1	THE DEMAND	2	THE DEFENSE
REGARDING HIS AUTHORITY		*23And when he was come into the temple, the chief priests and the elders of the people came unto him as he was teaching, and said, By what authority doest thou these things? and who gave thee this authority? (Mt. 21:23)*		*29And Jesus answered and said unto them, I will also ask of you one question, and answer me, and I will tell you by what authority I do these things. 30The baptism of John, was it from heaven, or of men? answer me. Mk. 11:29-30).*
	3	THE DILEMMA	4	THE DEFEAT
		5And they reasoned with themselves, saying, If we shall say, From heaven; he will say, Why then believed ye him not? 6But and if we say, Of men; all the people will stone us: for they be persuaded that John was a prophet (Lk.20:5-6).		*7And they answered, that they could not tell whence it was. 8And Jesus said unto them, Neither tell I you by what authority I do these things (Lk.20:7-8).*

	1	THE DECEIT	2	THE DENUNCIATION
REGARDING THE PAYING OF TRIBUTE		*15Then went the Pharisees, and took counsel how they might entangle him in his talk. 16And they sent out unto him their disciples with the Herodians, saying, Master, we know that thou art true, and teachest the way of God in truth, neither carest thou for any man: for thou regardest not the person of men. 17Tell us therefore, What thinkest thou? Is it lawful to give tribute unto Caesar, or not? (Mt. 22:15-17)*		*18But Jesus perceived their wickedness, and said, Why tempt ye me, ye hypocrites? (Mt. 22:18)*
	3	THE DEMAND	4	THE DEFEAT
		19Shew me the tribute money. And they brought unto him a penny. 20And he saith unto them, Whose is this image and superscription? (Mt. 22:19-20)		*21They say unto him, Caesar's. Then saith he unto them, Render therefore unto Caesar the things which are Caesar's; and unto God the things that are God's. 22When they had heard these words, they marvelled, and left him, and went their way (Mt. 22:21-22).*

		THE CONFRONTATION BY THE SADDUCEES: (MT. 22:24-28)	THE CLARIFICATION TO THE SADDUCEES
REGARDING THE RESURRECTION	**THEIR SILLY EXAMPLE**	Seven brothers married the same woman after the previous one had died. In the resurrection, whose wife would she be?	**Regarding The Glory Of The Resurrection:** *30For in the resurrection they neither marry, nor are given in marriage, but are as the angels of God in heaven (Mt. 22:30).*
	THEIR SERIOUS ERROR	**They Were Intolerant:** *23The same day came to him the Sadducees, which say that there is no resurrection, and asked him (Mt. 22:23).* **They Were Ignorant:** *29Jesus answered and said unto them, Ye do err, not knowing the scriptures, nor the power of God (Mt. 22:29).*	**Regarding The God Of The Resurrection:** *26And as touching the dead, that they rise: have ye not read in the book of Moses, how in the bush God spake unto him, saying, I am the God of Abraham, and the God of Isaac, and the God of Jacob? 27He is not the God of the dead, but the God of the living: ye therefore do greatly err (Mk. 12:26-27).*

TUESDAY: CHRIST'S CONFRONTATIONS
WITH THE PHARISEES AND SADDUCEES (Part Two)

SPECIFICS

A LAWYER AND THE COMMANDS OF GOD	A LAWYER AND THE KINGDOM OF GOD

REGARDING THE GREATEST COMMANDMENT

What The Lawyer Asked	[32]*And the scribe said unto him, Well, Master, thou hast said the truth: for there is one God; and there is none other but he:* [33]*And to love him with all the heart, and with all the understanding, and with all the soul, and with all the strength, and to love his neighbour as himself, is more than all whole burnt offerings and sacrifices.* [34]*And when Jesus saw that he answered discreetly, he said unto him, Thou art not far from the kingdom of God. And no man after that durst ask him any question* (Mk. 12:32-34).
[28]*And one of the scribes came, and having heard them reasoning together, and perceiving that he had answered them well, asked him, Which is the first commandment of all?* (Mk. 12:28)	
How The Savior Answered	

- **The Identity Of The Two Greatest Commands:** [37]*Jesus said unto him, Thou shalt love the Lord thy God with all thy heart, and with all thy soul, and with all thy mind.* [38]*This is the first and great commandment.* [39]*And the second is like unto it, Thou shalt love thy neighbour as thyself* (Mt. 22:37-39).

- **The Importance Of The Two Greatest Commands:** [40]*On these two commandments hang all the law and the prophets* (Mt. 22:40).

REGARDING THE IDENTITY OF THE MESSIAH

[41]*While the Pharisees were gathered together, Jesus asked them,* [42]*Saying, What think ye of Christ? whose son is he? They say unto him, The Son of David.* [43]*He saith unto them, How then doth David in spirit call him Lord, saying,* [44]*The LORD said unto my Lord, Sit thou on my right hand, till I make thine enemies thy footstool?* [45]*If David then call him Lord, how is he his son?* [46]*And no man was able to answer him a word, neither durst any man from that day forth ask him any more questions* (Mt. 22:41-46).

- **Jesus Points Out That The Messiah Is David's Son, Thus Affirming The Messiah's Humanity.** [41]While *the Pharisees were gathered together, Jesus asked them,* [42]*Saying, What think ye of Christ? whose son is he? They say unto him, The Son of David.* (Mt. 22:41-42)

- **Jesus Points Out The Fact That The Messiah Is Also David's Lord, Thus Affirming The Messiah's Deity.** [43]*He saith unto them, How then doth David in spirit call him Lord, saying,* [44]*The LORD said unto my Lord, Sit thou on my right hand, till I make thine enemies thy footstool?* [45]*If David then call him Lord, how is he his son?* [46]*And no man was able to answer him a word, neither durst any man from that day forth ask him any more questions.* (Mt. 22:43-46)

CHART # 28

SUBJECT

TUESDAY: JESUS BOTH PUBLICLY AND PRIVATELY CONDEMNS THE SCRIBES AND PHARISEES

SPECIFICS

PUBLIC CONDEMNATION (MT. 23:1-12)

1	The Wickedness Of These Men (Mt. 23:1-7)

- They do not practice what they preach (23:1-3)
- The place heavy burdens upon the people (23:4)
- They do everything for show (23:5, 7)
- They demand to occupy the place of prominence (23:6)

2	The Warning Against These Men (Mt. 23:8-12)

Jesus warns that whoever exalts himself will be humbled, and the one who humbles himself will be exalted!

PRIVATE CONDEMNATION (MT. 23:13-36)

THEIR PERVERSIONS AGAINST GOD (MT. 23:13-32)

1 First Transgression	**5 Fifth Transgression**
[13]*But woe unto you, scribes and Pharisees, hypocrites! for ye shut up the kingdom of heaven against men: for ye neither go in yourselves, neither suffer ye them that are entering to go in* (Mt. 23:13).	[23]*Woe unto you, scribes and Pharisees, hypocrites! for ye pay tithe of mint and anise and cummin, and have omitted the weightier matters of the law, judgment, mercy, and faith: these ought ye to have done, and not to leave the other undone.* [24]*Ye blind guides, which strain at a gnat, and swallow a camel* (Mt. 23:23-24).
2 Second Transgression	**6 Sixth Transgression**
[14]*Woe unto you, scribes and Pharisees, hypocrites! for ye devour widows' houses, and for a pretence make long prayer: therefore ye shall receive the greater damnation* (Mt. 23:14).	[25]*Woe unto you, scribes and Pharisees, hypocrites! for ye make clean the outside of the cup and of the platter, but within they are full of extortion and excess* (Mt. 23:25).
3 Third Transgression	**7 Seventh Transgression**
[15]*Woe unto you, scribes and Pharisees, hypocrites! for ye compass sea and land to make one proselyte, and when he is made, ye make him twofold more the child of hell than yourselves* (Mt. 23:15).	[27]*Woe unto you, scribes and Pharisees, hypocrites! for ye are like unto whited sepulchres, which indeed appear beautiful outward, but are within full of dead men's bones, and of all uncleanness* (Mt. 23:27).
4 Fourth Transgression	**8 Eighth Transgression**
[16]*Woe unto you, ye blind guides, which say, Whosoever shall swear by the temple, it is nothing; but whosoever shall swear by the gold of the temple, he is a debtor!* (Mt. 23:16)	[29]*Woe unto you, scribes and Pharisees, hypocrites! because ye build the tombs of the prophets, and garnish the sepulchres of the righteous,* [30]*And say, If we had been in the days of our fathers, we would not have been partakers with them in the blood of the prophets.* [31]*Wherefore ye be witnesses unto yourselves, that ye are the children of them which killed the prophets* (Mt. 23:29-31).

THEIR PUNISHMENT FROM GOD (MT. 23:33-36)

[33]*Ye serpents, ye generation of vipers, how can ye escape the damnation of hell?* [34]*Wherefore, behold, I send unto you prophets, and wise men, and scribes: and some of them ye shall kill and crucify; and some of them shall ye scourge in your synagogues, and persecute them from city to city:* [35]*That upon you may come all the righteous blood shed upon the earth, from the blood of righteous Abel unto the blood of Zacharias son of Barachias, whom ye slew between the temple and the altar.* [36]*Verily I say unto you, All these things shall come upon this generation* (Mt. 23:33-36).

TUESDAY: JESUS COMMENDS A POOR WIDOW, WEEPS OVER JERUSALEM AND DELIVERS HIS MT. OLIVET DISCOURSE

SPECIFICS

THE POOR WIDOW

- **When A Lot Was A Little:** *41And Jesus sat over against the treasury, and beheld how the people cast money into the treasury: and many that were rich cast in much* (Mk. 12:41).

- **When A Little Was A Lot:** *42And there came a certain poor widow, and she threw in two mites, which make a farthing. 43And he called unto him his disciples, and saith unto them, Verily I say unto you, That this poor widow hath cast more in, than all they which have cast into the treasury: 44For all they did cast in of their abundance; but she of her want did cast in all that she had, even all her living* (Mk. 12:42-44).

THE TEARS OVER JERUSALEM

- **The Desire** - What Jesus wants to do (23:37a): To gather and protect Israel

- **The Denial** - What Jesus could not do (23:37b): He had been rejected by Israel

- **The Desolation** - What Jesus must do (23:38-39): To remove His presence from Israel until The Great Tribulation

CONTENTS IN THE MT. OLIVET DISCOURSE

THE TWO PREDICTIONS

| 1 | The Great Tribulation |

- **The First Half (Mt. 24:1-8):** *8All these are the beginning of sorrows* (Mt. 24:8)

- **The Second Half (Mt. 24:9-28):** *21For then shall be great tribulation, such as was not since the beginning of the world to this time, no, nor ever shall be* (Mt. 24:21)

| 2 | The Second Coming |

- **The Return Of Christ (Mt. 24:29-30):** *30And then shall appear the sign of the Son of man in heaven: and then shall all the tribes of the earth mourn, and they shall see the Son of man coming in the clouds of heaven with power and great glory* (Mt. 24:30).

- **The Re-Gathering Of Israel (Mt. 24:31):** *31And he shall send his angels with a great sound of a trumpet, and they shall gather together his elect from the four winds, from one end of heaven to the other* (Mt. 24:31).

THE FIVE PARABLES

ONE	TWO	THREE	FOUR	FIVE
The Fig Tree	The Wise And Foolish Servant	The Ten Virgins	The Ten Talents	The Sheep And Goats
(Mt. 24:32-35)	(Mt. 24:36-51)	(Mt. 25:1-13)	(Mt. 25:14-30)	(Mt. 25:31-46)

CHART # 30

SUBJECT

WEDNESDAY: THE PREDICTIONS BY JESUS AND THE PLOTS AGAINST JESUS

SPECIFICS

THE PREDICTIONS

JESUS PREDICTED HIS SUFFERINGS, DEATH, AND RESURRECTION ON FOUR KEY OCCASIONS

1	**After Peter's Confession**	2	**After His Transfiguration**
[21]From that time forth began Jesus to shew unto his disciples, how that he must go unto Jerusalem, and suffer many things of the elders and chief priests and scribes, and be killed, and be raised again the third day (Mt. 16:21).		*[22]And while they abode in Galilee, Jesus said unto them, The Son of man shall be betrayed into the hands of men: [23]And they shall kill him, and the third day he shall be raised again. And they were exceeding sorry* (Mt. 17:22-23).	
3	**Just Prior To The Final Week**	4	**Wednesday Of The Final Week**
[17]And Jesus going up to Jerusalem took the twelve disciples apart in the way, and said unto them, [18]Behold, we go up to Jerusalem; and the Son of man shall be betrayed unto the chief priests and unto the scribes, and they shall condemn him to death, [19]And shall deliver him to the Gentiles to mock, and to scourge, and to crucify him: and the third day he shall rise again (Mt. 20:17-19).		*[1]And it came to pass, when Jesus had finished all these sayings, he said unto his disciples, [2]Ye know that after two days is the feast of the passover, and the Son of man is betrayed to be crucified* (Mt. 26:1-2).	

THE PLOTS

JESUS IS PLOTTED AGAINST ON TWO KEY OCCASIONS

* **The Plot By The Jewish Rulers:** *[3]Then assembled together the chief priests, and the scribes, and the elders of the people, unto the palace of the high priest, who was called Caiaphas, [4]And consulted that they might take Jesus by subtilty, and kill him. [5]But they said, Not on the feast day, lest there be an uproar among the people* (Mt. 26:3-5).

* **The Plot By The Traitor:** *[3]Then entered Satan into Judas surnamed Iscariot, being of the number of the twelve.* (Lk.22:3) *[14]Then one of the twelve, called Judas Iscariot, went unto the chief priests, [15]And said unto them, What will ye give me, and I will deliver him unto you? [16]And they covenanted with him for thirty pieces of silver. And from that time he sought opportunity to betray him* (Mt. 26:14-16).

THURSDAY: JESUS' FINAL PASSOVER (Part One)

SPECIFICS

THE PREPARATION

7Then came the day of unleavened bread, when the passover must be killed. 8And he sent Peter and John, saying, Go and prepare us the passover, that we may eat. 9And they said unto him, Where wilt thou that we prepare? 10And he said unto them, Behold, when ye are entered into the city, there shall a man meet you, bearing a pitcher of water; follow him into the house where he entereth in. 11And ye shall say unto the goodman of the house, The Master saith unto thee, Where is the guestchamber, where I shall eat the passover with my disciples? 12And he shall shew you a large upper room furnished: there make ready. 13And they went, and found as he had said unto them: and they made ready the passover (Lk.22:7-13).

THE CELEBRATION

EVENTS PRECEDING THE LORD'S SUPPER

1	The Love	2	The Desire
1Now before the feast of the passover, when Jesus knew that his hour was come that he should depart out of this world unto the Father, having loved his own which were in the world, he loved them unto the end (Jn. 13:1).		*14And when the hour was come, he sat down, and the twelve apostles with him. 15And he said unto them, With desire I have desired to eat this passover with you before I suffer: 16For I say unto you, I will not any more eat thereof, until it be fulfilled in the kingdom of God (Lk.22:14-16).*	

3	The Dispute	4	The Gentle Rebuke
24And there was also a strife among them, which of them should be accounted the greatest (Lk.22:24).		*25And he said unto them, The kings of the Gentiles exercise lordship over them; and they that exercise authority upon them are called benefactors. 26But ye shall not be so: but he that is greatest among you, let him be as the younger; and he that is chief, as he that doth serve (Lk.22:25-26).*	

5	The Promise	6	The Example
28Ye are they which have continued with me in my temptations. 29And I appoint unto you a kingdom, as my Father hath appointed unto me; 30That ye may eat and drink at my table in my kingdom, and sit on thrones judging the twelve tribes of Israel (Lk.22:28-30).		*3Jesus knowing that the Father had given all things into his hands, and that he was come from God, and went to God; 4He riseth from supper, and laid aside his garments; and took a towel, and girded himself. 5After that he poureth water into a bason, and began to wash the disciples' feet, and to wipe them with the towel wherewith he was girded (Jn. 13:3-5).*	

7	The Announcement	8	The Question
21And as they did eat, he said, Verily I say unto you, that one of you shall betray me (Mt. 26:21).		*22Then the disciples looked one on another, doubting of whom he spake. 23Now there was leaning on Jesus' bosom one of his disciples, whom Jesus loved. 24Simon Peter therefore beckoned to him, that he should ask who it should be of whom he spake. 25He then lying on Jesus' breast saith unto him, Lord, who is it? (Jn. 13:22-25)*	

9	The Answer	10	The Traitor
6Jesus answered, He it is, to whom I shall give a sop, when I have dipped it. And when he had dipped the sop, he gave it to Judas Iscariot, the son of Simon (Jn. 13:26).		*2And supper being ended, the devil having now put into the heart of Judas Iscariot, Simon's son, to betray him; 27And after the sop Satan entered into him. Then said Jesus unto him, That thou doest; do quickly. 28Now no man at the table knew for what intent he spake this unto him. 29For some of them thought, because Judas had the bag, that Jesus had said unto him, Buy those things that we have need of against the feast; or, that he should give something to the poor. 30He then having received the sop went immediately out: and it was night (Jn. 13:2, 27-30).*	

CHART # 32

SUBJECT

THURSDAY: JESUS' FINAL PASSOVER   (Part Two)

SPECIFICS

1	**EVENTS DURNING THE LORD'S SUPPER**

The Pattern

- **Jesus Holds Up The Bread Representing His Body:** *26And as they were eating, Jesus took bread, and blessed it, and brake it, and gave it to the disciples, and said, Take, eat; this is my body. 27And he took the cup, and gave thanks, and gave it to them, saying, Drink ye all of it* (Mt. 26:26-27).
- **Jesus Holds Up The Cup, Representing His Blood:** *28For this is my blood of the new testament, which is shed for many for the remission of sins.* (Mt. 26:28)

The Prediction

29But I say unto you, I will not drink henceforth of this fruit of the vine, until that day when I drink it new with you in my Father's kingdom (Mt. 26:29).

2	**EVENTS FOLLOWING THE LORD'S SUPPER**

The Bad News	The Good News

THE CELEBRATION

The Bad News

- **He Said All Would Desert Him:** *31Then saith Jesus unto them, All ye shall be offended because of me this night: for it is written, I will smite the shepherd, and the sheep of the flock shall be scattered abroad. 32But after I am risen again, I will go before you into Galilee* (Mt. 26:31-32).

- **He Said One Would Deny Him:** *33Peter answered and said unto him, Though all men shall be offended because of thee, yet will I never be offended. 34Jesus said unto him, Verily I say unto thee, That this night, before the cock crow, thou shalt deny me thrice. 35Peter said unto him, Though I should die with thee, yet will I not deny thee. Likewise also said all the disciples* (Mt. 26:33-35).

The Good News

JESUS ASSURES HIS DISCIPLES

1Let not your heart be troubled: ye believe in God, believe also in me. 2In my Father's house are many mansions: if it were not so, I would have told you. I go to prepare a place for you. 3And if I go and prepare a place for you, I will come again, and receive you unto myself; that where I am, there ye may be also. 27Peace I leave with you, my peace I give unto you: not as the world giveth, give I unto you. Let not your heart be troubled, neither let it be afraid (Jn. 14:1-3, 27).

JESUS ANSWERS HIS DISCIPLES

- ***Thomas:*** *"How can we know the way?"*
- ***Jesus:*** *6Jesus saith unto him, I am the way, the truth, and the life: no man cometh unto the Father, but by* me (Jn. 14:6).

- **Philip:** *"Show us the Father."*
- ***Jesus:*** *"He that hath seen me hath seen the Father."*

- **Judas (NOT ISCARIOT):** *22Judas saith unto him, not Iscariot, Lord, how is it that thou wilt manifest thyself unto us, and not unto the world?* (Jn. 14:22)
- **Jesus:** *23Jesus answered and said unto him, If a man love me, he will keep my words: and my Father will love him, and we will come unto him, and make our abode with him* (Jn. 14:23).

FRIDAY: JESUS' DISCOURSE ON FUTURE TRIBULATION AND THE EVER PRESENT TRINITY

SPECIFICS

HE SPOKE OF THE TRIBULATION THAT AWAITED BELIEVERS

[18]"If the world hates you, you know that it hated Me before it hated you. [19]"If you were of the world, the world would love its own. Yet because you are not of the world, but I chose you out of the world, therefore the world hates you. [20]"Remember the word that I said to you, `A servant is not greater than his master.' If they persecuted Me, they will also persecute you. If they kept My word, they will keep yours also (Jn. 15:18-20).

[1]"These things I have spoken to you, that you should not be made to stumble. [2]"They will put you out of the synagogues; yes, the time is coming that whoever kills you will think that he offers God service (Jn. 16:1-2).

MINISTRY OF THE FATHER

[2]"Every branch in Me that does not bear fruit He takes away; and every branch that bears fruit He prunes, that it may bear more fruit. [16]"You did not choose Me, but I chose you and appointed you that you should go and bear fruit, and that your fruit should remain, that whatever you ask the Father in My name He may give you (Jn. 15:2, 26).

[27]"for the Father Himself loves you, because you have loved Me, and have believed that I came forth from God (Jn. 16:27).

MINISTRY OF THE SON

[1]"I am the true vine, and My Father is the vinedresser. [3]"You are already clean because of the word which I have spoken to you. [4]"Abide in Me, and I in you. As the branch cannot bear fruit of itself, unless it abides in the vine, neither can you, unless you abide in Me. [5]"I am the vine, you are the branches. He who abides in Me, and I in him, bears much fruit; for without Me you can do nothing. [6]"If anyone does not abide in Me, he is cast out as a branch and is withered; and they gather them and throw them into the fire, and they are burned. [7]"If you abide in Me, and My words abide in you, you will ask what you desire, and it shall be done for you. [8]"By this My Father is glorified, that you bear much fruit; so you will be My disciples. [9]"As the Father loved Me, I also have loved you; abide in My love (Jn. 15:1, 3-9).

[33]"These things I have spoken to you, that in Me you may have peace. In the world you will have tribulation; but be of good cheer, I have overcome the world" (Jn. 16:33).

MINISTRY OF THE HOLY SPIRIT

[26]"But when the Helper comes, whom I shall send to you from the Father, the Spirit of truth who proceeds from the Father, He will testify of Me (Jn. 15:26).

[7]"Nevertheless I tell you the truth. It is to your advantage that I go away; for if I do not go away, the Helper will not come to you; but if I depart, I will send Him to you. [8]"And when He has come, He will convict the world of sin, and of righteousness, and of judgment: [9]" of sin, because they do not believe in Me; [10]"of righteousness, because I go to My Father and you see Me no more; [11]"of judgment, because the ruler of this world is judged. [12]"I still have many things to say to you, but you cannot bear them now. [13]"However, when He, the Spirit of truth, has come, He will guide you into all truth; for He will not speak on His own authority, but whatever He hears He will speak; and He will tell you things to come. [14]"He will glorify Me, for He will take of what is Mine and declare it to you. [15]"All things that the Father has are Mine. Therefore I said that He will take of Mine and declare it to you (Jn. 16:7-15).

HE SPOKE OF THE TRINITY THAT WOULD ASSIST BELIEVERS

CHART # 34

	SUBJECT

FRIDAY: JESUS' GREAT HIGH PRIESTLY PRAYER

	SPECIFICS

	THE FAITHFUL SON	**THE FRUITFUL SON**
HE PRAYS FOR HIMSELF: (JN. 17:1-5)	• **What He Asks:** [5]*"And now, O Father, glorify Me together with Yourself, with the glory which I had with You before the world was* (Jn. 17:5). • **Why He Asks:** [1]*Jesus spoke these words, lifted up His eyes to heaven, and said: "Father, the hour has come. Glorify Your Son, that Your Son also may glorify You* (Jn. 17:1).	• **He Had Given Eternal Life To All The Sent:** [2]*"as You have given Him authority over all flesh, that He should give eternal life to as many as You have given Him.* [3]*"And this is eternal life, that they may know You, the only true God, and Jesus Christ whom You have sent* (Jn. 17:2, 3). • **He Had Completed His Assignment:** [4]*"I have glorified You on the earth. I have finished the work which You have given Me to do* (Jn. 17:4).

HE PRAYS FOR HIS DISCIPLES: (JN. 17:6-19)	**JESUS' REPORT: HE REVIEWS HIS MINISTRY FOR THE DISCIPLES** • He has revealed the Father to them (17:6-7) • He has given the Father's words to them (17:8, 14) • He has prayed for them (17:9-10) • He has kept them safe, with the exception of Judas (17:12) • He has set himself apart for their sanctification (17:19) • He has sent them into the world (17:18) **JESUS' REQUESTS: HE PREVIEWS HIS FATHER'S FUTURE MINISTRY FOR THE DISCIPLES** • He asks that the Father unify them (17:11) • He asks that the Father impart joy to them (17:13) • He asks that the Father protect them (17:15-16) • He asks that the Father sanctify them (17:17)
HE PRAYS FOR HIS CHURCH: (17:20-26)	• He asks that the Father unify the church (17:20-21 a, 22) • He asks that the church honor the Son (17:21b) • He asks that the church display God's love (17:23) • He asks that the church experience God's love (17:25-26) • He asks that the church enjoy Christ's glory in heaven forever (17:24)

FRIDAY: JESUS' ORDEAL IN GETHSEMANE (Part One)

SPECIFICS

THE THREE APOSTLES	**Jesus Asks Peter, James, And John To Watch And Wait While He Prayed.** *[37]And He took with Him Peter and the two sons of Zebedee, and He began to be sorrowful and deeply distressed. [38]Then He said to them, "My soul is exceedingly sorrowful, even to death. Stay here and watch with Me"* (Mt. 26:37, 38).
THE ALARM	**Jesus Begins To Be Deeply Depressed And Troubled, Saying His Soul Was Overwhelmed With Sorrow To The Point Of Death.** *[37]And He took with Him Peter and the two sons of Zebedee, and He began to be sorrowful and deeply distressed. [38]Then He said to them, "My soul is exceedingly sorrowful, even to death. Stay here and watch with Me"* (Mt. 26:37, 38). *[33]And He took Peter, James, and John with Him, and He began to be troubled and deeply distressed.* *[34]Then He said to them, "My soul is exceedingly sorrowful, even to death. Stay here and watch"* (Mk. 14:33.34).
THE AGONY	**JESUS' FIRST PRAYER: (MATTHEW 26:39)** * **The Struggle:** *"Father, if it be thy will, let this cup pass from me"* * **The Submission:** *"Nevertheless, not my will be done but thine"* * **The Sleepers:** Jesus finds the three apostles asleep **JESUS' SECOND AND THIRD PRAYERS: (MATTHEW 26:42, 44)** * Similar circumstances as in the first prayer
THE ANGEL	*[43]Then an angel appeared to Him from heaven, strengthening Him* (Lk.22:43).

CHART # 36

SUBJECT

FRIDAY: JESUS' ORDEAL IN GETHSEMANE (Part Two)

SPECIFICS

THE ARREST

JESUS AND JUDAS

[47]*And while He was still speaking, behold, Judas, one of the twelve, with a great multitude with swords and clubs, came from the chief priests and elders of the people.* [48]*Now His betrayer had given them a sign, saying, "Whomever I kiss, He is the One; seize Him."* [49]*Immediately he went up to Jesus and said, "Greetings, Rabbi!" and kissed Him.* [50]*But Jesus said to him, "Friend, why have you come?" Then they came and laid hands on Jesus and took Him* (Mt. 26:47-50).

JESUS AND PETER

- **The Rashness:** [10]*Then Simon Peter, having a sword, drew it and struck the high priest's servant, and cut off his right ear. The servant's name was* Malchus (Jn. 18:10).
- **The Rebuke:** [52]*But Jesus said to him, "Put your sword in its place, for all who take the sword will perish by the sword* (Mt. 26:52).
- **The Reminder:** [53]*"Or do you think that I cannot now pray to My Father, and He will provide Me with more than twelve legions of angels?* (Mt. 26:53)

THE ABANDONMENT

- **By The Ten Apostles:** [50]*Then they all forsook Him and fled* (Mk. 14:50).
- **By A Young Man:** [51]*Now a certain young man followed Him, having a linen cloth thrown around his naked body. And the young men laid hold of him,* [52]*and he left the linen cloth and fled from them naked* (Mk. 14:51, 52).

CHART # 37

SUBJECT

FRIDAY: JESUS' UNFAIR TRIALS (Part One)

SPECIFICS

JESUS STANDS BEFORE ANNAS AND CAIAPHAS

1 STANDING BEFORE ANNAS, THE FORMER HIGH PRIEST

- **Jesus Is Bound:** [12]*Then the detachment of troops and the captain and the officers of the Jews arrested Jesus and bound Him.* [13]*And they led Him away to Annas first, for he was the father-in-law of Caiaphas who was high priest that year* (Jn. 18:12, 13).
- **Jesus Is Bullied:** [19]*The high priest then asked Jesus about His disciples and His doctrine.* [20]*Jesus answered him, "I spoke openly to the world. I always taught in synagogues and in the temple, where the Jews always meet, and in secret I have said nothing.* [21]*"Why do you ask Me? Ask those who have heard Me what I said to them. Indeed they know what I said*" (Jn. 18:19-21).
- **Jesus Is Buffeted:** [22]*And when He had said these things, one of the officers who stood by struck Jesus with the palm of his hand, saying, "Do You answer the high priest like that?"* (Jn. 18:22)

2 STANDING BEFORE CAIAPHAS, THE CURRENT HIGH PRIEST

[a] The Attempt

- **The Frantic Attempts:** [59]*Now the chief priests, the elders, and all the council sought false testimony against Jesus to put Him to death* (Mt. 26:59).
- **The Futile Attempts:** [60]*But found none. Even though many false witnesses came forward, they found none. But at last two false witnesses came forward* (Mt. 26:60) [57]*Then some rose up and bore false witness against Him, saying,* [58]*"We heard Him say, `I will destroy this temple made with hands, and within three days I will build another made without hands.'* [59]*"But not even then did their testimony agree* (Mk. 14:57-59).

[b] The Affirmation

[63]*But Jesus kept silent. And the high priest answered and said to Him, "I put You under oath by the living God: Tell us if You are the Christ, the Son of God!"* [64]*Jesus said to him, "It is as you said. Nevertheless, I say to you, hereafter you will see the Son of Man sitting at the right hand of the power, and coming in the clouds of heaven"* (Mt. 26:63, 64).

[c] The Accusation

[65]*Then the high priest tore his clothes, saying, "He has spoken blasphemy! What further need do we have of witnesses? Look, now you have heard His blasphemy!* [66]*"What do you think?" They answered and said, "He is deserving of death"* (Mt. 26:65-66).

[d] The Assaults

[67]*Then they spat in His face and beat Him; and others struck Him with the palms of their hands,* [68]*saying, "Prophesy to us, Christ! Who is the one who struck You?"* (Mt. 26:67, 68)

3 STANDING BEFORE THE ENTIRE SANHEDRIN

[1]*When morning came, all the chief priests and elders of the people plotted against Jesus to put Him to death* (Mt. 27:1).

CHART # 38

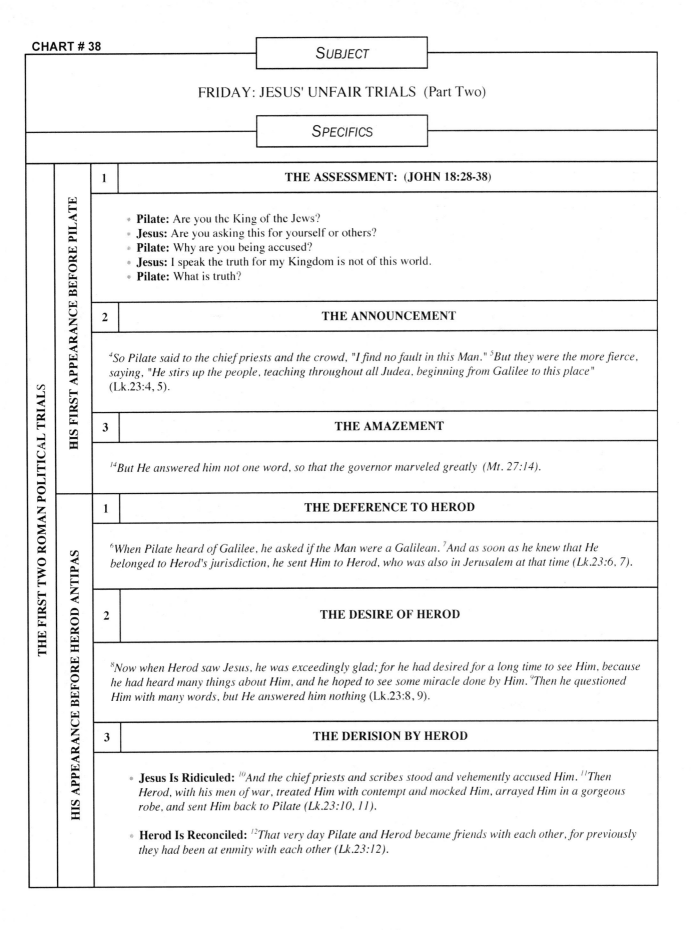

SUBJECT

FRIDAY: JESUS' UNFAIR TRIALS (Part Two)

SPECIFICS

THE FIRST TWO ROMAN POLITICAL TRIALS

HIS FIRST APPEARANCE BEFORE PILATE

1

THE ASSESSMENT: (JOHN 18:28-38)

* **Pilate:** Are you the King of the Jews?
* **Jesus:** Are you asking this for yourself or others?
* **Pilate:** Why are you being accused?
* **Jesus:** I speak the truth for my Kingdom is not of this world.
* **Pilate:** What is truth?

2

THE ANNOUNCEMENT

⁴So Pilate said to the chief priests and the crowd, "I find no fault in this Man." ⁵But they were the more fierce, saying, "He stirs up the people, teaching throughout all Judea, beginning from Galilee to this place" (Lk.23:4, 5).

3

THE AMAZEMENT

¹⁴But He answered him not one word, so that the governor marveled greatly (Mt. 27:14).

HIS APPEARANCE BEFORE HEROD ANTIPAS

1

THE DEFERENCE TO HEROD

⁶When Pilate heard of Galilee, he asked if the Man were a Galilean. ⁷And as soon as he knew that He belonged to Herod's jurisdiction, he sent Him to Herod, who was also in Jerusalem at that time (Lk.23:6, 7).

2

THE DESIRE OF HEROD

⁸Now when Herod saw Jesus, he was exceedingly glad; for he had desired for a long time to see Him, because he had heard many things about Him, and he hoped to see some miracle done by Him. ⁹Then he questioned Him with many words, but He answered him nothing (Lk.23:8, 9).

3

THE DERISION BY HEROD

* **Jesus Is Ridiculed:** *¹⁰And the chief priests and scribes stood and vehemently accused Him. ¹¹Then Herod, with his men of war, treated Him with contempt and mocked Him, arrayed Him in a gorgeous robe, and sent Him back to Pilate* (Lk.23:10, 11).

* **Herod Is Reconciled:** *¹²That very day Pilate and Herod became friends with each other, for previously they had been at enmity with each other* (Lk.23:12).

FRIDAY: JESUS' UNFAIR TRIALS   (Part Three)

1	**THE CONSENSUS**	**2**	**THE CUSTOM**

[13]Then Pilate, when he had called together the chief priests, the rulers, and the people, [14]said to them, "You have brought this Man to me, as one who misleads the people. And indeed, having examined Him in your presence, I have found no fault in this Man concerning those things of which you accuse Him; [15]"no, neither did Herod, for I sent you back to him and indeed nothing deserving of death has been done by Him (Lk.23:13-15).	*[15]Now at the feast the governor was accustomed to releasing to the multitude one prisoner whom they wished* (Mt. 27:15).

3	**THE CRIMINAL**	**4**	**THE CHOICE**

[19]who had been thrown into prison for a certain rebellion made in the city, and for murder (Lk.23:19).	*[17]Therefore, when they had gathered together, Pilate said to them, "Whom do you want me to release to you? Barabbas, or Jesus who is called Christ?'* (Mt. 27:17)

5	**THE CONSPIRACY**	**6**	**THE CRY**

[11]But the chief priests stirred up the crowd, so that he should rather release Barabbas to them (Mk. 15:11).	*[12]Pilate answered and said to them again, "What then do you want me to do with Him whom you call the King of the Jews?" [13]"So they cried out again, "Crucify Him!"[14] Then Pilate said to them, "Why, what evil has He done?" But they cried out all the more, "Crucify Him!"* (Mk. 15:12-14)

7	**THE CONCERN**	**8**	**THE CAPITULATION**

[19]When he was set down on the judgment seat, his wife sent unto him, saying. Have thou nothing to do with that just man; for I have suffered many things this day in a dream because of him (Mt. 27:19).	*[22]Then he said to them the third time, "Why, what evil has He done? I have found no reason for death in Him. I will therefore chastise Him and let Him go." [23]But they were insistent, demanding with loud voices that He be crucified. And the voices of these men and of the chief priests prevailed* (Lk.23:22, 23).

9	**THE CHASTENING**	**10**	**THE CLEANSING**

[1]So then Pilate took Jesus and scourged Him (Jn. 19:1).	*[24]When Pilate saw that he could not prevail at all, but rather that a tumult was rising, he took water and washed his hands before the multitude, saying, "I am innocent of the blood of this just Person. You see to it"* (Mt. 27:24).

11	**THE CURSE**	**12**	**THE CHRIST**

[25]And all the people answered and said, "His blood be on us and on our children" (Mt. 27:25).	*[4]Pilate then went out again, and said to them, "Behold, I am bringing Him out to you, that you may know that I find no fault in Him." [5]"Then Jesus came out, wearing the crown of thorns and the purple robe. And Pilate said to them, "Behold the Man!" [6]Therefore, when the chief priests and officers saw Him, they cried out, saying, "Crucify Him, crucify Him"' Pilate said to them, "You take Him and crucify Him, for I find no fault in Him" [7]The Jews answered him, "We have a law, and according to our law He ought to die, because He made Himself the Son of God"* (Jn. 19:4-7).

13	**THE CORRECTION**	**14**	**THE COURTYARD**

[8]Therefore, when Pilate heard that saying, he was the more afraid, [9]and went again into the Praetorium, and said to Jesus, "Where are You from?" But Jesus gave him no answer. [10]Then Pilate said to Him, "Are You not speaking to nit? Do You not know that I have power to crucify You, and power to release You?' "[11]Jesus answered, "You could have no power at all against Me unless it had been given you from above. Therefore the one who delivered Me to you has the greater sin" (Jn. 19:8-11).	*[12]From then on Pilate sought to release Him, but the Jews cried out, saying, "If you let this Man go, you are not Caesar's friend. Whoever makes himself a king speaks against Caesar." [13]When Pilate therefore heard that saying, he brought Jesus out and sat down in the judgment seat in a place that is called the Pavement, but in Hebrew, Gabbatha* (Jn. 19:12, 13).

THE FIRST TWO ROMAN POLITICAL TRIALS

THE MILITARY TRIAL

[27]Then the soldiers of the governor took Jesus into the Praetorium and gathered the whole garrison around Him [28]And they stripped Him and put a scarlet robe on Him. [29]When they had twisted a crown of thorns, they put it on His head, and a reed in His right hand. And they bowed the knee before Him and mocked Him, saying, "Hail, King of the Jews!" "[30]Then they spat on Him, and took the reed and struck Him on the head (Mt. 27:27-30).

CHART # 40

	SUBJECT

FRIDAY: THE DENIALS BY PETER AND THE DEATH OF JUDAS

	SPECIFICS

PETER'S DENIALS

1	THE SETTING INVOLVED

54But Peter followed Him at a distance, right into the courtyard of the high priest. And he sat with the servants and warmed himself at the fire (Mk. 14:54).

2	ME SIN INVOLVED

- **First Denial:** *66"Now as Peter was below in the courtyard, one of the servant girls of the high priest came. 67And when she saw Peter warming himself, she looked at him and said, "You also were with Jesus of Nazareth." 68But he denied it, saying, "I neither know nor understand what you are saying." And he went out on the porch, and a rooster crowed (Mk. 14:66-68).*
- **Second Denial:** *71And when he had gone out to the gateway, another girl saw him and said to those who were there, "This fellow also was with Jesus of Nazareth." 72But again he denied with an oath, "I do not know the Man!" (Mt. 26:71, 72)*
- **Third Denial:** *59Then after about an hour had passed, another confidently affirmed, saying, "Surely this fellow also was with Him, for he is a Galilean." (Lk.22:59) 71Then he began to curse and swear, "I do not know this Man of whom you speak!" (Mk. 14:71)*

3	THE SOUND INVOLVED

Immediately a rooster crowed (Mt. 26:74b).

4	THE SORROW INVOLVED

61And the Lord turned and looked at Peter. And Peter remembered the word of the Lord, how He had said to him, 'Before the rooster crows, you will deny Me three times.' 62So Peter went out and wept bitterly (Lk.22:61-62).

JUDAS' DEATH

1	THE BLOODY SILVER

- **The Despair Of Judas:** *3Then Judas, His betrayer, seeing that He had been condemned, was remorseful and brought back the thirty pieces of silver to the chief priests and elders, 4saying, "I have sinned by betraying innocent blood." And they said, "What is that to us? You see to it!" (Mt. 27:3-4)*
- **The Death Of Judas:** *5Then he threw down the pieces of silver in the temple and departed, and went and hanged himself (Mt. 27:5).*

2	THE BLOODY SOIL

The Deliberation By The Priests	The Decision By The Priests
6But the chief priests took the silver pieces and said, "It is not lawful to put them into the treasury, because they are the price of blood" (Mt. 27:6).	- **The Property They Found:** *7And they consulted together and bought with them the potter's field, to bury strangers in. 8Therefore that field has been called the Field of Blood to this day (Mt. 27:7-8).* - **The Prophecy They Fulfilled:** *9Then was fulfilled what was spoken by Jeremiah the prophet, saying, "And they took the thirty pieces of silver, the value of Him who was priced, whom they of the children of Israel priced, 10and gave them for the potter's field, as the LORD directed me" (Mt. 27:9-10).*

FRIDAY: THE CRUCIFIXION OF JESUS (Part One)

1	THE CARRIER OF THE CROSS	2	THE CONCERN REGARDING THE CROSS
	[26]*Now as they led Him away, they laid hold of a certain man, Simon a Cyrenian, who was coming from the country, and on him they laid the cross that he might bear it after Jesus* (Lk.23:26).		• **The pain of the maidens:** [27]*And there followed him a great company of people, and of women, which also bewailed and lamented him* (Lk.23:27). • **The prophecy of the Messiah:** [28]*But Jesus, turning to them, said, Daughters of Jerusalem, do not weep for Me, but weep for yourselves and for your children.* [29]*For indeed the days are coming in which they will say, Blessed are the barren, wombs that never bore, and breasts which never nursed!* [30]*Then they will begin to say to the mountains, Fall on us! and to the hills, Cover us'* [31]*For if they do these things in the green wood, what will be done in the dry?* (Lk.23:28-31)

3	THE CRIMINALS ON THE CROSS	4	THE CITATION ABOVE THE CROSS
	[32]*There were also two others, criminals, led with Him to be put to death* (Lk.23:32).		• **The Record:** *This is Jesus of Nazareth, the King of the Jews* • **The Request:** [20]*Then many of the Jews read this title, for the place where Jesus was crucified was near the city; and it was written in Hebrew, Greek, and Latin.* [21]*Therefore the chief priests of the Jews said to Pilate, "Do not write, `The King of the Jews,' but, 'He said, "I am the King of the Jews"* (Jn. 19:20-21). • **The Refusal:** [22]*Pilate answered, "What I have written, I have written"* (Jn. 19:22).

5	CLOTHING BELOW THE CROSS	6	COMFORTERS AROUND THE CROSS
	• **The Soldiers:** [23]*Then the soldiers, when they had crucified Jesus, took His garments and made four parts, to each soldier a part, and also the tunic. Now the tunic was without seam, woven from the top in one piece* (Jn. 19:23). • **The Scripture:** [24]*They said therefore among themselves, Let us not tear it, but cast lots for it, whose it shall be, that the Scripture might be fulfilled which says: They divided My garments among them, And for My clothing they cast lots. Therefore the soldiers did these things* (Jn. 19:24).		• Mary, His mother • Mary, wife of Cleopas • Mary Magdalene • Mother of James and Joseph • Mother of James and John Salome • John the apostle

7	THE FIRST CUP AT THE CROSS	8	THE CLOUD ABOVE THE CROSS
	[34]*They gave Him sour wine mingled with gall to drink. But when He had tasted it, He would not drink* (Mt. 27:34).		[45]*Now from the sixth hour until the ninth hour there was darkness over all the land* (Mt. 27:45).
	• **The Thieves:** [44]*Even the robbers who were crucified with Him reviled Him with the same thing* (Mt. 27:44). • **By The Passing Crowd:** [39]*And those who passed by blasphemed Him, wagging their heads* [40]*and saying, You who destroy the temple and build it in three days, save Yourself! If You are the Son of God, come down from the cross* (Mt. 27:39-40).		• **By The Jewish Rulers:** [4]*Likewise the chief priests also, mocking with the scribes and elders, said,* [42]*"He saved others; Himself He cannot save. If He is the King of Israel, let Him now come down from the cross, and we will believe Him.* [43]*"He trusted in God; let Him deliver Him now if He will have Him; for He said, 'I am the Son of God'* (Mt. 27:41-43). • **By The Soldiers:** [36]*The soldiers also mocked Him, coming and offering Him sour wine,* [37]*and saying, "If You are the King of the Jews, save Yourself"* (Lk.23:36-37).

CHART # 42

	SUBJECT

FRIDAY: THE CRUCIFIXION OF JESUS (Part Two)

	SPECIFICS

9	THE CRIES FROM THE CROSS

DURING THE SIX HOUR ORDEAL ON THE CROSS JESUS UTTERED SEVEN STATEMENTS

First 3 Hours 9:00 – Noon	1	*Father, forgive them, for they know not what they do (Lk.23:34)*
	2	*Verily I say unto thee, today thou shalt be with me in paradise (Lk.23:43)*
	3	*Woman, behold thy son! Behold thy mother (Jn. 19:26, 27)*
Final 3 Hours Noon – 3:00 PM	4	*My God, My God, why hast thou forsaken me? (Mt. 27:46)*
	5	*I thirst (Jn. 19:28)*
	6	*It is finished (Jn. 19:30)*
	7	*Father, into thy hands I commend my spirit (Lk.23:46)*

10	THE CONFUSION ABOUT THE CROSS	11	THE FINAL CUP AT THE CROSS

[47]*Some of those who stood there, when they heard that, said, "This Man is calling for Elijah!"* [48]*Immediately one of them ran and took a sponge, filled it with sour wine and put it on a reed, and offered it to Him to drink.* [49]*The rest said, "Let Him alone; let us see if Elijah will come to save Him "* (Mt. 27:47-49).

[29]*Now a vessel full of sour wine was sitting there; and they filled a sponge with sour wine, put it on hyssop, and put it to His mouth.* [30]*So when Jesus had received the sour wine, He said, "It is finished!" And bowing His head, He gave up His spirit* (Jn. 19:29-30).

FRIDAY: THOSE EVENTS IMMEDIATELY FOLLOWING JESUS' CRUCIFIXION

	SPECIFICS	

AT 3:00 PM

THE HEAVENLY ACTION

* **In Regards To The Temple:** [51]*Then, behold, the veil of the temple was torn in two from top to bottom* (Mt. 27:51 a).
* **In Regards To The Terrain:** *and the earth quaked, and the rocks were split* (Mt. 27:51b).
* **In Regards To The Tombs:** [52] *and the graves were opened; and many bodies of the saints who had fallen asleep were raised; and coming out of the graves after His resurrection, they went into the holy city and appeared to many* (Mt. 27:52-53).

THE HUMAN REACTION

* **The Confession Of The Centurion:** [54]*So when the centurion and those with him, who were guarding Jesus, saw the earthquake and the things that had happened, they feared greatly, saying, "Truly this was the Son of God!"* (Mt. 27:54)
* **The Contriteness Of The Crowd:** [4]*And all the people that came together to that sight, beholding the things which were done, smote their breasts, and returned* (Lk.23:48).

FROM 3:00 – 6:00 PM

The Jews' Request	The Soldiers' Response
[31]*Therefore, because it was the Preparation Day, that the bodies should not remain on the cross on the Sabbath (for that Sabbath was a high day), the Jews asked Pilate that their legs might be broken, and that they might be taken away* (Jn. 19:31).	[32]*Then the soldiers came and broke the legs of the first and of the other who was crucified with Him.* [33] *But when they came to Jesus and saw that He was already dead, they did not break His legs.* [34]*But one of the soldiers pierced His side with a spear, and immediately blood and water came out.* [35]*And he who has seen has testified, and his testimony is true; and he knows that he is telling the truth, so that you may believe.* [36]*For these things were done that the Scripture should be fulfilled, "Not one of His bones shall be broken."* [37]*And again another Scripture says, "They shall look on Him whom they pierced"* (Jn. 19:32-37).

PREPARING OF JESUS' BODY

* **The Role Of The Men:** [38]*After this, Joseph of Arimathea, being a disciple of Jesus, but secretly, for fear of the Jews, asked Pilate that he might take away the body of Jesus; and Pilate gave him permission. So he came and took the body of Jesus.* [39]*And Nicodemus, who at first came to Jesus by night, also came, bringing a mixture of myrrh and aloes, about a hundred pounds.* [40]*Then they took the body of Jesus, and bound it in strips of linen with the spices, as the custom of the Jews is to bury.* [41]*Now in the place where He was crucified there was a garden, and in the garden a new tomb in which no one had yet been laid.* [42]*So there they laid Jesus, because of the Jews' Preparation Day, for the tomb was nearby* (Jn. 19:38-42).
* **The Role Of The Women:** [55]*And the women who had come with Him from Galilee followed after, and they observed the tomb and how His body was laid.* [56]*Then they returned and prepared spices and fragrant oils. And they rested on the Sabbath according to the commandment* (Lk.23:55-56).

PLACING OF JESUS' BODY

* **The Garden:** [41]*Now in the place where He was crucified there was a garden, and in the garden a new tomb in which no one had yet been laid.* [42]*So there they laid Jesus, because of the Jews' Preparation Day, for the tomb was nearby* (Jn. 19:41-42).
* **The Grave Stone:** [59]*When Joseph had taken the body, he wrapped it in a clean linen cloth,* [60]*and laid it in his new, tomb which he had hewn out of the rock; and he rolled a large stone against the door of the tomb, and departed* (Mt. 27:59-60).

CHART # 44

<table>
<tr><td colspan="2" align="center">SUBJECT</td></tr>
<tr><td colspan="2" align="center">SATURDAY, SUNDAY: THOSE EVENTS PRECEDING JESUS' RESURRECTION</td></tr>
<tr><td colspan="2" align="center">SPECIFICS</td></tr>
</table>

SATURDAY

[62]*On the next day, which followed the Day of Preparation, the chief priests and Pharisees gathered together to Pilate,* [63]*saying, "Sir, we remember, while He was still alive, how that deceiver said, `After three days I will rise.'* [64]*"Therefore command that the tomb be made secure until the third day, lest His disciples come by night and steal Him away, and say to the people, `He has risen from the dead.' So the last deception will be worse than the first."* [65]*Pilate said to them, "You have a guard; go your way, make it as secure as you know how."* [66]*So they went and made the tomb secure, sealing the stone and setting the guard* (Mt. 27:62-66).

THE FIRST EASTER SUNDAY

1	**THE PREPARATION**	**2**	**THE MANIFESTATION**
[1]*Now when the Sabbath was past, Mary Magdalene, Mary the mother of James, and Salome bought spices, that they might come and anoint Him* (Mk. 16:1).		[2]*And behold, there was a great earthquake; for an angel of the Lord descended from heaven, and came and rolled back the stone from the door, and sat on it.* [3]*His countenance was like lightning, and his clothing as white as snow.* [4]*And the guards shook for fear of him, and became like dead men* (Mt. 28:2-4).	

3	**THE VISITATION**	**4**	**THE PROCLAMATION**
[2]*Very early in the morning, on the first day of the week, they came to the tomb when the sun had risen.* [3]*And they said among themselves, "Who will roll away the stone from the door of the tomb for us?"* [4]*But when they looked up, they saw that the stone had been rolled away: for it was very large* (Mk. 16:2-4).		[4]*And it happened, as they were greatly perplexed about this, that behold, two men stood by them in shining garments.* [5]*Then, as they were afraid and bowed their faces to the earth, they said to them, "Why do you seek the living among the dead?* [6]*He is not here, but is risen! Remember how He spoke - to you when He was still in Galilee,* [7]*saying, `The Son of Man must be delivered into the hands of sinful men, and be crucified, and the third day rise again.' "* (Lk.24:4-7) [7]*But go, tell His disciples and Peter that He is going before you into Galilee; there you will see Him, as He said to you."* [8]*So they went out quickly and fled from the tomb, for they trembled and were amazed. And they said nothing to anyone, for they were afraid* (Mk. 16:7-8).	

5	**THE SPECULATION**	**6**	**THE FALSIFICATION**
[8]And they remembered His words. [9]Then they returned from the tomb and told all these things to the eleven and to all the rest. [10]It was Mary Magdalene, Joanna, Mary the mother of James, and the other women with them, who told these things to the apostles. And their words seemed to them like idle tales, and they did not believe them (Lk.24:8-11).		[11]Now while they were going, behold, some of the guard came into the city and reported to the chief priests all the things that had happened. [12]When they had assembled with the elders and consulted together, they gave a large sum of money to the soldiers, [13]saying, "Tell them, `His disciples came at night and stole Him away while we slept.' [14]"And if this comes to the governor's ears, we will appease him and make you secure." [15]So they took the money and did as they were instructed; and this saying is commonly reported among the Jews until this day (Mt. 28:11-15).	

THE FINAL FORTY DAYS OF JESUS' EARTHLY MINISTRY

SPECIFICS

HIS GLORIOUS RESURRECTION

This Jesus hath God raised up, whereof we all are witnesses (Acts 2:32) Knowing that Christ being raised from the dead dieth no more; death hath no more dominion over him. (Rom. 6:9); For I delivered unto you first of all that which I also received, how that Christ died for our sins according to the scriptures; And that he was buried, and that he rose again the third day according to the scriptures (1 Cor. 15:3, 4).

HIS TEN RESURRECTION APPEARANCES

DURING THE FIRST DAY
- **First Resurrection Appearance**: To Mary Magdalene (Mk. 16:9-11; Jn. 20:11-18)
- **Second Resurrection Appearance:** To some women (Mt. 28:9, 10)
- **Third Resurrection Appearance:** To the Emmaus disciples (Mk. 16:12, 13; Lk.24:13-35)
- **Fourth Resurrection Appearance:** To Simon Peter (Lk.24:34; 1 Cor. 15:5)
- **Fifth Resurrection Appearance:** To the ten apostles in the Upper Room (Mk. 16:14; Lk.24:36-43; Jn. 20:19-25)

THE REMAINING FORTY
- **Sixth Resurrection Appearance:** To the eleven apostles in the Upper Room (Jn. 20:24-31)
- **Seventh Resurrection Appearance:** To seven apostles by the Galilean Sea (Jn. 21:1-25)
- **Eighth Resurrection Appearance:** To the eleven apostles plus 500 disciples on a Galilean mountain (Mt. 28:16-20; 1 Cor. 15:6; Mk. 16:15-18)
- **Ninth Resurrection Appearance:** To James, half-brother of Christ (Mk. 16:14-18; Lk.24:44-49; 1 Cor. 15:7)
- **Tenth Resurrection Appearance:** To the eleven apostles on Mt. Olivet (Lk.24:50-53; Mk. 16:19-20)

FINAL INSTRUCTIONS TO THE APOSTLES

And, being assembled together with them, commanded them that they should not depart from Jerusalem, but wait for the promise of the Father, which, saith he, ye have heard of me. For John truly baptized with water; but ye shall be baptized with the Holy Ghost not many days hence. When they therefore were come together, they asked of him, saying, Lord, wilt thou at this time restore again the kingdom to Israel? And he said unto them, It is not for you to know the times or the seasons, which the father hath put in his own power. But ye shall receive power, after that the Holy Ghost is come upon you: and ye shall be witnesses unto me both in Jerusalem, and in all Judaea, and in Samaria, and unto the uttermost part of the earth (Acts 1:4-8).

HIS ASCENSION INTO HEAVEN

So then after the Lord had spoken unto them, he was received up into heaven, and sat on the right hand of God (Mk. 16:19). And he led them out as far as to Bethany, and he lifted up his hands, and blessed them. And it came to pass, while he blessed them, he was parted from them, and carried up into heaven (Lk.24:50-51). And when he had spoken these things, while they beheld, he was taken up; and a cloud received him out of their sight. And while they looked stedfastly toward heaven as he went up, behold, two men stood by them in white apparel; Which also said, Ye men of Galilee, why stand ye gazing up into heaven? this same Jesus, which is taken up from you into heaven, shall so come in like manner as ye have seen him go into heaven (Acts 1:9-11).

Six:
GEOGRAPHICAL

Locating the various cities and places visited by Jesus and subsequent activities occurring there.

THE VARIOUS CITIES
AND PLACES VISITED BY JESUS

Bethabara:

A few miles north of Jericho, on the eastern bank of the Jordan River where John baptized Jesus (Jn. 1:28; Mt. 3:13-17).

BETHANY:

Fifteen furlongs, or one and three-fourths miles from Jerusalem on the eastern slope of the Mount of Olives. It is on the road to Jericho. Bethany was the Judean headquarters of Jesus, as Capernaum was his Galilean headquarters.

- Here He raised Lazarus from the dead (Jn. 11).
- Mary and Martha entertained Christ here (Lk. 10:38-42).
- Mary anointed His feet here (Jn. 12:1-11).
- It was also the home of Simon the leper (Mk. 14:3).
- Here Christ blessed His disciples just prior to His ascension from the Mount of Olives (Lk. 24:50).

BETHLEHEM:

Five miles south of Jerusalem

- It was the birthplace of both Mary and Joseph (Lk. 2:1-4).
- It was here Christ was born (Micah 5:2; Jn. 7:42; Lk. 2).

BETHPHAGE:

On the slopes of Mount Olivet between Bethany and Jerusalem. Here the triumphal entry began (Mt. 21:1-11; Mk. 11:1-11; Lk. 19:29-40).

BETHSAIDA:

Located at the place where the Jordan River enters the Sea of Galilee. It means "the place of catching."

- It was the home of Philip, Andrew, and Peter (Jn. 1:44).
- Jesus upbraided this city, along with others, for its unbelief (Lk. 10:11-14; Mt. 11:21).
- Here He also healed a blind man (Mk. 8:22-26).

BIREH:

Located fifteen miles north of Jerusalem and the first stopping place for caravans going from Jerusalem to Galilee, Bireh is thought to be the place where Jesus was found to be missing during His visit to the Temple at age 12 (Lk. 2:41-45).

CAESAREA PHILIPPI:

Situated at the base of Mount Hermon, northeast of the Galilean Sea. This was doubtless the farthest point north traveled by our Lord. Here He heard Simon Peter's great confession (Mt. 16:13-16).

CANA:

Four miles northeast of Nazareth, on the road to Tiberias.

- It was the hometown of Nathanael (Jn. 21:2).
- Here Jesus performed His first miracle, that of turning water into wine (Jn. 2:1-11).
- Here He also worked His second miracle, the healing of the nobleman's son (Jn. 4:46-54).

CAPERNAUM:

Located along the northwest shore of Galilee, two-and-a-half miles from where the Jordan River enters the lake.

- This became the Galilean headquarters of His earthly ministry (Mt. 4:13; 9:1).
- Here He chose Matthew (Mt. 9:9).
- Here He delivered His great Bread of Life sermon (Jn. 6:24-71).
- Here he performed nine of His recorded miracles:
  1. Healing of the centurion's servant (Mt. 8:5-13)
  2. Healing of Peter's mother-in-law (Mt. 8:14-15)
  3. Healing of a demoniac (Mk. 1:21-27)
  4. Healing of the palsied man who was lowered from the roof (Mk. 2:1-5)
  5. Healing of the woman with a bloody issue (Mt. 9:22)

6. Healing of Jairus' daughter (Mt. 9:25)

7. Healing of two blind men (Mt. 9:29)

8. Healing of a dumb demoniac (Mt. 9:33)

9. The miracle of the tribute money (Mt. 17:24-27)

CHORAZIN:

Two miles north of Capernaum. Christ pronounced judgment upon this city for its unbelief (Mt. 11:21-23).

EMMAUS:

About seven and a half miles west of Jerusalem. Here Christ appeared to two disciples after His resurrection and revealed Himself to them at the supper table (Lk. 24:13-31).

GERGESA:

Located on the northeastern shore of Galilee, where Jesus healed the demon-filled maniac of Gadara (Mk. 5:1-21).

GETHSEMANE:

Located across the Kidron Valley from the golden gate of Jerusalem. It was the garden place where He prayed just prior to His betrayal and arrest (Mt. 26:36-56; Jn. 18:1-14).

JENIN:

Twenty-four miles north of Samaria, where some believe Jesus healed the ten lepers (Lk. 17:11-19).

JERICHO:

Located seventeen miles northwest of Jerusalem near the Jordan River.

- Here Jesus healed a blind man named Bartimaeus (Lk. 18:35)
- Here Zacchaeus met Christ (Lk. 19:1-10)
- Jesus used this city to help illustrate His Good Samaritan parable (Lk. 10:30-37)

JERUSALEM:

The capital of God's world. It is situated on a rocky prominence about 2,500 feet above the Mediterranean and 3,800 feet above the Dead Sea. It is thirty-three miles east of the Mediterranean Sea and fourteen miles west of the Dead Sea.

- Jesus was dedicated here (Lk. 2:1-38)
- He attended the Passover at age twelve (Lk. 2:41-50)
- He cleansed the Temple (Jn. 2:13-17)
- He spoke to Nicodemus (Jn. 3:1-16)
- He healed a thirty-eight year old invalid (Jn. 5:8)
- He preached on the Holy Spirit during the feast of the tabernacles (Jn. 7:10-39)
- He forgave an adulterous woman (Jn. 8:1-11)
- He preached on the devil and his children (Jn. 8:33-59)
- He healed a man born blind (Jn. 9:7)
- He preached a sermon on the Good Shepherd (Jn. 10:1-18)
- He made His triumphal entry (Jn. 12:12-15)
- He cursed the fig tree (Mt. 21:19)
- He utterly condemned the wicked Pharisees (Mt. 23:1-36)
- He preached the Mt. Olivet discourse (Mt. 24-25)
- He wept over Jerusalem (Lk. 19:41; Mt. 23:37-39)
- He conducted the service in the Upper Room (Jn. 13-14)
- He preached on the vine and branches (Jn. 15-16)
- He prayed His great high priestly prayer (Jn. 17)
- He was arrested in Gethsemane (Mt. 26:47-56)
- He restored a severed ear (Lk. 22:51)
- He was condemned to death (Mt. 27:26)
- He was crucified (Mt. 27:27-50)
- He was buried (Mt. 27:57-60)
- He rose from the dead (Mt. 28:1-10)
- He visited the Upper Room for the first time after His resurrection (Lk. 24:36-43; Jn. 20:19-23)
- He visited the Upper Room for the third and final time (Mk. 16:14-18; Lk. 24:44-49)
- He ascended into heaven (Acts 1:4-11)

JORDAN RIVER:

It begins at the base of Mount Hermon, about 1,700 feet above sea level. From there it goes to the waters of Merom, some twelve miles down course. From there it flows the five miles to the Sea of Galilee, some 682 feet below sea level. Finally, it proceeds the sixty-five miles to the Dead Sea, 1,300 feet below sea level. Thus, during its eighty-two mile course, the Jordan River drops 3,000 feet. It was in the Jordan River that our Lord was baptized (Mt. 3:13-17).

KIDRON:

A valley, about two and three-fourths miles long, located immediately east of the wall of Jerusalem between the city and the Mount of Olives. Jesus crossed this valley en route to Gethsemane (Jn. 18:1).

MAGDALA:

Located three miles north of Tiberias on the western shore of the Galilean Sea (Mt. 15:39). This was the home of Mary Magdalene (Lk. 8:2; Mk. 16:9).

MOUNT HERMON:

Located some seventeen miles north of the Galilean Sea. It is by far the highest mountain in all Palestine, reaching 9,101 feet. Many believe this to be the "high mountain" of Matt. 17:1 where Christ was transfigured.

MOUNT OF OLIVES:

Located due east of Jerusalem, across from the Kidron Valley. Its height is 2,641 feet.

- Here Christ wept over Jerusalem (Lk. 19:41-44).
- Here He delivered His great sermon on prophecy (Mt. 25:24-25).
- Here He walked after the Passover in the Upper Room (Mt. 26:30; Mk. 14:26; Lk. 22:39).
- From here He ascended into heaven (Lk. 24:50-51; Acts 1:6-12).

MOUNT TABOR:

Located five and a half miles southeast of Nazareth. Its height is 1,843 feet above sea level. Some believe this was the mount of transfiguration instead of Mount Hermon. However, the text prefers the latter.

MOUNT ZION:

The height which rises close to the southwest corner of the old walled city. Here was located the Upper Room (Mk. 14:12-16; Lk. 22:7-13; Jn. 13-14).

NAIN:

A city some ten miles southeast of Nazareth, where Jesus raised the dead son of a sorrowing widow (Lk. 7:11).

NAZARETH:

Located about midway between the Sea of Galilee and the Mediterranean Sea.

- Both Joseph and Mary received the news from Gabriel concerning the virgin birth here (Lk. 1:26; Mt. 1:18-25).
- Here Jesus grew into manhood (Lk. 2:39-40, 51-52).
- Here He preached two sermons:
    1. After the first, on Isaiah 61, they attempted to kill Him (Lk. 4:16-30).
    2. After the second, He was totally rejected by the citizens (Mt. 13:53-58; Mk. 6:1-6).

SEA OF GALILEE:

This inland sea lake is thirteen miles long, seven and a half miles wide, and thirty-two miles in circumference. It is 700 feet below sea level, and its greatest depth is 200 feet.

- Beside this body of water, Jesus fed the 5,000 (Jn. 6:1-14).
- On the Mount of Beatitudes, He gave the Sermon on the Mount (Mt. 5-7).
- Here He calmed the wild stormy sea waters (Mt. 8:23-27).
- Here He walked on the water (Jn. 6:15-21).
- Here 2,000 hogs were drowned after He healed a maniac (Mk. 5:1-21).
- Here He performed His last miracle (Mk. 14:28; 16:7; Jn. 21).

SYCHAR:

Located some twenty-five miles due north of Jerusalem in Samaria. Here Jesus met the Samaritan woman at Jacob's well (Jn. 4).

Tyre:

A city located on the Mediterranean Sea, some twenty miles due west of Caesarea Philippi. Jesus healed the Syro-phoenician woman's daughter in this area (Mk. 3:8; Lk. 6:17).

Wilderness of Temptation:

The exact spot is unknown. However, some feel it may have been southeast of Jerusalem in the Dead Sea area (Mt. 4:1).

Seven:
POLITICAL & THEOLOGICAL

I dentifying the following political and religious groups referred to in the gospel accounts.

- ➤ Galileans

- ➤ Herodians

- ➤ Levites

- ➤ Pharisees

- ➤ Publicans

- ➤ Sadducees

- ➤ Sanhedrin

- ➤ Scribes

- ➤ Zealots

POLITICAL AND RELIGIOUS GROUPS REFERRED TO IN THE GOSPEL ACCOUNTS

GALILEANS:

The Galileans arose in northern Palestine, headed by Judas of Galilee, who led a rebellion against all foreign elements, advocating "Galilee for Galileans." They were the "extreme right" fanatics of their day. The anti-Roman position of the Galileans would have put them at odds with officials such as Pontius Pilate, who on one occasion felt forced to slaughter a number of them (Lk.13:1). Christ's enemies tried to identify both Him and His disciples with the Galileans (Mt. 6:69; Mk 14:70; Lk 23:6).

HERODIANS:

The Herodians were a political party who favored rule by the family of Herod. Though Jewish, they saw the rule of the Herods, under Roman oversight, as Israel's best chance for survival as a nation. They were therefore the "law and order" advocates of the day. They regarded Christ as a revolutionary fanatic and on three occasions joined the efforts of the Pharisees to silence him (Mk 3:6; 12:13; Mt. 22:16). Christ soundly condemned them (Mk 8:15; 12:13-17).

LEVITES:

The Levites were the descendants of Levi and were in charge of the Temple. Though quite prominent in Israelite history, they make only two appearances in the NT: The Jews sent some priests and Levites to check out the desert ministry of John the Baptist (John 1:19); Christ used them as an example of uncharitable religiosity in the parable of the Good Samaritan.

PHARISEES:

The Pharisees, who came to prominence around 100 B.C. during the time of the Maccabees, were known as the champions and guardians of Israel's written and oral law. As such they became the most bitter and hateful enemies of Christ. They numbered about 6,000 in Christ's day. John the Baptist called the Pharisees a "brood of snakes" (Matt. 3:7). Christ denounced them for letting their traditions negate the power of God's Word (Mt. 15:1-9; 23:1-36). He warned his followers about their false righteousness (Mt. 5:20), false teaching (Mt. 16:11), and false humility (Lk 18:10-14).

The Pharisees in turn condemned Christ for things such as associating with sinners (Mt. 9:11; Lk. 7:39; 15:2), healing on the Sabbath (Lk. 6:7; 14:1-6), and allowing His disciples to work on the Sabbath (Mt. 12:1-2). They despised Him because He refused to follow their traditions (Mt. 15:1-2).

They sought to entrap Him on various theological issues (Mt. 19:3; 22:15). They denied His miracles (Jn. 9:15-16). And, from early in His ministry, they sought to kill Him (Mt. 12:14; Jn. 11:47-53).

Nicodemus (Jn. 3:1) and Paul (Acts 23:6; Phil. 3:5) were Pharisees by birth and training.

PUBLICANS:

These public officials were authorized by Rome to collect taxes from the Jews for that Empire. Because of this, they were hated and despised by the Jews who associated them with terrible sinners (Mt. 9:11; 11:19), harlots (Mt. 21:31-32), and outright pagans (Mt. 18:17). Jesus was severely criticized by the Pharisees for eating with them (Mt. 9:10-11; Lk. 15:1-2). However, many Publicans apparently accepted the message of John the Baptist and were subsequently baptized (Lk. 3:12; 7:29). Jesus would later relate the parable of the humble Publican and the haughty Pharisee (Lk. 18:10-13). Finally, one of the most well known conversion accounts in the gospel records was that of a Publican named Zacchaeus (Lk. 19:2-10).

SADDUCEES:

Taking their name from Zadok, high priest during the reign of Solomon (1 Kings 2:35), the Sadducees came into prominence at about the same time as the Pharisees, a century before Christ. The Sadducees were the Jewish aristocrats of Christ's day and held most seats on the Sanhedrin. As the "insiders" of the priestly class, they accepted only the written Law and rejected the oral traditions popular with Pharisees. But both parties briefly set aside their differences to accomplish their common goal of getting rid of Christ.

John the Baptist lumped the Sadducees and Pharisees together, calling both of them a "brood of snakes" (Mt. 3:7). Christ, likewise, warned his followers to beware of the erroneous teachings of both Pharisees and Sadducees (Mt. 16:11).

The Sadducees, unlike the Pharisees, rejected the idea of the resurrection and an afterlife, and on at least one occasion they tried to ridicule Christ on this point (Mk. 12:18-27). Later, this difference of opinion was used by Paul to drive a wedge into the Pharisees' and Sadducees' united opposition to Christ (Acts 23:1-10).

SAMARITANS:

When the Assyrian king Sargon II took the northern kingdom of Israel into captivity in 722 B.C., he followed the Assyrian custom by leaving only the poorest and most uneducated Israelites behind and inviting other nations to come in and homestead the land vacated by those taken captive. These newcomers brought with them their pagan religions (2 Kings 17:24-33). As the Jews left in the land intermarried with them they came to be viewed as a separate race, neither Jew nor Gentile, and were held in contempt by Jews. (The name Samaritan comes from Samaria, the capital of the northern kingdom. In Christ's day the name referred to the entire territory between Judea and Galilee.)

The Samaritans offered to help rebuild the Temple in 536, but their offer was refused (Ezra 4:1-3). A century later, the Samaritan governor Sanballat tried to frustrate Nehemiah's rebuilding of Jerusalem's walls (Neh. 6:1-9). A complete break between the Jews and Samaritans occurred when the grandson of Eliashib the high priest married Sanballat's daughter, contrary to the statute prohibiting mixed marriages (Neh. 13:23-28). Since he refused to annul the marriage, he was promptly expelled from the priesthood and exiled. He retired to Samaria, where Sanballat built a temple for him on Mount Gerizim. This temple was destroyed by John Hyrcanus in 128 because the Samaritans had compromised with paganism under Antiochus Epiphanes IV by dedicating their temple to the Greek god Zeus.

By the time of the N.T., the hatred between Jews and Samaritans had reached its zenith (John 4:9; 8:48). Christ once ordered his disciples not to enter Samaria (Mt. 10:5), though He Himself ministered to Samaritans (Jn. 4:1-42). A Samaritan was the hero in one of Christ's parables (Lk. 10:30-37). When He healed 10 lepers, the only one who thanked him was a Samaritan (Lk. 17:11-19).

During Christ's final days of ministry, one village of Samaritans rejected Him because of His plans to go on to Jerusalem (Lk. 9:51-56). Just prior to His ascension, however, Christ commanded His disciples to proclaim the gospel in Samaria (Acts 1:8).

THE SANHEDRIN:

The Sanhedrin (the "high council," NLT) was the Jewish Supreme Court for both religious and legal matters. It may have come from the time of Moses (Num. 11:16-17) or of King Jehoshaphat (2 Chron. 19:8). It had 71 members, including: the high priest, who was president; the heads of the 24 priestly service divisions; scribes and lawyers; and elders, representing the laity. The word Sanhedrin comes from two Greek words: sun ("together with"), and hedro ("a sitting place"), thus referring to a group that sits in session. (Cathedral and ex cathedra have the same roots.)

Though the Jewish people trusted the Sanhedrin to render justice, when Christ stood before them prior to His crucifixion (Mt. 26:57-68; 27:1-2) the trial was unjust in several ways:

- They normally met in a semicircle with the prisoner standing in the midst, able to see them all. Jesus was blindfolded.

- Normally, two clerks were appointed--one to record the votes for acquittal, the other for conviction. In Christ's case this was not done.

- The arguments for acquittal were normally given first. There is no record of this happening in Christ's trial.

- If the vote was for acquittal, the prisoner was set free immediately; if the vote was for conviction, condemnation could not be pronounced until the following day. Christ was condemned the same day (Mt. 26:66).

Several leaders of the early church were also tried before the Sanhedrin (Acts 4:5-22; 5:21-40; 6:12-15; 22:30-23:10).

SCRIBES:

Scribes (also called "experts in religious law" — Mt. 22:35; Lk. 7:30) were the students, interpreters, and teachers of the O.T. Scriptures. Scribes had great power in Jewish society and were often called upon to settle disputes. They became bitter enemies of Christ, who grouped them with Pharisees, calling them both hypocrites (Mt. 23:13).

Scribes in the N.T. refused John's baptism (Lk. 7:30); tried to entrap Jesus on the issues of adultery (Jn. 8:3-12) and healing on the Sabbath (Lk. 6:7); demanded that Jesus perform signs (Mt. 12:38); and condemned Him for associating with sinners (Lk. 15:2).

Christ warned His disciples about the scribes' false righteousness (Mt. 5:20) and denounced the scribes for letting their traditions negate the power of God's Word (Mt. 16:21; 21:15; 23:1-36; Mk. 12:28-40).

ZEALOTS:

The Zealots were an intensely nationalistic sect, anti-Roman to the core, advocating that Israel should return to a theocratic form of government. They were the direct opposite of the tax collecting Publicans.

However, it is significant to observe that Jesus chose both a Zealot (Simon the Zealot, Lk. 6:15; Acts 1:13), and a Publican (Matthew, Mt. 9:9) to serve as two of His apostles!

Eight: NUMERICAL

The number of verses in the gospel accounts describing the twenty key events in the earthly life of Jesus.

THE NUMBER OF VERSES IN THE GOSPEL ACCOUNTS DESCRIBING THE TWENTY KEY EVENTS IN THE LIFE OF JESUS CHRIST

A CHRONOLOGICAL LISTING:

1. Birth (announcements to Zacharias, Mary, Joseph, shepherds and wise men): 120 verses
2. Baptism: 11 verses
3. Temptation: 26 verses
4. First temple cleansing: 10 verses
5. Call of Peter, Andrew, James, and John: 21 verses
6. Sending forth of the Twelve: 55 verses
7. Sending forth of the Seventy: 12 verses
8. Promise to build the church: 23 verses
9. Transfiguration: 24 verses
10. Anointing by Mary: 22 verses
11. Triumphal entry: 43 verses
12. Second temple cleansing: 12 verses
13. Confrontation with the Pharisees (final week): 130 verses
14. Upper room events: 134 verses
15. Great High Priestly prayer: 26 verses
16. Garden of Gethsemane: 71 verses
17. Unfair trials: 170 verses
18. Crucifixion: 93 verses
19. Resurrection and appearances: 137 verses
20. Ascension: 12 verses

A CONTENT LISTING:

(According to the number of verses used in describing the event)

1. Unfair trials: 170 verses
2. Resurrection and appearances: 137 verses
3. Upper room events: 134 verses
4. Confrontation with the Pharisees (final week): 130 verses
5. Birth: 120 verses

6. Crucifixion: 93 verses
7. Garden of Gethsemane: 71 verses
8. Sending forth of the Twelve: 55 verses
9. Triumphal entry: 43 verses
10. Temptation: 26 verses
11. Great High Priestly prayer: 26 verses
12. Transfiguration: 24 verses
13. Promise to build the church: 23 verses
14. Anointing by Mary: 22 verses
15. Call of Peter, Andrew, James, and John: 21 verses
16. Sending forth of the Seventy: 12 verses
17. Second temple cleansing: 12 verses
18. Ascension: 12 verses
19. Baptism: 11 verses
20. First temple cleansing: 10 verses

SEVEN IMPORTANT DIALOGUES OF CHRIST:

(According to verse content)
1. With Pilate: as described by 78 verses
2. With the rich young ruler: as described by 32 verses
3. With Nicodemus: as described by 21 verses
4. With the Samaritan woman: as described by 21 verses
5. With Cleopas: as described by 21 verses
6. With the woman taken in adultery: as described by 11 verses
7. With Zacchaeus: as described by 10 verses

TEN IMPORTANT MIRACLES OF CHRIST:

(According to verse content)
1. Feeding of the 5000: as described by 45 verses
2. Raising of Lazarus: as described by 44 verses
3. Restoring of the maniac of Gadara: as described by 41 verses
4. Healing of the man born blind: as described by 41 verses
5. Healing of the paralytic: as described by 30 verses
6. Healing of the demonic boy: as described by 30 verses
7. Walking on the water: as described by 22 verses
8. Healing of blind Bartimaeus: as described by 22 verses
9. Healing of the impotent man: as described by 16 verses
10. Second draught of fishes: as described by 14 verses

Three Important Parables of Christ:

(According to verse content)
1. The mysteries of the kingdom: as described by 101 verses
2. Some vicious vine keepers: as described by 37 verses
3. The missing sheep, coin, and Prodigal Son: 30 verses

Ten Important Sermons of Christ:

(According to verse content)
1. The Olivet Discourse: as described by 168 verses
2. The Sermon on the Mount: as described by 155 verses
3. The Abundance of Life sermon: as described by 60 verses
4. The Water of Life sermon: as described by 53 verses
5. The Bread of Life sermon: as described by 50 verses
6. The Light of Life sermon: as described by 48 verses
7. The Shepherd of Life sermon: as described by 39 verses
8. The Sermon on John the Baptist: as described by 35 verses
9. The Source of Life sermon: as described by 31 verses
10. The Way and the Truth and the Life sermon: as described by 31 verses

Nine:
PERSONAL

An alliterated outline overview of each of the four gospel records, namely, the books of:

- ➢ Matthew
- ➢ Mark
- ➢ Luke
- ➢ John

An Alliterated Outline Overview
of the Book of Matthew

- Preparation for
- Presentation of
- Prince of darkness and (verse)
- Preachers of
- Preaching by
- Principles of
- Power of
- Parables of
- Puzzle concerning
- Poverty of
- Plots and accusations against
- Provisions from
- Portrait of
- Pity of
- Provoking of
- Person of
- Pre-eminence of
- Petition to
- Parade for
- Purging by
- Pain of
- Predictions by
- Precious anointment upon
- Passover conducted by
- Prayers by
- Persecution suffered by
- Price paid by
- Placing of
- Proofs that
- Parting words from

A Topical Overview of Matthew's Gospel

I. Preparation for the King

   A. The First 2000 Years: The Genealogy Account From Abraham to Joseph and Mary (1:1-17)

      "The book of the generation of Jesus Christ, the son of David, the son of Abraham." (1:1)

   B. The Next Thirty Years

      1. The angel reassures Joseph (1:18-25)

      2. The wise men worship Jesus (2:1-12)

      3. The flight into Egypt (2:15-20)

      4. The settlement in Nazareth (2:21-23)

   C. The Final Few Months: The Ministry of John the Baptist (3:1-12)

      "In those days came John the Baptist, preaching in the wilderness of Judaea, And saying, Repent ye: for the kingdom of heaven is at hand." (3:1-2)

II. Presentation of the King (3:13-17)

"And Jesus, when he was baptized, went up straightway out of the water: and, lo, the heavens were opened unto him, and he saw the Spirit of God descending like a dove, and lighting upon him." (3:16)

III. Prince of Darkness and the King (4:1-11)

"Then was Jesus led up of the spirit into the wilderness to be tempted of the devil." (4:1)

IV. Preachers of the King

   A. The Call of Peter, Andrew, James and John (4:18-22)

   B. The Call of Matthew (9:9)

   The Commission of the Twelve (10:1-42)

      "And when he had called unto him his twelve disciples, he gave them power against unclean spirits, to cast them out, and to heal all manner of sickness and all manner of disease." (10:1)

V. Preaching by the King (4:12-17,23-25; 9:35-38; 11:1)

"And Jesus went about all the cities and villages, teaching in their synagogues, and preaching the gospel of the kingdom, and healing every sickness and every disease among the people. But

when he saw the multitudes, he was moved with compassion on them, because they fainted, and were scattered abroad, as sheep having no shepherd." (9:35-36)

VI. Principles of the King (5-7)

Jesus laid out His moral and spiritual standards during the Sermon on the Mount in regards to the Kingdom of Heaven.

A. Happiness and the Kingdom (5:1-12)

> *"Blessed are the poor in spirit: for theirs is the kingdom of heaven." (5:3)*

B. Citizens in the Kingdom (5:13-16)

> *"Ye are the salt of the earth ... ye are the light of the world."*

C. The King and the Kingdom (5:17-20)

> *"Think not that I am come to destroy the law, or the prophets: I am not come to destroy, but to fulfil." (5:17)*

D. Laws of the Kingdom

1. In regards to murder (5:21-26)
2. In regards to adultery (5:27-30)
3. In regards to divorce (5:31-32)
4. In regards to perjury (5:33-37)
5. In regards to retaliation (5:38-42)
6. In regards to forgiveness (5:43-48; 6:14-15)
7. In regards to giving (6:1-4)
8. In regards to fasting (6:16-18)
9. In regards to true riches (6:19-24)

   > *"But lay up for yourselves treasures in heaven, where neither moth nor rust doth corrupt, and where thieves do not break through nor steal." (6:20)*

10. In regards to anxiety and trust (6:25-34)

    > *"Therefore take no thought, saying, What shall we eat? or, What shall we drink? or, Wherewithal shall we be clothed? But seek ye first the kingdom of God, and his righteousness; and all these things shall be added unto you." (6:31, 33)*

11. In regards to judging (7:1-6)

    > *"Judge not, that ye be not judged." (7:1)*

12. In regards to false prophets and false profession (7:15-23)

    > *"Beware of false prophets, which come to you in sheep's clothing, but inwardly they are ravening wolves. Not every one that saith unto me, Lord, Lord, shall enter into the kingdom of heaven; but he that doeth the will of my Father which is in heaven." (7:15,21)*

E. The Golden Rule and the Kingdom

> *"Therefore all things whatsoever ye would that men should do to you, do ye even so to them: for this is the law and the prophets." (7:12)*

F. Entrance to the Kingdom (7:13-14)

"Enter ye in at the strait gate: for wide is the gate, and broad is the way, that leadeth to destruction, and many there be which go in thereat: Because strait is the gate, and narrow is the way, which leadeth unto life, and few there be that find it." (7:13-14)

G. The Wise Men and the Kingdom (7:24-27).

"Therefore whosoever heareth these sayings of mine, and doeth them, I will liken him unto a wise man, which built his house upon a rock." (7:24)

VII. Power of the King

There are 20 miracles of Christ recorded in Matthew's gospel.

A. Cleansing a leper (8:1-4)

B. Healing a centurion's servant (8:5-13)

C. Restoring Peter's mother-in-law (8:14-15)

D. Calming the stormy sea (8:23-27)

E. Delivering a Gadarene demoniac (8:28-34)

F. Healing a paralytic (9:1-8)

G. Healing a woman with an issue of blood (9:20-22)

H. Raising Jairus' daughter (9:18-19; 23-26)

I. Healing two blind men (9:27-31)

J. Delivering a dumb demoniac (9:32-33)

K. Restoring a withered hand (12:10-13)

L. Delivering a blind and dumb demoniac (12:22)

M. Feeding 5000 people (14:15-21)

N. Walking upon the water (14:25-33)

O. Delivering a demoniac girl (15:21-28)

P. Feeding 4000 people (15:32-38)

Q. Delivering a demoniac boy (17:14-18)

R. Arranging for a fish with a coin in its mouth (17:24-27)

S. Healing a blind man near Jericho (20:29-34)

T. Withering a fig tree (21:18-22)

VIII. Parables of the King

There are 26 parables recorded in Matthew's gospel:

A. Two houses in a hurricane (7:24-27)

B. Subduing a strong man (12:22-37)

C. The Sovereign Sower (13:1-9, 18-23)

D. Satan's tares in the Savior's field (13:24-30)

E. The mighty mustard seed (13:31-32)

F. The cook's leaven and the kingdom of heaven (13:33)

G. Finding a fortune in a field (13:44)

H. The price of a pearl (13:45-46)

I. Sorting out a sea catch (13:47-50)

J. A trained man and his treasure (13:52)

K. Feasting friends of the bridegroom (9:14-15)

L. A new cloth on an old cloth (9:16)

M. New wine and old bottles (9:17)

N. A generation of gripers (11:16-19)

O. The forgiven who couldn't forgive (18:21-35)

P. Eight spirits and a swept house (12:43-45)

Q. Readiness versus carelessness (24:42-51)

R. Defilement diagnosed (15:10-20)

S. Hourly workers and daily wages (20:1-16)

T. Two sons who reversed their roles (21:28-32)

U. The vicious vine keepers (21:33-46)

V. A wedding guest with no wedding garment (22:1-14)

W. The fig tree and the future (24:32-35)

X. Virgins, vessels, and vigilance (25:1-13)

Y. A traveler, three stewards and eight talents (25:14-30)

Z. Separating the sheep from the goats (25:31-46)

IX. Puzzle Concerning the King

In Jesus' hometown people were confused in regards to:

A. The nature of His spiritual family (12:46-50)

B. The source of His wisdom and power (13:53-58)

X. Poverty of the King (8:19-22)

"And Jesus saith unto him, The foxes have holes, and the birds of the air have nests; but the Son of man hath not where to lay his head." (8:20)

XI. Plots and Accusations Against the King

    A. The plots (12:14; 21:46; 22:15; 26:3-4; 14-15)

        "Then the Pharisees went out, and held a council against him, how they might destroy him." (12:14)

        "Then assembled together the chief priests, and the scribes, and the elders of the people, unto the palace of the high priest, who was called Caiaphas, And consulted that they might take Jesus by subtilty, and kill him." (26:3-4)

    B. The accusations (9:3, 34; 12:24)

        "And, behold, certain of the scribes said within themselves, This man blasphemeth. But the Pharisees said, He casteth out devils through the prince of the devils." (9:3, 34)

XII.   Provisions from the King

    "Come unto me, all ye that labour and are heavy laden, and I will give you rest. Take my yoke upon you, and learn of me; for I am meek and lowly in heart: and ye shall find rest unto your souls. For my yoke is easy, and my burden is light." (11:28-30)

XIII.   Portrait of the King

    "Behold my servant, whom I have chosen; my beloved, in whom my soul is well pleased: I will put my spirit upon him, and he shall shew judgment to the Gentiles. He shall not strive, nor cry; neither shall any man hear his voice in the streets. A bruised reed shall he not break, and smoking flax shall he not quench, till he send forth judgment unto victory." (12:18-20)

XIV.   Pity of the King

    A. Upon the impoverished

        "But when he saw the multitudes, he was moved with compassion on them, because they fainted, and were scattered abroad, as sheep having no shepherd. Then saith he unto his disciples, The harvest truly is plenteous, but the labourers are few; Pray ye therefore the Lord of the harvest, that he will send forth labourers into his harvest." (9:36-38)

    B. Upon the imprisoned

        1. The tenderness He displayed

        "Now when John had heard in the prison the works of Christ, he sent two of his disciples, And said unto him, Art thou he that should come, or do we look for another? Jesus answered and said unto them, Go and shew John again those things which ye do hear and see: The blind receive their sight, and the lame walk, the lepers are cleansed, and the deaf hear, the dead are raised up, and the poor have the gospel preached to them. And blessed is he, whosoever shall not be offended in me." (11:2-6)

        2. The tribute He delivered (11:7-15)

        "Verily I say unto you, Among them that are born of women there hath not risen a greater than John the Baptist: notwithstanding he that is least in the kingdom of heaven is greater than he." (11:11)

XV. Provoking of the King

    A. He pronounces judgment upon some cities (11:20-24)

        "Then began he to upbraid the cities wherein most of his mighty works were done, because they repented not." (11:20)

    B. He pronounces judgment upon some critics (23:1-36)

        "But woe unto you, scribes and Pharisees, hypocrites! for ye shut up the kingdom of heaven against men: for ye neither go in yourselves, neither suffer ye them that are entering to go in." (23:13)

XVI. Person of the King (16:13-23)

"When Jesus came into the coasts of Caesarea Philippi, he asked his disciples, saying, Whom do men say that I the Son of man am? And they said, Some say that thou art John the Baptist: some, Elias; and others, Jeremias, or one of the prophets. He saith unto them, But whom say ye that I am? And Simon Peter answered and said, Thou art the Christ, the Son of the living God." (16:13-16)

XVII. Pre-eminence of the King (17:1-13)

"And after six days Jesus taketh Peter, James, and John his brother, and bringeth them up into an high mountain apart, And was transfigured before them: and his face did shine as the sun, and his raiment was white as the light." (17:1-2)

XVIII.Petition to the King (20:20-28)

"Then came to him the mother of Zebedee's children with her sons, worshipping him, and desiring a certain thing of him. And he said unto her, What wilt thou? She saith unto him, Grant that these my two sons may sit, the one on thy right hand, and the other on the left, in thy kingdom." (20:20-21)

XIX. Parade for the King (21:1-11)

"And the disciples went, and did as Jesus commanded them, And brought the ass, and the colt, and put on them their clothes, and they set him thereon. And a very great multitude spread their garments in the way; others cut down branches from the trees, and strawed them in the way. And the multitudes that went before, and that followed, cried, saying, Hosanna to the son of David: Blessed is he that cometh in the name of the Lord; Hosanna in the highest." (21:6-9)

XX. Purging by the King (21:12-17)

"And Jesus went into the temple of God, and cast out all them that sold and bought in the temple, and overthrew the tables of the moneychangers, and the seats of them that sold doves, And said unto them, It is written, My house shall be called the house of prayer; but ye have made it a den of thieves." (21:12-13)

XXI. Pain of the King (23:37-39)

"O Jerusalem, Jerusalem, thou that killest the prophets, and stonest them which are sent unto thee, how often would I have gathered thy children together, even as a hen gathereth her chickens under her wings, and ye would not! " (23:3 7)

XXII. Predictions by the King (24)

A. In regards to the temple

"And Jesus went out, and departed from the temple: and his disciples came to him for to shew him the buildings of the temple. And Jesus said unto them, See ye not all these things? verily I say unto you, There shall not be left here one stone upon another, that shall not be thrown down." (24:1-2)

B. In regards to the tribulation (24:3-44)

"For then shall be great tribulation, such as was not since the beginning of the world to this time, no, nor ever shall be." (24:2 1)

XXIII. Precious Anointment Upon the King (26:6-13)

"There came unto him a woman having an alabaster box of very precious ointment, and poured it on his head, as he sat at meat." (26:7)

XXIV. Passover Conducted by the King (26:17-30)

"And as they were eating, Jesus took bread, and blessed it, and brake it, and gave it to the disciples, and said, Take, eat; this is my body. And he took the cup, and gave thanks, and gave it to them, saying, Drink ye all of it; For this is my blood of the new testament, which is shed for many for the remission of sins." (26:26-28)

XXV. Prayers by the King (26:36-46)

A. Key prayer at the beginning of His ministry

"At that time Jesus answered and said, I thank thee, O Father, Lord of heaven and earth, because thou hast hid these things from the wise and prudent, and hast revealed them unto babes. Even so, Father: for so it seemed good in thy sight. All things are delivered unto me of my Father: and no man knoweth the Son, but the Father; neither knoweth any man the Father, save the Son, and he to whomsoever the Son will reveal him." (11:25-27)

B. Key prayer at the conclusion of His ministry (26:36-46)

"Then cometh Jesus with them unto a place called Gethsemane, and saith unto the disciples, Sit ye here, while I go and pray yonder. And he went a little farther, and fell on his face, and prayed, saying, O my Father, if it be possible, let this cup pass from me: nevertheless not as I will, but as thou wilt." (26:36, 39)

XXVI. Persecution Suffered by the King

A. Betrayed by a follower (26:47-49; 27:1-10)

    1. The deceit of Judas Iscariot (26:47-49)

      "Now he that betrayed him gave them a sign, saying, Whomsoever I shall kiss, that same is he: hold him fast. And forthwith he came to Jesus, and said, Hail, master; and kissed him." (26:48-49)

    2. The death of Judas Iscariot (27:1-10)

      "Then Judas, which had betrayed him, when he saw that he was condemned, repented himself, and brought again the thirty pieces of silver to the chief priests and elders, And he cast down the pieces of silver in the temple, and departed, and went and hanged himself." (27:3, 5)

B. Denied by a friend

    1. The denials foretold (26:33-35)

      "Jesus said unto him, Verily I say unto thee, That this night, before the cock crow, thou shalt deny me thrice." (26:34)

    2. The denials fulfilled (26:58; 69-75)

      "Then began he to curse and to swear, saying, I know not the man. And immediately the cock crew." (26:74)

C. Mistreated by His foes

    1. At the hands of the High Priest (26:59-68)

      "Then did they spit in his face, and buffeted him; and others smote him with the palms of their hands, Saying, Prophesy unto us, thou Christ, Who is he that smote thee?" (26:67-68)

    2. At the hands of Pilate (27:11-26)

      "Then released he Barabbas unto them: and when he had scourged Jesus, he delivered him to be crucified." (27:26)

    3. At the hands of the soldiers (27:27-31)

      "And they stripped him, and put on him a scarlet robe. And when they had platted a crown of thorns, they put it upon his head, and a reed in his right hand: and they bowed the knee before him, and mocked him, saying, Hail, King of the Jews! And they spit upon him, and took the reed, and smote him on the head." (27:28-30)

XXVII. Price Paid by the King (27:31-56)

He freely gave His life on the cross to save us from our sins.

"And they crucified him, and parted his garments, casting lots: that it might be fulfilled which was spoken by the prophet, They parted my garments among them, and upon my vesture did they cast lots. Now from the sixth hour there was darkness over all the land unto the ninth hour. And about the ninth hour Jesus cried with a loud voice, saying, Eli, Eli, lama sabachthani? that is to say, My God, my God, why hast thou forsaken me? Jesus, when he had cried again with a loud voice, yielded up the ghost." (27:35, 45, 45-46, 50)

XXVIII. Placing of the King (27:57-66)

Joseph of Arimathaea secures the dead body of Jesus and places it in his own new tomb.

XXIX. Proofs That He is Indeed King (28:1-17)

The resurrected Christ makes His appearance before some women and His disciples.

XXX. Parting Words from the King (28:18-20)

"Go ye therefore, and teach all nations, baptizing them in the name of the Father, and of the Son, and of the Holy Ghost: Teaching them to observe all things whatsoever I have commanded you: and, lo, I am with you alway, even unto the end of the world. Amen." (28:19-20)

A Topical Overview of Mark's Gospel

I. Events in the Life of the Servant

A. His forerunner

1. The message of John the Baptist (1:1-8)

   "The voice of one crying in the wilderness, Prepare ye the way of the Lord, make his paths straight. John did baptize in the wilderness, and preach the baptism of repentance for the remission of sins." (1:3, 4)

2. The martyrdom of John the Baptist (6:4-29)

   "And immediately the king sent an executioner, and commanded his head to be brought: and he went and beheaded him in the prison." (6:27)

B. His baptism (1:9-11)

"And straightway coming up out of the water, he saw the heavens opened, and the Spirit like a dove descending upon him." (1:10)

C. His temptation (1:12, 13)

"And he was there in the wilderness forty days, tempted of Satan; and was with the wild beasts; and the angels ministered unto him." (1:13)

D. His disciples

1. Their call
   a. The first five: Andrew, Peter, James, John and Matthew (1:16-20; 2:13, 14)
   b. The final twelve (3:13-21)

      "And he goeth up into a mountain, and calleth unto him whom he would: and they came unto him. And he ordained twelve, that they should be with him, and that he might send them forth to preach." (3:13, 14)

2. Their commission (6:7-13, 30, 31)
   a. The orders

      "And he called unto him the twelve, and began to send them forth by two and two; and gave them power over unclean spirits." (6:7)

   b. The obedience

      "And they went out, and preached that men should repent. And they cast out many devils, and anointed with oil many that were sick, and healed them." (6:12, 13)

E. His visit to Nazareth (6:1-6)

"And when the sabbath day was come, he began to teach in the synagogue: and many hearing him were astonished, saying, From whence hath this man these things? and what wisdom is this which is given unto him, that even such mighty works are wrought by his hands? But Jesus, said unto them, A prophet is not without honour, but in his own country, and among his own kin, and in his own house." (6:2, 4)

F. His predictions regarding the cross and empty tomb (9:30-32; 10:32-34)

"For he taught his disciples, and said unto them, The Son of man is delivered into the hands of men, and they shall kill him; and after that he is killed, he shall rise the third day." (9:31) "And they shall mock him, and shall scourge him, and shall spit upon him, and shall kill him: and the third day he shall rise again." (10:34)

G. His blessing upon some children (10:13-16)

"And he took them up in his arms, put his hands upon them, and blessed them." (10:16)

H. His transfiguration (9:1-13)

"And his raiment became shining, exceeding white as snow; so as no fuller on earth can white them." (9:3)

I. His meeting with the rich young ruler (10:17-22)

"And one of the multitude answered and said, Master, I have brought unto thee my son, which hath a dumb spirit." (9:17)

J. His request from James and John (10:35-45)

"They said unto him, Grant unto us that we may sit, one on thy right hand, and the other on thy left hand, in thy glory." (10:37)

K. His Triumphal Entry (11:1-11)

"And many spread their garments in the way: and others cut down branches off the trees, and strawed them in the way. And they that went before, and they that followed, cried, saying, Hosanna; Blessed is he that cometh in the name of the Lord." (11:8, 9)

L. His cleansing of the Temple (11:15-19)

"And they come to Jerusalem: and Jesus went into the temple, and began to cast out them that sold and bought in the temple, and overthrew the tables of the moneychangers, and the seats of them that sold doves; And he taught, saying unto them... Is it not written, My house shall be called of all nations the house of prayer? but ye have made it a den of thieves." (11:15, 17)

M. His commending of a scribe (12:28-34)

"And one of the scribes came, and having heard them reasoning together, and perceiving that he had answered them well, asked him, Which is the first commandment of all? And Jesus answered him, The first of all the commandments is, Hear, O Israel; The Lord our God is one Lord: And thou shalt love the Lord thy God with all thy heart, and with all thy soul, and with all thy mind, and with all thy strength: this is the first commandment. And the second is like, namely this, Thou shalt love thy neighbour as thyself. There is none other command-

ment greater than these. And the scribe said unto him, Well, Master, thou hast said the truth: for there is one God; and there is none other but he; And when Jesus saw that he answered discreetly, he said unto him, Thou art not far from the kingdom of God. And no man after that durst ask him any question." (12:28-32, 34)

N. His commending of a poor widow (12:41-44)

"And he called unto him his disciples, and saith unto them, Verily I say unto you, That this poor widow hath cast more in, than all they which have cast into the treasury." (12:43)

O. His anointing in Bethany (14:3-9)

"And being in Bethany in the house of Simon the leper, as he sat at meat, there came a woman having an alabaster box of ointment of spikenard very precious; and she brake the box, and poured it on his head." (14:3)

P. His final Passover Supper (14:12-25)

"And as they did eat, Jesus took bread, and blessed, and brake it, and gave to them, and said, Take, eat: this is my body. And he took the cup, and when he had given thanks, he gave it to them: and they all drank of it. And he said unto them, This is my blood of the new testament, which is shed for many. Verily I say unto you, I will drink no more of the fruit of the vine, until that day that I drink it new in the kingdom of God." (14:22-24)

Q. His ordeal in Gethsemane (14:32-42)

"And they came to a place which was named Gethsemane: and he saith to his disciples, Sit ye here, while I shall pray. And saith unto them, My soul is exceeding sorrowful unto death: tarry ye here, and watch. And he said, Abba, Father, all things are possible unto thee; take away this cup from me: nevertheless not what I will, but what thou wilt." (14:32, 34, 36)

R. His betrayal by Judas

1. As foretold

"And Judas Iscariot, one of the twelve, went unto the chief priests, to betray him unto them. And as they sat and did eat, Jesus said, Verily I say unto you, One of you which eateth with me shall betray me." (14:10, 18)

2. As fulfilled

"And he that betrayed him had given them a token, saying, Whomsoever I shall kiss, that same is he; take him, and lead him away safely. And as soon as he was come, he goeth straightway to him, and saith, Master, master; and kissed him." (14:44, 45)

S. His denials by Peter

1. As foretold (14:27-31)

"And Jesus saith unto him, Verily I say unto thee, That this day, even in this night, before the cock crow twice, thou shalt deny me thrice." (14:30)

2. As fulfilled (14:66-72)

"But he began to curse and to swear, saying, I know not this man of whom ye speak. And the second time the cock crew. And Peter called to mind the word that Jesus said unto him, Before the cock crow twice, thou shalt deny me thrice. And when he thought thereon, he wept." (14:71, 72)

T. His abandonment by all (14:50-52)

"And they all forsook him, and fled." (14:50)

U. His unfair trials (14:53-65; 15:1-20)

1. Before the high priest (14:53-65)

"And the chief priests and all the council sought for witness against Jesus to put him to death; and found none. And some began to spit on him, and to cover his face, and to buffet him, and to say unto him, Prophesy: and the servants did strike him with the palms of their hands." (14:55, 65)

2. Before Pilate (15:1-15)

"And so Pilate, willing to content the people, released Barabbas unto them, and delivered Jesus, when he had scourged him, to be crucified." (15:15)

3. Before the soldiers (15:16-20)

"And they clothed him with purple, and platted a crown of thorns, and put it about his head, And began to salute him, Hail, King of the Jews! And they smote him on the head with a reed, and did spit upon him, and bowing their knees worshipped him." (15:17-19)

V. His cruel crucifixion (15:21-41)

"And they bring him unto the place Golgotha, which is, being interpreted, The place of a skull. And it was the third hour, and they crucified him. And with him they crucify two thieves; the one on his right hand, and the other on his left. And at the ninth hour Jesus cried with a loud voice, saying, Eloi, Eloi, lama sabachthani? which is, being interpreted, My God, my God, why hast thou forsaken me? And Jesus cried with a loud voice, and gave up the ghost. And the veil of the temple was rent in twain from the top to the bottom. And when the centurion, which stood over against him, saw that he so cried out, and gave up the ghost, he said, Truly this man was the Son of God." (15:22, 25, 27, 34, 37-39)

W. His burial (15:42-47)

"Joseph of Arimathaea, an honourable counsellor, which also waited for the kingdom of God, came, and went in boldly unto Pilate, and craved the body of Jesus. And he bought fine linen, and took him down, and wrapped him in the linen, and laid him in a sepulchre which was hewn out of a rock, and rolled a stone unto the door of the sepulchre." (15:43, 46)

X. His resurrection (16:1-18)

1. The announcement (16:1-8)

"And entering into the sepulchre, they saw a young man sitting on the right side, clothed in a long white garment; and they were affrighted. And he saith unto them, Be not affrighted: Ye seek Jesus of Nazareth, which was crucified: he is risen; he is not here: behold the place where they laid him." (16:5, 6)

2. The appearances (16:9-18)

a. Before Mary Magdalene (16:9-11)

b. Before two disciples (16:12, 13)

c. Before eleven apostles (16:14-18)

Y. His ascension (16:19, 20)

> *"So then after the Lord had spoken unto them, he was received up into heaven, and sat on the right hand of God." (16:19)*

II. Miracles Performed by the Servant

A. Freeing a demoniac at Capernaum (1:23-28)

B. Healing Peter's mother-in-law (1:29-31)

C. Healing a leper (1:40-45)

D. Healing a paralytic (2:3-12)

E. Restoring a withered hand (3:1-5)

F. Stilling a storm (4:35-41)

G. Freeing a demoniac at Gadara (5:1-20)

H. Raising Jairus' daughter (5:22-24, 35-43)

I. Healing a woman with an issue of blood (5:25-34)

J. Feeding of the 5,000 (6:35-44)

K. Walking on the water (6:45-52)

L. Healing a deaf and dumb man (7:31-37)

M. Freeing a demoniac girl (7:24-30)

N. Feeding of the 4,000 (8:1-9)

O. Healing a blind man (8:22-26)

P. Freeing a demoniac boy (9:14-29)

Q. Healing blind Bartimaeus (10:46-52)

R. Withering of a fruitless fig tree (11:12-14)

III. Parables Related By the Servant

A. New cloths and wine versus old garments and wineskins (2:21, 22)

B. A house divided against itself (3:22-27)

C. The sower and the seed (4:1-8; 14-20)

D. The function of a lamp (4:21, 22)

E. The seed growing secretly (4:26-29)

F. The grain of mustard seed (4:30-32)

G. Inward defilement (7:14-23)

H. The wicked vineyard keepers (12:1-9)

I. The rejected stone (12:10, 11)

J. The fruitless fig tree (13:28, 29)

K. The watchful servant (13:34-37)

IV. Subjects Discussed By the Servant

A. Discipleship (8:34-38)

B. Divorce (10:1-13)

C. Faith (11:20-24)

D. Fasting (2:19, 20)

E. Forgiveness (11:25, 26)

F. Hell (9:42-50)

G. Humility (9:33-37; 10:42-45)

H. Heaven (8:15-21)

I. Rewards (10:28-31)

J. Riches (10:23-27)

K. Sectarianism (9:38-41)

L. Unpardonable sin (3:28-30)

V. Discourses Delivered By the Servant

A. By the seaside (4:1-34)

"And he began again to teach by the sea side: and there was gathered unto him a great multitude, so that he entered into a ship, and sat in the sea; and the whole multitude was by the sea on the land." (4:1)

B. On a mountain (13:1-37)

"And as he sat upon the mount of Olives over against the temple, Peter and James and John and Andrew asked him privately, Tell us, when shall these things be? and what shall be the sign when all these things shall be fulfilled? And Jesus answering them began to say, Take heed lest any man deceive you." (13:3-5)

A TOPICAL OVERVIEW OF LUKE'S GOSPEL

I. The Explanation: Luke explains to his friend Theophilus his reason for twisting an account of the Son of man (1:1-4).

II. The Annunciations: There were a number of heavenly birth announcements concerning both Jesus and John the Baptist.

    A. Those announcements preceding Jesus' birth

        1. Zacharias and Gabriel (Lk.1:5-25)

        "But the angel said unto him, Fear not, Zacharias: for thy prayer is heard; and thy wife Elisabeth shall bear thee a son, and thou shalt call his name John... For he shall be great in the sight of the Lord, and shall drink neither wine nor strong drink; and he shall be filled with the Holy Ghost, even from his mother's womb ... And, behold, thou shalt be dumb, and not able to speak, until the day that these things shall be performed, because thou believest not my words, which shall be fulfilled in their season." (1:13, 15, 20)

        2. Mary and Gabriel (1:26-38)

        "And the angel said unto her, Fear not, Mary: for thou hast found favour with God. And, behold, thou shalt conceive in thy womb, and bring forth a son, and shalt call his name JESUS ... Then said Mary unto the angel, How shall this be, seeing I know not a man? And the angel answered and said unto her, The Holy Ghost shall come upon thee, and the power of the Highest shall overshadow thee: therefore also that holy thing which shall born of thee shall be called the Son of God." (1:30-31, 34-35)

        3. Mary and Elisabeth (1:39-56)

        "And Mary arose in those days, and went into the hill country with haste, into a city of Juda...And it came to pass, that, when Elisabeth heard the salutation of Mary, the babe leaped in her womb; and Elisabeth was filled with the Holy Ghost ... And Mary said, My soul doth magnify the Lord." (1:39, 41, 46)

        4. Zacharias and the infant John (1:57-80)

        "And his father Zacharias was filled with the Holy Ghost, and prophesied, saying, Blessed be the Lord God of Israel; for he hath visited and redeemed his people ... And thou, child, shalt be called the prophet of the Highest: for thou shalt go before the face of the Lord to prepare his ways; To give knowledge of salvation unto his people by the remission of their sins ... And the child grew, and waxed strong in spirit, and was in the deserts till the day of his shewing unto Israel." (1:67-68, 76-77, 80)

        5. Mary and Joseph (2:1-7)

        "And Joseph also went up from Galilee, out of the city of Nazareth, into Judaea, unto the city of David, which is called Bethlehem; (because he was of the house and lineage of

David:) To be taxed with Mary his espoused wife, being great with child. And so it was, that, while they were there, the days were accomplished that she should be delivered. And she brought forth her firstborn son, and wrapped him in swaddling clothes, and laid him in a manger; because there was no room for them in the inn." (2:4-7)

B. Those announcements following Jesus' birth

    1. The shepherds and the angels (2:8-15)

    "And the angel said unto them, Fear not: for, behold, I bring you good tidings of great joy, which shall be to all people. For unto you is born this day in the city of David a Saviour, which is Christ the Lord." (2:10-11)

    2. The shepherds and the infant Jesus (2:16-20)

    "And they came with haste, and found Mary, and Joseph, and the babe lying in a manger ... And the shepherds returned, glorifying and praising God for all the things that they had heard and seen, as it was told unto them." (2:16, 20)

    3. Simeon and the infant Jesus (2:21-35)

    "And it was revealed unto him by the Holy Ghost, that he should not see death, before he had seen the Lord's Christ. And he came by the Spirit into the temple: and when the parents brought in the child Jesus, to do for him after the custom of the law, Then took he him up in his arms, and blessed God, and said, Lord, now lettest thou thy servant depart in peace, according to thy word: For mine eyes have seen thy salvation." (2:26-30)

    4. Anna and the infant Jesus (2:36-38)

    "And she coming in that instant gave thanks likewise unto the Lord, and spake of him to all them that looked for redemption in Jerusalem." (2:38)

III. The Preparation: The quiet boyhood of Jesus prepared Him for His role as the perfect Son of man.

A. As seen in the home of His mother (2:39-40, 51-52)

"And the child grew, and waxed strong in spirit, filled with wisdom: and the grace of God was upon him ... And he went down with them, and came to Nazareth, and was subject unto them: but his mother kept all these sayings in her heart ... And Jesus increased in wisdom and stature, and in favour with God and man." (2:40, 51-52)

B. As seen in the house of His father (2:41-50)

"And it came to pass, that after three days they found him in the temple, sitting in the midst of the doctors, both hearing them, and asking them questions ... And when they saw him, they were amazed: and his mother said unto him, Son, why hast thou thus dealt with us? behold, thy father and I have sought thee sorrowing ... And he said unto them, How is it that ye sought me? wist ye not that I must be about my Father's business?" (2:46, 48-49)

IV. The Anticipation: John's preaching caused great interest in the promised appearance of Jesus. (3:1-20)

"And he came into all the country about Jordan, preaching the baptism of repentance for the remission of sins; As it is written in the book of the words of Esaias the prophet, saying, The voice of one crying in the wilderness, Prepare ye the way of the Lord, make his paths straight. Every

valley shall be filled, and every mountain and hill shall be brought low; and the crooked shall be made straight, and the rough ways shall be made smooth; And all flesh shall see the salvation of God ... And as the people were in expectation, and all men mused in their hearts of John, whether he were the Christ, or not; John answered, saying unto them all, I indeed baptize you with water; but one mightier than I cometh, the latchet of whose shoes I am not worthy to unloose: he shall baptize you with the Holy Ghost and with fire" (3:3-6, 15-16)

V. The Validation: The Father now gives official approval of Jesus. (3:21-22)

"Now when all the people were baptized, it came to pass, that Jesus also being baptized, and praying, the heaven was opened, And the Holy Ghost descended in a bodily shape like a dove upon him, and a voice came from heaven, which said, Thou art my beloved Son; in thee I am well pleased." (3:21-22)

VI. The Documentation: Luke traces the genealogy of Jesus through Nathan, the second son of King David. (3:23-38)

VII. The Temptation: Jesus is tempted on three occasions by Satan. (4:1-13)

    A. First temptation— *"turn stones into bread!" (4:3)*

    B. Second temptation— *"worship me!" (4:7)*

    C. Third temptation— *"leap from the temple pinnacle!" (4:9)*

VIII. The Proclamation: Jesus preaches His message throughout the land.

"And Jesus returned in the power of the Spirit into Galilee: and there went out a fame of him through all the region round about. And he taught in their synagogues, being glorified of all ... And it came to pass afterward, that he went throughout every city and village, preaching and shewing the glad tidings of the kingdom of God: and the twelve were with him." (4:14-15; 8:1)

    A. The sermons He delivered

        1. The message at Nazareth on Isa. 61

        "And he came to Nazareth, where he had been brought up: and, as his custom was, he went into the synagogue on the sabbath day, and stood up for to read. And there was delivered unto him the book of the prophet Esaias. And when he had opened the book, he found the place where it was written, The Spirit of the Lord is upon me, because he hath anointed me to preach the gospel to the poor; he hath sent me to heal the brokenhearted, to preach deliverance to the captives, and recovering of sight to the blind, to set at liberty them that are bruised, To preach the acceptable year of the Lord. And he closed the book, and he gave it again to the minister, and sat down. And the eyes of all them that were in the synagogue were fastened on him. And he began to say unto them, This day is this scripture fulfilled in your ears. And all bare him witness, and wondered at the gracious words which proceeded out of his mouth. And they said, Is not this Joseph's son? And he said unto them, Ye will surely say unto me this proverb, Physician, heal thyself: whatsoever we have heard done in Capernaum, do also here in thy country. And he said, Verily

I say unto you, No prophet is accepted in his own country. But I tell you of a truth, many widows were in Israel in the days of Elias, when the heaven was shut up three years and six months, when great famine was throughout all the land; But unto none of them was Elias sent, save unto Sarepta, a city of Sidon, unto a woman that was a widow. And many lepers were in Israel in the time of Eliseus the prophet; and none of them was cleansed, saving Naaman the Syrian. And all they in the synagogue, when they heard these things, were filled with wrath, And rose up, and thrust him out of the city, and led him unto the brow of the hill whereon their city was built, that they might cast him down headlong. But he passing through the midst of them went his way." (4:16-30)

2. The Sermon on the Mount (6:17-49; 12:22-34; 14:34-35; 16:17)

"And he closed the book, and he gave it again to the minister, and sat down. And the eyes of all them that were in the synagogue were fastened on him ... And came down to Capernaum, a city of Galilee, and taught them on the sabbath days.... And Jesus rebuked him, saying, Hold thy peace, and come out of him. And when the devil had thrown him in the midst, he came out of him, and hurt him not... And he arose out of the synagogue, and entered into Simon's house. And Simon's wife's mother was taken with a great fever; and they besought him for her ... And he said unto his disciples, Therefore I say unto you, Take no thought for your life, what ye shall eat; neither for the body, what ye shall put on ... But rather seek ye the kingdom of God; and all these things shall be added unto you." (4:20, 31, 35, 38; 12:22, 31)

3. The Mt. Olivet Discourse (19:43-44; 21:5-38)

"And as some spake of the temple, how it was adorned with goodly stones and gifts, he said, As for these things which ye behold, the days will come, in the which there shall not be left one stone upon another, that shall not be thrown down. And they asked him, saying, Master, but when shall these things be? and what sign will there be when these things shall come to pass? And he said, Take heed that ye be not deceived: for many shall come in my name, saying, I am Christ; and the time draweth near: go ye not therefore after them... Then said he unto them, Nation shall rise against nation, and kingdom against kingdom: And great earthquakes shall be in divers places, and famines, and pestilences; and fearful sights and great signs shall there be from heaven ... And there shall be signs in the sun, and in the moon, and in the stars; and upon the earth distress of nations, with perplexity; the sea and the waves roaring; Men's hearts failing them for fear, and for looking after those things which are coming on the earth: for the powers of heaven shall be shaken. And then shall they see the Son of man coming in a cloud with power and great glory." (21:5-8, 10-11, 25-27)

B. The subjects He discussed

1. Covetousness (12:13-15; 16:14-15)
2. Discipleship (9:23-26, 57-62; 14:25-33)
3. Faith (17:5-6)
4. False religious profession (13:22-30)
5. Forgiveness (17:3-4)
6. Future suffering, crucifixion and resurrection (9:22, 44-45; 17:25; 18:31-34)
7. Greatness (9:46-48; 22:24-30)
8. Great White Judgment Throne (12:2-5)

9. Holy Spirit (12:10-12)

10. Last Day conditions (17:22-37)

11. Mission of Christ (12:49-53)

12. Repentance and confession (12:8-9; 13:1-5)

13. Rewards (18:28-30; 22:28-30)

14. Sectarianism (9:49-50)

15. Signs of the times (12:54-57)

16. Spiritual relationships (8:19-21)

17. Unbelief and coming judgment (11:29-32)

18. Watchfulness (12:35-40)

IX. The Eulogization: Jesus pays great homage to the imprisoned John the Baptist. (7:19-29)

    A. The concern from John

        "And John calling unto him two of his disciples sent them to Jesus, saying, Art thou he that should come? or look we for another?" (7:19)

    B. The comfort for John

        "Then Jesus answering said unto them, Go your way, and tell John what things ye have seen and heard; how that the blind see, the lame walk, the lepers are cleansed, the deaf hear, the dead are raised, to the poor the gospel is preached." (7:22)

    C. The commendation of John

        "For I say unto you, Among those that are born of women there is not a greater prophet than John the Baptist: but he that is least in the kingdom of God is greater than he." (7:28)

X. The Deputation: Jesus calls and commissions His followers.

    A. The twelve apostles

        1. Their call (5:1-11, 27-29; 6:13-16)

        "And it came to pass in those days, that he went out into a mountain to pray, and continued all night in prayer to God. And when it was day, he called unto him his disciples: and of them he chose twelve, whom also he named apostles." (6:12-13)

        2. Their commission (9:1-11)

        "Then he called his twelve disciples together, and gave them power and authority over all devils, and to cure diseases. And he sent them to preach the kingdom of God, and to heal the sick ... And they departed, and went through the towns, preaching the gospel, and healing every where." (9:1-2, 6)

    B. The seventy Disciples (10:1-24)

        "After these things the LORD appointed other seventy also, and sent them two and two before his face into every city and place, whither he himself would come. Therefore said he unto them, The harvest truly is great, but the labourers are few: pray ye therefore the Lord of the harvest, that he would send forth labourers into his harvest ... And into whatsoever city ye enter, and they receive you, eat such things as are set before you: And heal the sick that are therein, and say unto them, The kingdom of God is come nigh unto you ... And the seventy

returned again with joy, saying, Lord, even the devils are subject unto us through thy name."
(10:1-2, 8-9, 17)

XI.   The Demonstrations: Jesus exhibits His mighty power by performing many miracles as recorded by Luke.

    A. Casting out of demons

        1. A man at Capernaum (4:31-37)

        2. Mary Magdalene (8:2-3)

        3. The maniac of Gadara (8:26-40)

        4. A boy at the base of Mt. Hermon (9:37-43)

        5. A man somewhere in Galilee (11:14)

    B. Raising the dead

        1. The widow's son at Nain (7:11-18)

        2. Jairus' daughter in Galilee (8:41-42. 49-56)

    C. Feeding the hungry (9:12-17)

    D. Healing the sick

        1. Peter's mother-in-law (4:38-39)

        2. A leper (5:12-15)

        3. Ten lepers (17:11-19)

        4. A paralytic (5:17-26)

        5. A paralyzed hand (6:6-11)

        6. A centurion's servant (7:1-10)

        7. A woman with an issue of blood (8:43-48)

        8. A woman with an 18-year infirmity (13:10-17)

        9. A man with dropsy (14:1-6)

        10. A blind man (18:35-43)

    E. Calming the sea (8:22-25)

XII.   The Illustrations: Jesus illustrated both His message and mission through parables.

    A. The cloth and the wine (5:36-39)

    B. The two debtors (7:40-50)

    C. The sower and the soil (8:4-15)

    D. The mustard seed (13:18-19)

    E. The leaven (13:20-21)

    F. The lighted lamp (8:16-18; 11:33-36)

    G. The Good Samaritan (10:25-37)

    H. The generous father (11:11-13)

    I. The persistent friend (11:5-8)

J. The divided kingdom (11:16-23)

K. Reformation with regeneration (11:24-26)

L. The rich fool (12:16-21)

M. The faithful and faithless servants (12:41-48)

N. The fruitless fig tree (13:6-9)

O. The ambitious guest (14:7-14)

P. The great supper (14:16-24)

Q. The lost sheep (15:1-7)

R. The lost coin (15:8-10)

S. The lost son (15:11-32)

T. The unjust steward (16:1-13)

U. The rich man and Lazarus (16:19-31)

V. When our best is but the least (17:7-10)

W. The persistent widow (18:1-8)

X. The publican and the Pharisee (18:9-14)

Y. The ten pounds (19:11-27)

Z. The angry vineyard owner (10:9-18)

AA. The budding fig tree (21:29-32)

XIII. The Verification: (9:18-21)

"And it came to pass, as he was alone praying, his disciples were with him: and he asked them, saying, Whom say the people that I am? They answering said, John the Baptist; but some say, Elias; and others say, that one of the old prophets is risen again. He said unto them, But whom say ye that I am? Peter answering said, The Christ of God." (9:18-20)

XIV. The Invitations: On two special occasions Jesus issued a personal invitation.

A. To a rich young ruler (18:18-27)

"And a certain ruler asked him, saying, Good Master, what shall I do to inherit eternal life, Now when Jesus heard these things, he said unto him, Yet lackest thou one thing: sell all that thou hast, and distribute unto the poor, and thou shalt have treasure in heaven: and come, follow me. And when he heard this, he was very sorrowful: for he was very rich." (18:18, 22-23)

B. To a rich tax collector (19:1-10)

1. Zacchaeus, the sinner (19:1-2)
2. Zacchaeus, the seeker (19:3-4)
3. Zacchaeus, the sought (19:5-6)
4. Zacchaeus, the saved (19:7-10)

XV. **The Intolerance:** Jesus witnesses a two-fold example of gross intolerance on a certain occasion.

A. As demonstrated by the Samaritans, directed toward the Saviour (9:51-53)

"And they did not receive him, because his face was as though he would go to Jerusalem." (9:53)

B. As demonstrated by the apostles, directed toward the Samaritans (9:54-56)

"And when his disciples James and John saw this, they said, Lord, wilt thou that we command fire to come down from heaven, and consume them, even as Elias did?" (9:54)

XVI. **The Clarification:** Jesus gently corrects Martha during a visit with her and her sister Mary. (10:38-42)

A. Martha's complaint

"But Martha was cumbered about much serving, and came to him, and said, Lord, dost thou not care that my sister hath left me to serve alone? bid her therefore that she help me." (10:40)

B. Jesus' correction

"And Jesus answered and said unto her, Martha, Martha, thou art careful and troubled about many things: But one thing is needful: and Mary hath chosen that good part, which shall not be taken away from her." (10:41-42)

XVII. **The Consecration:** Some children are brought to Jesus for Him to bless them.

XVIII. The Lamentation: Jesus weeps over Jerusalem on two occasions.

A. First occasion (13:34-35)

"O Jerusalem, Jerusalem, which killest the prophets, and stonest them that are sent unto thee; how often would I have gathered thy children together, as a hen doth gather her brood under her wings, and ye would not! Behold, your house is left unto you desolate: and verily I say unto you, Ye shall not see me, until the time come when ye shall say, Blessed is he that cometh in the name of the Lord." (13:34-35)

B. Second occasion (19:41-44)

"And when he was come near, he beheld the city, and wept over it." (19:41)

XIX. **The Presentation:** Jesus presents Himself during the triumphal entry on Palm Sunday. (19:28-40)

"And as he went, they spread their clothes in the way. And when he was come nigh, even now at the descent of the mount of Olives, the whole multitude of the disciples began to rejoice and praise God with a loud voice for all the mighty works that they had seen; Saying, Blessed be the King that cometh in the name of the Lord: peace in heaven, and glory in the highest." (19:36-38)

XX. **The Observations:** Jesus' comments concerning those who presented their gifts in the temple. (21:1-4)

  A. The shallow gifts

   "And he looked up, and saw the rich men casting their gifts into the treasury." (21:1)

  B. The sacrificial gift

   "And he saw also a certain poor widow casting in thither two mites. And he said, Of a truth I say unto you, that this poor widow hath cast in more than they all: For all these have of their abundance cast in unto the offerings of God: but she of her penury hath cast in all the living that, she had." (21:2-4)

XXI. **The Confrontations:** Jesus was often confronted and accused by the wicked Jewish rulers.

  A. They said he was a blasphemer (5:21)

  B. They accused him of having a demon (11:15)

  C. They criticized him in various areas:

   1. For associating with sinners (5:30-32; 7:36-39)
   2. For not observing their ceremonial fastings (5:33-35)
   3. For not observing their ceremonial washings (11:37-38)
   4. For allowing his disciples to pluck grain for food on the Sabbath (6:1-5)
   5. For healing on the Sabbath (6:6-11)

  D. They challenged his authority (20:1-8)

  E. They attempted to trap him.

   1. Concerning the paying of tribute (20:21-26)
   2. Concerning the resurrection of the dead (20:27-40)
   3. Concerning the Messiah (20:41-44)

XXII. **The Condemnation:** Jesus utterly condemns the wicked Jewish leaders. (11:39-54; 20:45-47)

"Woe unto you, scribes and Pharisees, hypocrites! for ye are as graves which appear not, and the men that walk over them are not aware of them... Woe unto you! for ye build the sepulchres of the prophets, and your fathers killed them... Woe unto you, lawyers! for ye have taken away the key of knowledge: ye entered not in yourselves, and them that were entering in ye hindered." (11:44, 47, 52)

"Beware of the scribes, which desire to walk in long robes, and love greetings in the markets, and the highest seats in the synagogues, and the chief rooms at feasts; Which devour widows' houses, and for a shew make long prayers: the same shall receive greater damnation." (20:46-47)

XXIII. **The Symbolization:** Jesus uses the bread and wine in the Upper Room to symbolize His impending death. (22:7-23)

"And he took the cup, and gave thanks, and said, Take this, and divide it among yourselves: For I say unto you, I will not drink of the fruit of the vine, until the kingdom of God shall come. And he took bread, and gave thanks, and brake it, and gave unto them, saying, This is my body which is given for you: this do in remembrance of me. Likewise also the cup after supper, saying, This cup is the new testament in my blood, which is shed for you." (22:17-20)

XXIV. The Supplications: Jesus prayed often while upon this earth.

A. His personal prayers—Jesus prayed:

1. At His baptism (3:21)
2. In the wilderness (5:16)
3. Before choosing the Twelve (6:12)
4. During His transfiguration (9:29)
5. After hearing the report of the returning Seventy (10:21-22)
6. Before giving the model prayer (11:1)
7. In the Upper Room for Peter— *"And the Lord said, Simon, Simon, behold, Satan hath desired to have you, that he may sift you as wheat: But I have prayed for thee, that thy faith fail not: and when thou art converted, strengthen thy brethren." (22:31-32)*
8. In the Garden— *"And he was withdrawn from them about a stone's cast, and kneeled down, and prayed, Saying, Father, if thou be willing, remove this cup from me: nevertheless not my will, but thine, be done. And there appeared an angel unto him from heaven, strengthening him. And being in an agony he prayed more earnestly: and his sweat was as it were great drops of blood falling down to the ground." (22:41-44)*
9. On the cross— *"Then said Jesus, Father, forgive them; for they know not what they do." (23:34) "And when Jesus had cried with a loud voice, he said, Father, into thy hands I commend my spirit." (23:46)*

B. His pattern prayer— *"And he said unto them, When ye pray, say, Our Father which art in heaven, Hallowed be thy name. Thy kingdom come. Thy will be done, as in heaven, so in earth. Give us day by day our daily bread. And forgive us our sins; for we also forgive every one that is indebted to us. And lead us not into temptation; but deliver us from evil." (11:2-4)*

C. His points on prayer

1. Whom we should pray for (6:28-29)
2. When we should pray (18:1)
3. Why we should pray (11:9-10; 21:36; 22:40)

XXV. The Repudiation: Jesus is betrayed and denied by two followers.

A. The betrayal by Judas (22:1-6, 47-48)

B. The denials by Peter (22:31-38, 54-62)

XXVI. The Interrogation: Jesus is arrested in Gethsemane and subjected to various unfair trials.

A. Before the high priest (22:54, 63-65)

B. Before the Sanhedrin (22:66-71)

C. Before Pilate for the first time (23:4)

D. Before Herod Antipas (23:8-12)

E. Before Pilate for the second time (23:13-25)

XXVII. **The Brutalization:** Jesus is crucified. (23:26-49)

A. The trip to the cross (23:26-3 1)

"And as they led him away, they laid hold upon one Simon, a Cyrenian, coming out of the country, and on him they laid the cross, that he might bear it after Jesus. And there followed him a great company of people, and of women, which also bewailed and lamented him. But Jesus turning unto them said, Daughters of Jerusalem, weep not for me, but weep for yourselves, and for your children." (23:26-28)

B. The travail on the cross (23:32-49)

   1. The compassion shown by Jesus for sinners

      a. For the crucifers

        "Then said Jesus, Father, forgive them; for they know not what they do. And they parted his raiment, and cast lots." (23:34)

      b. For the crucified (23:40-43)

        He saves the repentant dying thief

   2. The contempt shown by sinners for Jesus

      "And the people stood beholding. And the rulers also with them derided him, saying, He saved others; let him save himself, if he be Christ, the chosen of God. And the soldiers also mocked him, coming to him, and offering him vinegar, And saying, If thou be the king of the Jews, save thyself... And one of the malefactors which were hanged railed on him, saying, If thou be Christ, save thyself and us" (23:35-37, 39)

C. The testimony concerning the cross (23:47)

"Now when the centurion saw what was done, he glorified God, saying, Certainly this was a righteous man." (23:47)

XXVIII. **The Authorization:** Joseph of Arimathaea receives permission from Pilate to remove the body of Jesus. (23:50-53)

"And he took it down, and wrapped it in linen, and laid it in a sepulchre that was hewn in stone, wherein never man before was laid." (23:53)

XXIX. **The Dedication:** (23:54-56)

"And the women also, which came with him from Galilee, followed after, and beheld the sepulchre, and how his body was laid. And they returned, and prepared spices and ointments; and rested the sabbath day according to the commandment." (23:55-56)

XXX.   **The Vindication:** Jesus' claims of deity are vindicated through His glorious resurrection from the dead. (24:1-48)

A. The announcement (24:1-12)

"And they began to accuse him, saying, We found this fellow perverting the nation, and forbidding to give tribute to Caesar, saying that he himself is Christ a King. And Pilate asked him, saying, Art thou the King of the Jews? And he answered him and said, Thou sayest it. Then said Pilate to the chief priests and to the people, I find no fault in this man. And they were the more fierce, saying, He stirreth up the people, teaching throughout all Jewry, beginning from Galilee to this place. When Pilate heard of Galilee, he asked whether the man were a Galilaean. And as soon as he knew that he belonged unto Herod's jurisdiction, he sent him to Herod, who himself also was at Jerusalem at that time." (23:2-7)

B. The appearances (24:13-48)

1. Jesus appears before two disciples on the Emmaus Road (24:13-35)

"Then he said unto them, O fools, and slow of heart to believe all that the prophets have spoken: Ought not Christ to have suffered these things, and to enter into his glory? And beginning at Moses and all the prophets, he expounded unto them in all the scriptures the things concerning himself... And their eyes were opened, and they knew him; and he vanished out of their sight. And they said one to another, Did not our heart burn within us, while he talked with us by the way, and while he opened to us the scriptures?" (24:25-27, 31-32)

2. Jesus appears before ten apostles in the Upper Room (24:36-48)

"But they were terrified and affrighted, and supposed that they had seen a spirit. And he said unto them, Why are ye troubled? and why do thoughts arise in your hearts? Behold my hands and my feet, that it is I myself: handle me, and see; for a spirit hath not flesh and bones, as ye see me have. And when he had thus spoken, he shewed them his hands and his feet. And while they yet believed not for joy, and wondered, he said unto them, Have ye here any meat? And they gave him a piece of a broiled fish, and of an honeycomb. And he took it, and did eat before them." (24:37-43)

XXXI.   The Exhortation: (24:49)

"And, behold, I send the promise of my Father upon you: but tarry ye in the city of Jerusalem, until ye be endued with power from on high." (24:49)

XXXII.   The Finalization: (24:50-51)

"And he led them out as far as to Bethany, and he lifted up his hands, and blessed them. And it came to pass, while he blessed them, he was parted from them, and carried up into heaven." (24:50-51)

XXXIII.   The Celebration: (24:52-53)

"And they worshipped him, and returned to Jerusalem with great joy: And were continually in the temple, praising and blessing God. Amen." (24:52-53)

A Topical Overview of John's Gospel

I. The Nature of the Son of God

"In the beginning was the Word, and the Word was with God, and the Word was God. The same was in the beginning with God." (1:1, 2)

II. The Incarnation of the Son of God

"And the Word was made flesh, and dwelt among us, (and we beheld his glory, the glory as of the only begotten of the Father,) full of grace and truth." (1:14)

III. The Two-fold Work of the Son of God

    A. His work in Creation

        "All things were made by him; and without him was not any thing made that was made." (1:3)

    B. His work in Redemption (1:4-5, 9-13, 29)

        "The next day John seeth Jesus coming unto him, and saith, Behold the Lamb of God, which taketh away the sin of the world." (1:29)

IV. The 12-Fold Witness to the Son of God

    A. The Testimony of John the Baptist (1:6-8, 15-36; 3:22-36; 5:33-35)

        1. What John said about himself

            a. He was sent by God the Father to introduce God the Son (1:6-8, 15, 19-26, 34)

            b. He felt totally unworthy to do this (1:27, 30; 3:30)

            c. His joy was, however, fulfilled in doing this (1:27, 30; 3:30)

        2. What John said about his Savior

            a. He was indeed the Son of God (1:34)

            b. He was indeed the Jewish Messiah (1:19-26)

            c. He was the source of all light and life (1:6-8; 3:36)

            d. He was the giver of grace (1:16-17)

            e. He came to take away our sins (1:29, 35)

            f. He came from the Father (3:34b)

            g. He came to reveal the Father (1:18; 3:28-29)

            h. He is dearly loved by the Father (3:35)

            i. He was totally anointed by the Spirit (1:32-33)

B. The testimony of the Savior Himself

"But I have greater witness than that of John: for the works which the Father hath given me to finish, the same works that I do, bear witness of me, that the Father hath sent me." (5:36)

C. The testimony of the Father (5:37-38)

"And the Father himself, which hath sent me, hath borne witness of me. Ye have neither heard his voice at any time, nor seen his shape." (5:37)

D. The testimony of the Scriptures

"Search the scriptures; for in them ye think ye have eternal life: and they are they which testify of me." (5:39)

E. The testimony of Nathanael

"Nathanael answered and saith unto him, Rabbi, thou art the Son of God; thou art the King of Israel." (1:49)

F. The testimony of the Samaritan woman

"Come, see a man, which told me all things that ever I did: is not this the Christ?" (4:29)

G. The testimony of Peter

"And we believe and are sure that thou art that Christ, the Son of the living God." (6:69)

H. The testimony of a former blind man (9:35-38)

"And he said, Lord, I believe. And he worshipped him." (9:38)

I. The testimony of Martha (11:27)

"She saith unto him, Yea, Lord: I believe that thou art the Christ, the Son of God, which should come into the world." (11:27)

J. The testimony of Thomas

"And Thomas answered and said unto him, My LORD and my God." (20:28)

K. The testimony of John the Apostle

"But these are written, that ye might believe that Jesus is the Christ, the Son of God; and that believing ye might have life through his name." (20:31)

V. The Zeal of the Son of God

"And the Jews' passover was at hand, and Jesus went up to Jerusalem. And found in the temple those that sold oxen and sheep and doves, and the changers of money sitting: And when he had made a scourge of small cords, he drove them all out of the temple, and the sheep, and the oxen; and poured out the changers' money, and overthrew the tables; And said unto them that sold doves, Take these things hence; make not my Father's house an house of merchandise. And his disciples remembered that it was written, The zeal of thine house hath eaten me up." (2:13-17)

VI. The Claims of the Son of God

A. In regard to His Father

1. That He had shared His Father's glory before the world was created (17:5)
2. That He had been sent by the Father (7:29; 8:16, 42)
3. That He was indwelled by the Father (14:10-11)
4. That He was loved by the Father (10:17; 17:24)
5. That He was sealed by the Father (6:27)
6. That He came to do the will of His Father (6:38)
7. That He came to speak the words of His Father (7:16; 17:14)
8. That He came to perform and complete the works of His Father (9:4; 17:4)
9. That He would return to His Father (16:28)

B. In regard to Himself

1. That He was equal with God (5:18; 9:35-37; 10:30)
2. That He was the Messiah (4:26)
3. That He was the King of the Jews (18:3 7)
4. That He existed before Abraham (8:58)

C. In regard to all humanity

1. That He was the Water of Life (4:10, 14; 7:38)
2. That He was the Bread of Life (6:33, 35, 48, 51)
3. That He was the Light of the world (8:12; 12:35-36, 46)
4. That He was the only Door of the Sheep (10:7-8; 13:6)
5. That He was the Good Shepherd (10:11, 14)
6. That He was the Resurrection and the Life (11:25)
7. That He was the Way, the Truth, and the Life (14:6; 18:37)
8. That He was the true Vine (15:1)
9. That He came to save sinners (3:17; 12:47)
10. That He would eventually raise all men (5:21, 25, 28-29; 6:39-40, 44, 54)
11. That He would eventually judge all men (5:22, 27)
12. That He had overcome the world (16:33)

VII. The Key Dialogues of the Son of God

A. With Nathanael (1:47-51)

B. With Nicodemus (3:1-21)

C. With the Samaritan woman (4:5-42)

D. With a woman taken in the act of adultery (8:3-11)

E. With a man born blind (9:35-39)

F. With Martha (11:20-27, 39-40)

G. With Simon Peter

1. First occasion (6:66-69)
2. Second occasion (13:36-38)
3. Third occasion (21:15-22)

H. With the Jewish High Priest (18:19-23)

I. With Pilate (18:33-38; 19:8-11)

J. With Mary Magdalene (20:11-17)

K. With Thomas (20:24-29)

VIII. **The Miracles of the Son of God**

A. Turning water into wine (2:1-11)

B. Healing of the nobleman's son (4:46-54)

C. Healing of the impotent man (5:1-16)

D. Feeding of the 5000 (6:1-14)

E. Walking on the water (6:15-21)

F. Healing of the man born blind (9:1-7)

G. Raising of Lazarus (11:39-44)

H. Preparing a great catch of fish (21:5-6)

IX. **The Sermons of the Son of God**

A. The Source of Life sermon (5:17-47)

"For as the Father hath life in himself; so hath he given to the Son to have life in himself." (5:26)

B. The Bread of Life sermon (6:22-59)

"And Jesus said unto them, I am the bread of life: he that cometh to me shall never hunger; and he that believeth on me shall never thirst." (6:35)

C. The Waters of Life sermon (7:14-39)

"In the last day, that great day of the feast, Jesus stood and cried, saying, If any man thirst, let him come unto me, and drink." (7:37)

D. The Light of Life sermon (8:12-59)

"Then spake Jesus again unto them, saying, I am the light of the world: he that followeth me shall not walk in darkness, but shall have the light of life." (8:12)

E. The Shepherd of Life sermon (10:1-18)

"I am the good shepherd: the good shepherd giveth his life for the sheep." (10:11)

F. The Lord of Life sermon (13:6-20)

"Ye call me Master and Lord: and ye say well; for so I am." (13:13)

G. The Reassurance in Life sermon (14:1-31)

> *"Let not your heart be troubled: ye believe in God, believe also in me ... Peace I leave with you, my peace I give unto you: not as the world giveth, give I unto you. Let not your heart be troubled, neither let it be afraid." (14:1, 27)*

H. The Abundance of Life sermon (15, 16)

> *"I am the vine, ye are the branches: He that abideth in me, and I in him, the same bringeth forth much fruit: for without me ye can do nothing." (15:5)*

X. The Triumphal Entry of the Son of God (12:12-15)

> *"On the next day much people that were come to the feast, when they heard that Jesus was coming to Jerusalem, Took branches of palm trees, and went forth to meet him, and cried, Hosanna: Blessed is the King of Israel that cometh in the name of the Lord. And Jesus, when he had found a young ass, sat thereon; as it is written, Fear not, daughter of Sion: behold, thy King cometh, sitting on an ass's colt." (12:12-15)*

XI. The Anointing of the Son of God (12:1-8)

> *"Then took Mary a pound of ointment of spikenard, very costly, and anointed the feet of Jesus, and wiped his feet with her hair: and the house was filled with the odour of the ointment." (12:3)*

XII. The High Priestly Prayer of the Son of God (17)

> *"These words spake Jesus, and lifted up his eyes to heaven, and said, Father, the hour is come; glorify thy Son, that thy Son also may glorify thee." (17:1)*

XIII. The Arrest of the Son of God (18:1-12)

> *"When Jesus had spoken these words, he went forth with his disciples over the brook Kidron, where was a garden, into the which he entered, and his disciples ... Judas then, having received a band of men and officers from the chief priests and Pharisees, cometh thither with lanterns and torches and weapons... Then the band and the captain and officers of the Jews took Jesus, and bound him." (18:1, 3, 12)*

XIV. The Sufferings of the Son of God

A. Misunderstood (2:18-21; 6:42, 52)

B. Rejected by His family (7:5)

C. Abandoned by His followers (6:66)

D. Threatened (5:18; 7:1; 8:59; 10:31)

E. Slandered (8:48, 52; 9:24)

F. Plotted against (11:47-53)

G. Betrayed by Judas (18:2-5)

H. Denied by Peter (18:25-27)

I. Interrogated

   1. By the High Priest (18:19)
   2. By Pilate (18:33-38; 19:10)

J. Slapped (18:22)

K. Scourged (19:1)

L. Ridiculed (19:2-3)

M. Buffeted (19:3)

XV. The Crucifixion of the Son of God (19:16-30)

"And he bearing his cross went forth into a place called the place of a skull, which is called in the Hebrew Golgotha: Where they crucified him, and two other with him, on either side one, and Jesus in the midst. And Pilate wrote a title, and put it on the cross. And the writing was JESUS OF NAZARETH THE KING OF THE JEWS." (19:17-19)

XVI. The Resurrection Appearances of the Son of God

A. Before Mary Magdalene (20:11-18)

"Jesus saith unto her, Woman, why weepest thou? whom seekest thou? She, supposing him to be the gardener, saith unto him, Sir, if thou have borne him hence, tell me where thou hast laid him, and I will take him away. Jesus saith unto her, Mary. She turned herself, and saith unto him, Rabboni; which is to say, Master." (20:15-16)

B. Before ten apostles (20:19-23)

"Then the same day at evening, being the first day of the week, when the doors were shut where the disciples were assembled for fear of the Jews, came Jesus and stood in the midst, and saith unto them, Peace be unto you." (20:19)

C. Before Thomas (20:26-29)

"And after eight days again his disciples were within, and Thomas with them: then came Jesus, the doors being shut, and stood in the midst, and said, Peace be unto you." (20:26)

D. Before seven apostles (21:1-23)

"After these things Jesus shewed himself again to the disciples at the sea of Tiberias; and on this wise shewed he himself. There were together Simon Peter, and Thomas called Didymus, and Nathanael of Cana in Galilee, and the sons of Zebedee, and two other of his disciples." (21:1-2)

CPSIA information can be obtained at www.ICGtesting.com
Printed in the USA
BVOW060253060912

299699BV00003B/1/P